D0742482

Financial Derivatives

This book offers a succinct account of the principles of financial derivatives pricing. The first chapter provides readers with an intuitive exposition of basic random calculus. Concepts such as volatility and time, random walks, geometric Brownian motion, and Itô's lemma are discussed heuristically. The second chapter develops generic pricing techniques for assets and derivatives, determining the notion of a stochastic discount factor or pricing kernel, and then uses this concept to price conventional and exotic derivatives. The third chapter applies the pricing concepts to the special case of interest rate markets, namely, bonds and swaps, and discusses factor models and term-structure-consistent models. The fourth chapter deals with a variety of mathematical topics that underlie derivatives pricing and portfolio allocation decisions, such as mean-reverting processes and jump processes, and discusses related tools of stochastic calculus, such as Kolmogorov equations, martingales techniques, stochastic control, and partial differential equations.

Jamil Baz is Head of Global Fixed Income Research at Deutsche Bank, London. Prior to this appointment, he was a Managing Director at Lehman Brothers. Dr. Baz is a Research Fellow at Oxford University, where he teaches financial economics. He has degrees from the Ecole des Hautes Etudes Commerciales (Diplôme), the London School of Economics (MSc), MIT (SM), and Harvard University (AM, PhD).

George Chacko is Associate Professor in the Finance Faculty of Harvard Business School. He has degrees from MIT (SB), the University of Chicago (MBA), and Harvard University (PhD). Professor Chacko's research continues to focus on optimal portfolio choice and consumption decisions in a dynamic framework.

Financial Derivatives

Pricing, Applications, and Mathematics

JAMIL BAZ

Deutsche Bank

GEORGE CHACKO

Harvard Business School

CAMBRIDGE
UNIVERSITY PRESS

PUBLISHED BY THE PRESS SYNDICATE OF THE UNIVERSITY OF CAMBRIDGE
The Pitt Building, Trumpington Street, Cambridge, United Kingdom

CAMBRIDGE UNIVERSITY PRESS
The Edinburgh Building, Cambridge CB2 2RU, UK
40 West 20th Street, New York, NY 10011-4211, USA
477 Williamstown Road, Port Melbourne, VIC 3207, Australia
Ruiz de Alarcón 13, 28014 Madrid, Spain
Dock House, The Waterfront, Cape Town 8001, South Africa

http://www.cambridge.org

First published 2004

Printed in the United States of America

Typeface Times Ten 10/13.5 pt.   *System* LATEX 2_ε [TB]

A catalog record for this book is available from the British Library.

Library of Congress Cataloging in Publication Data
Baz, Jamil.
Financial derivatives : pricing, applications, and mathematics / Jamil Baz,
George Chacko.
p. cm.
Includes bibliographical references and index.
ISBN 0-521-81510-X
1. Derivative securities.   I. Chacko, George.   II. Title.
HG6024.A3B396   2003
332.63′2 – dc21
2002041452

ISBN 0 521 81510 X hardback

To Maurice and Elena   J.B.
To my parents   G.C.

Contents

Acknowledgments

We are as ever in many people's debt. Both authors are lucky to have worked with or been taught by eminent experts such as John Campbell, Sanjiv Das, Jerome Detemple, Ken Froot, Andrew Lo, Franco Modigliani, Vasant Naik, Michael Pascutti, Lester Seigel, Peter Tufano, Luis Viceira, and Jean-Luc Vila. A list, by no means exhaustive, of colleagues who have read or influenced this manuscript includes Richard Bateson, Eric Briys, Robert Campbell, Marcel Cassard, Didier Cossin, François Degeorge, Lev Dynkin, David Folkerts-Landau, Vincent Koen, Ravi Mattu, Christine Miqueu-Baz, Arun Muralidhar, Prafulla Nabar, Brian Pinto, David Prieul, Vlad Putyatin, Nassim Taleb, Michele Toscani, Sadek Wahba, and Francis Yared. Special thanks are due to Tarek Nassar, Saurav Sen, Feng Li, and Dee Luther for diligent help with the manuscript. The biggest debt claimant to this work is undoubtedly Robert Merton, whose influence pervades this manuscript, including the footnotes; as such, because there is no free lunch, he must take full responsibility for all serious mistakes, details of which should be forwarded directly to him.

Introduction

This book is about risk and derivative securities. In our opinion, no one has described the issue more eloquently than Jorge Luis Borges, an intrepid Argentinian writer. He tells a fictional story of a lottery in ancient Babylonia. The lottery is peculiar because it is compulsory. All subjects are required to play and to accept the outcome. If they lose, they stand to lose their wealth, their lives, or their loved ones. If they win, they will get mountains of gold, the spouse of their choice, and other wonderful goodies.

It is easy to see how this story is a metaphor of our lives. We are shaped daily by doses of randomness. This is where the providential financial engineer intervenes. The engineer's thoughts are along the following lines: to confront all this randomness, one needs artificial randomness of opposite sign, called derivative securities. And the engineer calls the ratio of these two random quantities a hedge ratio.

Financial engineering is about combining the Tinker Toys of capital markets and financial institutions to create custom risk-return profiles for economic agents. An important element of the financial engineering process is the valuation of the Tinker Toys; this is the central ingredient this book provides.

We have written this book with a view to the following two objectives:

- to introduce readers with a modicum of mathematical background to the valuation of derivatives

- to give them the tools and intuition to expand upon these results when necessary

By and large, textbooks on derivatives fall into two categories: the first is targeted toward MBA students and advanced undergraduates, and the second aims at finance or mathematics PhD students. The former tend to score high on breadth of coverage but do not go in depth into any specific area of derivatives. The latter tend to be highly rigorous and therefore limit the audience. While this book is closer to the second category, it strives to simplify the mathematical presentation and make it accessible to a wider audience. Concepts such as measure, functional spaces, and Lebesgue integrals are avoided altogether in the interest of all those who have a good knowledge of mathematics but yet have not ventured into advanced mathematics.

The target audience includes advanced undergraduates in mathematics, economics, and finance; graduate students in quantitative finance master's programs as well as PhD students in the aforementioned disciplines; and practitioners afflicted with an interest in derivatives pricing and mathematical curiosity.

The book assumes elementary knowledge of finance at the level of the Brealey and Myers corporate finance textbook. Notions such as discounting, net present value, spot and forward rates, and basic option pricing in a binomial model should be familiar to the reader. However, very little knowledge of economics is assumed, as we develop the required utility theory from first principles.

The level of mathematical preparation required to get through this book successfully comprises knowledge of differential and integral calculus, probability, and statistics. In calculus, readers need to know basic differentiation and integration rules and Taylor series expansions, and should have some familiarity with differential equations. Readers should have had the standard year-long sequence in probability and statistics. This includes conventional, discrete, and continuous probability distributions and related notions, such as their moment generating functions and characteristic functions.

The outline runs as follows:

1. Chapter 1 provides readers with the mathematical background to understand the valuation concepts developed in Chapters 2 and 3. It provides an intuitive exposition of basic random

calculus. Concepts such as volatility and time, random walks, geometric Brownian motion, and Itô's lemma are exposed heuristically and given, where possible, an intuitive interpretation. This chapter also offers a few appetizers that we call paradoxes of finance: these paradoxes explain why forward exchange rates are biased predictors of future rates; why stock investing looks like a free lunch; and why success in portfolio management might have more to do with luck than with skill.

2. Chapter 2 develops generic pricing techniques for assets and derivatives. The chapter starts from basic concepts of utility theory and builds on these concepts to derive the notion of a stochastic discount factor, or pricing kernel. Pricing kernels are then used as the basis for the derivation of all subsequent pricing results, including the Black-Scholes/Merton model. We also show how pricing kernels relate to the hedging, or dynamic replication, approach that is the origin of all modern valuation principles. The chapter concludes with several applications to equity derivatives to demonstrate the power of the tools that are developed.

3. Chapter 3 specializes the pricing concepts of Chapter 3 to interest rate markets; namely bonds, swaps, and other interest rate derivatives. It starts with elementary concepts such as yield-to-maturity, zero-coupon rates, and forward rates; then moves on to naïve measures of interest rate risk such as duration and convexity and their underlying assumptions. An overview of interest rate derivatives precedes pricing models for interest rate instruments. These models fall into two conventional families: factor models, to which the notion of price of risk is central, and term-structure-consistent models, which are partial equilibrium models of derivatives pricing. The chapter ends with an interpretation of interest rates as options.

4. Chapter 4 is an expansion of the mathematical results in Chapter 1. It deals with a variety of mathematical topics that underlie derivatives pricing and portfolio allocation decisions. It describes in some detail random processes such as random walks, arithmetic and geometric Brownian motion, mean-reverting processes and jump processes. This chapter also includes an exposition of the rules of Itô calculus and contrasts it with the

competing Stratonovitch calculus. Related tools of stochastic calculus such as Kolmogorov equations and martingales are also discussed. The last two sections elaborate on techniques widely used to solve portfolio choice and option pricing problems: dynamic programming and partial differential equations.

We think that one virtue of the book is that the chapters are largely independent. Chapter 1 is essential to the understanding of the continuous-time sections in Chapters 2 and 3. Chapter 4 may be read independently, though previous chapters illuminate the concepts developed in each chapter much more completely.

Why Chapter 4 is at the end and not the beginning of this book is an almost aesthetic undertaking: Some finance experts think of mathematics as a way to learn finance. Our point of view is different. We feel that the joy of learning is in the process and not in the outcome. We also feel that finance can be a great way to learn mathematics.

1

Preliminary Mathematics

This chapter presents a brief overview of the technical language of modern finance. In the apparatus that we shall use, expressions such as *Random Walk*, *Brownian Motion*, and *Itô Calculus* may carry a shroud of mystery in the readers' minds. In an attempt to lift this shroud, we will be guilty of oversimplification and make no apology for that. Topics discussed in this chapter will be revisited and fleshed out in more detail in Chapter 4.

1.1 RANDOM WALK

Picture a particle moving on a line. Define X_t as the position of the particle at time t, with $X_0 = 0$. The particle moves one step forward $(+1)$ or backward (-1) with equal probability at each instant of time, and successive steps are independent. At $t = 1$

$$\Pr[X_1 = -1] = \Pr[X_1 = 1] = 1/2$$

See Figure 1.1.

Similarly at $t = 2$, the particle can be at the positions $-2, 0, 2$ with probabilities $1/4$, $1/2$, and $1/4$ respectively (see Figure 1.2). At $t = 3$, the values for X and their respective probabilities are

x	$\Pr[X_3 = x]$
-3	1/8
-1	3/8
$+1$	3/8
$+3$	1/8

We can calculate the expected value, variance, and standard deviation for X_t as of time zero. For example:

$$\mathbb{E}[X_1] = \left(\tfrac{1}{2} \times (-1)\right) + \left(\tfrac{1}{2} \times 1\right) = 0$$

$$Var[X_1] = \mathbb{E}[X_1 - \mathbb{E}X_1]^2 = \left(\tfrac{1}{2} \times (-1 - 0)^2\right) + \left(\tfrac{1}{2} \times (1 - 0)^2\right) = 1$$

$$SD[X_1] = \sqrt{Var[X_1]} = 1$$

Similarly,

$$\mathbb{E}[X_2] = \left(\tfrac{1}{4} \times (-2)\right) + \left(\tfrac{1}{2} \times 0\right) + \left(\tfrac{1}{4} \times 2\right) = 0$$

$$Var[X_2] = \mathbb{E}[X_2 - \mathbb{E}X_2]^2$$

$$= \tfrac{1}{4} \times (-2 - 0)^2 + \tfrac{1}{2}(0 - 0)^2 + \tfrac{1}{4} \times (2 - 0)^2 = 2$$

$$SD[X_2] = \sqrt{Var[X_2]} = \sqrt{2}$$

$$t = 0$$

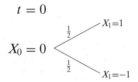

Figure 1.1

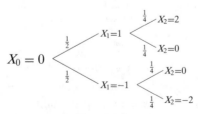

Figure 1.2

Using a similar logic, we can find the expected value, variance, and standard deviation of X_t, conditional on $X_0 = 0$, for any $t > 0$:

	X_1	X_2	X_3	...	X_n
Expected Value $\mathbb{E}_0[X_t]$	0	0	0	...	0
Variance $Var_0[X_t]$	1	2	3		n
Standard Deviation $\sqrt{Var_0[X_t]}$	1	$\sqrt{2}$	$\sqrt{3}$		$\sqrt{n}$

We can generalize the above example. Now the variable X can go up a step with probability p or down a step with probability $q = 1 - p$. The step size is σ.

We can calculate the mean, variance, and standard deviation of X_1 as before. We now have

$$\mathbb{E}[X_1] = (p - q)\sigma = \mu$$

$$\mathbb{E}[X_1^2] = p\sigma^2 + q\sigma^2 = \sigma^2$$

$$Var[X_1] = \mathbb{E}X_1^2 - (\mathbb{E}X_1)^2 = 4\sigma^2 pq$$

$$SD[X_1] = \sqrt{Var[X_1]} = 2\sigma\sqrt{pq}$$

Define $\mu = (p - q)\sigma$. The variable μ is called the drift of X. X is said to follow a random walk with drift when $p \neq q$, and a driftless random walk when $p = q = 1/2$. In general we have

$$E[X_n] = n(p - q)\sigma = n\mu$$

$$Var[X_n] = 4\sigma^2 npq$$

$$SD[X_n] = \sqrt{Var[X_n]} = 2\sigma\sqrt{npq}$$

If the particle takes one step per unit of time then $n = t$, where t is the number of units of time. We see that the mean of a random walk is proportional to time, whereas the standard deviation is proportional to the square root of time. The latter result stems from the independence of the increments in a random walk. In a financial context, stock returns are often modeled as random walks. If $R_{t-1,t}$ represents the return on a stock between $t - 1$ and t, then the return over T periods is

$$R_{0,T} = R_{0,1} + R_{1,2} + \cdots + R_{T-1,T}$$

Returns in successive periods are assumed to be independent. This means that

$$Var\,[R_{0,T}] = Var\,[R_{0,1} + R_{1,2} + \cdots + R_{T-1,T}]$$
$$= Var\,[R_{0,1}] + Var\,[R_{1,2}] + \cdots + Var\,[R_{T-1,T}]$$

Additionally, if the return in each period has a constant variance of σ^2, then

$$Var\,[R_{0,T}] = \sigma^2 T$$

and

$$SD\,[R_{0,T}] = \sigma\sqrt{T}$$

In finance, the standard deviation of a stock's returns is referred to as its *volatility*.

1.2 ANOTHER TAKE ON VOLATILITY AND TIME

We now give another perspective of volatility and time (Figure 1.3). X follows a two-dimensional random walk. The step size is σ. The angle θ_i at step i is random. After two steps, the distance D between the departure point X_0 and X_2 is given by

$$D^2 = (X_0 C)^2 + (X_2 C)^2$$

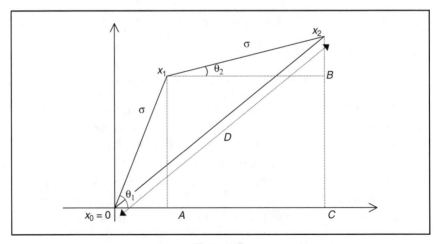

Figure 1.3

But

$$X_0C = X_0A + AC = X_0A + X_1B = \sigma\cos\theta_1 + \sigma\cos\theta_2$$

and

$$X_2C = X_2B + BC = X_2B + X_1A = \sigma\sin\theta_2 + \sigma\sin\theta_1$$

It follows that

$$\begin{aligned}
D^2 &= \sigma^2[(\cos\theta_1 + \cos\theta_2)^2 + (\sin\theta_1 + \sin\theta_2)^2] \\
&= \sigma^2[\cos^2\theta_1 + \sin^2\theta_1 + \cos^2\theta_2 + \sin^2\theta_2 \\
&\quad + 2(\sin\theta_1\sin\theta_2 + \cos\theta_1\cos\theta_2)]
\end{aligned}$$

Recall the equalities

$$\cos^2\theta_1 + \sin^2\theta_1 = 1$$
$$\cos\theta_1\cos\theta_2 + \sin\theta_1\sin\theta_2 = \cos(\theta_1 - \theta_2)$$

Using these equalities yields

$$D^2 = \sigma^2[2 + 2\cos(\theta_1 - \theta_2)]$$

Because the cosine term equals zero on average, we get

$$E(D^2) = 2\sigma^2$$
$$SD(D) = \sigma\sqrt{2}$$

1.3 A FIRST GLANCE AT ITÔ'S LEMMA

Recall the experiment discussed in the previous section (see Figure 1.4). It is easy to check that if we represent the process for X as shown in Figure 1.5, where $\mu \equiv (p - q)\sigma$, we get the same drift and volatility for each process.

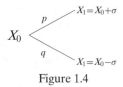

Figure 1.4

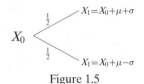

Figure 1.5

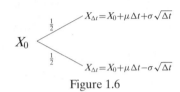

Figure 1.6

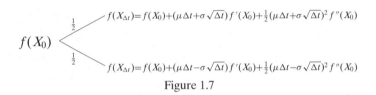

Figure 1.7

The second process can be expressed as

$$X_1 = X_0 + \mu \pm \sigma$$

or

$$\Delta X = \mu + \sigma \varepsilon$$

where $\Delta X = X_1 - X_0$ and $\varepsilon = 1$ or -1 with probability 1/2 for each outcome.

We now represent the binomial tree for a change in X given a time interval Δt (see Figure 1.6). The process for the binomial tree can be written as

$$\Delta X = X_{\Delta t} - X_0 = \mu \Delta t + \sigma \varepsilon \sqrt{\Delta t}$$

where the random variable ε keeps the same properties as above. Now, how can the variation on a function $f(X)$ be expressed? This is the question solved by Itô's lemma. A simple Taylor expansion to the second order gives the result shown in Figure 1.7.

For a small Δt, we may choose to neglect terms in $(\Delta t)^n$ (with $n > 1$) to get the outcome shown in Figure 1.8. In shorthand notation,

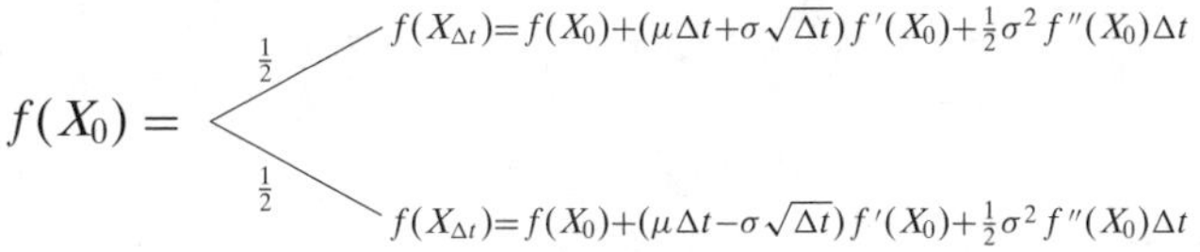

$$f(X_0) = \begin{cases} \dfrac{1}{2} & f(X_{\Delta t})=f(X_0)+(\mu\Delta t+\sigma\sqrt{\Delta t})f'(X_0)+\frac{1}{2}\sigma^2 f''(X_0)\Delta t \\[3ex] \dfrac{1}{2} & f(X_{\Delta t})=f(X_0)+(\mu\Delta t-\sigma\sqrt{\Delta t})f'(X_0)+\frac{1}{2}\sigma^2 f''(X_0)\Delta t \end{cases}$$

Figure 1.8

$$\Delta f(X) = f(X_{\Delta t}) - f(X_0) = [\mu f'(X_0) + \frac{1}{2}\sigma^2 f''(X_0)]\Delta t$$
$$+ \sigma\varepsilon f'(X_0)\sqrt{\Delta t}$$

This is the simplest expression of Itô's lemma.

1.4 CONTINUOUS TIME: BROWNIAN MOTION; MORE ON ITÔ'S LEMMA

The smaller the time interval, the better Itô's lemma approximates $\Delta f(X)$. In the process of this shrinkage, Δt gets partitioned into smaller and smaller time intervals and a larger and larger number of binomial realizations occur as a result. Chapter 4 shows that in this passage to continuous time, the random variable ε ends up converging toward a standard normal variable $\phi \sim N(0, 1)$ which has a normal distribution with mean zero and variance one. We call an infinitesimal time interval dt. The random process in continuous time can be written as

$$dX(t) = \mu dt + \sigma\phi\sqrt{dt}, \text{ with } X(0) = x_0$$

The process X is said to follow an arithmetic Brownian motion (with drift). The above expression is commonly written as

$$dX(t) = \mu dt + \sigma dW(t)$$

where $dW(t) \equiv \phi\sqrt{dt}$ is called a Wiener increment. Naturally

$$\mathbb{E}[dW] = \mathbb{E}\left[\phi\sqrt{dt}\right] = \mathbb{E}[\phi]\sqrt{dt} = 0$$
$$Var[dW] = Var\left[\phi\sqrt{dt}\right] = Var[\phi]\,dt = dt$$

It follows that

$$\mathbb{E}[dX] = \mu dt$$
$$Var[dX] = \sigma^2 dt$$

Example 1.1. There is a 95% probability that ϕ is in the $[-1.96, 1.96]$ interval. With $\mu = 2\%$, $\sigma = 1\%$, and $dt = 1$, dX will be in the $[0.04\%; 3.96\%]$ interval with 95% probability.

More generally, a variable X is said to follow an Itô process if

$$dX = \mu(t, X)dt + \sigma(t, X)dW$$

where $\mu(t, X)$ is the drift function and $\sigma(t, X)$ is the volatility for an increment in X. Of particular interest in finance is the so-called geometric Brownian motion where $\mu(t, X) = \mu X$ and $\sigma(t, X) = \sigma X$, where μ and σ are constants. The process can be written as

$$dX = \mu Xdt + \sigma XdW$$

This process is used to describe the return dynamics of a wide range of assets. For example, we can assume that a stock price follows a geometric Brownian motion. This simply states that we assume the returns to the stock price to follow a normal distribution. Let S be the stock price. Then the process can be written as

$$\frac{dS}{S} = \mu dt + \sigma dW$$

where μdt is the deterministic drift term and σdW, or $\sigma\phi\sqrt{dt}$, is the random term. For $\mu = 10\%$, $dt = 1$, and $\sigma = 30\%$, the stock return dS/S is

$$\frac{dS}{S} = 0.1 + 0.3\phi$$

where $\phi \sim N(0, 1)$. If ϕ turns out to be 1, then $dS/S = 0.4$. If $\phi = -0.5$, then $dS/S = -0.05$. From this it can be seen that dS/S has a normal distribution with mean μdt, variance $\sigma^2 dt$, and volatility $\sigma\sqrt{dt}$. This means that as time elapses, the probability density function shifts and flattens. With a positive drift term, the passage of time can transform the density function of stock returns as shown in Figure 1.9.

For general Itô processes of the form

$$dX = \mu(t, X)dt + \sigma(t, X)dW$$

Itô's lemma turns out to be similar to the primitive version in the previous section. For a function $f(t, X)$ (where f is at least twice

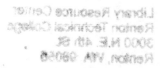

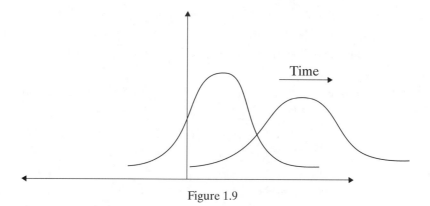

Figure 1.9

differentiable on X and once differentiable on t):

$$df(t, X) = \left[\frac{\partial f}{\partial t} + \frac{\partial f}{\partial X}\mu(t, X) + \frac{1}{2}\frac{\partial^2 f}{\partial X^2}\sigma^2(t, X)\right] dt + \frac{\partial f}{\partial X}\sigma(t, X)dW$$

For a geometric Brownian motion, it is therefore

$$df(t, X) = \left[\frac{\partial f}{\partial t} + \frac{\partial f}{\partial X}\mu X + \frac{1}{2}\frac{\partial^2 f}{\partial X^2}\sigma^2 X^2\right] dt + \frac{\partial f}{\partial X}\sigma X dW$$

Example 1.2. A stock price process S follows the random motion

$$\frac{dS}{S} = \mu dt + \sigma dW$$

We are interested in the process followed by $d(\log S)$. Set $f(t, S) = \log S$. Then

$$\frac{\partial f}{\partial S} = \frac{1}{S}; \frac{\partial f}{\partial t} = 0; \frac{\partial^2 f}{\partial S^2} = \frac{-1}{S^2}$$

Applying Itô's lemma for the geometric Brownian motion, we obtain

$$d(\log S) = \left(\mu - \frac{\sigma^2}{2}\right) dt + \sigma dW$$

This allows us to derive an explicit formulation for the evolution of a stock price. Integrating between 0 and T the above expression

$$\int_0^T d(\log S) = \left(\mu - \frac{\sigma^2}{2}\right)\int_0^T dt + \sigma \int_0^T dW$$

we get

$$\log(S_T) - \log(S_0) = \left(\mu - \frac{\sigma^2}{2}\right) T + \sigma\left(W(T) - W(0)\right)$$

Taking exponentials and noting that $W(0) = 0$, we have an expression for S_T as a function of S_0 for a geometric Brownian motion:

$$S_T = S_0 \exp\left[\left(\mu - \frac{\sigma^2}{2}\right) T + \sigma W(T)\right]$$

$$= S_0 \exp\left[\left(\mu - \frac{\sigma^2}{2}\right) T + \sigma\epsilon\sqrt{T}\right]$$

We have just shown that

$$dS/S = \mu dt + \sigma dW \Rightarrow S_T = S_0 \exp\left\{\left(\mu - \tfrac{1}{2}\sigma^2\right) T + \sigma W(T)\right\}$$

It is tempting to try solving the equation on the left by observing that $dS/S = d\log S$, leading to the erroneous answer $S_T = S_0 \exp\{\mu t + \sigma W\}$. However, since S is stochastic (random), dS/S is not equal to $d\log S$, and we have to use Itô's lemma to get the correct answer. Itô's lemma tells us that $d\log S = \left(\mu - \tfrac{1}{2}\sigma^2\right) dt + \sigma dW$. Since this is "linear" in the derivatives, we can indeed integrate it as in normal Newtonian calculus to get the correct answer.

1.5 TWO-DIMENSIONAL BROWNIAN MOTION

Let asset prices X and Y follow geometric Brownian motions:

$$\frac{dX}{X} = \mu_X dt + \sigma_X dW_X$$

$$\frac{dY}{Y} = \mu_Y dt + \sigma_Y dW_Y$$

Each asset return is characterized by its own drift term μ and volatility term σ. Also note that the Wiener process is not the same in each equation. If $dW_X = dW_Y$, then both returns would be perfectly correlated. This is because dX/X would then be a deterministic function of dY/Y:

$$\frac{dX}{X} = \left(\mu_X - \frac{\sigma_X}{\sigma_Y}\mu_Y\right) dt + \frac{\sigma_X}{\sigma_Y}\frac{dY}{Y}$$

Asset returns are generally not perfectly correlated (i.e., $dW_X \neq dW_Y$). If $dW_X = \phi_X\sqrt{dt}$ and $dW_Y = \phi_Y\sqrt{dt}$, with $\phi_X, \phi_Y \sim N(0,1)$ and $\mathbb{E}[dW_X dW_Y] = \mathbb{E}[\phi_X\phi_Y]\,dt = \rho dt$ where, by definition, $\rho \equiv \mathbb{E}[\phi_X\phi_Y]$ and $-1 \leq \rho \leq 1$.

1.6 BIVARIATE ITÔ'S LEMMA

Itô's lemma for the two-dimensional geometric Brownian motion above is given by:

$$df(t, X, Y)$$
$$= \left(\frac{\partial f}{\partial t} + \frac{\partial f}{\partial X}\mu_X X + \frac{\partial f}{\partial Y}\mu_Y Y + \frac{\partial^2 f}{\partial X \partial Y}\rho\sigma_X\sigma_Y XY + \frac{1}{2}\frac{\partial^2 f}{\partial X^2}\sigma_X^2 X^2 \right.$$
$$\left. + \frac{1}{2}\frac{\partial^2 f}{\partial Y^2}\sigma_Y^2 Y^2 \right) dt + \frac{\partial f}{\partial X}\sigma_X X dW_X + \frac{\partial f}{\partial Y}\sigma_Y Y dW_Y$$

This can be seen by simply applying Taylor's theorem to a function of three variables.

Example 1.3. As above, two asset prices follow equations

$$\frac{dX}{X} = \mu_X dt + \sigma_X dW_X$$
$$\frac{dY}{Y} = \mu_Y dt + \sigma_Y dW_Y$$

The correlation between returns is ρ. What random process does the ratio $f(X, Y) = X/Y$ follow?

$$\frac{\partial f}{\partial X} = \frac{1}{Y}; \frac{\partial f}{\partial Y} = -\frac{X}{Y^2}; \frac{\partial f}{\partial t} = 0; \frac{\partial^2 f}{\partial X^2} = 0; \frac{\partial^2 f}{\partial Y^2} = \frac{2X}{Y^3};$$
$$and \ \frac{\partial^2 f}{\partial X \partial Y} = -\frac{1}{Y^2}$$

The result follows directly:

$$df = \left(\mu_X - \mu_Y - \rho\sigma_X\sigma_Y + \sigma_Y^2 \right) f dt + \sigma_X f dW_X - \sigma_Y f dW_Y$$

Also note that if we define

$$dW_f \equiv \frac{\sigma_X dW_X - \sigma_Y dW_Y}{\sigma_f}$$

with $\sigma_f \equiv \sqrt{\sigma_X^2 + \sigma_Y^2 - 2\rho\sigma_X\sigma_Y}$, then

$$\mathbb{E}(dW_f) = \frac{\sigma_X}{\sigma_f}\mathbb{E}(dW_X) - \frac{\sigma_Y}{\sigma_f}\mathbb{E}(dW_Y) = 0$$

and

$$Var(dW_f) = \frac{\sigma_X^2}{\sigma_f^2}Var(dW_X) + \frac{\sigma_Y^2}{\sigma_f^2}Var(dW_Y) - \frac{2\sigma_X\sigma_Y}{\sigma_f^2}Cov(dW_X, dW_Y)$$

$$= \frac{\sigma_X^2}{\sigma_f^2}dt + \frac{\sigma_Y^2}{\sigma_f^2}dt - \frac{2\sigma_X\sigma_Y}{\sigma_f^2}\rho dt = dt$$

and we can write more concisely

$$\frac{df}{f} = \mu_f dt + \sigma_f dW_f$$

with $\mu_f = \mu_X - \mu_Y - \rho\sigma_X\sigma_Y + \sigma_Y^2$.

1.7 THREE PARADOXES OF FINANCE

We illustrate the results discussed thus far with three paradoxes. These paradoxes elaborate in turn upon three fields of finance: exchange rate forecasting, stock outperformance, and skill and luck in the money-management industry.

1.7.1 Paradox 1: Siegel's Paradox

We give a simple example to motivate our discussion of Siegel's paradox. Let the €/$ exchange rate today be 1. For the sake of simplicity, assume the euro will be worth either $1.25 or $0.80 in one year, with equal probability for each outcome. This means that the expected value of the euro is $(0.5*1.25) + (0.5*0.80) = \$1.025$. However, an equivalent statement of the problem is that the dollar in one year will be worth either €0.80 or €1.25 with equal probability for each outcome. We face the paradoxical situation where one euro is expected to be worth $1.025 and one dollar is expected to be worth €1.025 in a year.

In the setting of a continuous-time process, if the €/$ exchange rate η follows a geometric Brownian motion

$$\frac{d\eta}{\eta} = \mu dt + \sigma dW$$

then the $/€ exchange rate is $f(\eta) = 1/\eta$. To write the process for $f(\eta)$, we use Itô's lemma. Note that $f_\eta = -1/\eta^2$ and $f_{\eta\eta} = 2/\eta^3$. f is not an explicit function of time, and so $f_t = 0$. A straightforward application of Itô's lemma gives

$$df = \left[-\frac{1}{\eta^2}\mu\eta + 0 + \frac{1}{2}\frac{2}{\eta^3}\sigma^2\eta^2 \right] dt - \frac{1}{\eta^2}\sigma\eta dW$$

Hence

$$\frac{df}{f} = \left(\sigma^2 - \mu\right) dt - \sigma dW$$

For the expected exchange rate and its inverse to be equal as in the example above, we want $\mathbb{E}[d\eta/\eta] = \mathbf{E}[df/f]$. Since dW is zero on average, we have $\mathbb{E}[d\eta/\eta] = \mu dt$ and $\mathbb{E}[df/f] = \left(\sigma^2 - \mu\right) dt$. A trader can assign the €/$ exchange rate and the $/€ exchange rate the same expected value if $\sigma^2 = 2\mu$.

We now discuss two implications of Siegel's paradox:

1. Looking at the simple example in Paradox 1, one conclusion is that investors need to keep part of their currency exposure unhedged. If an American holds €1, then the euro is expected to be worth $1.025. Simultaneously, a European owning $1 can expect it to be worth €1.025. It appears there are gains for both investors keeping their currency holdings (at least partly) unhedged.

2. Forward exchange rates cannot be unbiased predictors of future spot exchange rates. To be an unbiased predictor, the forward €/$ exchange rate at time t, $F(t)$ needs to be by definition the expected value of the €/$ exchange rate at $t + 1$. So, $F(t) = \mathbb{E}[\eta_{t+1}]$. If forwards were unbiased predictors of future spot rates, then this should also apply to the $/€ exchange rate: $1/F(t) = \mathbb{E}[1/\eta_{t+1}]$. But this can never happen in an uncertain world. This mathematical result:

$$\frac{1}{\mathbb{E}[\eta_{t+1}]} \geq \mathbb{E}\left[\frac{1}{\eta_{t+1}}\right]$$

is known as Jensen's inequality. Viewed in our context, it states that forward currency trades can be "profitable" on average.

1.7.2 Paradox 2: The Stock, Free-Lunch Paradox

Say you have to choose at time t between investing in a goverment bond or in the stock market. The question is: What is the probability that the stock investment will outperform the bond investment by time T? Say the value of the stock index S follows a geometric Brownian motion:

$$\frac{dS}{S} = \mu dt + \sigma dW$$

If invested in a zero-coupon bond, the amount S over time period $T - t$ will yield $S(t) \exp\{R(T - t)\}$ where R is the zero-coupon rate on a bond maturing in $T - t$ periods. The probability p that the stock investment outperforms the bond investment is

$$p = \Pr\left[S(t) \exp\left\{ \left(\mu - \frac{\sigma^2}{2}\right)(T - t) + \sigma\phi\sqrt{T - t} \right\} \right.$$
$$\left. > S(t) \exp\{R(T - t)\} \right]$$

A little algebra shows that

$$p = \Phi\left[\left(\frac{\mu - R}{\sigma} - \frac{\sigma}{2}\right)\sqrt{T - t}\right]$$

where Φ is the cumulative standard normal distribution.

To illustrate the result, say the risk premium of a stock index over zero-coupon bonds, that is, $\mu - r$, is 5.6% and index volatility is 20%. Then

$$p = \Phi[0.18\sqrt{T - t}]$$

Table 1.1 gives the probability p of outperformance of stocks as a function of the holding period.

The probability of outperformance goes to 100% as the holding period goes to infinity. However, if the investor wanted to buy insurance against the risk of the stock investment underperforming the bond investment, as the reader will discover in the next chapter, the hedging investment is a put option on the stock index purchased at

Table 1.1.

Holding Period $T - t$ in Years	Probability p in %
1	57
2	60
5	66
10	72
20	79
50	90
100	96

time t with strike price $S(t) \exp\{R(T - t)\}$ and expiring at T. The investor would realize in dismay that the price of such insurance increases with the time to expiration! It appears, paradoxically, that the insurance market is assigning a higher and higher price to an event with probability shrinking to zero. This is just an illustration of the growing insurance premium that hedgers are willing to pay as the hedging horizon increases.

1.7.3 Paradox 3: The Skill Versus Luck Paradox

Is outperformance versus an index a signal of managerial talent or the result of market randomness? The question is more than academic considering the size of the money management industry today. This section attempts to give no more than a stylized answer (see Ambarish and Seigel, 1996). Consider a money manager whose portfolio value P follows the motion

$$\frac{dP}{P} = \mu_P dt + \sigma_P dW_P$$

The money manager is trying to beat an index

$$\frac{dI}{I} = \mu_I dt + \sigma_I dW_I$$

dW_P and dW_I have correlation ρ. With $F(P, I) = R = P/I$ denoting relative performance, it follows from Example 1.3 that

$$\frac{dR}{R} = \left(\mu_P - \mu_I + \sigma_I^2 - \sigma_I \sigma_P \rho\right) dt + \sigma_P dW_P - \sigma_I dW_I$$

As in Example 1.3, we can define a Wiener process W_R so that $\sigma_R dW_R = \sigma_P dW_P - \sigma_I dW_I$ with $\sigma_R^2 = \sigma_P^2 + \sigma_I^2 - 2\rho\sigma_P\sigma_I$.

Now define $\mu_R = \mu_P - \mu_I + \sigma_I^2 - \sigma_I\sigma_P\rho$. We therefore have

$$\frac{dR}{R} = \mu_R dt + \sigma_R dW_R$$

with $R(0) = P_0/I_0$. We can state the value of the process at time t:

$$R_t = R_0 \exp\left[\left(\mu_R - \frac{1}{2}\sigma_R^2\right)t\right]\exp\left(\sigma_R\phi\sqrt{t}\right)$$

Without loss of generality, we may take $R_0 = 1$.

$$R_t > 1 \Rightarrow \log R_t = \left(\mu_R - \frac{1}{2}\sigma_R^2\right)t + \sigma_R\phi\sqrt{t} > 0$$

$$\Rightarrow t > \frac{\sigma_R^2\phi^2}{\left(\mu_R - \frac{1}{2}\sigma_R^2\right)^2}$$

The realization of ϕ defines the confidence interval with which one can predict the above inequality. For example, when $\phi = 1$, the confidence interval is 84%.

Table 1.2. *Probability of Outperformance in $t = 1$ Year ($\sigma_P = 25\%$; $\sigma_I = 15\%$; $\rho = 90\%$)*

$\mu_P - \mu_I$	**Probability in %**
0%	44
3%	53
6%	62
9%	70
12%	78
15%	84

Table 1.3. *Time it Takes to Outperform Versus Confidence Level ($\sigma_P = 25\%$; $\sigma_I = 15\%$; $\rho = 90\%$; $\mu_P - \mu_I = 3\%$)*

Term (years)	**Confidence Level in %**
1	53
25	65
50	70
75	74
100	78
200	86
300	90

Alternatively, based on the above, the probability of beating the index is

$$\Phi \left[\frac{\left(\mu_R - \frac{1}{2}\sigma_R^2 \right) \sqrt{t}}{\sigma_R} \right]$$

Tables 1.2 and 1.3 illustrate these points. Table 1.3 states that, if a portfolio manager outperforms the index by 3% per year on average and under the volatility and correlation conditions described above, it would take 300 years for this manager to outperform the index with 90% probability.

2

Principles of Financial Valuation

This chapter introduces the fundamentals of security pricing. It begins with a discussion on utility theory and risk and introduces the stochastic discount factor, or pricing kernel, as the fundamental determinant of all security prices. Some basic applications are introduced as examples and to help develop martingale pricing principles. This is initially accomplished in a discrete-time setting and then taken to continuous time. The stochastic discount factor and martingale pricing are subsequently used to develop various option-pricing results. Throughout the chapter, every effort is made to relate the mathematics of pricing to the underlying economic concepts.

2.1 UNCERTAINTY, UTILITY THEORY, AND RISK

One of the most important concepts in finance is that of *risk*. The fact that there is so much risk in the world is what makes finance a very complicated subject. As we will see later, the existence of financial markets and institutions can be explained by the need to control risk in our lives. Therefore, before we can dive into the theory of finance, we must first understand what risk is and how it affects us. The mathematical characterization of risk is one of the main goals of economic theory and the building block of modern finance theory. In this section, we will present the basics of this theory.

Generally, when thinking of risk, we think of an uncertain factor affecting our "happiness" in a negative manner. For example, a homeowner may be very concerned about the risk of fire destroying his home. A person commuting to work may be concerned about the risk of traffic conditions or the weather making him late for work. The two key elements that comprise risk are uncertainty and how that uncertainty affects "happiness."

Uncertainty refers to the fact that we do not know for certain the outcome of a particular event. For example, we do not know for certain what the weather will be like tomorrow when we commute to work. As another example, we do not know when lightning will strike a house. In economics, uncertainty is characterized using probability theory. We use random variables to characterize the uncertainty associated with an uncertain event. For example, we may characterize all uncertainty associated with our commute to work by a random variable x_t, which represents the time in minutes it takes to commute to work on a given day. The subscript t on the random variable indicates that repeated draws occur through time from the distribution characterizing that random variable. Therefore, if $x_t \sim N(30, 4)$, that is, a normal random variable with mean of 30 and standard deviation of 2, we could say that our expected commute time to work for any given day is 30 minutes and that there is a 95% chance that it will take between 26 and 34 minutes to get to work on any given day. Of course, a normal distribution cannot be the true distribution for the commute time because this distribution allows for negative commute times. In other words, the normal distribution gives positive probabilities to negative commute times, which does not make physical sense. Therefore, better distributional assumptions for x_t would be the lognormal or chi-squared distributions. However, the convenient properties of the normal distribution make it very attractive to use even with events where it may not make physical sense to do so. With the lightning strike example above, we may want to characterize the event of a lightning strike as a draw from a Poisson distribution. Alternatively, we may consider the time between lightning strikes to be approximately normally distributed.

Of course, uncertainty by itself is not a sufficient description of risk. For example, we may be uncertain as to what the winning lottery number will be tomorrow, but if we have not entered the lottery then this is not a source of risk. Therefore, for an uncertain event to represent risk, it must somehow affect our well-being or happiness. In economics, we use the expression *utility* to represent happiness. Mathematically, we can represent the happiness that we get from things such as consumption of goods by functions called utility functions, or preference functions. For example, the utility from purchasing (consuming) a television could be represented by the utility function

$$u(C_t) = C_t^2 \tag{2.1}$$

where $u(C_t)$ represents the level of utility at time t and C_t represents the number of televisions purchased at time t.

Now, it may seem as though we could use any arbitrary function to represent a utility function, but this is not completely true. Utility functions have to satisfy two basic mathematical properties. First, a utility function must be a monotonically increasing function. Intuitively, this means that if we get utility from consuming a good, then the more of that good we consume the more utility we must get from it. However, it seems unreasonable to assume that we would get the same utility from consumption of the tenth television as from the first television. For most of us, one or two televisions in the home is enough so that the tenth television in a home adds very little to our happiness. This characteristic is captured by the concept of diminishing marginal utility. Marginal utility is the incremental utility that one gets from each additional unit of consumption, and it can be calculated by simply taking the derivative of the utility function. Therefore, for the utility function given in (2.1) above, the marginal utility function is given by

$$u'(C_t) = 2C_t \tag{2.2}$$

The second mathematical property that utility functions must satisfy is that they have diminishing marginal utility functions, in other words, marginal utility functions should be monotonically decreasing functions. Notice that while the utility function in (2.1) satisfies the condition that utility functions be increasing functions, it does not satisfy the diminishing marginal utility condition.

A commonly used utility function that satisfies both conditions is the log utility function given by

$$u(C_t) = \log C_t \tag{2.3}$$

With the log utility function, utility is increasing in consumption, but marginal utility is decreasing in consumption.

Now that we have discussed the concepts of uncertainty and utility, we are ready to introduce the definition of risk. Risk is simply uncertainty about anything that either directly or indirectly affects our utility. Another way of stating this is that something is considered risky if it makes us uncertain about our level of utility in the future. So if utility is determined by consumption (as we will assume for the remainder of the book), and something makes future consumption uncertain, then that something represents risk to us. For example, the performance of the economy may represent risk to us if the economy affects our level of consumption because our uncertainty about the performance of the economy translates into uncertainty in our consumption level, and thus uncertainty about our utility. However, the arrival time of a flight arriving in Hong Kong does not represent risk to most of us because it does not make us more uncertain about our utility.

Since we have a way of quantifying uncertainty and our preferences, there should be a way of quantifying the level of risk we face and our attitude toward risk. We demonstrate how this is done through an example. Suppose that it is time $t - 1$ today and that our utility function for time t consumption is given by (2.3). Assume, however, that we are uncertain about our level of consumption; therefore, we face risky consumption because we are uncertain about it and it affects our utility. Assume furthermore that the uncertainty in consumption is characterized by a Bernoulli distribution

$$C_t = \varepsilon \tag{2.4}$$

where ε represents a Bernoulli random variable that takes on the value 5 with probability $1/2$ and the value 10 with probability $1/2$. Figure 2.1 depicts how this uncertainty in consumption translates to uncertainty in utility, or risk.

Suppose we are in the "good" state and we have a consumption level of 10. Then, our utility level is $\log 10$ utils (for the remainder of the book, we will refer to a unit of utility as a *util*). However, if we are in the "bad" state, then we have a utility level of $\log 5$ utils. Therefore, our utility level is also characterized by a Bernoulli distribution. One natural way of characterizing our level of utility under uncertainty is by our expected level of utility. Since the good and bad states occur with probability $1/2$ each, our expected level of utility at time t is given

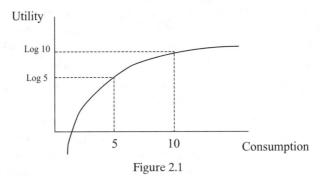

Figure 2.1

by

$$\mathbb{E}[u(C_t)] = \frac{1}{2}\log 10 + \frac{1}{2}\log 5 \approx 1.956 \text{ utils} \qquad (2.5)$$

Let's compare this to the level of utility achieved at the expected level of consumption. Our expected level of consumption at time t is given by

$$\mathbb{E}[C_t] = \frac{1}{2}(10) + \frac{1}{2}(5) = 7.5 \text{ units} \qquad (2.6)$$

Our utility level at this level of consumption is $\log 7.5 \approx 2.015$. Note that this is higher than the expected level of utility. Why? This is because the utility function is a nonlinear function, and for nonlinear functions

$$\mathbb{E}[u(C_t)] \neq u(\mathbb{E}[C_t]) \qquad (2.7)$$

which states that expected utility of consumption is not equal to the utility of expected consumption. More specifically, for concave functions (which all utility functions are due to the diminishing marginal utility condition)

$$\mathbb{E}[u(C_t)] \leq u(\mathbb{E}[C_t]) \qquad (2.8)$$

This is known as Jensen's inequality.

Example 2.1. Suppose that someone were willing to sell us an insurance contract that allowed us to lock in, or hedge, the level of consumption at time t at the level of consumption that we expect to have, 7.5. This contract takes out all the uncertainty from consumption. Would we be willing to take this contract? Yes, because it would increase our expected level of utility from 1.956 to 2.015. This demonstrates precisely why there is value in insurance, or hedging risk. By locking in the level of consumption to that which we expected to have, our utility increases. How much would we be willing to pay the insurer for this contract? Well, we would be willing to pay up to

$$2.015 - 1.956 = .059 \ utils$$

Of course, we need to translate this into units of the consumption good since we cannot literally give away units of utility. Since 2.015 utils correspond to 7.5 units of the consumption good, and 1.956 utils correspond to

$$u^{-1}(1.956) = \exp 1.956 = 7.071$$

units of the consumption good, we can conclude that we would be willing to pay up to

$$7.5 - 7.071 = .429$$

units of the consumption good at time t in return for the insurance contract.

In this example, if we could lock in a level of consumption of 7.5, all risk would be eliminated because we would no longer be uncertain about how much we would consume at time t, and therefore our utility at time t. This indicates that a good way to measure the amount of risk is the level of dispersion of the distribution characterizing that risk. When there is no dispersion, such as when consumption is known to be a sure 7.5 units, then there is no risk. However, when there is some dispersion in consumption, as in when consumption has a 50–50 chance of being 10 units or 5 units, we face risk, and the greater the dispersion the more risk we face. A natural way to measure the level of dispersion of uncertain consumption or utility is the standard deviation (or, equivalently, the variance) of consumption or utility. When consumption was a sure 7.5 units, the standard deviation of consumption was zero, and therefore, we faced no risk. However, when consumption was either 5 or 10 units, the standard deviation was

$$\sqrt{\frac{1}{2}(10 - 7.5)^2 + \frac{1}{2}(5 - 7.5)^2} = 2.5 \qquad (2.9)$$

and we faced risk.

Now, intuitively, we would expect that since there is a gain in utility from hedging risk, the gain should be higher in the presence of greater risk. Let's check our intuition by increasing the risk in Example 2.1 and recalculating the gain in utility from hedging this risk. In order to increase the risk we face, we need to increase the standard deviation of consumption. Therefore, suppose consumption at time t is now a Bernoulli random variable that takes on the value 5 with probability $1/2$ and 15 with probability $1/2$. The standard deviation of consumption is now

$$\sqrt{\frac{1}{2}(15 - 10)^2 + \frac{1}{2}(5 - 10)^2} = 5$$

so the risk has indeed increased. Our expected level of utility is

$$\frac{1}{2}\log 15 + \frac{1}{2}\log 5 \approx 2.159 \text{ utils}$$

The expected level of consumption is 10 units. If we could hedge consumption at this level, our expected utility would be $\log 10 \approx 2.303$ utils. Therefore, the gain from hedging risk is

$$2.303 - 2.159 = 0.144 \text{ utils}$$

which is indeed greater than the 0.059 utils that we gained when hedging a lower amount of risk. This also indicates that we would be willing to pay a higher price in terms of the units of consumption good in order to have the insurance contract.

2.2 RISK AND THE EQUILIBRIUM PRICING OF SECURITIES

The future price of a security is a source of risk for two reasons. First, we are uncertain as to what that price will be. Second, it affects our utility because if the price of the security is high and we are invested in it, then we can consume more from the proceeds of selling that security, and thus our utility will be higher (since a utility function is monotonically increasing). Alternatively, if the price is low, we will consume less from the proceeds of selling the security and our utility will be lower. In this section, we relate the concept of risk which was introduced in the previous section to the pricing of financial securities.

We first consider the following problem. An individual who invests his savings into the stock market and lives off of the dividends is trying to decide how to allocate his funds between two stocks. How should he allocate his wealth? The individual has a total amount of wealth M and will invest that wealth into stock 1 and/or stock 2. Stock 1 pays a dividend of δ_1 dollars per share of stock 1 owned, while stock 2 pays a dividend of δ_2 dollars per share. The individual's utility function is a function of two arguments: the dividend received from his investment in stock 1 and the dividend received from his investment in stock 2. The utility function is given by $U(\delta_1 N_1, \delta_2 N_2)$. Here, N_1 represents the number of shares of stock 1 he decides to purchase, while N_2 represents the number of shares of stock 2. Therefore $\delta_1 N_1$ represents the dividend that the individual receives from stock 1 and, similarly, $\delta_2 N_2$ represents the dividend received from stock 2.

The question of how to allocate the investor's wealth between the two stocks is formalized by the following static optimization problem:

$$\max_{N_1, N_2} U(\delta_1 N_1, \delta_2 N_2) \qquad (2.10)$$

subject to the following constraint:

$$M \geq p_1 N_1 + p_2 N_2 \qquad (2.11)$$

where p_1 and p_2 represent the current prices of stocks 1 and 2, respectively. This simply states that the individual attempts to maximize his utility U by deciding how many shares, N_1 and N_2, of each stock to purchase. Of course he cannot simply buy all of the existing shares in the market. So the constraint, which we call a budget constraint, says that the number of shares of each stock he buys multiplied by their respective prices must not be greater than his wealth.

To solve this equation we use a Lagrange multiplier, λ, to write the problem as one simple optimization problem over the two control variables:

$$\max_{N_1, N_2} U(\delta_1 N_1, \delta_2 N_2) + \lambda \left[M - p_1 N_1 - p_2 N_2 \right]$$

To solve this optimization problem, we take first-order conditions with respect to each of the control variables, N_1, N_2:

$$N_1 : \quad U_1' - \lambda p_1 = 0$$
$$N_2 : \quad U_2' - \lambda p_2 = 0$$

Here U'_1 represents the first derivative of the utility function with respect to the first argument, while U'_2 represents the first derivative of the utility function with respect to the second argument. Therefore, U'_1 and U'_2 represent marginal utilities with respect to the number of shares of each stock owned. We can solve for λ in both equations:

$$\lambda = \frac{U'_1}{p_1}; \qquad \lambda = \frac{U'_2}{p_2}$$

Since both expressions on the right-hand side (RHS) equate to λ, they must be equal to each other. Therefore, we have the following result from the investor's optimization problem:

$$\frac{U'_1}{p_1} = \frac{U'_2}{p_2}$$

$$\frac{U'_1}{U'_2} = \frac{p_1}{p_2} \qquad (2.12)$$

Equation (2.12) is one of the most fundamental relations in financial economics. It states that if the investor acts optimally, the ratio of prices of the two securities equals the ratio of marginal utilities of the prices of those two stocks. The ratio of marginal utilities, U'_1/U'_2, is such an important expression that it has a special name. It is typically referred to as the *marginal rate of substitution* between the two stocks.

To see how this problem works for an actual utility function, let's use an actual utility function and put numbers in to verify (2.12). The utility function is assumed to be of the form

$$U(\delta_1 N_1, \delta_2 N_2) = \frac{(\delta_1 N_1)^{1-\gamma} - 1}{1 - \gamma} + \frac{(\delta_2 N_2)^{1-\gamma} - 1}{1 - \gamma}$$

Utility functions of this form are known as *power utility functions* because utility is determined by raising the utility-inducing quantity to some power. In this case the power is $1 - \gamma$. The term γ is known as the coefficient of risk aversion, because as γ rises the individual becomes more risk averse, that is, he demands more compensation for bearing greater volatility. If $\gamma = 0$, then the individual is *risk-neutral*; that is, he demands no additional compensation for bearing volatility, no matter how great that volatility may be. So, from (2.12), the price ratio of the two securities for power utility is given by

$$\frac{p_1}{p_2} = \frac{\delta_1 \left(\delta_1 N_1 \right)^{-\gamma}}{\delta_2 \left(\delta_2 N_2 \right)^{-\gamma}} \tag{2.13}$$

Notice from this relation that if the dividends received from stock 2 are higher than those of stock 1, then as γ increases, that is, as the investor becomes more risk averse, the price of stock 2 becomes higher. This is because as the investor becomes more risk averse, he prefers to invest in the higher dividend stock. As his demand for that stock increases, so does its price. Similarly, if the dividend per share, δ_2, is higher for stock 2, then the price of stock 2 will increase relative to stock 1's price. This is because the investor always prefers the higher-dividend-paying stock to the lower-dividend-paying stock, since the higher-dividend-paying stock gives him greater utility. This increases the demand for stock 2 relative to stock 1 and therefore increases stock 2's price relative to that of stock 1.

Example 2.2. Using (2.13), we can construct a numerical example. Suppose the individual has $10,000 to invest (so $M = 10,000$), and his risk aversion coefficient is 2. If stock 1's price is $50 and pays a dividend of $2 per share, and stock 2's price is $25 and pays a dividend of $5 per share, then the number of shares bought by the investor is determined by

$$\frac{N_2}{N_1} = \frac{2}{\sqrt{5}} = 0.8944$$

So, the individual would buy 0.8944 times as many shares of stock 2 as of stock 1. With wealth of $10,000, this means that the individual would buy

$$\frac{10,000}{0.8944(25) + 50} = 138.1966$$

shares of stock 1 and $0.8944 \times 138.1966 = 123.6068$ shares of stock 2.

Of course, in the above example, the amount of risk of the two securities was zero. Now, we would like to see how the introduction of uncertainty into the economic environment affects the pricing relation (2.12). To do so, we first provide a description of the uncertainty in the environment. Figure 2.2 provides a possible characterization of this uncertainty.

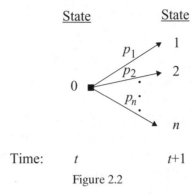

Figure 2.2

At time t all current prices are known; however, it is uncertain what prices are going to be tomorrow, time $t + 1$. At time $t + 1$, the economy can move into one of n possible states from today. Each state of the economy is characterized by a different set of prices for securities. The probability of each state occurring is given by p_ω where $\omega = 1, \ldots, n$. Since these are probabilities, we have the relation

$$\sum_{\omega=1}^{n} p_\omega = 1$$

Now consider once again the problem of an investor who is trying to decide how to invest his savings. However, this time he has to choose among securities with the future being uncertain. We will use the characterization of uncertainty given in Figure 2.2, with $n = 2$ (only 2 possible future states at time $t + 1$). The probabilities of moving to states 1 or 2 are given by p_1 and p_2. In addition, his choice of securities is different. In this economy, there exist 2 Arrow-Debreu securities whose prices are given as $A(1)$ and $A(2)$. An Arrow-Debreu security, $A(\omega)$, is defined as a security that pays \$1 if state ω is realized at time $t + 1$. For example, if the economy moves into state 2 at time $t + 1$, then security $A(2)$ is worth \$1, while security $A(1)$ is worth \$0. The investor's problem is to maximize his utility by consuming his wealth at times t and $t + 1$ and investing his wealth appropriately in the collection of Arrow-Debreu securities between times t and $t + 1$. His utility function is given by

$$U = u(C_t) + \mathbb{E}_t \left[u(C_{t+1}(\omega)) \right]$$

where C_t represents how much consumption the investor chooses at time t and $C_{t+1}(\omega)$ represents how much consumption the investor chooses at time $t+1$ in state ω. Notice that in this utility function, because the future is uncertain, the investor maximizes the *expected* value of future utility. Beginning with an initial wealth of W_t, he first decides how much to consume out of this initial wealth. Then, he invests the remaining amount of his wealth in the Arrow-Debreu securities. Let $N(1)$ represent the number of shares bought of $A(1)$ and $N(2)$ represent the number of shares purchased of $A(2)$. At time $t+1$, the state of the economy is realized and some of his Arrow-Debreu securities pay off \$1 each. He then uses all of these proceeds for consumption. Therefore, his optimization problem is the following:

$$\max_{C_t,\, C_{t+1},\, N(1),\, N(2)} u(C_t) + \mathbb{E}_t\left[u(C_{t+1}(\omega))\right] \tag{2.14}$$

subject to the budget constraint

$$M_t = A(1)N(1) + A(2)N(2) + C_t \tag{2.15}$$

To solve this problem, first notice that

$$C_{t+1}(\omega) = N(\omega)$$

for $\omega = 1, 2$. To see why, suppose that state 1 is realized, that is, $\omega = 1$. Then any proceeds in security 2 are worth 0. If $N(1)$ shares of $A(1)$ were purchased, then these shares are worth exactly $N(1)$ since each share pays off exactly \$1. Therefore, the investor's utility-maximizing consumption is to consume all of these proceeds, $C_{t+1}(1) = N(1)$. Similar arguments apply if state $\omega = 2$ is realized instead of state 1. Using this relation we can substitute for $C_{t+1}(\omega)$ in (2.14).

$$\max_{C_t,\, C_{t+1},\, N(1),\, N(2)} u(C_t) + \mathbb{E}_t\left[u(N(\omega))\right] \tag{2.16}$$

In addition, from (2.15) we can express C_t as

$$C_t = M_t - A(1)N(1) - A(2)N(2) \tag{2.17}$$

We can rearrange (2.17) and substitute into (2.16) to reduce the optimization problem to

$$\max_{N(1),\, N(2)} u(M_t - A(1)N(1) - A(2)N(2)) + \mathbb{E}_t\left[u(N(\omega))\right]$$

We can rewrite the expectation $\mathbb{E}_t[u(N(\omega))]$ using the probabilities p_1 and p_2 of moving into each state:

$$\mathbb{E}_t[u(N(\omega))] = p_1 u(N(1)) + p_2 u(N(2))$$

Therefore, the optimization problem can be written as

$$\max_{N(1),\,N(2)} u(M_t - A(1)N(1) - A(2)N(2)) + p_1 u(N(1)) + p_2 u(N(2))$$

The first-order conditions with respect to $N(1)$ and $N(2)$ are given as

$$N(1): \quad A(1)u'(C_t) = p_1 u'(C_{t+1})$$
$$N(2): \quad A(2)u'(C_t) = p_2 u'(C_{t+1})$$

Therefore, we have derived the price today of each Arrow-Debreu security.

$$A(1) = p_1 \frac{u'(C_{t+1}(\omega))}{u'(C_t)}$$

$$A(2) = p_2 \frac{u'(C_{t+1}(\omega))}{u'(C_t)}$$

Notice that the ratio of marginal utilities once again appears in this pricing relationship as it did in Example 2.1. However, this time it is not the ratio of marginal utilities across securities but the ratio of marginal utilities across time. This ratio is called the *intertemporal marginal rate of substitution*. It is also referred to as the *state price density* and the *pricing kernel*.

The above equations yield a fundamental result: the price of an Arrow-Debreu security is simply the product of the intertemporal marginal rate of substitution and the probability of the state occurring in which the Arrow-Debreu security pays off \$1. This result is quite powerful because it applies not just in this example, but in any situation with uncertainty. One can see a bit of that generality by extending the above example to n possible states and n Arrow-Debreu securities. In this case we would obtain the result

$$A(\omega) = p_\omega \frac{u'(C_{t+1}(\omega))}{u'(C_t)} \qquad \omega = 1, \ldots, n \qquad (2.18)$$

Now, the question is, how can we use this result to price securities other than Arrow-Debreu securities, that is, securities with arbitrary payoff structures? Suppose we go back to our two-state example and introduce a new security into the economy. Unlike the Arrow-Debreu security, this security pays off \$1 no matter which state of the economy is realized at time $t + 1$. We call such a security a risk-free bond because its payoff is the same regardless of what state occurs. Thus, an investor experiences no risk by investing in such an asset.

How would we calculate the price of a risk-free bond at time t? We do so by a replication argument. Let's call the price of the risk-free bond at time t as $P(t, t + 1)$. The $t + 1$ refers to the fact that the bond matures at time $t + 1$. Notice that the risk-free bond can be replicated by a portfolio of two Arrow-Debreu securities, one share of $A(1)$ and one share of $A(2)$. This portfolio exactly matches the payoff of the risk-free bond since the portfolio too pays \$1 regardless of which state occurs. Therefore, this portfolio must also have the same price as the risk-free bond. Why? This is because if its price were different from that of the risk-free bond, we would have an *arbitrage* opportunity present in the economy. When an arbitrage opportunity is present, it means that riskless profits can be made through some trading strategy. In this specific case, if the portfolio of Arrow-Debreu securities differs in price from the price of the risk-free bond, then the arbitrage strategy would be to buy the lower priced one and sell short the higher priced one. Since each has the exact same payoff profile, this trade would leave us with zero net risk (the risk of one cancels the other's risk because we have bought and sold in equal quantities the same payoff profile). However, we would make a profit because we are buying at a low price and selling at a high price. Since arbitrage conditions cannot exist in an economy, the price of the risk-free bond equals the price of the portfolio. Using (2.18), the price of the portfolio is simply

$$P(t, t + 1) = A(1) + A(2) = p_1 \frac{u'(C_{t+1}(1))}{u'(C_t)} + p_2 \frac{u'(C_{t+1}(2))}{u'(C_t)}$$

$$P(t, t + 1) = \mathbb{E}_t^{\mathbb{P}} \left[\frac{u'(C_{t+1}(\omega))}{u'(C_t)} \right]$$

Therefore, the price of a risk-free bond is simply the expected value, taken with respect to the probability measure $\mathbb{P} = \{p_1, p_2\}$, of the intertemporal marginal rate of substitution. The interest rate r_t is now defined using the reciprocal of the bond price.

$$1 + r_t = \frac{1}{P(t, t + 1)}$$

Therefore, we have the fundamental relation

$$\frac{1}{1+r_t} = \mathbb{E}_t^{\mathbb{P}}\left[\frac{u'(C_{t+1}(\omega))}{u'(C_t)}\right] \tag{2.19}$$

that defines the interest rate in any economy. So, suppose that the probability of state 1 occurring is 1/4, while the probability of state 2 occurring is 3/4. Also assume that the pricing kernel equals 0.95 for state 1 and 0.92 for state 2. Then using the previous formulas, we can calculate the bond price

$$P(t, t+1) = \frac{1}{4}(.95) + \frac{3}{4}(.92) = .9275$$

The interest rate is then given by

$$r_t = \frac{1}{.9275} - 1 = 7.82\%$$

Thus, we see that the pricing of a bond and the determination of interest rates is simple to do once the set of Arrow-Debreu prices, the prices of Arrow-Debreu securities, are known. But what about a security that has some arbitrarily complicated payoff pattern, rather than the simple payoff pattern of a bond? Suppose that a security has a payoff function, or future price function, given by $f_{t+1}(\omega)$ where $\omega = 1, \ldots, n$. Can this security be replicated by a portfolio of Arrow-Debreu securities? Yes! Consider the portfolio that consists of holding $N(\omega) = f_{t+1}(\omega), \omega = 1, \ldots, n$, Arrow-Debreu securities. This portfolio exactly replicates the security. The price of the portfolio of Arrow-Debreu securities at time t is given by

$$f_t = \sum_{\omega=1}^{n} p_\omega \frac{u'(C_{t+1}(\omega))}{u'(C_t)} f_{t+1}(\omega) \tag{2.20}$$

$$f_t = \mathbb{E}_t^{\mathbb{P}}\left[\frac{u'(C_{t+1}(\omega))}{u'(C_t)} f_{t+1}(\omega)\right] \tag{2.21}$$

Equation (2.21) is one of the most important pricing formulas in finance. It basically allows us to calculate the price of any security today using that security's payoff structure at some future point.

Two major implications fall out from (2.20) and (2.21) that we will use regularly throughout the book. First, take (2.21) and multiply through by $u'(C_t)$. This basically gives the following relation:

$$u'(C_t) f_t = \mathbb{E}_t^{\mathbb{P}}\left[u'(C_{t+1}(\omega)) f_{t+1}(\omega)\right] \tag{2.22}$$

Any sequence of random variables $\{G_t\}$ that satisfies the relation $G_t = \mathbb{E}_t[G_{t+1}]$ is known as a martingale. Notice that in (2.22), $u'(C_t)f_t$ satisfies exactly this definition. Therefore, we have the relation that the price of any asset multiplied by marginal utility is a martingale. If we normalize current marginal utility to 1, then the relation can be restated as the product of any asset price and the pricing kernel is a martingale.

The second major implication, and one that is more useful, comes from rewriting (2.20) by transforming the probabilities. Notice that both the probability p_ω and the pricing kernel $\frac{u'(C_{t+1}(\omega))}{u'(C_t)}$ vary with the state ω. Consequently, we can try to transform the probabilities used in (2.20) to simplify the pricing relation.

The pricing equation (2.20) is a weighted sum of all the possible outcomes for the asset price, in various states of the world ω at time $t+1$. Since $\{p_\omega\}$ is a set of probabilities and u is a utility function, we have $p_\omega > 0$ and $u' > 0$ for all ω. Hence the weights are all positive. To make them look like a set of probabilities, we also need to ensure that they sum to 1. Keeping this in mind, we try the transformation

$$q_\omega = \frac{p_\omega \frac{u'(C_{t+1}(\omega))}{u'(C_t)}}{\sum_{\omega=1}^{n} p_\omega \frac{u'(C_{t+1}(\omega))}{u'(C_t)}}$$

It is easy to verify that indeed $0 < q_\omega < 1$ for each ω, and $\sum_\omega q_\omega = 1$. Thus, $\mathbb{Q} = \{q_\omega : \omega = 1, \dots, n\}$ represents a set of probabilities on the possible future states of the world. Additionally, note that $p_\omega = 0 \Leftrightarrow q_\omega = 0$, meaning that the two sets of probabilities agree on what is impossible. Probability measures that satisfy this property are called "equivalent probability measures."

From the definition of interest rates, we note that

$$\sum_{\omega=1}^{n} p_\omega \frac{u'(C_{t+1}(\omega))}{u'(C_t)} = \frac{1}{1+r_t}$$

Using this, we can rewrite the equivalent probabilities as

$$q_\omega = p_\omega \frac{u'(C_{t+1}(\omega))}{u'(C_t)}(1+r_t) \tag{2.23}$$

Under this transformation, (2.20) can be rewritten as

$$f_t = \sum_{\omega=1}^{n} p_\omega \frac{u'(C_{t+1}(\omega))}{u'(C_t)} f_{t+1}(\omega)$$

$$= \sum_{\omega=1}^{n} p_\omega \frac{u'(C_{t+1}(\omega))}{u'(C_t)} (1 + r_t) \frac{1}{1 + r_t} f_{t+1}(\omega)$$

$$= \sum_{\omega=1}^{n} q_\omega \frac{1}{1 + r_t} f_{t+1}(\omega)$$

$$f_t = \mathbb{E}_t^{\mathbb{Q}} \left[\frac{f_{t+1}(\omega)}{1 + r_t} \right] \tag{2.24}$$

The resulting equation once again has a simple interpretation. It states that the price of a security today is simply the expected price of the security in the future discounted back to today by the risk-free rate. Because the risk-free rate is used to discount the future payoff of the security, the q_ω probabilities are commonly known as *risk-neutral probabilities*. This terminology is used because even though the security is risky, the investor prices the security today as if he does not care about risk: He discounts back the risky payoff in the future at a risk-free rate. So, the investor is acting as if his utility function were a risk-neutral one.

The transformation coefficient, $\frac{u'(C_{t+1}(\omega))}{u'(C_t)}(1 + r_t)$, that relates q_ω and p_ω is known as the *Radon-Nikodym derivative*. This term is used generally to refer to any transformation coefficient that relates two sets of probabilities.

Now, let's do two examples to illustrate how to use risk-neutral probabilities to price assets.

Example 2.3. Suppose we have a stock with the payoff structure shown in Figure 2.3. The stock is liquidated in one period and pays off $1 if state 1 occurs, $2 if state 2 occurs, $3 if state 3 occurs, $4 if state 4 occurs, and $5 if state 5 occurs. We will assume that each state is equally likely to occur so that the probability of any state occurring is 20%. What is the price of this security today if the pricing kernel takes on the values 0.98, 0.96, 0.94, 0.92, and 0.9 for states 1 to 5, respectively?

To answer this question, let's first calculate the risk-neutral probability of each state using (2.23). Then we can use (2.24) to calculate the price of the security today. First, we need to calculate the risk-free rate, r_t. This

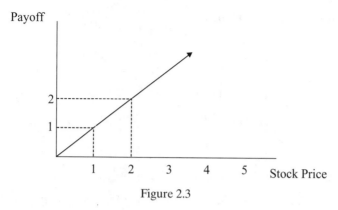

Figure 2.3

is given by the following set of calculations:

$$\frac{1}{1+r_t} = \mathbb{E}_t^{\mathbb{P}}\left[\frac{u'(C_{t+1}(\omega))}{u'(C_t)}\right]$$
$$= \frac{1}{5}(.98) + \frac{1}{5}(.96) + \frac{1}{5}(.94) + \frac{1}{5}(.92) + \frac{1}{5}(.9)$$
$$= .94$$

Therefore, we have

$$1 + r_t = 1.0638$$
$$r_t = 6.38\%$$

Now, we can calculate the risk-neutral probabilities using (2.23):

$$q_1 = p_1 \frac{u'(C_{t+1}(1))}{u'(C_t)}(1 + 6.38\%) = .2(.98)(1.0638) = .2085$$

Similarly, q_2, q_3, q_4, and q_5 are calculated as

$$q_2 = .2(.96)(1.0638) = .2043$$
$$q_3 = .2(.94)(1.0638) = .2$$
$$q_4 = .2(.92)(1.0638) = .1957$$
$$q_5 = .2(.90)(1.0638) = .1915$$

With these risk-neutral probabilities, we can now apply (2.24) to obtain the price of the security today:

$$f_t = \mathbb{E}_t^{\mathbb{Q}} \left[\frac{f_{t+1}(\omega)}{1 + r_t} \right]$$

$$= \frac{1}{1.0638} \left[q_1 \, f_{t+1}(1) + \ldots + q_5 \, f_{t+1}(5) \right]$$

$$= .94 \left[.2085(1) + .2043(2) + .2(3) + .1957(4) + .1915(5) \right]$$

$$= 2.78$$

Therefore, the current price of the stock is $2.78.

Example 2.4. Now consider a call option written on this same stock with a strike price of $3. Figure 2.4 gives the payoffs of the call option for each possible state of the economy. The call option pays off $0 in states 1, 2, and 3 and pays $1 in state 4 and $2 in state 5. What is the price of this call option?

Since the economy is the same as the one we used above in pricing the stock, we can use the risk-neutral probabilities and the interest rate calculated above in order to price the option.

$$f_t = \mathbb{E}_t^{\mathbb{Q}} \left[\frac{f_{t+1}(\omega)}{1 + r_t} \right]$$

$$= \frac{1}{1.0638} \left[q_1 \, f_{t+1}(1) + \ldots + q_5 \, f_{t+1}(5) \right]$$

$$= .94 \left[.2085(0) + .2043(0) + .2(0) + .1957(1) + .1915(2) \right]$$

$$= .54$$

Therefore, the price of the option is $0.54.

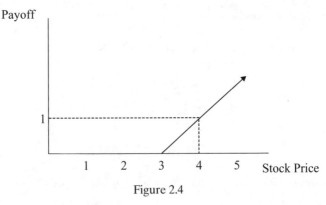

Figure 2.4

These two examples illustrate the power of the approach using risk-neutral probabilities. The price of any security, regardless of how complicated the payoff structure is, can be calculated by simply knowing the pricing kernel and the actual probabilities of future states.

2.3 THE BINOMIAL OPTION-PRICING MODEL

Now that we know how to build simple discrete-time models of security prices, let's apply that knowledge to the pricing of derivatives. In the previous section, we developed, through an example, a one-period price for an option on a stock. In this section, we extend that model to a multiperiod option-pricing model known commonly as the "binomial option-pricing model." The starting point for the model will be the simple one-period Bernoulli model developed before. However, now we attach several Bernoulli models together consecutively to form the binomial model. Figure 2.1 depicts this model. In this figure, the total time covered by the model is of length T. This length of time is split into n subperiods. Thus, each subperiod covers a period of time of length T/n.

The problem we face is the following. Suppose that we have a stock, with price S_t, an expected return of μ, and a subperiod volatility of σ. Now suppose we wish to purchase a contract that has the following payoff structure at the maturity date of that contract, time T:

$$\max[0, S_T - K]$$

where K represents the strike price of the contract, which is determined at the inception of the contract. Such a contract is known as a "call option." More specifically, it is known as a European call option because the contract expires only at the maturity date of the contract. Another type of option is the American call option, which has the same payoff structure but which can expire at any time before the maturity date (the owner of the option can exercise the option any time he chooses).

We will only be dealing with European options in this section. In order to price this option, we will use a multiperiod model. Initially, we will keep things simple by working out a two-period version of the model in Figure 2.3. This is depicted in Figure 2.5. We assume that it is currently time 0, and the option is scheduled to mature in two periods at time period 2. Our strategy for calculating the price of the option is as follows. We will first calculate the price of the option at maturity,

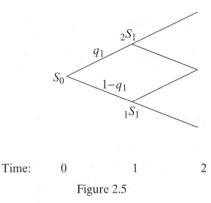

Time: 0   1   2

Figure 2.5

time 2, and then work backward through the tree by calculating the price of the option at each node to the left of the nodes at maturity. Then, when we have worked backward through the tree to the point where we have the option's price at the node at time 0, we will have calculated the price of the option today.

So, we first need to calculate the price of the option at maturity. To do this, we need the price of the stock at time 2, as the price of the option at time 2 depends only on the stock's price at that time. So, given that the price of the stock today is S_0, we need to calculate the prices of the stock at each of the three nodes at time 2. To do this, let us first calculate the price of the stock at each of the two nodes at time 1, and then from there we can calculate the price of the stock at each node at time 2.

The price of the stock at each node is explicitly determined by the first two moments of the stock's return dynamics. Specifically, we know the first two moments, R, which represents one plus the risk-free rate, and σ^2, of the stock price's risk-neutral dynamics, and we have three free variables in the model that must be set so that the model of the stock price process also has the same moments. The three free variables are the up/down probabilities and the stock prices at the up and down nodes. Denote the up and down probabilities at time 1 to be q_1 and $1 - q_1$, respectively, and denote the up and down stock price values at the up and down nodes to be $_2S_1$ and $_1S_1$, respectively.[1] Then we have

---

[1] In the term $_2S_1$, the subscript to the right represents the time (or horizontal displacement) and the subscript to the left represents the node (or vertical displacement) at that particular time.

the following two equations from the moment conditions:

$$q_1 u + (1 - q_1)d = R$$
$$q_1 (u - R)^2 + (1 - q_1)(d - R)^2 = \sigma^2$$

where u denotes the proportional return from time 0 to the up node at time 1 and d denotes the proportional return to the down node. Therefore, $u = {}_2S_1/S_0$ and $d = {}_1S_1/S_0$. In addition, we use r to denote the risk-free rate for one time period.

In these equations, we set the first moment equal to the risk-free rate rather than μ, the stock's true expected return, because we are interested in risk-neutral probabilities. From (2.23), these are given by $q_1 = p_1 \frac{u'(C_{t+1}(H))}{u'(C_t)}(1 + r_t)$ and $1 - q_1 = (1 - p_1)\frac{u'(C_{t+1}(L))}{u'(C_t)}(1 + r_t)$, where p_1 and $1 - p_1$ represent the true probabilities. As shown in (2.24), the advantage of using risk-neutral probabilities is that we can then discount all cash flows at the risk-free rate. Therefore, the price of the option at time 0 on the tree can be calculated by discounting the value of the option at time 2 back to time 0 at the risk-free rate. This is precisely the strategy we will use.

Since we have three variables and only two equations, infinitely many solutions exist. To pick a solution, we impose an additional constraint

$$q = 1 - q = \frac{1}{2}$$

for all probabilities on the tree. This constraint is not required. We impose it simply because an additional constraint is needed, and this particular one leads to simple solutions for the remaining variables. With this constraint, along with the two moment conditions, we can solve for u and d. The solutions are

$$u = R + \sigma$$
$$d = R - \sigma$$

Here, we will require that $\sigma < R$ to ensure that the stock price does not become negative. Now, it is easy to calculate the value of the stock throughout the tree. Starting with S_0, R, and σ as given

$$_1S_1 = S_0(R - \sigma)$$
$$_2S_1 = S_0(R + \sigma)$$
$$_1S_2 = S_0(R - \sigma)^2 \qquad (2.25)$$
$$_2S_2 = S_0(R - \sigma)(R + \sigma)$$
$$_3S_2 = S_0(R + \sigma)^2$$

With the values of the stock price known at the ending nodes, we can then calculate the payoff of the call option. At each node, the call option will have a payoff that is determined by the value of the stock at that node. Denote $_1F_2$, $_2F_2$, and $_3F_2$ the payoffs of the call option at nodes 1, 2, and 3, respectively, at time 2. Since the price of the option must equal its payoff at maturity, $_1F_2$, $_2F_2$, and $_3F_2$, also denote the prices of the option at time 2.

Now that we have the values of the option at time 2, we need to work backward through the tree to calculate the value of the option today, time 0. Since the risk-neutral probabilities have already been calculated, this is easy to do using (2.24). At time 1, we have the following option prices:

$$_1F_1 = \frac{_1F_2 + _2F_2}{2R}$$
$$_2F_1 = \frac{_2F_2 + _3F_2}{2R}$$

Then, from the prices of the option at time 1, we can calculate the time 0 price of the option

$$F_0 = \frac{_1F_1 + _2F_1}{2R}$$

Thus, we have calculated the current value of the call option with nothing more as inputs than the current stock price, the stock's return volatility, and the interest rate.

Example 2.5. Let's try a numerical example to see precisely how this would work. Suppose we have a stock whose current price is $30, its return volatility is 10% per month, and the interest rate is 1% per month. What would be the price of a call option written on this stock with a maturity of two months and a strike price of $31?

We'll use a simple two-period model and let each period represent one month. We will also use the assumption that the up/down risk-neutral probabilities are 1/2. Then, the up and down proportions are given by

$$u = 1.11$$
$$d = .91$$

From (2.25), it is easy to calculate the stock price at time 2:

$$_1 S_2 = \$24.843$$
$$_2 S_2 = \$30.303$$
$$_3 S_2 = \$36.963$$

From these stock prices, we can determine the payoff of the call option. The option pays off $\max[0, S_T - 31]$. *Therefore, the values of the call option at time 2 are simply*

$$_1 F_2 = \$0$$
$$_2 F_2 = \$0.303$$
$$_3 F_2 = \$6.963$$

Now, we can work backward through the tree. The values of the option at time 1 are

$$_1 F_1 = \$0.15$$
$$_2 F_1 = \$3.597$$

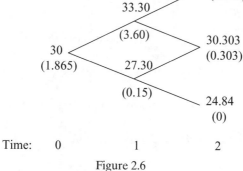

Time: 0   1   2

Figure 2.6

Therefore the current, time 0, value of the option is

$$\$1.865$$

Figure 2.6 shows the complete binomial tree with stock prices listed above the nodes and option prices listed below the nodes in parentheses.

2.4 LIMITING OPTION-PRICING FORMULA

Although it is simple to do two-period models to calculate option prices, it is not very accurate. That is because stocks trade almost continuously, and as a result they can take on more than just three values at the maturity of the option. Therefore, in the option-pricing example given in Example 2.5, to be more precise in calculating the value of the option, we should use a tree where one period represents a much shorter duration than one month. As we make the duration of each period shorter, more levels in the tree are needed for the tree to span the whole time period till the option's maturity, which allows the stock price to realize more potential values at the option's maturity date. This increases the realism of the model and, thus, its accuracy. Therefore, in this section we will calculate the general formula for the call option for an n-level binomial tree model.

This general price for a call option in an n-level tree was originally done in Cox, Ross, and Rubinstein (1979). To see what such a formula might look like, we first calculate the price of an option for $n = 1, 2$, and 3. It is obvious from here that the value of a call option is given simply by

$$C_0 = \frac{1}{R} \left[{}_1C_1 p + {}_2C_1 (1 - p) \right]$$
$$= \frac{1}{R} \left[\max(0, dS - K) p + \max(0, uS - K)(1 - p) \right]$$

For $n = 2$, we can follow the same set of calculations to derive

$$C_0 = \frac{1}{R} \left[{}_1C_2 p^2 + {}_2C_2 p(1 - p) + {}_3C_2 (1 - p)^2 \right]$$
$$= \frac{1}{R^2} \left[\max(0, d^2 S - K) p^2 + 2\max(0, udS - K) p(1 - p) \right.$$
$$\left. + \max(0, u^2 S - K)(1 - p)^2 \right]$$

Similarly, for $n = 3$, we obtain the relation

$$C_0 = \frac{1}{R^3}[\max\left(0, d^3 S - K\right) p^3 + 3\max\left(0, ud^2 S - K\right) p^2(1 - p)$$
$$+ 3\max\left(0, u^2 dS - K\right) p(1 - p)^2 + \max\left(0, u^3 S - K\right) (1 - p)^3]$$

It is easy to infer from this pattern what the formula for the n-level tree will be. This is given by

$$C_0 = \frac{1}{R^n} \sum_{i=0}^{n} \binom{n}{i} \max\left(0, u^i d^{n-i} S - K\right) p^{n-i}(1 - p)^i \qquad (2.26)$$

Suppose we now fix the time to expiration for the option to be of length T. In this case, for an n-level tree, the length of time of a single period is given by $T/n \equiv h$. One question we may want to ask is what (2.26) looks like as we take the limit $n \longrightarrow \infty$. This question can also be interpreted as what happens to (2.26) as the length of each period approaches zero, $T/n \longrightarrow 0$, the continuous-time limit.

To answer the question as to the continuous-time limit, we first need to determine what sequence we choose for u, d, and R, the three free variables at each node of the tree, as $n \longrightarrow \infty$. As shown by Cox, Ross, and Rubinstein (1979), if we choose these variables such that

$$u = \exp(\sigma \sqrt{h})$$
$$d = \exp(-\sigma \sqrt{h})$$
$$R = \exp(rh)$$

where σ is the volatility over one period and $r = R - 1$ is the interest rate over one period, then the Black-Scholes/Merton formula for the price of a call option results. While the proof of this is not shown here, this formula is derived in the next section using traditional continuous-time methods rather than as the limit of a sequence of discrete-time prices.

2.5 CONTINUOUS-TIME MODELS

As we mentioned in the previous section, because stocks and other financial securities trade very frequently, a two-period model, or even a model in which the periods are longer than a day or so, could result in inaccurate pricing results. For this reason, in this section and the remaining sections of the chapter, we turn to continuous-time models of financial asset prices, where we assume that assets are traded on a continuous basis. Thus, we assume that asset prices evolve on a continuous basis. This assumption initially complicates the modeling of asset prices because we are forced to use stochastic differential equations, but as it turns out, elegant, closed-form solutions can be obtained in some cases for asset prices. The Black-Scholes model for option prices is one such solution that we will focus on in this section.

2.5.1 The Black-Scholes/Merton Model – Pricing Kernel Approach

Our goal here is to derive a closed-form solution for the price of an option on a stock if the stock price evolves on a continuous basis. Therefore, suppose that we have a derivative security on a stock with an expiration date that is a time τ in the future. The derivative's payoff structure is assumed to be $H(T, S)$, where S represents the stock price, T represents maturity date, and H represents a general but deterministic and sufficiently well-behaved payoff function. We will show that if the stock price evolves continuously in a particular way, closed-form solutions exist for certain types of payoff structures. The crux of the argument, as will be repeatedly demonstrated, is that if the price of the derivative is a deterministic function of the stock price at maturity, then it must be a deterministic function of the stock price today.

We assume that the evolution of the stock price is described by the following stochastic differential equation:

$$\frac{dS_t}{S_t} = \mu dt + \sigma dW_t \qquad (2.27)$$

Here, S_t represents the stock price at time t, μ represents the instantaneous expected return of the stock, σ represents the instantaneous standard deviation of the stock's return, or volatility, and W_t is a Wiener process. μ and σ are assumed to be constant. Equation (2.27) is known as a geometric Brownian motion process. The conditional density of the stock price is lognormal under such a process. Indeed, by Itô's lemma

$$d \log S_t = \frac{d(\log S_t)}{dS_t} dS_t + \frac{1}{2} \frac{d^2(\log S_t)}{dS_t^2} d \langle S \rangle_t$$

$$= \frac{1}{S_t}(\mu S_t dt + \sigma S_t dW_t) + \frac{1}{2}\left(\frac{-1}{S_t^2}\right)\sigma^2 S_t^2 dt$$

$$= (\mu - \frac{1}{2}\sigma^2)dt + \sigma dW_t$$

We make one more assumption: namely, that the instantaneous interest, or the yield of an instantaneously maturing bond, is constant and denoted by r. Therefore, the price of any zero-coupon bond has the following dynamics:

$$\frac{dP}{P} = r dt$$

which simply states that the instantaneous expected return of any bond is simply the risk-free rate. This is true because bonds have no embedded interest rate risk since the interest rate is assumed constant.

Now, we need to derive the process for the price of the derivative security. Let $F_t = F(t, S_t)$ denote the price of the derivative at time t. The derivative expires at time T, so $\tau = T - t$ represents the time to expiration. Since the derivative's price is a function of S_t, by Itô's lemma, we have the following stochastic process for the derivative's price:

$$dF_t = \frac{\partial F_t}{\partial S_t} dS_t + \frac{1}{2} \frac{\partial^2 F_t}{\partial S_t^2} d \langle S \rangle_t + \frac{\partial F_t}{\partial \tau} d\tau$$

$$= \left[\mu S_t \frac{\partial F_t}{\partial S_t} + \frac{1}{2}\sigma^2 S_t^2 \frac{\partial^2 F_t}{\partial S_t^2} - \frac{\partial F_t}{\partial \tau}\right] dt + \sigma S_t \frac{\partial F_t}{\partial S_t} dW_t \quad (2.28)$$

From (2.28), we can see that the Wiener process on the option price is the same as the Wiener process on the stock. As we will see later, this turns out to be an important result.

Now that we have the derivative's price dynamics, the next step is to determine the risk premium in the economy. The risk premium tells us how much people charge for bearing the risk inherent in the option. From Section 2.2, we know that the risk premium is dependent on the utility functions of agents in the economy and it is characterized by the pricing kernel, or marginal rate of substitution. Therefore, we will start by assuming a process for the pricing kernel. It has been shown by Harrison and Kreps that the existence of a pricing kernel is guaranteed if markets are arbitrage-free.[2] Let ξ_t denote the level of marginal utility in the economy at time t.[3] We assume that the dynamics of ξ_t are determined by

$$\frac{d\xi_t}{\xi_t} = f(\xi_t, S_t)dt + g(\xi_t, S_t)dW_t \tag{2.29}$$

where $f(\xi_t, S_t)$ and $g(\xi_t, S_t)$ are general functions. To determine the pricing kernel, we need to determine these functions.

To determine $f(\xi_t, S_t)$, we start from (2.21). This relation tells us that the product of the price of any traded security and the pricing kernel is a martingale. While this was derived in discrete time, it holds in continuous time as well. Therefore, let's take the product of the pricing kernel and the riskless money market account: $\xi_t P_t$. This product must be a martingale. If we apply Itô's lemma, we can calculate the dynamics of $\xi_t P_t$:

$$
\begin{aligned}
d(\xi_t P_t) &= \xi_t dP_t + P_t d\xi_t + d\langle \xi, P \rangle_t \\
&= \xi_t (r P_t dt) + P_t \left[f(\xi_t, S_t)\xi_t dt + g(\xi_t, S_t)\xi_t dW_t \right] \\
&= \xi_t P_t \left[(r + f(\xi_t, S_t)) dt + g(\xi_t, S_t)dW_t \right]
\end{aligned}
\tag{2.30}
$$

Since $\xi_t P_t$ is a martingale, the drift term in (2.30) must be zero. Therefore, we have the result

$$f(\xi_t, S_t) = -r$$

Therefore (2.29) can be written as

$$\frac{d\xi_t}{\xi_t} = -rdt + g(\xi_t, S_t)dW_t \tag{2.31}$$

We now proceed to solve for $g(\xi_t, S_t)$. Again, from (2.21), we know that the product of the price of the stock and the pricing kernel is a

---

[2] The uniqueness of a pricing kernel is guaranteed in markets that are complete. See Section 2.2 for more details on complete markets.

[3] Then, ξ_T / ξ_t would represent the marginal rate of substitution from time t to time T.

martingale, since the stock is a traded security. If we apply Itô's lemma, we can calculate the dynamics of $\xi_t S_t$:

$$
\begin{aligned}
d(\xi_t S_t) &= \xi_t dS_t + S_t d\xi_t + d\langle \xi, S \rangle_t \\
&= \xi_t (\mu S_t dt + \sigma S_t dW_t) + S_t (-r\xi_t dt + \xi_t g(\xi_t, S_t) dW_t) \\
&\quad + \sigma \xi_t S_t g(\xi_t, S_t) dt \\
&= \xi_t S_t (\mu - r + \sigma g(\xi_t, S_t)) \, dt + \xi_t S_t [\sigma + g(\xi_t, S_t)] \, dW_t \quad (2.32)
\end{aligned}
$$

Once again, since $\xi_t S_t$ must be a martingale, it must be the case that the drift of (2.32) must be zero. This restriction leads to the following equation:

$$
\mu - r + \sigma g(\xi_t, S_t) = 0; \Rightarrow g(\xi_t, S_t) = -\frac{\mu - r}{\sigma}
$$

Notice that $-g(\xi_t, S_t)$ is equal to the excess return over risk, a type of Sharpe ratio. The negative of the pricing kernel's diffusion component is often called the *market price of risk* for the Wiener process because it can be interpreted as the equilibrium excess return demanded by investors per unit of risk borne. Thus, we have fully solved for the dynamics of the pricing kernel:

$$
\frac{d\xi_t}{\xi_t} = -r dt - \frac{\mu - r}{\sigma} dW_t \quad (2.33)
$$

Two important points about the pricing kernel should be noted. First, the form of the pricing kernel used here and the interpretation of the drift and diffusion terms is universal. Therefore, even when we go to more complicated economic settings, we will find that the expected instantaneous return of the pricing kernel is the risk-free rate while the diffusion component(s) represent the market price(s) of risk.

Another important point is that the marginal rate of substitution in the economy has been determined here without any knowledge of the underlying preferences, or utility functions, in the economy. This is a very powerful statement because it allows us to accomplish pricing without having to be concerned with subjective quantities like preference functions. These situations only arise in special circumstances, discussed in Section 2.2. In these circumstances, we obtain what is known as *preference-free* pricing relationships.

With the pricing kernel specified, we can now derive the fundamental valuation equation. This can be accomplished in two ways. We can use (2.21), utilizing the option as the traded security. We can alternatively use what is known as Girsanov's theorem. Both approaches are economically equivalent, and we present both here.

To apply Girsanov's theorem, first note that if the market price of risk is known for any security, the risk premium for that security can be eliminated, in other words, we can construct a new stochastic process for the security where the security has no risk premium. Such a stochastic process would only exist in an economy where investors are fully risk-neutral, so they would not require a risk premium for bearing risk. Thus, what we will do is to transform all stochastic processes in the economy to the form they would have if the economy were risk-neutral (many people term this transformation *risk-neutralizing* the economy), and Girsanov's theorem tells us how to do this transformation.

Girsanov's theorem simply states that when an economy with a pricing kernel defined by (2.31) is transformed to a risk-neutral economy, any stochastic process X (whether X is the price of a traded security or not) whose dynamics are characterized by

$$\frac{dX_t}{X_t} = h_1(X_t)dt + h_2(X_t)dW \qquad (2.34)$$

in the original economy becomes transformed to the process

$$\frac{dX_t}{X_t} = \left[h_1(X_t) - g(\xi_t, S_t)h_2(X_t)\right]dt + h_2(X_t)dW^* \qquad (2.35)$$

where W^* is simply a Wiener process in the risk-neutral economy.

We will now apply Girsanov's theorem to derive the fundamental valuation equation for the price of a derivative security. The dynamics of the price of a derivative security are given by (2.28). The price of the derivative essentially represents the variable X in (2.34). The pricing kernel in the economy is given by (2.33). Therefore, applying Girsanov's theorem gives the stochastic process for the derivative security in a risk-neutral economy:

$$
\frac{dF_t}{F_t} = \frac{1}{F_t} \left[\mu S_t \frac{\partial F_t}{\partial S_t} + \frac{1}{2}\sigma^2 S_t^2 \frac{\partial^2 F_t}{\partial S_t^2} - \frac{\partial F_t}{\partial \tau} - \frac{\mu - r}{\sigma} \sigma S_t \frac{\partial F_t}{\partial S_t} \right] dt
$$
$$
+ \frac{\sigma S_t}{F_t} \frac{\partial F_t}{\partial S_t} dW_t^*
$$
$$
= \frac{1}{F_t} \left[\mu S_t \frac{\partial F_t}{\partial S_t} + \frac{1}{2}\sigma^2 S_t^2 \frac{\partial^2 F_t}{\partial S_t^2} - \frac{\partial F_t}{\partial \tau} - (\mu - r) S_t \frac{\partial F_t}{\partial S_t} \right] dt
$$
$$
+ \frac{\sigma S_t}{F_t} \frac{\partial F_t}{\partial S_t} dW_t^*
$$
$$
= \frac{1}{F_t} \left[r S_t \frac{\partial F_t}{\partial S_t} + \frac{1}{2}\sigma^2 S_t^2 \frac{\partial^2 F_t}{\partial S_t^2} - \frac{\partial F_t}{\partial \tau} \right] dt + \frac{\sigma S_t}{F_t} \frac{\partial F_t}{\partial S_t} dW_t^*
$$

In a risk-neutral economy, we know that the expected return of any traded security must equal the risk-free rate. Since a derivative security by definition is a traded security, its expected instantaneous return therefore must equal the risk-free rate:

$$
r = \mathbb{E}_t^* \left[\frac{dF_t}{F_t} \right]
$$

The expected instantaneous return of dF/F is simply the drift term of the stochastic process. So, we have

$$
r = \frac{1}{F_t} \left[r S_t \frac{\partial F_t}{\partial S_t} + \frac{1}{2}\sigma^2 S_t^2 \frac{\partial^2 F_t}{\partial S_t^2} - \frac{\partial F_t}{\partial \tau} \right]
$$
$$
r F = \frac{1}{2}\sigma^2 S_t^2 \frac{\partial^2 F_t}{\partial S_t^2} + r S_t \frac{\partial F_t}{\partial S_t} - \frac{\partial F_t}{\partial \tau} \tag{2.36}
$$

This last equation is the fundamental valuation equation for the price of any traded security. We now show the derivation of (2.36) using (2.21) a third time. This time, we will multiply the pricing kernel with the price of the option: $\xi_t F_t$. Once again, since the derivative is a traded security, this product should be a martingale, that is, the stochastic process defining the product should have a drift of zero. The stochastic process defining $\xi_t F_t$ is calculated using Itô's lemma:

$$d(\xi_t F_t) = \xi_t dF_t + F_t d\xi_t + d\langle \xi, F \rangle_t$$

$$= \xi_t \left\{ \left[\mu S_t \frac{\partial F_t}{\partial S_t} + \frac{1}{2}\sigma^2 S_t^2 \frac{\partial^2 F_t}{\partial S_t^2} - \frac{\partial F_t}{\partial \tau} \right] dt + \sigma S_t \frac{\partial F_t}{\partial S_t} dW_t \right\}$$

$$+ F_t \left[-r\xi_t dt - \frac{\mu - r}{\sigma} \xi_t dW_t \right] - (\mu - r)\xi_t S_t \frac{\partial F_t}{\partial S_t} dt$$

$$= \xi_t \left[\mu S_t \frac{\partial F_t}{\partial S_t} + \frac{1}{2}\sigma^2 S_t^2 \frac{\partial^2 F_t}{\partial S_t^2} - \frac{\partial F_t}{\partial \tau} - rF_t - (\mu - r)S_t \frac{\partial F_t}{\partial S_t} \right] dt$$

$$+ \xi_t \left[\sigma S_t \frac{\partial F_t}{\partial S_t} - \frac{\mu - r}{\sigma} F_t \right] dW_t \qquad (2.37)$$

In (2.37), the restriction that the drift of the process be zero leads to the equation

$$\frac{1}{2}\sigma^2 S_t^2 \frac{\partial^2 F_t}{\partial S_t^2} + rS_t \frac{\partial F_t}{\partial S_t} - \frac{\partial F_t}{\partial \tau} - rF_t = 0 \qquad (2.38)$$

This partial differential equation (PDE) is the fundamental Black-Scholes/Merton valuation equation determining the value of a derivative security. Note that in deriving this partial differential equation, no mention was made of the contractual terms of the derivative. The payoff structure was left quite general. The only assumptions used were the geometric Brownian motion assumption on the stock price and the assumption of a constant interest rate. In addition, note that the expected return, μ, of the stock does not enter into the valuation formula; only its volatility matters. Therefore, the expected return could be any value, but the price of the derivative security would end up being the same.

Since the fundamental valuation equation, (2.38), was derived for a general payoff structure, how do various payoff structures result in different derivatives prices? The explanation is that the particular payoff structure serves as the boundary condition(s) for the equation. To illustrate how this works, let us derive the price for a European call option. The call option matures at time T and has a payoff function $\max[0, S_T - K]$ at maturity, where K is the strike price of the option. Then, at the maturity date of the option, it must be the case that

$$F_T = \max[0, S_T - K] \qquad (2.39)$$

This equation then serves as the boundary condition for the PDE in (2.38). Now, we can solve the partial differential equation, and the solution will be the price of the option.

We start by first transforming variables. Let $Y_t = \log S_t$. Under this transformation, the partial differential equation and boundary condition become

$$\frac{1}{2}\sigma^2\frac{\partial^2 F_t}{\partial Y_t^2} + (r - \frac{1}{2}\sigma^2)\frac{\partial F_t}{\partial Y_t} - \frac{\partial F_t}{\partial \tau} - rF_t = 0 \qquad (2.40)$$

subject to the boundary condition $F_T = \max[0, e^{Y_T} - K]$. We will solve (2.40) by guessing a solution form for this equation:

$$F_t = e^{Y_t}\Pi_{1,t} - Ke^{-r\tau}\Pi_{2,t}$$

where $\Pi_{1,t}$ and $\Pi_{2,t}$ are functions that satisfy the respective boundary conditions

$$\Pi_{1,T} = 1_{\{Y_T \geq \log K\}}$$
$$\Pi_{2,T} = 1_{\{Y_T \geq \log K\}}$$

Notice that with these boundary conditions our guess satisfies the original boundary condition, (2.39). Since (2.38) is a linear PDE, each of the components of the guess, $e^{Y_t}\Pi_{1,t}$ and $Ke^{-r\tau}\Pi_{2,t}$, must individually satisfy the PDE as well. Therefore, if we substitute $e^{Y_t}\Pi_{1,t}$ into the PDE and simplify, we obtain another PDE that must be satisfied by $\Pi_{1,t}$:

$$\frac{1}{2}\sigma^2\frac{\partial^2 \Pi_{1,t}}{\partial Y_t^2} + \left(r + \frac{1}{2}\sigma^2\right)\frac{\partial \Pi_{1,t}}{\partial Y_t} - \frac{\partial \Pi_{1,t}}{\partial \tau} = 0 \qquad (2.41)$$

subject to the boundary condition $\Pi_{1,T} = 1_{\{Y_T \geq \log K\}}$. It is easy to see that (2.41) has the form of the Kolmogorov backward equation for the process

$$dY_t = (r + \frac{1}{2}\sigma^2)dt + \sigma dW_t \qquad (2.42)$$

The boundary condition, therefore, indicates that $\Pi_{1,t}$ is the probability that $Y_t \geq \log K$ if Y_t is governed by the process in (2.42).[4]

---

[4] For the Kolmogorov backward equation, different boundary conditions indicate different interpretations. For example, if the boundary condition were $\Pi_{1,T} = 1_{\{S_T = x\}}$, where x is an arbitrary stock price, then the solution would be a density function. If the boundary condition had the form $\Pi_{1,T} = e^{i\omega S_T}$, where $i = \sqrt{-1}$ and ω is a dummy

Of course, since (2.42) is simply an arithmetic Brownian motion process, we know that the conditional density of $Y_T \mid Y_t$ is the normal density function:

$$Y_T \sim N(Y_t + (r + \frac{1}{2}\sigma^2)\tau, \sigma^2\tau)$$

The probability that $Y_T \geq \log K$ is equivalent to the probability that $X_T \geq \frac{\log K - Y_0 - (r + \frac{1}{2}\sigma^2)\tau}{\sigma\sqrt{\tau}}$ where X_T is a standard normal variable. Therefore, if we let $\Phi(\cdot)$ represent the standard normal distribution function, we have the result that

$$\text{Prob}\left(X_T \geq \frac{\log K - Y_t - (r + \frac{1}{2}\sigma^2)\tau}{\sigma\sqrt{\tau}}\right)$$

$$= 1 - \Phi\left(\frac{\log K - Y_t - (r + \frac{1}{2}\sigma^2)\tau}{\sigma\sqrt{\tau}}\right) = \Phi\left(\frac{Y_t + (r + \frac{1}{2}\sigma^2)\tau - \log K}{\sigma\sqrt{\tau}}\right)$$

Therefore, if we transform from Y_t back to S_t, we have the solution for $\Pi_{1,t}$:

$$\Pi_{1,t} = \Phi\left(\frac{\log S_t + (r + \frac{1}{2}\sigma^2)\tau - \log K}{\sigma\sqrt{\tau}}\right) = \Phi\left(\frac{\log \frac{S_t}{K} + (r + \frac{1}{2}\sigma^2)\tau}{\sigma\sqrt{\tau}}\right)$$

Similarly, $Ke^{-r\tau}\Pi_{2,t}$ must satisfy (2.38), so we can substitute $Ke^{-r\tau}\Pi_{2,t}$ into (2.38) to obtain a PDE for $\Pi_{2,t}$:

$$\frac{1}{2}\sigma^2\frac{\partial^2\Pi_{1,t}}{\partial Y_t^2} + (r - \frac{1}{2}\sigma^2)\frac{\partial\Pi_{1,t}}{\partial Y_t} - \frac{\partial\Pi_{1,t}}{\partial\tau} = 0 \qquad (2.43)$$

subject to the boundary condition $\Pi_{2,T} = 1_{\{Y_T \geq \log K\}}$. As with $\Pi_{1,T}$, (2.43) has the form of the Kolmogorov backward equation for the process

$$dY_t = (r - \frac{1}{2}\sigma^2)dt + \sigma dW_t \qquad (2.44)$$

Again, the boundary condition for $\Pi_{2,T}$ indicates that it is the probability that $Y_T \geq \log K$ if Y_t is governed by (2.44). Because (2.44) is an arithmetic Brownian motion process

$$Y_T \sim N(Y_t + (r - \frac{1}{2}\sigma^2)\tau, \sigma^2\tau)$$

---

variable, then the solution would be a characteristic function. Finally, if the boundary condition is $\Pi_{1,T} = 1_{\{S_T \geq x\}}$, then the solution is the probability that $S_T \geq x$.

The probability that $Y_T \geq \log K$ is equivalent to the probability that $X_T \geq \frac{\log K - Y_0 - (r - \frac{1}{2}\sigma^2)\tau}{\sigma\sqrt{\tau}}$ where X_T is a standard normal variable. Therefore

$$\text{Prob} \left(X_T \geq \frac{\log K - Y_t - (r - \frac{1}{2}\sigma^2)\tau}{\sigma\sqrt{\tau}} \right)$$

$$= 1 - \Phi \left(\frac{\log K - Y_t - (r - \frac{1}{2}\sigma^2)\tau}{\sigma\sqrt{\tau}} \right) = \Phi \left(\frac{Y_t + (r - \frac{1}{2}\sigma^2)\tau - \log K}{\sigma\sqrt{\tau}} \right)$$

If we transform from Y_t back to S_t, we have the solution for $\Pi_{2,t}$:

$$\Pi_{2,t} = \Phi \left(\frac{\log S_t + (r - \frac{1}{2}\sigma^2)\tau - \log K}{\sigma\sqrt{\tau}} \right) = \Phi \left(\frac{\log \frac{S_t}{K} + (r - \frac{1}{2}\sigma^2)\tau}{\sigma\sqrt{\tau}} \right)$$

Thus, the closed-form solution for the option price is given by

$$F_t = S_t \Phi \left(\frac{\log \frac{S_t}{K} + (r + \frac{1}{2}\sigma^2)\tau}{\sigma\sqrt{\tau}} \right) - K e^{-r\tau} \Phi \left(\frac{\log \frac{S_t}{K} + (r - \frac{1}{2}\sigma^2)\tau}{\sigma\sqrt{\tau}} \right)$$

$$(2.45)$$

This solution was originally derived by Black and Scholes (1973) and Merton (1973).

2.5.2 The Black-Scholes/Merton Model – Probabilistic Approach

The approach in the previous section utilized the dynamics of the pricing kernel to derive the partial differential equation that governs the behavior of all derivative securities, and we solved this PDE for the particular case of a European call option. In this subsection, we utilize the so-called probabilistic approach to derive the same solution. Specifically, we utilize (2.24) to write the price of the option as a function of the expectations operator under the risk-neutral probability measure. Then, we explictly evaluate this expectation by integrating over a density function. The result will be the same solution as that derived in (2.45).

We start as in the previous section with a derivative security that has a payoff structure represented by $H(T, S)$. Letting $F_t = F(t, S_t)$ represent the price of the derivative at time t and assuming the derivative expires at time T, we can use (2.24) to write down its price at time t:

$$F_t = \mathbb{E}_t\left[\int_t^T \frac{\xi_T}{\xi_t} H(w, S)dw\right] = \mathbb{E}_t^{\mathbb{Q}}\left[\int_t^T e^{-\int_t^w r_v dv} H(w, S)dw\right] \quad (2.46)$$

where $\mathbb{Q}$ denotes that the expectation is taken under the risk-neutral probability measure. From this point, we can calculate the price of the security by evaluating the expectation, that is, by integrating $\int_t^T e^{-\int_t^w r_v dv} H(w, S)dw$ over a density function.

We illustrate this procedure by deriving the Black-Scholes/Merton solution for the price of a call option that was calculated in the previous section using a PDE approach. The call option is European and pays off

$$H(T, S) = F_T = \max[0, S_T - K]$$

at time T, the expiration date of the option. K is the strike price, and the interest rate, r, is assumed to be constant. The price dynamics of the stock price are assumed to be geometric Brownian motion:

$$\frac{dS_t}{S_t} = \mu dt + \sigma dW_t$$

While stochastic process for the stock price is important, what we really need is the risk-neutral stochastic process for the stock price, because in (2.46), we evaluate the conditional expectation with respect to the risk-neutral probabilities for stock price movements. Under the risk-neutral probability measure, the expected return of all traded assets is simply the risk-free rate. Therefore, the risk-neutral stock price process is given by

$$\frac{dS_t}{S_t} = rdt + \sigma dW_t^{\mathbb{Q}}$$

Furthermore, by Itô's lemma, the risk-neutral log stock price is then given by

$$d\log S_t = (r - \frac{1}{2}\sigma^2)dt + \sigma dW_t^{\mathbb{Q}}$$

Since the log stock price is simply arithmetic Brownian motion, the conditional density of the log stock price is given by

$$\log S_T \mid \log S_t \sim N[\log S_t + (r - \frac{1}{2}\sigma^2)\tau, \sigma^2\tau]$$

where $\tau = T - t$.

Now we are prepared to price the call option. From (2.46), the call option price can be written as

$$F_t = e^{-r\tau} E_t^Q [\max(0, S_T - K)]$$

To calculate a closed-form solution for the option price, we need to evaluate the conditional expectation. We first rewrite the expression above in terms of the log stock price:

$$F_t = e^{-r\tau} E_t^Q [\max(0, \exp(\log S_T) - K)]$$

Now, using the conditional density of the risk-neutral log stock price, we can re-express the conditional expectation as an integral over the conditional density of the log stock price:

$$F_t = e^{-r\tau} \int_{\log K}^{\infty} [\exp(\log S_T) - K] \frac{1}{\sqrt{2\pi\sigma^2\tau}}$$

$$\times \exp\left[-\frac{\left[\log S_T - \log S_t - (r - \frac{1}{2}\sigma^2)\tau\right]^2}{2\sigma^2\tau} \right] d\log S_T$$

We can simplify this expression to

$$F_t = \frac{1}{\sqrt{2\pi\sigma^2\tau}} e^{-r\tau}$$

$$\times \int_{\log K}^{\infty} \exp\left[\log S_T - \frac{\left[\log S_T - \log S_t - (r - \frac{1}{2}\sigma^2)\tau\right]^2}{2\sigma^2\tau} \right]$$

$$\times d\log S_T - K \frac{1}{\sqrt{2\pi\sigma^2\tau}} e^{-r\tau}$$

$$\times \int_{\log K}^{\infty} \exp\left[-\frac{\left[\log S_T - \log S_t - (r - \frac{1}{2}\sigma^2)\tau\right]^2}{2\sigma^2\tau} \right] d\log S_T \quad (2.47)$$

The two integrals are in the form of distribution functions. We will deal with each integral individually and rewrite the terms inside of the integrals so that each is in the form of a standard normal distribution function. We start with the first integral. We start with the transformation $Z = \log \frac{S_T}{S_t}$. With this transformation, the integral can be written as

$$\frac{1}{\sqrt{2\pi\sigma^2\tau}} e^{-r\tau} S_t \int_{\log \frac{K}{S_t}}^{\infty} \exp\left[Z - \frac{\left[Z - (r - \frac{1}{2}\sigma^2)\tau\right]^2}{2\sigma^2\tau} \right] dZ$$

Combining the expressions in the exponential yields

$$\frac{1}{\sqrt{2\pi\sigma^2\tau}}e^{-r\tau}S_t$$

$$\times \int_{\log\frac{K}{S_t}}^{\infty} \exp\left[\frac{2Z\sigma^2\tau - Z^2 + 2Z(r - \frac{1}{2}\sigma^2)\tau - (r - \frac{1}{2}\sigma^2)^2\tau^2}{2\sigma^2\tau}\right]dZ$$

Simplifying the numerator of the exponential then gives

$$\frac{1}{\sqrt{2\pi\sigma^2\tau}}e^{-r\tau}S_t \int_{\log\frac{K}{S_t}}^{\infty} \exp\left[\frac{-Z^2 + 2Z(r + \frac{1}{2}\sigma^2)\tau - (r - \frac{1}{2}\sigma^2)^2\tau^2}{2\sigma^2\tau}\right]dZ$$

We now complete the square in the numerator of the exponential by adding and subtracting $2r\sigma^2\tau^2$. After rearranging, we can then write the expression as

$$\frac{1}{\sqrt{2\pi\sigma^2\tau}}e^{-r\tau}S_t$$

$$\times \int_{\log\frac{K}{S_t}}^{\infty} \exp\left[r\tau - \frac{Z^2 - 2Z(r + \frac{1}{2}\sigma^2)\tau + (r + \frac{1}{2}\sigma^2)^2\tau^2}{2\sigma^2\tau}\right]dZ$$

Thus, completing the square gives

$$\frac{1}{\sqrt{2\pi\sigma^2\tau}}S_t \int_{\log\frac{K}{S_t}}^{\infty} \exp\left[-\frac{[Z - (r + \frac{1}{2}\sigma^2)\tau]^2}{2\sigma^2\tau}\right]dZ$$

We now make a second transformation. If we let $Y = \frac{Z - (r + \frac{1}{2}\sigma^2)\tau}{\sigma\sqrt{\tau}}$, then the expression can be simplified to

$$S_t \int_{\frac{\log\frac{K}{S_t} - (r + \frac{1}{2}\sigma^2)\tau}{\sigma\sqrt{\tau}}}^{\infty} \frac{1}{\sqrt{2\pi}} \exp\left[-\frac{Y^2}{2}\right]dY$$

Now the the integral is simply the value of the standard normal distribution evaluated at $-\frac{\log\frac{K}{S_t} - (r + \frac{1}{2}\sigma^2)\tau}{\sigma\sqrt{\tau}}$. Therefore, we have the result that (2.47) can be written as

$$F_t = S_t\Phi\left(\frac{\log\frac{S_t}{K} + (r + \frac{1}{2}\sigma^2)\tau}{\sigma\sqrt{\tau}}\right) - K\frac{1}{\sqrt{2\pi\sigma^2\tau}}e^{-r\tau}$$

$$\times \int_{\log K}^{\infty} \exp\left[\frac{[\log S_T - \log S_t - (r - \frac{1}{2}\sigma^2)\tau]^2}{2\sigma^2\tau}\right]d\log S_T$$

using the fact that $1 - \Phi(x) = \Phi(-x)$, where $\Phi(x)$ represents the standard normal distribution evaluated at x.

We will now similarly try to simplify the second integral in this expression so that it can be written in terms of a standard normal distribution. We first make the transformation $Y = \frac{\log S_T - \log S_t - (r - \frac{1}{2}\sigma^2)\tau}{\sigma\sqrt{\tau}}$. Doing so gives the result

$$Ke^{-r\tau} \int_{\frac{\log \frac{K}{S_t} - (r - \frac{1}{2}\sigma^2)\tau}{\sigma\sqrt{\tau}}}^{\infty} \frac{1}{\sqrt{2\pi}} \exp\left[-\frac{Y^2}{2}\right] dY$$

Once again, the integral has been transformed to a standard normal distribution. Therefore, we can write the complete option price as

$$F_t = S_t \Phi\left(\frac{\log \frac{S_t}{K} + (r + \frac{1}{2}\sigma^2)\tau}{\sigma\sqrt{\tau}}\right) - Ke^{-r\tau} \Phi\left(\frac{\log \frac{S_t}{K} + (r - \frac{1}{2}\sigma^2)\tau}{\sigma\sqrt{\tau}}\right)$$

which is the same result derived at the end of Section 2.5.1. However, here we used a probabilistic approach to solve for the option price rather than solving a partial differential equation.

2.5.3 The Black-Scholes/Merton Model – Hedging Approach

In this subsection, we rederive the fundamental valuation equation derived in previous sections for the price of any derivative security but using the original hedging methodology employed in Black and Scholes (1972) and Merton (1973). The advantage to this approach is that it gives strong intuition as to the economics underlying the valuation of these securities. We will see that the payoff of the derivative security can be exactly replicated using a dynamic portfolio of the stock and a risk-free bond. Therefore, if the condition of no-arbitrage holds in the economy, it must be the case that the price of the portfolio must at all times equal the value of the derivative security.

We start off with the usual assumptions. The stock price, S, is characterized by a geometric Brownian motion process with instantaneous expected return of μ and an instantaneous volatility of σ. The interest rate is assumed constant at r. Therefore, the dynamics of the riskless asset are given by

$$\frac{dB_t}{B_t} = r dt$$

where B_t represents the value of the riskless asset at time t. The derivative security has a price at time t of F_t, and its payoff structure is given by $H(T, S)$. By Itô's lemma, we can derive the dynamics of the derivative security:

$$dF_t = \left[\mu S_t \frac{\partial F_t}{\partial S_t} + \frac{1}{2}\sigma^2 S_t^2 \frac{\partial^2 F_t}{\partial S_t^2} - \frac{\partial F_t}{\partial \tau} \right] dt + \sigma S_t \frac{\partial F_t}{\partial S_t} dW_t$$

Now, we will attempt to construct a dynamic trading strategy that replicates the instantaneous movements of the derivative security. We will try to do so using just the stock and bond. Suppose we invest an amount X_t into the derivative security. With an amount X_t, we can buy $\frac{X_t}{F_t}$ units of the derivative security. Then, as time evolves, the change in our investment value is given by

$$
\begin{aligned}
dX_t &= \frac{X_t}{F_t} dF_t \\
&= \frac{X_t}{F_t} \left[\mu S_t \frac{\partial F_t}{\partial S_t} + \frac{1}{2}\sigma^2 S_t^2 \frac{\partial^2 F_t}{\partial S_t^2} - \frac{\partial F_t}{\partial \tau} \right] dt + \sigma S_t \frac{X_t}{F_t} \frac{\partial F_t}{\partial S_t} dW_t \quad (2.48)
\end{aligned}
$$

Instead, suppose we took the same amount of investment and invested it into the stock and a riskless bond such that a fraction of our investment equal to $\frac{S_t}{F_t} \frac{\partial F_t}{\partial S_t}$ is held in the stock and the remaining fraction, $1 - \frac{S_t}{F_t} \frac{\partial F_t}{\partial S_t}$, is invested in the riskless bond.[5] In such a case, the dynamics of our investment portfolio would be given by

$$
\begin{aligned}
dX_t &= \frac{\frac{S_t}{F_t} \frac{\partial F_t}{\partial S_t} X_t}{S_t} dS_t + \frac{(1 - \frac{S_t}{F_t} \frac{\partial F_t}{\partial S_t}) X_t}{B_t} dB_t \\
&= \frac{S_t}{F_t} \frac{\partial F_t}{\partial S_t} X_t \mu dt + \frac{S_t}{F_t} \frac{\partial F_t}{\partial S_t} X_t \sigma dW_t + (1 - \frac{S_t}{F_t} \frac{\partial F_t}{\partial S_t}) X_t r dt \\
&= \left[\mu X_t \frac{S_t}{F_t} \frac{\partial F_t}{\partial S_t} + (1 - \frac{S_t}{F_t} \frac{\partial F_t}{\partial S_t}) X_t r \right] dt + \sigma X_t \frac{S_t}{F_t} \frac{\partial F_t}{\partial S_t} dW_t \quad (2.49)
\end{aligned}
$$

Notice that the risk of the two investments is exactly the same. In (2.48) and (2.49), the Wiener processes are the same and the volatilities of the portfolios are equal. Therefore, the risk borne by undertaking each of these investments is the same, and the expected return of the two investments must be the same as well. This follows from a simple no-arbitrage condition that says two investments of equal risk must have

---

[5] If one of these fractions is negative, it can be interpreted as short-selling that security and using the proceeds to purchase the other security.

equal expected returns. Otherwise, a risk-free profit can be made by investing in the investment with the higher expected return and short-selling the investment with the lower expected return. Therefore, if the expected returns are equal, we can take the drift terms from (2.48) and (2.49) and equate them:

$$\frac{X_t}{F_t}\left[\mu S_t\frac{\partial F_t}{\partial S_t}+\frac{1}{2}\sigma^2 S_t^2\frac{\partial^2 F_t}{\partial S_t^2}-\frac{\partial F_t}{\partial \tau}\right]=\left[\mu X_t\frac{S_t}{F_t}\frac{\partial F_t}{\partial S_t}+(1-\frac{S_t}{F_t}\frac{\partial F_t}{\partial S_t})X_t r\right]$$

$$\mu S_t\frac{\partial F_t}{\partial S_t}+\frac{1}{2}\sigma^2 S_t^2\frac{\partial^2 F_t}{\partial S_t^2}-\frac{\partial F_t}{\partial \tau}=\mu S_t\frac{\partial F_t}{\partial S_t}+r F_t-r S_t\frac{\partial F_t}{\partial S_t}$$

$$\frac{1}{2}\sigma^2 S_t^2\frac{\partial^2 F_t}{\partial S_t^2}+r S_t\frac{\partial F_t}{\partial S_t}-\frac{\partial F_t}{\partial \tau}=r F_t$$

The last expression is precisely the same PDE, (2.38), derived in Section 2.5.1. The PDE can now be solved in exactly the same way as that solved in Section 2.5.1.

Thus, we see that the derivative security can be exactly replicated by a dynamic trading strategy utilizing the stock and the riskless bond. A market in which one has the ability to synthetically replicate one security using a dynamic portfolio of other traded securities is known as a *complete* market. In complete markets, it has been proven by Harrison and Kreps (1979) that a unique pricing kernel exists.

2.6 EXOTIC OPTIONS

In this section we apply the continuous-time techniques developed in the previous sections to the pricing of more complex instruments, sometimes termed exotic options. Despite the seeming complexity of these securities, it will be demonstrated that the simple application of the principles that we have learned so far is all that is necessary to price these securities. Thus, this section can be viewed as providing further examples of continuous-time pricing techniques.

With all the securities that we work with, the underlying is assumed to be a stock price with dynamics characterized by geometric Brownian motion

$$\frac{dS_t}{S_t}=\mu dt+\sigma dW_t$$

unless indicated otherwise. While other processes may be used as well, this form is the most commonly used because it does not allow for negative prices and leads to tractable equations for the pricing of derivatives. The interest rate in all the cases considered in this section is assumed to be constant and denoted by r. In the next chapter we will introduce stochastic interest rates.

2.6.1 Digital Options

A digital option is one whose payoff at its expiration date T is given by

$$1_{\{S_T \geq K\}} M$$

Thus, it pays off a fixed amount M if the stock price at expiration exceeds K; otherwise it pays nothing. We can compute the price of a digital option as we did the price of a call option in Section 2.5.1. First, we know that the risk-neutral log price process for the stock is given by

$$d \log S_t = (r - \frac{1}{2}\sigma^2)dt + \sigma dW_t$$

If we let F_t represent the price of a digital option at time t, then we have the following expression for its price:

$$F_t = e^{-r\tau} E_t^Q [\max(0, M_{\{S_T \geq K\}})]$$

where $\tau = T - t$. As we did in Section 2.5.2, we can rewrite this as an integral over a normal density function:[6]

$$F_t = e^{-r\tau} \int_{\log K}^{\infty} \frac{M}{\sqrt{2\pi\sigma^2\tau}}$$
$$\times \exp\left[-\frac{[\log S_T - \log S_t - (r - \frac{1}{2}\sigma^2)\tau]^2}{2\sigma^2\tau}\right] d\log S_T$$

If we now transform this integral using the transformation rule $Z_T = \frac{\log S_T - \log S_t - (r - \frac{1}{2}\sigma^2)\tau}{\sigma\sqrt{\tau}}$, we can rewrite the price as

$$F_t = M e^{-r\tau} \int_{\frac{\log K - \log S_t - (r - \frac{1}{2}\sigma^2)\tau}{\sigma\sqrt{\tau}}}^{\infty} \frac{1}{\sqrt{2\pi}} \exp\left[-\frac{Z_T^2}{2}\right] dZ_T$$

---

[6] We know that for geometric Brownian motion the log stock price has a conditional normal density function given by

$$\log S_T \mid \log S_t \sim N[\log S_t + (r - \frac{1}{2}\sigma^2)\tau, \sigma^2\tau]$$

We now have a standard normal density function as the integrand. Therefore, we can rewrite the integral as

$$F_t = M e^{-r\tau} \left[1 - \Phi \left(\frac{\log \frac{K}{S_t} - (r - \frac{1}{2}\sigma^2)\tau}{\sigma \sqrt{\tau}} \right) \right]$$

$$= M e^{-r\tau} \Phi \left(\frac{\log \frac{S_t}{K} + (r - \frac{1}{2}\sigma^2)\tau}{\sigma \sqrt{\tau}} \right)$$

Thus, we have derived the price of a digital option by applying the probabilistic pricing technique.

2.6.2 Power Options

We now derive the prices of two types of securities: power securities and power options. Power securities pay the owner of the security the value of the stock at expiration raised to some prespecified power, S_T^n. Power options in turn pay the owner the same payoff as a power security less a strike price only if the the value of the underlying is greater than the strike price:

$$\max [0, S_T^n - K]$$

We first tackle the pricing of the power security. Suppose we denote F_t as the value of the power security. We could price this security using either the probabilistic approach or the PDE approach. We will use the PDE approach here for pedagogical purposes. The price of the option satisfies the same Black-Scholes/Merton PDE

$$\frac{1}{2}\sigma^2 S_t^2 \frac{\partial^2 F_t}{\partial S_t^2} + r S_t \frac{\partial F_t}{\partial S_t} - \frac{\partial F_t}{\partial \tau} - r F_t = 0$$

but with boundary condition given by $F_T = S_T^n$. To derive a solution for this PDE, we will take the same route taken in Section 2.5.1 by first guessing a solution form. We guess the following solution form:

$$F_t = A(\tau) S_t^n$$

where the function $A(\tau)$ is a function of the time to expiration only and not of the stock price. Substituting this solution form into the PDE leads to the following ordinary differential equation (ODE) for the function A:

$$\frac{dA}{d\tau} = (n-1)(\frac{1}{2}\sigma^2 n + r)A$$

with boundary condition $A(0) = 1$. This is a first-order, linear ODE which can be solved easily. The solution is given by

$$A(\tau) = \exp\left[(n-1)(\frac{1}{2}\sigma^2 n + r)\tau\right]$$

Therefore, the price of the power security is given by

$$F_t = \exp\left[(n-1)(\frac{1}{2}\sigma^2 n + r)\tau\right] S_t^n$$

Given the price of the power security, we now derive the price of the power option, H_t. The stochastic process for S_t^n is given by

$$dS_t^n = nS_t^{n-1}(\mu S_t dt + \sigma S_t dW_t) + \frac{1}{2}n(n-1)S_t^{n-2}\sigma^2 S_t^2 dt$$

$$= \left[n\mu + \frac{1}{2}n(n-1)\sigma^2\right]S_t^n dt + n\sigma S_t^n dW_t$$

From Section 2.5.1, we know that the pricing kernel is characterized by the process

$$\frac{d\xi_t}{\xi_t} = -rdt - \frac{\mu - r}{\sigma}dW_t$$

By Itô's lemma, we know that the price of the power derivative is given by the process

$$dH_t = \frac{\partial H_t}{\partial S_t^n}dS_t^n + \frac{1}{2}\frac{\partial^2 H_t}{\partial S_t^{n2}}d\langle S^n\rangle_t - \frac{\partial H_t}{\partial \tau}dt$$

$$= \left\{\frac{\partial H_t}{\partial S_t^n}\left[n\mu + \frac{1}{2}n(n-1)\sigma^2\right]S_t^n + \frac{1}{2}\frac{\partial^2 H_t}{\partial S_t^{n2}}n^2\sigma^2 S_t^{n2} - \frac{\partial H_t}{\partial \tau}\right\}dt$$

$$+ n\sigma S_t^n \frac{\partial H_t}{\partial S_t^n}dW_t$$

Since $H_t\xi_t$ must be a martingale, it must have a drift term of zero. Since we have derived the stochastic processes for ξ_t and H_t in the previous two equations, we can use Itô's lemma to calculate the drift of $H_t\xi_t$ and set it equal to zero. Doing so gives the PDE

$$\frac{1}{2}n^2\sigma^2 S_t^{n2}\frac{\partial^2 H_t}{\partial S_t^{n2}} + \left[nr + \frac{1}{2}n(n-1)\sigma^2\right]S_t^n\frac{\partial H_t}{\partial S_t^n} - \frac{\partial H_t}{\partial \tau} = rH_t$$

with the boundary condition $H_T = \max[0, S_T^n - K]$. Notice that this PDE and boundary condition are exactly as those for the call option but with S_t, r, and σ replaced by $S_t^n, rn + \frac{1}{2}n(n-1)\sigma^2$, and σn, respectively. Therefore, by analogy with the solution for the call option price, we have the following solution for the price of a power option:

$$F_t = S_t \Phi \left(\frac{\log \frac{S_t^n}{K} + (rn + \frac{1}{2}n(n-1)\sigma^2 + \frac{1}{2}\sigma^2 n^2)\tau}{\sigma n \sqrt{\tau}} \right)$$

$$- Ke^{-[nr + \frac{1}{2}n(n-1)\sigma^2]\tau} \Phi \left(\frac{\log \frac{S_t^n}{K} + (rn + \frac{1}{2}n(n-1)\sigma^2 - \frac{1}{2}\sigma^2 n^2)\tau}{\sigma n \sqrt{\tau}} \right)$$

Thus, we have derived closed-form solutions for the price of a power security and the power option using the simple pricing techniques derived above.

2.6.3 Asian Options

Asian options are options where the terminal payoff is a function of the average of the stock price over the length of the option. The question then remains as to how the term *average* is defined. In this section, we will deal with continuous geometric averaging, though options with arithmetic averaging are more commonly found in the market. Consequently, the Asian option that we consider has the following payoff function:

$$\max[0, Y_T - K]$$

where the term $Y_t = \exp[\frac{1}{T}\int_0^t \log S_v \, dv]$ represents the continuous geometric average of the stock price.[7] For this option, the averaging period is the time that the option was first written, time 0, to the time the option expires, time T. Thus, T represents the time to expiration of the option when the option was first written.

The Asian option's payoff function can be rewritten as

$$\max[0, e^{\log Y_T} - K]$$

---

[7] If we were using arithmetic averaging, the payoff function would be

$$\max\left[0, \frac{1}{\tau}\int_t^T S_v \, dv - K\right]$$

Therefore, the price of the Asian option today, F_t, can be written as

$$F_t = E_t^q \left[e^{-r\tau} \max(0, e^{\log Y_T} - K) \right] \qquad (2.50)$$

$$= e^{-r\tau} E_t^q \left[\max(0, e^{\log Y_T} - K) \right] \qquad (2.51)$$

As we have done previously, we would like to convert this expectation to an integral over a density function. However, here the density function of $\log Y_T$ is not immediately obvious. Therefore, we must first derive this density function. To do so, we first write out the full risk-neutral dynamics of $\log Y_t$:

$$d \log Y_t = \frac{1}{T} \log S_t \, dt$$

$$d \log S_t = (r - \frac{1}{2}\sigma^2)dt + \sigma \, dW_t$$

Under these dynamics, we can calculate the characteristic function of $\log Y_T$ at all times t and then invert this characteristic function to obtain the conditional (time t) density function. The characteristic function at time t of $\log Y_T$ is given by $\phi_t(\omega) = E_t^q \left[e^{i\omega \log Y_T} \right]$ where $i = \sqrt{-1}$. We can calculate the characteristic function by utilizing the fact that it satisfies the Kolmogorov backward equation

$$\frac{1}{2}\sigma^2 \frac{\partial^2 \phi_t}{\partial (\log S_t)^2} + (r - \frac{1}{2}\sigma^2)\frac{\partial \phi_t}{\partial (\log S_t)} - \frac{\partial \phi_t}{\partial \tau} + \frac{1}{T} \log S_t \frac{\partial \phi_t}{\partial \log Y_t} = 0$$

where $\tau = T - t$. The boundary condition for the characteristic equation is given by $\phi_T = e^{i\omega \log Y_T}$. The solution to this PDE can be calculated by first guessing the following solution form:

$$\phi_t = \exp[A(\tau) \log S_t + i\omega \log Y_t + B(\tau)]$$

where the functions $A(\tau)$ and $B(\tau)$ are functions of only time to maturity and the other constants in the PDE. Substituting this solution form into the PDE and separating variables results in two ordinary differential equations:

$$\frac{dA}{d\tau} = \frac{1}{T}i\omega$$

$$\frac{dB}{d\tau} = \frac{1}{2}\sigma^2 A^2 + (r - \frac{1}{2}\sigma^2)A$$

with the boundary conditions $A(0) = B(0) = 0$. Since these are simply linear ODEs, their solutions can be computed by well-known methods.

They are given by

$$A(\tau) = \frac{1}{T} i\omega\tau$$

$$B(\tau) = \frac{1}{6}\sigma^2 \frac{1}{T^2}(i\omega)^2 \tau^3 + \frac{1}{2}(r - \frac{1}{2}\sigma^2)\frac{1}{T}i\omega\tau^2$$

Thus, we have derived the characteristic function for $\log Y_T$:

$$\phi_t = \exp\left[\left(\frac{\tau}{T}\log S_t + \log Y_t + \frac{(r - \frac{1}{2}\sigma^2)\tau^2}{2T}\right)i\omega + \frac{\sigma^2\tau^3}{6T^2}(i\omega)^2\right]$$

Since the characteristic function for a normal distribution, $N(\mu, \sigma^2)$, is given by $\exp[\mu i\omega + \frac{1}{2}\sigma^2(i\omega)^2]$, we can see from the form of the characteristic function for $\log Y_T$ that its distribution function is given by

$$\log Y_T \mid \log Y_t \sim N\left[\left(\frac{\tau}{T}\log S_t + \log Y_t + \frac{(r - \frac{1}{2}\sigma^2)\tau^2}{2T}\right), \frac{\sigma^2\tau^3}{6T^2}\right]$$

Consequently, the conditional density function for $\log Y_T$ is given by

$$\sqrt{\frac{6T^2}{2\pi\sigma^2\tau^3}} \exp\left[-\frac{\left[\log Y_T - (\frac{\tau}{T}\log S_t + \log Y_t + \frac{(r-\frac{1}{2}\sigma^2)\tau^2}{2T})\right]^2}{2\left(\frac{\sigma^2\tau^3}{6T^2}\right)}\right]$$

Now that we know the conditional density function of $\log Y_T$, we are prepared to write (2.50) as an integral over this density function:

$$F_t = e^{-r\tau}\int_{\log K}^{\infty} e^{\log Y_T} \sqrt{\frac{6T^2}{2\pi\sigma^2\tau^3}}$$

$$\times \exp\left[-\frac{\left[\log Y_T - (\frac{\tau}{T}\log S_t + \log Y_t + \frac{(r-\frac{1}{2}\sigma^2)\tau^2}{2T})\right]^2}{2\left(\frac{\sigma^2\tau^3}{6T^2}\right)}\right]$$

$$\times d\log Y_T - Ke^{-r\tau}\int_{\log K}^{\infty}\sqrt{\frac{6T^2}{2\pi\sigma^2\tau^3}}$$

$$\times \exp\left[-\frac{\left[\log Y_T - (\frac{\tau}{T}\log S_t + \log Y_t + \frac{(r-\frac{1}{2}\sigma^2)\tau^2}{2T})\right]^2}{2\left(\frac{\sigma^2\tau^3}{6T^2}\right)}\right] d\log Y_T$$

We will tackle this expression one integral at a time. The first integral can be rewritten as

$$e^{-r\tau + \frac{3T^2}{\sigma^2\tau^3}\left[\frac{a\sigma^2\tau^3}{3T^2} + \frac{\sigma^4\tau^6}{36T^4}\right]} \sqrt{\frac{6T^2}{2\pi\sigma^2\tau^3}}$$

$$\times \int_{\log K}^{\infty} \exp\left[-\frac{\left[\log Y_T - \left(a + \frac{\sigma^2\tau^3}{6T^2}\right)\right]^2}{2\left(\frac{\sigma^2\tau^3}{6T^2}\right)}\right] d\log Y_T$$

where $a = \frac{\tau}{T}\log S_t + \log Y_t + \frac{(r-\frac{1}{2}\sigma^2)\tau^2}{2T}$. If we now make the transformation

$$Z = \frac{\sqrt{6}T\left[\log Y_T - \left(a + \frac{\sigma^2\tau^3}{6T^2}\right)\right]}{\sigma\tau^{3/2}}$$

then the integral may be expressed as

$$e^{-r\tau + \frac{3T^2}{\sigma^2\tau^3}\left[\left(\frac{\tau}{T}\log S_t + \log Y_t + \frac{(r-\frac{1}{2}\sigma^2)\tau^2}{2T}\right)\frac{\sigma^2\tau^3}{3T^2} + \frac{\sigma^4\tau^6}{36T^4}\right]}$$

$$\times \frac{1}{\sqrt{2\pi}} \int_{\frac{\sqrt{6}T\left[\log K - \left(a + \frac{\sigma^2\tau^3}{6T^2}\right)\right]}{\sigma\tau^{3/2}}}^{\infty} \exp\left[-\frac{Z^2}{2}\right] dZ$$

Since the integral is now a standard normal distribution, we can re-express this term as

$$e^{-r\tau + \frac{3T^2}{\sigma^2\tau^3}\left[\left(\frac{\tau}{T}\log S_t + \log Y_t + \frac{(r-\frac{1}{2}\sigma^2)\tau^2}{2T}\right)\frac{\sigma^2\tau^3}{3T^2} + \frac{\sigma^4\tau^6}{36T^4}\right]}$$

$$\times \Phi\left(\frac{\sqrt{6}T\left[\log \frac{S_t^{\tau/T}}{K} + \log Y_t + \frac{(r-\frac{1}{2}\sigma^2)\tau^2}{2T} + \frac{\sigma^2\tau^3}{6T^2}\right]}{\sigma\tau^{3/2}}\right)$$

Meanwhile, using the transformation

$$Z = \frac{\sqrt{6}T\left[\log Y_T - \left(\frac{\tau}{T}\log S_t + \log Y_t + \frac{(r-\frac{1}{2}\sigma^2)\tau^2}{2T}\right)\right]}{\sigma\tau^{3/2}},$$

we can rewrite the second integral as

$$\frac{Ke^{-r\tau}}{\sqrt{2\pi}} \int_{\frac{\sqrt{6}T\left[\log K - \left(\frac{\tau}{T}\log S_t + \log Y_t + \frac{(r-\frac{1}{2}\sigma^2)\tau^2}{2T}\right)\right]}{\sigma\tau^{3/2}}}^{\infty} \exp\left[-\frac{Z^2}{2}\right] dZ$$

which is simply

$$\frac{Ke^{-r\tau}}{\sqrt{2\pi}} \Phi \left(\frac{\sqrt{6}T \left[\log \frac{S_t^{\tau/T}}{K} + \log Y_t + \frac{(r-\frac{1}{2}\sigma^2)\tau^2}{2T} \right)}{\sigma\tau^{3/2}} \right)$$

Thus, we have the result that the price of the option is given by

$$F_t = e^{-r\tau + \frac{3T^2}{\sigma^2\tau^3} \left[\left(\frac{\tau}{T} \log S_t + \log Y_t + \frac{(r-\frac{1}{2}\sigma^2)\tau^2}{2T} \right) \frac{\sigma^2\tau^3}{3T^2} + \frac{\sigma^4\tau^6}{36T^4} \right]}$$

$$\times \Phi \left(\frac{\sqrt{6}T \left[\log \frac{S_t^{\tau/T}}{K} + \log Y_t + \frac{(r-\frac{1}{2}\sigma^2)\tau^2}{2T} + \frac{\sigma^2\tau^3}{6T^2} \right)}{\sigma\tau^{3/2}} \right)$$

$$- \frac{Ke^{-r\tau}}{\sqrt{2\pi}} \Phi \left(\frac{\sqrt{6}T \left[\log \frac{S_t^{\tau/T}}{K} + \log Y_t + \frac{(r-\frac{1}{2}\sigma^2)\tau^2}{2T} \right)}{\sigma\tau^{3/2}} \right)$$

2.6.4 Barrier Options

In this section, we price barrier options. As with standard European options, a barrier option has a prespecified (contractual) payoff function at its expiration date, T. This payoff function depends on the value of the underlying stock price at the expiration date as well as the time series of stock prices leading up to that date. Specifically, the option depends on whether or not the stock price breached a certain price level, called a *barrier*, during the life of the option. Barriers can be set such that the option expires if the barrier is breached, termed a *knock-out option*, or becomes live if the barrier is breached, termed a *knock-in option*. Barriers can be set above or below the value of the stock price on the date, t, the option contract is written. If the barrier is set above the stock price at time t, and the option expires upon breaching the barrier, the option is called an *up-and-out option*. If the option becomes live when this barrier is crossed, then the option is termed an *up-and-in option*. Alternatively, the barrier could be set below the stock price at time t. If the option expires when this barrier is crossed, then it is termed a *down-and-out option*, while if the option becomes live upon crossing this barrier, then it is called a *down-and-in*. For this section, we will focus on utilizing the pricing techniques developed in Section 2.5 to first price an up-and-out call option and then to price an up-and-in call option.

The up-and-out option has the following feature: The barrier is set at a level b which is greater than the current stock price S_t and greater than the strike price K.[8] If the stock price ever reaches the barrier, the option expires worthless. If the barrier is not crossed during the life of the option, then the option has a payoff $\max[S_T - K, 0]$.

We make the usual assumptions regarding the stock price process (geometric Brownian motion) and the interest rate (constant). Then, the log stock price process under the risk-neutral probability measure is given by

$$d \log S_t = (r - \frac{1}{2}\sigma^2)dt + \sigma dW_t$$

and we know that $\log S_T \mid \log S_t$ is distributed normally with mean $(r - \frac{1}{2}\sigma^2)\tau$ and variance $\sigma^2\tau$, where $\tau = T - t$. To price the option, we need to know the risk-neutral probability that the stock price will be greater than the exercise price at time T and the maximum stock price between t and T will be less than b, the value of the barrier.

We could start from the risk-neutral stock price process given above to calculate this probability. However, this is difficult to do. Instead, we will first solve for this probability for the case of zero drift in the log stock price process and then modify the result to incorporate a drift of $r - \frac{1}{2}\sigma^2$. Thus, we temporarily assume that the log stock price under the risk-neutral measure is characterized by the following dynamics:

$$d \log S_t = \sigma dW_t \tag{2.52}$$

and the current value of $\log S_t$ is zero, that is, $S_t = 1$. Under these dynamics, $\log S_T \mid \log S_t \sim N(0, \sigma^2\tau)$. Using (2.24), we now write down

---

[8] Notice that if the barrier were set below the exercise price, the up-and-out option would have a price of zero. This is because it would be impossible for the option to end up in the money without crossing the barrier. But if it crosses the barrier, the option becomes dead.

the price of the option at time t as

$$F_t = e^{-r\tau} \mathbb{E}_t^{\mathbb{Q}} \left[\max \left\{ e^{\log S_T} - K, 0 \right\} \right]$$

$$= e^{-r\tau} \int_{\log K}^{\infty} e^{\log S_T} d\tilde{F}(\log S_T \mid M_T \leq b)$$

$$- Ke^{-r\tau} \int_{\log K}^{\infty} d\tilde{F}(\log S_T \mid M_T \leq b) \qquad (2.53)$$

where M_T represents the maximum price that the stock takes on between time t and T, where $\tilde{F}$ represents the zero-drift density function, and F will be used to denote the true density function, with mean $r - \frac{1}{2}\sigma^2$.

So, the first step is to evaluate $\tilde{F}(\log S_T \mid M_T \leq b)$, the probability distribution of the stock price given that the stock price does not breach the barrier b. From the definition of a probability distribution, we know that

$$\tilde{F}(\log S_T \mid M_T \leq b) = \Pr(\log S_T \leq x \mid M_T \leq b)$$

Using the fact that

$$\Pr(\log S_T \leq x) = \Pr(\log S_T \leq x \mid M_T \leq b) + \Pr(\log S_T \leq x \mid M_T > b)$$

we can write

$$\tilde{F}(\log S_T \mid M_T \leq b) = \Pr(\log S_T \leq x) - \Pr(\log S_T \leq x \mid M_T > b) \qquad (2.54)$$

From (2.54), we can use the reflection principle to rewrite the distribution function as

$$\tilde{F}(\log S_T \mid M_T \leq b) = \Pr(\log S_T \leq x) - \Pr(\log S_T \geq 2b - x)$$

$$= \Pr(\log S_T \leq x) - \Pr(\log S_T < x - 2b) \qquad (2.55)$$

The two probabilities on the RHS are easy to calculate given (2.52):

$$\Pr(\log S_T \leq x) = \Phi\left(\frac{x}{\sigma\sqrt{\tau}}\right)$$

$$\Pr(\log S_T \geq x - 2b) = \Phi\left(\frac{x - 2b}{\sigma\sqrt{\tau}}\right)$$

where $\Phi(\cdot)$ represents the cumulative standard normal distribution. Therefore, the conditional density function $d\tilde{F}(\log S_T \mid M_T \leq b)$ can be calculated as the derivative of (2.55):

$$d\tilde{F}\,(\log S_T \mid M_T \le b)$$

$$= \frac{1}{\sigma\sqrt{2\pi\tau}} \exp\left[-\frac{\log^2 S_T}{2\sigma^2\tau}\right] d\log S_T - \frac{1}{\sigma\sqrt{2\pi\tau}} \exp\left[-\frac{(\log S_T - 2b)^2}{2\sigma^2\tau}\right] d\log S_T$$

The density function is a combination of two normal density functions.

However, this density function was calculated under the assumption of zero drift for the log stock price and $\log S_t = 0$. We now need to factor in the fact that the risk-neutral log stock price has a drift of $r - \frac{1}{2}\sigma^2$ and that $\log S_t \neq 0$. To do so, we utilize the fact that for any variable $Z \sim N(0, \sigma^2)$, multiplying its density function by $\exp\left[\frac{\mu}{\sigma^2} Z - \frac{1}{2}\frac{\mu^2}{\sigma^2}\right]$ transforms Z to a normal distribution with a mean of μ, $Z \sim N(\mu, \sigma^2)$.[9] So, to convert the density function calculated above with zero drift to one with a drift of $r - \frac{1}{2}\sigma^2$ we simply have to multiply the density function by

$$\exp\left[\frac{(r - \frac{1}{2}\sigma^2)\tau + \log S_t}{\sigma^2\tau} \log S_T - \frac{1}{2}\frac{[(r - \frac{1}{2}\sigma^2)\tau + \log S_t]^2}{\sigma^2\tau}\right]$$

Therefore, the relevant (nonzero drift) density function, $dF(\log S_T \mid M_T \le b)$, for pricing the option is given by

$$\frac{1}{\sigma\sqrt{2\pi\tau}} e^{-\frac{1}{2\sigma^2\tau}\left((\log S_T)^2 - 2[(r - \frac{1}{2}\sigma^2)\tau + \log S_t]\log S_T + [(r - \frac{1}{2}\sigma^2)\tau + \log S_t]^2\right)} d\log S_T$$

$$- \frac{1}{\sigma\sqrt{2\pi\tau}} e^{-\frac{1}{2\sigma^2\tau}\left((\log S_T - 2b)^2 - 2[(r - \frac{1}{2}\sigma^2)\tau + \log S_t]\log S_T + [(r - \frac{1}{2}\sigma^2)\tau + \log S_t]^2\right)} d\log S_T$$

---

[9] This is easy to verify. The original density function $f(Z)$ is given by

$$f(Z) = \frac{1}{\sigma\sqrt{2\pi}} \exp\left[-\frac{Z^2}{2\sigma^2}\right]$$

If we multiply this density function by $\exp\left[\frac{\mu}{\sigma^2} Z - \frac{1}{2}\frac{\mu^2}{\sigma^2}\right]$, we have the result

$$f(Z) = \frac{1}{\sigma\sqrt{2\pi}} \exp\left[-\frac{(Z - \mu)^2}{2\sigma^2}\right]$$

With this result we can rewrite the option's price, (2.53), as

$$
\frac{e^{-r\tau}}{\sigma\sqrt{2\pi\tau}}\int_{\log K}^{\log b} e^{\log S_T} e^{-\frac{1}{2\sigma^2\tau}\left(\log^2 S_T - 2[(r-\frac{1}{2}\sigma^2)\tau+\log S_t]\log S_T+[(r-\frac{1}{2}\sigma^2)\tau+\log S_t]^2\right)}
$$

$$
\times \, d\log S_T - \frac{e^{-r\tau}}{\sigma\sqrt{2\pi\tau}}
$$

$$
\times \int_{\log K}^{\log b} e^{\log S_T} e^{-\frac{1}{2\sigma^2\tau}\left((\log S_T-2b)^2 - 2[(r-\frac{1}{2}\sigma^2)\tau+\log S_t]\log S_T+[(r-\frac{1}{2}\sigma^2)\tau+\log S_t]^2\right)}
$$

$$
\times \, d\log S_T - \frac{Ke^{-r\tau}}{\sigma\sqrt{2\pi\tau}}
$$

$$
\times \int_{\log K}^{\log b} e^{-\frac{1}{2\sigma^2\tau}\left(\log^2 S_T - 2[(r-\frac{1}{2}\sigma^2)\tau+\log S_t]\log S_T+[(r-\frac{1}{2}\sigma^2)\tau+\log S_t]^2\right)}
$$

$$
\times \, d\log S_T + \frac{Ke^{-r\tau}}{\sigma\sqrt{2\pi\tau}}
$$

$$
\times \int_{\log K}^{\log b} e^{-\frac{1}{2\sigma^2\tau}\left((\log S_T-2b)^2 - 2[(r-\frac{1}{2}\sigma^2)\tau+\log S_t]\log S_T+[(r-\frac{1}{2}\sigma^2)\tau+\log S_t]^2\right)}
$$

$$
\times \, d\log S_T
$$

To calculate the option price, we need to evaluate these four integrals. We do this one integral at a time.

The first integral can be rewritten as

$$
\int_{\log K}^{\log b} e^{-\frac{1}{2\sigma^2\tau}\left(\log^2 S_T - 2[(r-\frac{1}{2}\sigma^2)\tau+\log S_t+\sigma^2\tau]\log S_T+[(r-\frac{1}{2}\sigma^2)\tau+\log S_t]^2\right)} d\log S_T
$$

We first complete the square in the exponential. This gives

$$
e^{r\tau+\log S_t}\int_{\log K}^{\log b} e^{-\frac{1}{2\sigma^2\tau}\left(\log S_T-[(r-\frac{1}{2}\sigma^2)\tau+\log S_t+\sigma^2\tau]\right)^2} d\log S_T
$$

If we make the transformation

$$
Y = \frac{\log S_T - [(r-\frac{1}{2}\sigma^2)\tau + \log S_t + \sigma^2\tau]}{\sigma\sqrt{\tau}}
$$

then we get

$$
\sigma\sqrt{\tau}e^{r\tau+\log S_t}\int_{\frac{\log K-[(r-\frac{1}{2}\sigma^2)\tau+\log S_t+\sigma^2\tau]}{\sigma\sqrt{\tau}}}^{\frac{\log b-[(r-\frac{1}{2}\sigma^2)\tau+\log S_t+\sigma^2\tau]}{\sigma\sqrt{\tau}}} \exp\left[-\frac{Y^2}{2}\right] dY
$$

Since we now have a standard normal density function, this expression can be written as

$$\sigma\sqrt{2\pi\tau}\,e^{r\tau+\log S_t}\left[\Phi(\frac{\log\frac{S_t}{K}+(r+\frac{1}{2}\sigma^2)\tau}{\sigma\sqrt{\tau}})-\Phi(\frac{\log\frac{b}{K}+(r+\frac{1}{2}\sigma^2)\tau}{\sigma\sqrt{\tau}})\right]$$

Therefore, the first term of the option price is given by

$$S_t\left[\Phi\left(\frac{\log\frac{S_t}{K}+(r+\frac{1}{2}\sigma^2)\tau}{\sigma\sqrt{\tau}}\right)-\Phi\left(\frac{\log\frac{b}{K}+(r+\frac{1}{2}\sigma^2)\tau}{\sigma\sqrt{\tau}}\right)\right] \quad (2.56)$$

We now calculate the second integral in the option price. The process is the same as that used for the first integral, so we will skip many of the details. This integral can be written as

$$e^{A(\tau)}\int_{\log K}^{\log b}e^{-\frac{1}{2\sigma^2\tau}\left(\log S_T-[\log S_t+(r+\frac{1}{2}\sigma^2)\tau+b]\right)^2}d\log S_T$$

where

$$A(\tau)=r\tau+\frac{r-\frac{1}{2}\sigma^2}{\sigma^2}+\frac{b}{\sigma^2\tau}\log S_t-S_t-b$$

Therefore, applying the transformation

$$Y=\frac{\log S_T-[\log S_t+(r+\frac{1}{2}\sigma^2)\tau+b]}{\sigma\sqrt{\tau}}$$

gives the following expression:

$$\sigma\sqrt{\tau}e^{A(\tau)}\int_{\frac{\log K-[\log S_t+(r+\frac{1}{2}\sigma^2)\tau+b]}{\sigma\sqrt{\tau}}}^{\frac{\log b-[\log S_t+(r+\frac{1}{2}\sigma^2)\tau+b]}{\sigma\sqrt{\tau}}}\exp\left[-\frac{1}{2}Y^2\right]dY$$

Therefore, the second term in the option price may be written as

$$-S_t^{\frac{b}{\sigma^2\tau}-1}e^{\frac{2r-\sigma^2}{2\sigma^2}-b}\left[\Phi\left(\frac{\log\frac{S_t}{K}+(r+\frac{1}{2}\sigma^2)\tau+b}{\sigma\sqrt{\tau}}\right)\right.$$
$$\left.-\Phi\left(\frac{\log\frac{b}{K}+(r+\frac{1}{2}\sigma^2)\tau+b}{\sigma\sqrt{\tau}}\right)\right] \quad (2.57)$$

Similarly, the third integral in the option price expression may be written as

$$\int_{\log K}^{\log b}e^{-\frac{1}{2\sigma^2\tau}\left(\log S_T-[(r-\frac{1}{2}\sigma^2)\tau+\log S_t]\right)^2}d\log S_T$$

With the transformation $Y = \frac{\log S_T - [(r - \frac{1}{2}\sigma^2)\tau + \log S_t]}{\sigma\sqrt{\tau}}$, we can then write the third term in the option price as

$$
-Ke^{-r\tau}\left[\Phi\left(\frac{\log\frac{S_t}{K} + (r - \frac{1}{2}\sigma^2)\tau}{\sigma\sqrt{\tau}}\right) - \Phi\left(\frac{\log\frac{b}{K} + (r - \frac{1}{2}\sigma^2)\tau}{\sigma\sqrt{\tau}}\right)\right]
$$

(2.58)

Finally, the fourth integral may be written as

$$
e^{\frac{2(r - \frac{1}{2}\sigma^2)\tau + \log S_t}{\sigma^2\tau}} \int_{\log K}^{\infty} e^{-\frac{1}{2\sigma^2\tau}\left(\log S_T - [(r - \frac{1}{2}\sigma^2)\tau + 2b + \log S_t]\right)^2} d\log S_T
$$

Using the transformation $Y = \frac{\log S_T - [(r - \frac{1}{2}\sigma^2)\tau + 2b + \log S_t]}{\sigma\sqrt{\tau}}$, we can write the fourth term of the option price as

$$
Ke^{-r\tau}e^{\frac{2(r - \frac{1}{2}\sigma^2)\tau + \log S_t}{\sigma^2\tau}}\left[\Phi\left(\frac{\log\frac{S_t}{K} + (r - \frac{1}{2}\sigma^2)\tau + 2b}{\sigma\sqrt{\tau}}\right)\right.
$$
$$
\left. - \Phi\left(\frac{\log\frac{b}{K} + (r - \frac{1}{2}\sigma^2)\tau + 2b}{\sigma\sqrt{\tau}}\right)\right]
$$

Combining this expression with (2.56), (2.57), and (2.58) gives the total price of an up-and-out barrier option.

To price an up-and-in barrier option, notice that a portfolio containing an up-and-in option and an up-and-out option (where the barriers are the same value) is equivalent to a standard European call option. Therefore, the price of an up-and-in barrier is simply the Black-Scholes/Merton formula less the expression for the price of an up-and-out option derived above.

3

Interest Rate Models

This chapter analyzes fixed-income securities. There are two goals for this chapter. The first is to see how the valuation principles developed in Chapter 2 can be usefully applied to an extremely important class of assets (in fact the largest asset class in the world after real estate). This leads to the development of discrete-time and continuous-time term structure models. The second goal is to introduce the basic financial securities that trade in the fixed-income markets as well as the tools required for basic analysis of these securities such as duration and convexity.

3.1 INTEREST RATE DERIVATIVES: NOT SO SIMPLE

Why are interest rate derivatives so different that a new chapter is needed to analyze them? A simple example will give you a hint. Recall the price of a European call on a non-dividend-paying asset in a Black-Scholes economy:

$$C_{EU}(t, S, T, K) = S\Phi(d_1) - Ke^{-r(T-t)}\Phi(d_2)$$

with

$$d_1 \equiv \frac{\log(S/K) + \left(r + \frac{1}{2}\sigma^2\right)(T-t)}{\sigma\sqrt{T-t}}$$
$$d_2 \equiv d_1 - \sigma\sqrt{T-t}$$

We want to price a European call on a one-year Treasury bill with the following parameters: $S = 95.12$, $K = 100$, $r = 5\%$, $\sigma = 15\%$, and $(T - t) = 1$ year. Plugging these parameter values in the Black-Scholes formula, we get $C_{EU} = 5.71$. However, you may have noticed that, because the one-year Treasury bill price can only converge to 100, the call is worth nothing at expiration and is therefore worth nothing anytime before expiration. The correct answer is thus $C_{EU} = 0$. The Black-Scholes formula appears to be assigning a value of 5.71 to a worthless option.

What went wrong with the Black-Scholes formula? Remember the random process for asset prices in the Black-Scholes model:

$$\frac{dS}{S} = \mu dt + \sigma dW$$

Two underlying assumptions of this process are of concern when it comes to pricing interest rate derivatives:

1. The term structure of interest rates is flat and deterministic.
2. The standard deviation of returns increases linearly in time, that is, σ is constant.

These assumptions need to be substantially revised to account for a reasonable behavior of interest rate instruments: first, it seems incongruous to model interest rate derivatives in a world of constant interest rates. Second, because riskless bonds converge to par, the uncertainty gets resolved as we get closer to maturity. The variance of the return should hence decrease, not increase, with time.

Throughout the chapter, we shall therefore search for an interest model that will:

1. Use realistic, yet parsimonious, assumptions;
2. Generate term structure scenarios in line with market observations (upward sloping, downward sloping, humped); and
3. Be arbitrage-free.

This all sounds fairly complex. In Robert Merton's words, interest rate derivatives are complicated because the underlying asset (e.g., a bond) is so simple. Contrary to stocks, riskless bonds converge to face value. Meanwhile, interest rates should be positive and volatility, as outlined above, drops with time to maturity. These are the "simple intricacies" we need to deal with.

Before getting into the modeling of the term structure, we give a basic description of bonds and interest rate derivatives in the next three sections.

3.2 BONDS AND YIELDS

3.2.1 Prices and Yields to Maturity

Consider a bond paying fixed riskless cash flows $C_1, C_2, \ldots, C_T$ at periods $1, 2, \ldots, T$. The bond price is $P(0, T)$. An investor who buys this bond will therefore pay P and receive the cash flows $C_1, C_2, \ldots, C_T$ in the future. The net present value of the investment is the discounted value of the cash flows, $C_1, C_2, \ldots, C_T$ minus the initial bond price P.

The *yield to maturity* y is the single discount rate that, when applied to all cash flows, gives a net present value of zero. Formally

$$P(0, T) = \frac{C_1}{1+y} + \frac{C_2}{(1+y)^2} + \cdots + \frac{C_T}{(1+y)^T}$$

Example 3.2.1. A bond priced at 103 pays annual coupons of 7% of a principal of 100 for the next four years. The bond pays the principal at the end of year four. What is the annual yield to maturity?

The annual yield to maturity y solves the equation

$$103 = \frac{7}{1+y} + \frac{7}{(1+y)^2} + \frac{7}{(1+y)^3} + \frac{107}{(1+y)^4}$$

We find $y = 6.13\%$.

When a bond pays a coupon rate C on a face value F and pays the principal F at maturity, the price-yield relationship can be rewritten as

$$P = \frac{CF}{1+y} + \frac{CF}{(1+y)^2} + \cdots + \frac{CF}{(1+y)^T} + \frac{F}{(1+y)^T}$$

Because the first T terms of the right-hand side of the equation follow a geometric progression, we can write

$$\frac{P}{F} = \frac{C}{y}(1 - (1+y)^{-T}) + (1+y)^{-T}$$

When the coupon rate is equal to the yield to maturity ($C = y$), the price of the bond is equal to face value ($P = F$). The bond is then said to be a *par bond*. If $C > y$, as in the above example, $P > F$. The bond is called a *premium bond*. If $C < y$, the price is lower than face value and the bond is called a *discount bond*. The *yield curve* is a pervasive concept in the financial industry; the curve represents yields to maturity of bonds as a function of the maturity of these bonds. We build a yield curve in the following example.

Example 3.2.2(a). The government of country XYZ has five domestic bonds outstanding. All bonds have a principal of 100 and pay a constant coupon. All bonds are riskless. See Table 3.1. To find the bond yields,

Table 3.1

	Maturity (years)	Coupon Rate (%)	Price
Bond A	1	5.00	100.91
Bond B	2	6.00	103.02
Bond C	3	7.50	107.54
Bond D	4	5.25	101.18
Bond E	5	8.00	112.72

we proceed as in Example 3.2.1. The yield y_E of bond E, for instance, is the solution of

$$112.72 = \frac{8}{1 + y_E} + \frac{8}{(1 + y_E)^2} + \frac{8}{(1 + y_E)^3} + \frac{8}{(1 + y_E)^4} + \frac{108}{(1 + y_E)^5}$$

y_E is equal to 5.06%. In similar fashion, we find $y_A = 4.05\%$; $y_B = 4.39\%$; $y_C = 4.745\%$; and $y_D = 4.92\%$ (Figure 3.1).

Can the yield curve be used for arbitrage purposes? In other words, can we infer from a bond yield whether the bond is cheap or expensive?

To build on Example 3.2.2(a), say a new bond (call it B') has just been issued by the government of country XYZ. The bond has a two-year maturity, a 12% coupon rate, and trades at 114.29. You can check that the yield to maturity of that bond is $y_{B'} = 4.38\%$. Comparing bonds B and B', it would therefore appear that B' may be more "expensive" than B (because $y_{B'} = 4.38\% < y_B = 4.39\%$ even though both bonds have the same maturity). If B' is indeed more "expensive" than B, then

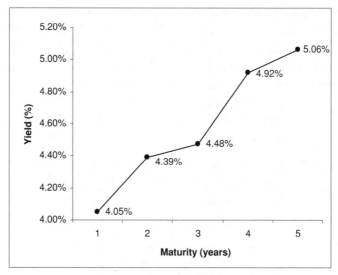

Figure 3.1. Coupon stripping – yield to maturity from coupon rates

a strategy involving a purchase of B and a sale of B' should generate profits.

As the next subsection shows, such an arbitrage is impossible.

3.2.2 Discount Factors, Zero-Coupon Rates, and Coupon Bias

We now infer from an existing set of bonds the discount factors appropriate for cash flows according to their maturity. This should help us decide whether bond B' of the previous subsection is overpriced or not. We use the data in Example 3.2.2 to clarify this point.

Example 3.2.2(b). We want to obtain the discount rates R_1, R_2, R_3, R_4, and R_5 corresponding to cash flows from periods $1, \ldots, 5$ respectively. The $R_i's$ $(i = 1 \ldots 5)$ solve the following equations:

$$100.91 = \frac{105}{1 + R_1}$$

$$103.02 = \frac{6}{1 + R_1} + \frac{106}{(1 + R_2)^2}$$

$$107.52 = \frac{7.5}{1 + R_1} + \frac{7.5}{(1 + R_2)^2} + \frac{107.5}{(1 + R_3)^3}$$

$$101.18 = \frac{5.25}{1 + R_1} + \frac{5.25}{(1 + R_2)^2} + \frac{5.25}{(1 + R_3)^3} + \frac{105.25}{(1 + R_4)^4}$$

$$112.72 = \frac{8}{1 + R_1} + \frac{8}{(1 + R_2)^2} + \frac{8}{(1 + R_3)^3} + \frac{8}{(1 + R_4)^4} + \frac{108}{(1 + R_5)^5}$$

These equations can be solved successively to get: $R_1 = 4.05\%$; $R_2 = 4.40\%$; $R_3 = 4.78\%$; $R_4 = 4.95\%$; $R_5 = 5.12\%$.

R_i ($i = 1 \ldots 5$) is called the i-year *zero-coupon rate*, because R_i is used to discount any i^{th} period cash flow, as if this cash flow were the single payment from an i-year zero-coupon bond. (A *zero-coupon bond* is a bond that pays only one cash flow, at maturity.)

We can now evaluate the mispricing, if any, of bond B'. The market price of bond B' should be

$$\frac{12}{1.0405} + \frac{12}{(1.044)^2} = 114.29$$

which is exactly the price at which it is trading (see previous subsection). Hence, bond B' is well priced, despite displaying a yield that is different from the yield of bond B. Note that B and B', while having the same maturity, have different coupons. The difference in yields for same maturity bonds is attributed to the so-called coupon bias. The coupon bias illustrates why zero-coupon rates are useful for decision making, whereas yields are a rather insignificant measure of a bond return. Yields are merely a harmonic mean; zero-coupon rates are a pricing system.

Indeed, if bond B' had not been priced in accordance with R_1 and R_2, the mispricing could have been arbitraged away, as the following example shows.

Example 3.2.2(b) contd. Assume the price of bond B' were 115 instead of 114.29. One could then execute the following transaction:

Sell a bond B'
Buy 112/106 bonds B
Buy 5.66/105 bonds A

The cash-flow table for the transaction is

Periods	0	1	2
Sell Bond B'	115.00	−12.00	−112.00
Buy 112/106 bonds B	−108.85	6.34	112.00
Buy 5.66/105 bonds A	−5.44	5.66	0.00
Total	0.71	0.00	0.00

The riskless profit from the transaction is 0.71. This is exactly the difference between the traded price (115) and the correct price (114.29). Lastly, note that discount factors δ_i are defined as

$$\delta_i = (1 + R_i)^{-i}$$

In this instance, $\delta_1 = 0.961$; $\delta_2 = 0.917$; $\delta_3 = 0.869$; $\delta_4 = 0.824$; and $\delta_5 = 0.779$.

The preceding example shows that zero-coupon rates, not yields to maturity, should be used to value bonds. More generally, if there are T bonds in an economy: $B_1, \ldots, B_T$ where the subscript i denotes maturity and if bond B_i has price P_i and pays cash flows $C_{i1}, C_{i2}, \ldots, C_{ii}$, at periods $1, 2, \ldots, i$, then the solution for discount factors (and therefore zero-coupon rates) can be expressed in matrix form as

$$C\Delta = P \Rightarrow \Delta = C^{-1}P$$

where

$$\Delta \equiv \begin{bmatrix} \delta_1 \\ \delta_2 \\ \vdots \\ \delta_T \end{bmatrix}; C \equiv \begin{bmatrix} C_{11} & 0 & \cdots & 0 \\ C_{21} & C_{22} & \cdots & 0 \\ \vdots & \vdots & & \vdots \\ C_{T1} & C_{T2} & \cdots & C_{TT} \end{bmatrix}; P \equiv \begin{bmatrix} P_1 \\ P_2 \\ \vdots \\ P_3 \end{bmatrix}$$

This procedure allows us to calculate T zero-coupon rates. To obtain a full zero-coupon curve, fairly complex interpolation, and smoothing interpolation techniques, that we shall not discuss here, are used.

Last, note that it is easy to artificially manufacture zero-coupon bonds out of existing coupon bonds. The technique, called *coupon stripping*, consists of creating linear combinations of short and long existing bonds that would result in aggregate in the desired zero-coupon bond. We revert back to Example 3.2.2 to illustrate the stripping technique.

Example 3.2.2(c). A bank wants to create two-year zero-coupon bonds out of the existing set of bonds in Example 3.2.2(a). Consider a portfolio composed of

(i) a short position (i.e., a sale) of 6/105 bond A
(ii) a long position (i.e., a purchase) of one bond B

The cash flow in and out of the portfolio is

Periods	0	1	2
Sell 6/105 bond A	5.76	−6	0
Buy bond B	−103.02	6	106
Total	97.25	0	106

The resulting portfolio is an "artificial" two-year zero coupon. Not surprisingly, the zero-coupon rate, R_2, given by the equation

$$97.25 = \frac{106}{(1 + R_2)^2}$$

turns out to be 4.40%, which is the rate already found in Example 3.2.2(b). The bank is likely to market 100/106 of this bond so that the amount paid at maturity is 100. This two-year zero with face value 100 has a price of $100/106 \times 97.25 = 91.75$. This is, as should be expected, $100 \times \delta_2$, where δ_2, the discount factor calculated in Example 3.2.2(b), is today's value of one currency unit two years from now. All zero coupons till year 5 can be priced following similar arguments. If Q_i is the value today of a zero coupon paying 100 in year i, then we find: $Q_1 = 96.11$; $Q_2 = 91.75$; $Q_3 = 86.93$; $Q_4 = 82.43$; and $Q_5 = 77.91$.

3.2.3 Forward Rates

A *forward transaction* is the purchase or the sale of a security for future delivery at a pre-agreed price. Let $_m f_n$ be the yield on a zero-coupon bond (i.e., the zero-coupon rate) delivered in m periods and maturing in n periods ($n > m$). To replicate a forward purchase of the zero-coupon bond, one can buy n-year zero-coupon bonds and sell m-year zero-coupon bonds so as to be left with a long position m years from now maturing at time n.

If both bonds promise a cash flow of 100 at maturity, then the price of the m-year zero-coupon is

$$P_m = \frac{100}{(1 + R_m)^m}$$

Similarly

$$P_n = \frac{100}{(1 + R_n)^n}$$

The replication strategy consists in buying an n-year zero-coupon bond and selling $\frac{(1+R_m)^m}{(1+R_n)^n}$ of the m-year zero-coupon bond. Cash flows resulting from this strategy are shown below.

Period	0	m	n
Sell $\frac{(1+R_m)^m}{(1+R_n)^n}$ m-year bond	$\frac{100}{(1+R_n)^n}$	$\frac{-100(1+R_m)^m}{(1+R_n)^n}$	
Buy one n-year bond	$\frac{-100}{(1+R_n)^n}$		100
Total	0	$\frac{-100(1+R_m)^m}{(1+R_n)^n}$	100

We have thus created a synthetic zero-coupon starting n years forward and lasting $(n - m)$ years thereafter. The forward rate $_m f_n$ is given by the present value relationship

$$\frac{100(1 + R_m)^m}{(1 + R_n)^n} = \frac{100}{(1 +_m f_n)^{n-m}}$$

Therefore

$$_m f_n = \sqrt[n-m]{\frac{(1 + R_n)^n}{(1 + R_m)^m}} - 1$$

An equivalent way of thinking about forward rates is that based on the information at time 0, we should be indifferent between investing a dollar for n years and investing a dollar for two successive periods of m and $n - m$ years. In other words:

$$(1 + R_n)^n = (1 + R_m)^m (1 +_m f_n)^{n-m} \Rightarrow _m f_n = \sqrt[n-m]{\frac{(1 + R_n)^n}{(1 + R_m)^m}} - 1$$

as before.

Example 3.2.2(d). We use the zero-coupon rates to calculate $_1 f_2$, $_2 f_3$, $_3 f_4$, and $_4 f_5$. These rates are called the "short forwards" because

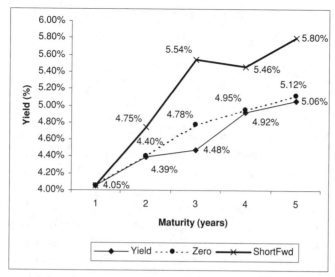

Figure 3.2. Relation between yield to maturity, zero-coupon rates, and short forward rates

they apply to one period ($n - m = 1$). The general formula for forwards yields the following results:

$$_1 f_2 = \frac{(1 + R_2)^2}{1 + R_1} - 1 = 4.75\%$$

$$_2 f_3 = \frac{(1 + R_3)^3}{(1 + R_2)^2} - 1 = 5.54\%$$

$$_3 f_4 = \frac{(1 + R_4)^4}{(1 + R_3)^3} - 1 = 5.46\%$$

$$_4 f_5 = \frac{(1 + R_5)^5}{(1 + R_4)^4} - 1 = 5.80\%$$

Also note that $_0 f_1 = R_1 = 4.05\%$ because a one-year forward starting today is the one-year zero-coupon rate. In general and for the same reason, $_0 f_i = R_i$, the i-year zero-coupon rate. The graph in Figure 3.2 shows the yields to maturity, zero-coupon rates, and short forward rates derived in Example 3.2.2.

Note that the short forward curve is above the zero-coupon curve. This is because the zero-coupon curve is upward sloping. A simple proof can be given along these lines:

$$R_t > R_{t-1}$$
$$\Leftrightarrow (1 + R_t)^t > (1 + R_{t-1})^t$$
$$\Leftrightarrow (1 + R_{t-1})^{t-1}(1 +_{t-1} f_t) > (1 + R_{t-1})^t$$
$$\Leftrightarrow {}_{t-1} f_t > R_{t-1}$$

The third line follows from the general forward equation. It can be shown similarly that when the zero-coupon curve is downward sloping, the short forward curve is below the zero-coupon curve. When the zero-coupon curve is flat, both curves are identical.

A question of interest is whether forward rates can predict future rates. Theories of the term structure and of interest rate expectations will be expanded in Section 3.5. Another question relates to the way we priced bonds and forward transactions throughout this section. Recall from Example 3.2.2 that we started with a set of existing bonds with one-, two-, three-, four-, and five-year maturities. Then we price a new two-year bond relative to the existing set of bonds. Similarly, we calculated forward rates, taking the existing bond prices as a given. In linear algebra parlance, the set of five bonds are a basis. But nowhere in this section have we tried to justify or explain these bond prices. How bonds are priced is a topic we shall deal with in Section 3.6 and in subsequent sections. For now, we shall discuss naive models of interest rate risk and, in particular, the notions of duration and convexity.

3.3 NAIVE MODELS OF INTEREST RATE RISK

3.3.1 Duration

Duration is a measure of the sensitivity of bond price to a change in interest rates. We revisit the bond of Section 3.2. This bond pays fixed, riskless cash flows $C_1, C_2, \ldots, C_T$ at periods $1, 2, \ldots, T$. We postulate a flat term structure of interest rates, that is, the yield-to-maturity curve, the zero-coupon curve, and the forward curve are all flat and identical. The price P of this bond is

$$P = \frac{C_1}{1+r} + \frac{C_2}{(1+r)^2} + \cdots + \frac{C_T}{(1+r)^T} = \sum_{i=1}^{T} \frac{C_i}{(1+r)^i} \qquad (3.1)$$

You can think of r as the yield to maturity, the zero-coupon rate, or the forward rate. The reason we can afford to be fuzzy about the definition of r is that, as noted above, the term structure is flat and therefore, all rates are the same and all nuances vanish. For convenience, we shall call r "the" interest rate.

Differentiating P with respect to r gives

$$\frac{dP}{dr} = \frac{-C_1}{(1+r)^2} - \frac{2C_2}{(1+r)^3} - \cdots - \frac{TC_T}{(1+r)^{T+1}} = \frac{-1}{1+r}\sum_{i=1}^{T}\frac{iC_i}{(1+r)^i}$$

(3.2)

We multiply both sides of the equation by dr/P to get

$$\frac{dP}{P} = -\frac{1}{1+r}\frac{\sum_{i=1}^{T}\frac{iC_i}{(1+r)^i}}{\sum_{i=1}^{T}\frac{C_i}{(1+r)^i}}dr$$

(3.3)

We define *duration D* as

$$D \equiv \frac{\sum_{i=1}^{T}\frac{iC_i}{(1+r)^i}}{\sum_{i=1}^{T}\frac{C_i}{(1+r)^i}}$$

(3.4)

The relationship between bond price relative changes and interest rate changes can therefore be formulated as

$$\frac{dP}{P} = \frac{-D}{1+r}dr$$

(3.5)

D is called the *Macaulay duration*, after F. R. Macaulay, who suggested this measure of interest rate risk in 1938. As shown in the definition, the duration is the weighted average time (expressed in years) until maturity of a bond, with the weights being the present values of the cash flows divided by the bond price. Indeed, (3.4) can be rewritten as

$$D \equiv \sum_{i=1}^{T} i \times \frac{C_i}{(1+r)^i/P}$$

(3.6)

Another interpretation of duration can be given from rewriting (3.5):

$$D = \frac{\ln P}{d\ln\frac{1}{1+r}} = \frac{d\ln P_T}{d\ln P_1}$$

(3.7)

where $P_1 \equiv \frac{1}{1+r}$ is the price of a one-year zero-coupon bond with face value of one. Duration is then interpreted as the elasticity of the bond price vis-à-vis a one-year zero-coupon bond price.

We give examples on how to calculate a duration and how to infer bond price changes resulting from rate changes.

Example 3.3.1(a). We calculate the duration of a bond paying an 8% coupon for five years, with principal repayment of 100 at the end of year five. The interest rate is 10%. Relevant calculations are shown in

Table 3.2

Period	Cash Flows	Discount Factor	Discounted Cash Flows	Discounted Cash Flows × Time
1	8	$(1.1)^{-1}$	7.2727	7.2727
2	8	$(1.1)^{-2}$	6.6116	13.2231
3	8	$(1.1)^{-3}$	6.0105	18.0316
4	8	$(1.1)^{-4}$	5.4641	21.8564
5	108	$(1.1)^{-5}$	67.0595	335.2975
		TOTAL	92.4184	395.6814

Table 3.2. We use the duration definition in (3.4). The numerator is given by the total of column 5:

$$\sum_{i=1}^{5} \frac{iC_i}{(1+r)^i} = 395.6814$$

The denominator, that is, the bond price, is the total of column 4:

$$\sum_{i=1}^{5} \frac{C_i}{(1+r)^i} = 92.4184$$

The duration of the bond is therefore

$$D = \frac{395.6814}{92.4184} = 4.28 \; years$$

Example 3.3.1(b). Refer to Example 3.3.1(a). There is an interest rate hike from 10% to 10.1%. What is the resulting bond price change?
  We apply equation (3.5) to get

$$\frac{price \; change}{92.4184} = \frac{-4.28}{1.1} \times 0.1\%$$

Hence, the price change is −0.3596. The new price predicted by equation (3.5) is 92.4184 − 0.3596 = 92.0588.

It is a matter of simple algebra to derive a closed-form formula for the duration of a bond with a constant coupon rate and a final payment. Denote by P the bond price, A the face value, C the coupon rate, T the time to maturity, P_C the present value of the coupon payments, and P_A the present value of the principal payment. Then

$$P = P_C + P_A$$

with

$$P_C = \sum_{i=1}^{T} \frac{FC}{(1+r)^i} = FC \frac{1-(1+r)^{-T}}{r} \tag{3.8}$$

and

$$P_A = A(1+r)^{-T} \tag{3.9}$$

From (3.5)

$$D = -\frac{(1+r)}{P} \frac{dP}{dr} = -\frac{1+r}{P} \left(\frac{dP_C}{dr} + \frac{dP_A}{dr} \right) \tag{3.10}$$

From (3.8) and (3.9)

$$\frac{dP_C}{dr} = \frac{-P_C}{r} + \frac{TCP_A}{r(1+r)} \tag{3.11}$$

and

$$\frac{dP_A}{dr} = \frac{-AT}{(1+r)^{T+1}} = \frac{-P_A T}{1+r} \tag{3.12}$$

combining (3.10), (3.11), and (3.12), we obtain the closed-form formula[1] for D:

$$D = \frac{P_C}{P} \left(1 + \frac{1}{r} \right) + \frac{P_A}{P} \left(1 - \frac{C}{r} \right) T \tag{3.13}$$

Special cases of this formula include

1. ZERO-COUPON BONDS: In this case, $P_A = P$, $C = 0$, and $P_C = 0$. It follows that $D = T$. The duration of a zero coupon is equal to its maturity. This can also be seen from the duration formula in

---

[1] See Babcock (1984).

(3.4) which reduces to

$$D = \frac{TC_T}{(1+r)^T} \bigg/ \frac{C_T}{(1+r)^T} = T \qquad (3.14)$$

2. PERPETUITIES: There is no final repayment ($P_A = 0$ and $P_C = P$) in this case; we thus obtain

$$D = \frac{1+r}{r} \qquad (3.15)$$

3. PAR BONDS: By definition of a par bond, $C = r$ and $P = A$. Then by (3.8) and (3.13)

$$D = \left(1 - (1+r)^{-T}\right)\left(1 + \frac{1}{r}\right) \qquad (3.16)$$

Another conventional measure of duration, called *modified duration* and denoted D_{mod}, is defined as

$$D_{\text{mod}} \equiv \frac{D}{1+r}$$

so that

$$\frac{dP}{P} = -D_{\text{mod}} \times dr$$

It follows that the modified duration of a perpetuity is $1/r$ and that of a par bond is $\frac{1-(1+r)^{-T}}{r}$, which is simply the annuity factor for a stream of constant annuity payments.

Example 3.3.2. Interest rates are at a 5% level. What is the duration of (i) a 7-year zero-coupon bond paying 100 at maturity? (ii) a perpetuity paying a yearly coupon of 8%? (iii) a 10-year bond paying a 5% coupon with face value 100?

    (i) By (3.14), the duration is seven years.
    (ii) By (3.15), the duration is $1.05/0.05 = 21$ years. The coupon information is irrelevant!
    (iii) By (3.16), the duration is $\frac{1-(1.05)^{-10}}{0.05} \times 1.05 = 8.11$ years.

It can be shown with some tedious algebra that duration increases with maturity (except for deep discount bonds) and decreases with coupon size and with the level of interest rates. That duration increases with bond maturity makes intuitive sense. When the coupon rate is higher or when interest rates rise, the value of early cash flows increases relative to late cash flows. This makes the bond effectively "shorter"; in other words, it reduces its duration.

Example 3.3.3(a). How does a maturity change affect the duration of a 10-year par bond in a 10% interest rate environment?
From (3.16)

$$\frac{\partial D}{\partial T} = \frac{(1+r)\ln(1+r)}{r}(1+r)^{-T}$$

with $r = 0.1$ and $T = 10$, $\partial D/\partial T = 0.404$. When maturity decreases by one day, duration decreases by about 4/10 of a day.

Example 3.3.3(b). How does an interest rate change modify the duration of a perpetuity when interest rates are at 5%?
From (3.15)

$$\frac{\partial D}{\partial r} = \frac{-1}{r^2} = -400$$

When rates decrease by ten basis points (0.1%), the duration of the perpetuity increases by 4.8 months (4/10 of a year).

It is possible to calculate the duration of nonstandard bonds such as mortgages or the duration of altogether different asset classes, such as equity and derivatives. We provide a few examples to show how the duration concept can be extended beyond standard bonds.

Example 3.3.4. Consider an option-free mortgage with level yearly payments of M. The price of the mortgage is the present value of these payments:

$$P = \frac{M}{1+r} + \frac{M}{(1+r)^2} + \cdots + \frac{M}{(1+r)^T} = M\frac{1-(1+r)^{-T}}{r}$$

Then

$$\frac{dP}{dr} = \frac{-P}{r} + \frac{MT}{r(1+r)^{T+1}}$$

The duration of the mortgage is thus

$$D = \frac{-(1+r)}{P}\frac{dP}{dr} = \frac{1+r}{r} - \frac{T}{(1+r)^T - 1}$$

Note that this formula is equivalent to the duration of a perpetuity for an infinite maturity $(T \to \infty)$.

Example 3.3.5: The Duration of Equity. This concept may sound a bit exotic in the sense that interest rates contribute less to the volatility of stock prices than, say, the volatility of government bond prices. We shall see in Example 3.3.6 that this is not necessarily the case. We define δ as the initial dividend, g as the growth rate of this dividend, and r as the rate of return required by equity investors $(r > g)$. Then the equity price P is[2]

$$P = \frac{\delta}{r - g} \tag{3.17}$$

The interest rate sensitivity of the stock price is

$$P = \frac{-\delta}{(r - g)^2}$$

and its duration can then be directly calculated:[3]

$$D = \frac{-dP}{r} \times \frac{1}{P} = \frac{1}{r - g} \tag{3.18}$$

From (3.17) and (3.18), we may conclude that

$$D = \frac{P}{\delta} = \frac{1}{dividend\ yield}$$

---

[2] This formula has been obtained by setting

$$P = \int_0^\infty \delta e^{gt} e^{-rt} dt = \frac{\delta}{r - g}$$

Alternatively, a discrete-time formulation could have yielded a similar result:

$$P = \sum_{i=1}^\infty \frac{(1 + g)^{i-1} \delta}{(1 + r)^i} = \frac{\delta}{r - g}$$

although the interpretation is slightly different in discrete time.

[3] Because we operate in continuous time, $D = -dP/dr * 1/P$ (and not $\frac{-dP}{dr} \frac{1+r}{P}$). To convince yourself, calculate

$$D = \frac{\int_0^\infty t\delta e^{gt} e^{-rt} dt}{\int_0^\infty \delta e^{gt} e^{-rt} dt}$$

to find $1/r - g$ as stated in (3.18).

The dividend yield of various stock indices is typically between 1% and 5%. This would mean that equity duration is between 20 and 100 years. This range is high compared to most empirical estimates of duration (2 to 10 years). One reason is that a rise in interest rates is often caused by a rise in inflation expectations. These in turn cause dividends to rise. To the extent these movements are comparable, a rise in interest rate caused by a rise in expected inflation will have little effect on the stock price.

We can amend our equations to reflect the various components of interest rate risk. We model the required rate of return and the dividend growth rate as follows:[4]

$$r = R + \pi^e + \rho(R, \pi^e) \qquad (3.19)$$

$$g = g_0 + aR + b\pi^e \qquad (3.20)$$

where g_0 is exogenous growth, R is the real rate, π^e expected inflation, and ρ the equity risk premium. From (3.17), $P = P(r, g)$. Therefore

$$\frac{dP}{P} = d \ln P = \frac{\partial \ln P}{\partial r} dr + \frac{\partial \ln P}{\partial g} dg \qquad (3.21)$$

From (3.18), (3.19), and (3.20)

$$\frac{\partial \ln P}{\partial r} = \frac{-1}{r - g} = -D \qquad (3.22)$$

$$\frac{\partial \ln P}{\partial g} = \frac{1}{r - g} = D \qquad (3.23)$$

$$dr = dR + d\pi^e + \frac{\partial \rho}{\partial R} dR + \frac{\partial \rho}{\partial \pi^e} d\pi^e \qquad (3.24)$$

and

$$dg = dg_0 + a\,dR + b\,d\pi^e \qquad (3.25)$$

---

[4] See Leibowitz et al. (1989) for a detailed discussion of this model.

From equations (3.21)–(3.25), it follows that

$$\frac{dP}{P} = -D(dr - dg)$$
$$= -D\left\{ \left(1 - a + \frac{\partial \rho}{\partial R}\right) dR + \left(1 - b + \frac{\partial \rho}{\partial \pi^e}\right) d\pi^e - dg_0 \right\} \quad (3.26)$$

Equation (3.26) shows three sources of stock price change:

a. *Real interest rates: The "real rate duration" is $D(1 - a + \partial \rho/R)$*
b. *Expected inflation: The "expected inflation duration" is $D(1 - b + \partial \rho/\partial \pi^e)$*
c. *Exogenous growth: The "exogenous growth duration" is $-D$, that is, if growth increases by 1% and is not induced by interest rate changes, the stock price grows by D% (or 20% to 100% as stated above).*

Note that, of the three components of stock price change, only the first two are interest rate risk components. It is difficult, a priori, to decide on the sign of a, $\partial \rho/\partial R$, and $\partial \rho/\partial \pi^e$, because it will depend on the nature of the interest rate shock.[5] By contrast, because b is an inflation pass-through factor, it is close to one.[6] The implication is that real rate duration is likely to be far higher than expected inflation duration. For example, if $a = \partial \rho/\partial R = \partial \rho/\partial \pi^e = 0$; $b = 0.8$ and $D = P/d = 40$, then the real interest duration is 40 years, whereas the expected inflation duration is $40 \times (1 - 0.8) = 8$ years. Remember, however, that a stock price is, more often than not, perturbed by non-interest rate variables. In equation (3.26), even though exogenous growth duration and real rate duration are comparable in magnitude, g_0 is subject to more shocks (for most stocks) than the real interest rate and will therefore be a major contributor to stock price changes. As noted at the beginning of this example, this need not be the case. Consider a financial institution with a balance sheet populated exclusively by fixed-income instruments. To such an

---

[5] For example, an increase in real interest rates can be prompted by a restrictive monetary policy. This could prompt savings to increase at the expense of consumption, thus reducing aggregate demand, profitability, and dividends. In this scenario, $a < 0$. But an increase in real rates can also be induced by a higher productivity of capital, in which case dividends should increase ($a > 0$). See Leibowitz et al. (1989).

[6] Leibowitz et al. (1989) estimate it at 0.8.

institution, interest rate risk is the major source of risk. We now discuss the duration of equity in financial institutions in a stylized example.

Example 3.3.6. Duration of Equity in Financial Institutions. Consider the simplified balance sheet of a bank:

	Assets			Liabilities	
	Market Value	Duration		Market Value	Duration
Bond A	100	11 years	Bond B	90	5.5 years
			Equity	10	?

Interest rates are at a 10% level. What is the effect of an interest rate hike to 11%? We use equation (3.5) to get the new values of bond A and bond B:

$$\text{Change in value of bond } A = \frac{-11}{1.1} \times 100 \times 0.01 = -10$$
$$\text{Change in value of bond } B = \frac{-5.5}{1.1} \times 90 \times 0.01 = -4.5$$

The balance sheet after the rate hike is shown in this tabulation:

	Assets		Liabilities
	Market Value		Market Value
Bond A	90	Bond B	85.5
		Equity	4.5

Equity value has been more than halved by a 1% increase in interest rates.[7] If A, L, and E are the market values of bond A, bond B, and equity, respectively, and if D_A, D_L, and D_E are the corresponding durations, then

$$\frac{dA}{dr} = \frac{d(B+E)}{dr} \tag{3.27}$$

$$\text{i.e., } \frac{-(1+r)}{A}\frac{dA}{dr} = \frac{-(1+r)}{A}\frac{dL}{dr} \times \frac{L}{L} - \frac{(1+r)}{A}\frac{dE}{dr} \times \frac{E}{E}$$

$$\text{i.e., } AD_A = LD_L + ED_E$$

---

[7] Implicit in this example is the joint assumption of unlimited liability and "rich" shareholders. This allows us to treat liability cash flows as riskless and equity as the difference between the asset and the liability. If shareholders enjoy limited liability, equity is then a call on assets with exercise price equal to the face value of the debt.

Suppose the initial values of these parameters are: $A = 100$; $L = 90$;
$D_A = 11$; $D_L = 5.5$; $E = 4.5$. From equation (3.27), $D_E = 60.5$ years. As
evidenced by the new balance sheet, equity stands to "bleed" when in-
terest rates rise. From the same equation (3.27), we can infer the hedging
rule for immunizing equity against interest rate changes (i.e., $D_E = 0$):

$$D_A = \frac{L}{A} D_L \tag{3.28}$$

Rule (3.28) means that the duration of the assets should be reduced
from 11 years to $90/100 \times 5.5 = 4.95$ years. This can be accomplished
by selling a proportion of bond A holdings and buying with the proceeds
low-duration bonds.

Example 3.3.7. Duration of an Option. The duration of an option can be
computed along the same lines as ordinary bonds. If we define effective
duration D^* as $-\frac{dP}{dr}\frac{1}{P}$ (this is similar to modified duration for a simple
bond), then

$$D_V^* = \frac{-1}{V}\frac{dV}{dr} = \frac{-1}{V}\frac{dV}{dP}\frac{dP}{dr} = \frac{1}{V}\frac{dV}{dP}D_P^* P \tag{3.29}$$

where D_V^* is the effective duration of the option, V the price of the option,
P the price of the underlying asset, and D_P^* the effective duration of the
asset. Stated differently

$$D_V^* = \Omega D_P^*$$

where Ω is the elasticity of the option, that is, the relative price change of
the option induced by the relative price change of the underlying

$$\Omega = \frac{dV/V}{dP/P}$$

Ω can also be viewed as the product of the option delta ($\Delta_V = dV/dP$)
and the ratio of the underlying price to the option price (P/V)

$$\Omega = \Delta \times \frac{P}{V}$$

For instance, a 1-year call on a 10-year bond worth 100 is worth 4.
The delta of the call is 0.52 and the effective duration of the underlying

bond is 7.1 years. The duration of the call option is

$$D_V^* = \Omega D_P^* = \Delta \times \frac{P}{V} \times D_P^* = 0.52 \times \frac{100}{4} \times 7.1 = 92.3 \; years$$

Throughout the examples, we used extensively equation (3.5). The differential term dr belies three assumptions:

1. Changes in interest rates are infinitesimal;
2. The term structure of interest rates is flat (r has no maturity subscript); and
3. Changes in the term structure are parallel.

In the next subsection, we relax assumption (1) and discuss the notion of convexity. Then we show why assumptions (2) and (3) taken together can generate riskless arbitrage.

3.3.2 Convexity

Equation (3.5)

$$\frac{dP}{P} = \frac{-D}{1+r} dr$$

can be Taylor-expanded to one term as

$$\hat{P}(r) = P_0 - \frac{D(r_0) P_0}{1+r}(r - r_0) \tag{3.30}$$

where $\hat{P}(r)$ and r (resp. P_0 and r_0) are the new (resp. old) price-yield combination. In equation (3.30), the new bond price P is a linear function of the new interest rate r. But bond prices are a hyperbolic function of interest rates. Equation (3.30) or equivalently (3.5) will display a bias, as Example 3.3.8 will show.

Example 3.3.8. Consider a one-year zero-coupon bond with a face value of 1. Its "true" price P can be expressed as $P(r) = \frac{1}{1+r}$. With an initial interest rate $r_0 = 10\%$, $P_0 = 1/1.1$, and $D(r_0, P_0) = 1$ year, equation (3.30) gives the following price estimate:

$$\hat{P}(r) = \frac{1}{1.1} - \frac{1/1.1}{1.1}(r - 0.1) = \frac{120}{121} - \frac{100r}{121}$$

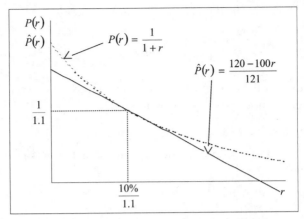

Figure 3.3. Two portfolios with same duration but different convexities

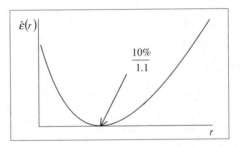

Figure 3.4. Convexity bias

The bias $\hat{\varepsilon}(r)$ is the difference between the true price and the duration-predicted price:

$$\hat{\varepsilon}(r) = P(r) - \hat{P}(r) = \frac{1}{1+r} + \frac{100r}{121} - \frac{120}{121}$$

$P(r)$, $\hat{P}(r)$, and $\hat{\varepsilon}(r)$ are plotted in Figures 3.3 and 3.4.

The bias in Example 3.3.8 is the difference between a function and its first-order approximation. A Taylor expansion on the function $P(r)$

gives the following expression:

$$P(r) = P(r_0) + \frac{dP}{dr} \Big|_{r=r_0} (r - r_0) + \frac{1}{2} \frac{d^2 P}{dr^2} \Big|_{r=r_0} (r - r_0)^2$$
$$+ \frac{1}{6} \frac{d^3 P}{dr^3} \Big|_{r=r_0} (r - r_0)^3 + \cdots \tag{3.31}$$
$$= P(r_0) + \sum_{i=1}^{\infty} \frac{d^i P}{dr^i} \frac{(r - r_0)^i}{i!}$$

We shall limit ourselves to the first two terms of the expansion to get

$$\Delta P = P'(r_0)\Delta r + \frac{P''(r_0)}{2}(\Delta r)^2 + o(\Delta r^2) \tag{3.32}$$

where $\Delta P \equiv P - P_0$ and $\Delta r = r - r_0$. Neglecting higher-order terms and dividing through by P, we get the expression of relative price change as a function of a duration term and a "convexity" term

$$\frac{\Delta P}{P} = -D_{\mathrm{mod}} \Delta r + \frac{\kappa}{2}(\Delta r)^2 \tag{3.33}$$

with $D_{\mathrm{mod}} \equiv -\frac{dP}{dr} \frac{1}{P}$ as seen before, and the *convexity* κ defined as

$$\kappa \equiv \frac{1}{P} \frac{d^2 P}{dr^2} \tag{3.34}$$

For a bond with fixed, riskless cash flows, we can differentiate (3.1) twice with respect to r to get

$$\frac{d^2 P}{dr^2} = \frac{2C_1}{(1+r)^3} + \frac{3C_2}{(1+r)^4} + \cdots + \frac{T(T+1)C_T}{(1+r)^{T+2}} \tag{3.35}$$

Convexity is in the case

$$\kappa = \frac{\sum_{i=1}^{T} \frac{i(i+1)C_i}{(1+r)^{i+2}}}{\sum_{i=1}^{T} \frac{C_i}{(1+r)^i}} \tag{3.36}$$

Duration is a linear approximation to the sensitivity of bond prices to changes in the intererest rate. Convexity provides a second-order correction in estimating the true sensitivity.

Example 3.3.9(a). Calculate the duration and the convexity of a bond paying a 10% annual coupon for five years with a principal repayment of 100 at the end of year five. Interest rates are at a 10% level.

We calculate the relevant quantities in Table 3.3.

From (3.4), we get the value of the duration: Duration $= 416.99/$
$100 = 4.1699$ *years.*

Table 3.3

Period	Cash Flows	Discount Factor	DCF	DCF × Time	DCF × (Time + 1)
1	10	$(1.1)^{-1}$	9.09	9.09	18.18
2	10	$(1.1)^{-2}$	8.26	16.53	49.59
3	10	$(1.1)^{-3}$	7.51	22.54	90.16
4	10	$(1.1)^{-4}$	6.83	27.32	136.60
5	110	$(1.1)^{-5}$	68.3	341.51	2049.04
		TOTAL	100	416.99	2343.57

Convexity obtains from equation (3.36). This corresponds to the total of column 6 divided by $[Price \times (1 + r)^2]$. *(Note that the physical unit of measure of convexity is* $(years)^2$.*)*

$$\kappa = \frac{2,343.57}{100 \times (1.1)^2} = 19.3683 \ (years)^2$$

Example 3.3.9(b). Consider the bond described in Example 3.3.9(a). Accounting for both the duration and the convexity effects, what is the new bond price if interest rates rise from 10% to 11%?

We use equation (3.33):

$$\frac{\Delta P}{P} = \frac{-D}{1+r}\Delta r + \frac{\kappa}{2}(\Delta r)^2 = \frac{-4.1699}{1.1} \times 1\% + \frac{19.3683}{2} \times (1\%)^2$$
$$= -3.7908\% + 0.0968\% = -3.6940\%$$

The new price is therefore 96.306.

Example 3.3.9(c). We compare the duration prediction and the combined duration-convexity prediction for change in the bond price, for interest rate changes away from their initial 10% level. As in Example 3.3.9(a), the reference bond is a 10% coupon, five-year maturity bond with face value 100.

Interest Rate/Price	12%	11%	9%	8%
Actual price	92.7904	96.3041	103.8897	107.9854
Duration prediction	92.4184	96.2092	103.7908	107.5816
Duration/convexity prediction	92.8058	96.3061	103.8876	107.9689

Convexity, like duration, generally increases with maturity and decreases with the coupon and interest rate levels. We illustrate the effect of maturity and interest rates with the following examples.

Example 3.3.10(a). What is the convexity of a zero-coupon bond? How is it affected by maturity and interest rates?
   From (3.36), a direct calculation shows that

$$\kappa = \frac{T(T+1)}{(1+r)^2} \tag{3.37}$$

for a zero-coupon bond. Therefore

$$\frac{\partial \kappa}{\partial T} = \frac{2T+1}{(1+r)^2} > 0$$

and

$$\frac{\partial \kappa}{\partial r} = \frac{-2(1+r)T(T+1)}{(1+r)^4} < 0$$

Example 3.3.10(b). What is the convexity of a perpetuity? How does it react to a change in interest rates?
   The price of a perpetuity paying C per year is

$$P = \sum_{i=1}^{\infty} \frac{C}{(1+r)^i} = \frac{C}{r}$$

Hence, $dP/dr = -C/r^2$ and $d^2 P/dr^2 = 2C/r^3$. Convexity is calculated using (3.34):

$$\kappa = \frac{d^2 P}{dr^2} \times \frac{1}{P} = \frac{2}{r^2} \tag{3.38}$$

Convexity will therefore decrease with rates

$$\frac{d\kappa}{dr} = \frac{-4}{r^3} < 0$$

3.3.3 The Free Lunch in the Duration Model

The duration model, as pointed out, assumed parallel shifts of a flat term structure of interest rates. We now question whether these types of movements of the term structure are acceptable. In our parlance, "acceptable" means that the term structure changes that we postulate disallow riskless arbitrage. If such an arbitrage is made possible by our assumptions, then these assumptions need to be revised to reflect the simple reality of bond markets: there are very few riskless arbitrage opportunities around.

The presumption of a free lunch in the duration model arises from the fact that two portfolios having the same value and the same duration will generally have different convexities. In a world where movements in a flat term structure are parallel, a strategy where one purchases the high-convexity portfolio and sells the low-convexity portfolio should always make money.

Example 3.3.11. Consider a portfolio (portfolio A) of 5-year zero-coupon bonds. Portfolio B is invested in 1-year and 10-year zero-coupon bonds. The relative weights on 1-year and 10-year zeros are chosen so that portfolios A and B have the same value and the same modified duration. Portfolio B is then called a "barbell portfolio." If portfolio A consists of one 5-year zero-coupon worth P_5, and portfolio B comprises q_1 1-year zero coupons worth P_1 each and q_{10} 10-year zero coupons worth P_{10} each, and if $D_{\text{mod } i}$ is the modified duration of an i-year zero-coupon bond, then we have

$$P_1 q_1 + P_{10} q_{10} = P_5 \; (\textit{equal value constraint})$$
$$P_1 q_1 D_{\text{mod } 1} + P_{10} q_{10} D_{\text{mod } 10} = P_5 D_{\text{mod } 5} \; (\textit{duration-matching constraint})$$

This system of two equations with two unknowns (q_1 and q_{10}) determines the composition of the barbell portfolio. If all bonds have a face *value of 100 and interest rates are at 5%, then*

$$P_1 = 100 \times (1.05)^{-1} = 95.238$$
$$P_5 = 100 \times (1.05)^{-5} = 78.353$$
$$P_{10} = 100 \times (1.05)^{-10} = 61.391$$
$$D_{\text{mod } 1} = \frac{1}{1.05} = 0.952 \text{ year}$$
$$D_{\text{mod } 5} = \frac{5}{1.05} = 4.762 \text{ years}$$
$$D_{\text{mod } 10} = \frac{10}{1.05} = 9.524 \text{ years}$$

The equations simplify to

$$95.238q_1 + 61.391q_{10} = 78.353$$
$$90.703q_1 + 584.676q_{10} = 373.108$$

We find $q_1 = 0.457$ and $q_{10} = 0.567$.

Which of portfolio A or portfolio B is more convex? It turns out that barbell portfolios (portfolio B in this case) are more convex. From equation (3.37): $\kappa = T(T+1)/(1+r)^2$. The convexities κ_1, κ_5, and κ_{10} of 1-year, 5-year, and 10-year zero-coupon bonds are 1.81, 27.21, and 99.77, respectively. The convexity of portfolio B is therefore[8]

$$\kappa_B = \frac{P_1 q_1 \kappa_1 + P_{10} q_{10} \kappa_{10}}{P_1 q_1 + P_{10} q_{10}}$$
$$= \frac{(95.238 \times 0.457 \times 1.81) + (61.391 \times 0.567 \times 99.77)}{(95.238 \times 0.457 + 61.391 \times 0.567)} = 44.85$$

whereas the convexity of portfolio A is $\kappa_A = \kappa_5 = 27.21$.

As illustrated by Figure 3.5, under the assumptions of the duration model (i.e., parallel displacements of a flat yield curve), one can create a money machine out of the following arbitrage: Sell a bond of

---

[8] If κ_1 and κ_2 are the convexities of two bonds P_1 and P_2 respectively, then it is easy to check that the convexity of the portfolio $\alpha_1 P_1 + \alpha_2 P_2$ is given by

$$\kappa = \frac{\alpha_1 P_1 \kappa_1 + \alpha_2 P_2 \kappa_2}{\alpha_1 P_1 + \alpha_2 P_2}$$

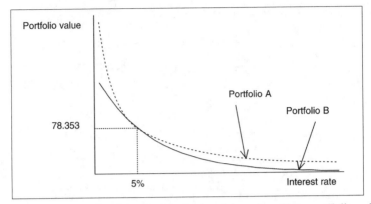

Figure 3.5. The free lunch in the duration model – value of two portfolios with the same duration but different convexities can react differently to changes in interest rate, and it is possible to arbitrage away this difference.

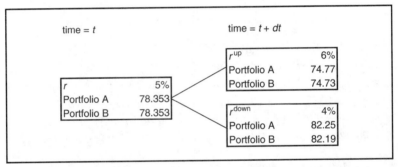

Figure 3.6. The free lunch in the duration model – case of binomial interest rate movement

intermediate maturity and buy against it a barbell portfolio with the same value and modified duration.

To illustrate the point further, say the term structure follows a binomial distribution whereby it moves instantaneously from 5% to either 4% or 6% (Figure 3.6). Then, on either node of the tree as the reader may check, portfolio A is more valuable than portfolio B.

Example 3.3.11 just showed a flaw in the assumption of a parallel displacement of a flat yield curve: This assumption cannot support an arbitrage-free set of prices. Two remarks, one technical, the second more general, are in order: First, why is a barbell portfolio more convex than an intermediate-maturity bond? The mathematical explanation can be found in equation (3.37):

$$\kappa = \frac{T(T+1)}{(1+r)^2}$$

From this equation, we can infer that the convexity of a zero-coupon bond increases at an increasing pace with its maturity:

$$\frac{\partial^2 \kappa}{\partial T^2} = \frac{2}{(1+r)^2} > 0$$

For the sake of argument, let us assume a flat term structure of interest rates. We form a barbell of two zero-coupon bonds of maturities $t - \Delta t$ and $t + \Delta t$. We want to prove that this barbell is more convex than a t-year zero-coupon bond with equivalent value and modified duration.

The modified durations for the short, intermediate, and long zero coupons are, respectively, $\frac{t-\Delta t}{1+r}$, $\frac{t}{1+r}$, and $\frac{t+\Delta t}{1+r}$. As before, we have

$$P_s q_s + P_l q_l = P_i q_i \text{ (price matching)}$$

$$\frac{t - \Delta t}{1+r} P_s q_s + \frac{t + \Delta t}{1+r} P_l q_l = P_i q_i \text{ (duration matching)}$$

where the subscripts s, i, and l refer to the short, intermediate, and long zero coupons. It follows that

$$P_s q_s = P_l q_l = \frac{P_i q_i}{2}$$

The market value weights for short and long zeros in the barbell are 50%. From (3.37), the convexity of the barbell portfolio B is therefore

$$\kappa_B = \frac{(t + \Delta t)(t + \Delta t + 1) + (t - \Delta t)(t - \Delta t + 1)}{2(1+r)^2} = \frac{t^2 + t + (\Delta t)^2}{(1+r)^2}$$

whereas the convexity of the intermediate bond portfolio A is

$$\kappa_A = \frac{t^2 + t}{(1+r)^2}$$

It follows that $\kappa_A < \kappa_B$ and that the convexity difference is proportional to the square of the difference between the maturity of the long zero coupon and that of the short zero coupon. Figure 3.7 illustrates the argument.

We close this section with a general remark on arbitrage-free movements of the term structure. As stated before, the assumption of parallel

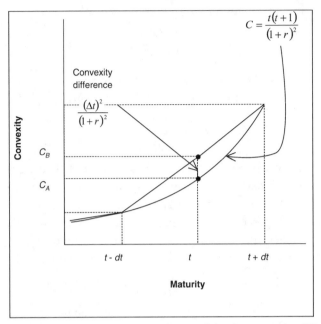

Figure 3.7. The free lunch in the duration model – the convexity difference

shifts of a flat term structure of interest rates is not acceptable because it allow riskless arbitrage transactions. Under this assumption, we would have, as in Example 3.3.11, a portfolio dominate another portfolio even though both have equal value. Hence the need for more sophisticated interest rate models: In Example 3.3.11, one can imagine a number of scenarios where portfolio A would be dominated by portfolio B. Think of a steepening of the zero-coupon curve in the 5- to 10-year portion: If the 10-year rate rises with the 5-year and 1-year rates unmoved, then the "arbitrage strategy" would lose money. The assumptions behind the duration model cannot account for such a scenario. It is in this sense that the duration model is naive. Remember, though, that "all models are wrong, but some are useful." If its popular appeal in the financial sector is any guide, the duration model is certainly deserving despite its flawed assumptions.

3.4 AN OVERVIEW OF INTEREST RATE DERIVATIVES

This section describes the main features of interest rate derivatives. We discuss in turn bonds with embedded options, forward rate agreements,

Eurodollar futures, interest rate swaps, currency swaps, caps, floors, and swaptions.

3.4.1 Bonds with Embedded Options

Bonds can sometimes be bought back by the issuer at a prespecified "call" price. Such bonds are known as *callable bonds*. For example, a "30 non-call 10" (or a 30-year bond that cannot be called during the first 10 years) may have the call schedule shown in Table 3.4. This bond is *multicallable*. Starting in year 10, the issuer has the right to buy the bond at the call price. Because the issuer owns the right, the investor needs to be compensated for the right conceded to the issuer. In this case, the right consists of a 30-year call option on the bond with exercise prices specified in Table 3.4, and with exercise rights yearly starting from year 10. These options are called *Bermudan* options. If P_C, P, and V_C designate the values of the 30 noncall 10 bond, the 30-year noncallable bond (a bond with identical characteristics but without a call feature), and the Bermudan call, respectively, then it must be that

$$P_C = P - V_C \qquad (3.39)$$

Everything else being equal, the callable bond will carry a higher coupon than the noncallable version of this bond to compensate the investor for the short option position. Note that the price of a callable bond is *less* than the price of a noncallable bond. This seemingly counter-intuitive fact can be resolved by observing that the optionality feature enhances the *yield* of the callable bond, thereby reducing the price.

A *puttable* bond is different in that the investor has the right to sell the bond back to the issuer at a prespecified price. A "10 nonput

Table 3.4

Year	Call Price
10	107
11	106
12	105
13	104
14	103
>15	102

5" (or a 10-year bond that cannot be put to the issuer before year 5) may have, for example, a single exercise date at the end of year 5 at 99. The investor's right in this case is a 5-year European put on what would then be a 5-year bond at an exercise price of 99. If P_π, P, and V_π designated the values of the 10 non-put 5 bond, the 10-year nonputtable bond (with otherwise identical characteristics), and the European put, respectively, then we have

$$P_\pi = P + V_\pi \qquad (3.40)$$

Everything else being equal, the puttable bond will carry a lower coupon than the nonputtable bond to compensate the issuer for the put owned by the investor.

Typically, a bond which is callable at par will be called by the issuer if interest rates are lower than at issuance. The issuer can then refinance itself at lower rates. Conversely, a bond which is puttable at par will be sold by the investor to the issuer if interest rates are higher than at issuance. The investor can then reinvest the cash at higher rates.

3.4.2 Forward Rate Agreements

Forward rate agreements (FRAs) are over-the-counter contracts whereby two parties agree at time zero on a rate of interest to be paid on a loan starting at time m and maturing at time n. The buyer of the FRA receives the difference between the prevailing rate at time n and the strike rate prespecified in the contract for a given period (typically three months) multiplied by a notional amount. Thus, the buyer of the FRA makes money when rates increase. The payment takes place conventionally at time n and therefore needs to be discounted. The payment follows the money market convention which consists in dividing the number of days in the interest accrual period by 360 days. The reference rate is typically the three-month LIBOR (the London interbank offered rate), which is the rate paid by large international banks on interbank loans.

The timetable can be drawn as shown in Figure 3.8. With payoff at time m equal to

$$\frac{1}{1 + L(m, m, n)\frac{n-m}{360}} \times \left[L(m, m, n) - \overline{R} \right] \times \frac{n-m}{360} \times A \qquad (3.41)$$

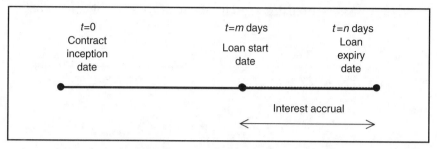

Figure 3.8. Timetable for FRA

where $L(m, m, n)$ is the LIBOR rate as of time m on a loan starting at time m and expiring at time n, $\overline{R}$ is the prespecified strike rate, and A is the notional principal. If, at time 0, $\overline{R}$ is set at the forward LIBOR prevailing for a loan that starts at time m and ends at time n, in other words, if

$$\overline{R} = L(0, m, n) \tag{3.42}$$

then, as will be shown below, the value at inception of the FRA is zero. This FRA is called an $m \times n$ FRA. The replication of an FRA is somewhat similar to the replication used to determine forward rates in Section 3.2. We assume that money can be borrowed and lent at LIBOR. Note that, under this assumption, the payoff at time m of the FRA in (3.41) is equivalent to a payoff at time n equal to

$$\left[L(m, m, n) - \overline{R}\right] \times \frac{n - m}{360} \times A \tag{3.43}$$

since the cash flow received at time m can be reinvested at the then prevailing LIBOR $L(m, m, n)$ till time n (if this cash flow is negative, the cash outflow can be borrowed at the same rate $L(m, m, n)$).

The replication strategy parallels the construction of the forward rate contract as discussed in Section 3.2:

1. Borrow $\frac{\left(1 + \overline{R} \times \frac{n-m}{360}\right)A}{1 + L(0,0,n) \times \frac{n}{360}}$ at time 0 for n days;
2. Deposit $\frac{A}{1 + L(0,0,m) \times \frac{m}{360}}$ at time 0 for m days;
3. Deposit at time m the proceeds from the above deposit for $(n - m)$ days.

The cash flows from this portfolio are summarized in this tabulation:

Time (days)	Cash Flow at $t = 0$	$t = m$	$t = n$
Step 1	$\frac{\left(1+\overline{R}\frac{n-m}{360}\right)A}{1+L(0,0,n)\frac{n}{360}}$		$-\left(1+\overline{R}\times\frac{n-m}{360}\right)A$
Step 2	$\frac{-A}{1+L(0,0,m)\frac{m}{360}}$	A	
Step 3		$-A$	$\left[1+L(m,m,n)\frac{n-m}{360}\right]\times A$
TOTAL	$\frac{\left(1+\overline{R}\frac{n-m}{360}\right)A}{1+L(0,0,n)\frac{n}{360}}-\frac{A}{1+L(0,0,m)\frac{m}{360}}$	0	$\left[L(m,m,n)-\overline{R}\right]\frac{n-m}{360}A$

It can be seen that the portfolio replicates exactly the cash flow from the FRA in (3.43) at time n. If the FRA is to have a zero value at inception, we need to set $\overline{R}$ so that the initial cash flows from the portfolio equal zero:

$$\frac{\left(1+\overline{R}\times\frac{n-m}{360}\right)\times A}{1+L(0,0,n)\times\frac{n}{360}} - \frac{A}{1+L(0,0,m)\times\frac{m}{360}} = 0 \qquad (3.44)$$

Hence the value of $\overline{R}$

$$\overline{R} = \left[\frac{1+L(0,0,n)\times\frac{n}{360}}{1+L(0,0,m)\times\frac{m}{360}} - 1\right]\times\frac{360}{n-m} \qquad (3.45)$$

The reader can easily check that the expression in (3.45) corresponds to the forward LIBOR as of time 0 for a loan between time m and time n, that is $L(0,m,n)$. This verifies equation (3.42).

Example 3.4.1. The three-month and six-month LIBORs are respectively equal to 4% and 4.2%. The first three months amount to 91 days, whereas the following three months amount to 92 days. What is the strike rate $\overline{R}$ on a 3×6 FRA?

We have $m = 91$; $n = 91 + 92 = 183$; $L(0,0,91) = 4\%$; and $L(0, 0, 183) = 4.2\%$. It follows that

$$\overline{R} = \left(\frac{1+4.2\%\times\frac{183}{360}}{1+4\%\times\frac{91}{360}} - 1\right)\times\frac{360}{92} = 4.35\%$$

3.4.3 Eurostrip Futures

Eurostrip futures contracts are traded on major exchanges such as the LIFFE and the Chicago Mercantile Exchange. At expiration date T, the payoff is defined as

$$\text{Futures settlement price} = 100 \times (1 - L_T) \qquad (3.46)$$

where L_T is the $3m$-LIBOR at time T. At $t < T$, we can infer from the futures price before expiration $F(t, T, T + 3m)$ the forward three-month LIBOR $L(t, T, T + 3m)$. This follows directly from (3.46):

$$L(t, T, T + 3m) = 1 - \frac{F(t, T, T + 3m)}{100} \qquad (3.47)$$

For a number of major currencies such as the USD, a one-basis-point move of the LIBOR or, equivalently, a 0.01 move of the futures price (one tick) is worth 25 USD per contract.

Example 3.4.2. One day prior to its expiration, the Eurodollar futures contract quoted 96.3. The one-day futures three-month LIBOR is therefore $1 - \frac{96.3}{100} = 3.7\%$. At expiration date, the Eurodollar futures quoted 96.35, indicating a spot three-month LIBOR at 3.65%. If a trader is long one contract, the gain on this contract is 5 basis points $\times$ 25 = 125 USD over the last day.

Note that the contract is cash settled on the last trading day. The performance of Eurostrip futures, unlike forward rate agreements, is guaranteed by the exchanges where they are traded. There is little worry among market participants about counterparties' creditworthiness, that is, whether these counterparties will be solvent should they settle on a contract.

3.4.4 The Convexity Adjustment

A major difference between FRAs and futures stems from the fact that the payoff of a futures contract is linear, whereas it is nonlinear for an FRA (see Figure 3.9). Indeed, an $m \times n$ FRA can be viewed as an m-day forward zero-coupon bond with maturity $(n - m)$ days. The price-yield relationship in the FRA case is similar to that of a bond. For example, dollar-based investors expecting a rate decline may try to take advantage of this view by paying LIBOR and receiving the fixed strike rate of a USD FRA or alternatively, may purchase a Eurodollar futures contract. As shown in Figure 3.9, no matter where the rate goes in the future, the value of the forward rate agreement will be higher than the value of the futures contract if the strike rate is the

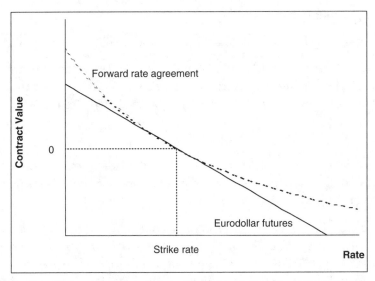

Figure 3.9. Convexity adjustment – price-yield relationship at the inception of futures and FRA contracts

same for both contracts. Because the investor is paying LIBOR and receiving fixed on both contracts, the strike rate must be lower in the FRA than in the futures contract to eliminate the advantage from the FRA nonlinear payoff. In other words, the forward rate is lower than the futures rate. The nonlinearity advantage is called the *convexity advantage*: strictly speaking, the advantage stems from all the higher order moments of the price-yield function (recall that the convexity is just the second-order moment). We provide a numerical example to illustrate the so-called convexity advantage.

Example 3.4.3. As in Example 3.4.1, the three-month and six-month LIBORs are 4% and 4.2%, respectively, and $m = 91; n = 183$. The strike rate of the 3×6 FRA is $\overline{R} = 4.35\%$, and $A = 100\,million\,USD$. We want to calculate the convexity advantage of this FRA over an "equivalent" futures contract. By equivalent, we mean a contract with the same interest rate sensitivity and the same strike rate. Let us posit an investor seeking to profit from a decline in rates. This investor will sell an FRA and will have the following payoff at maturity of the FRA:

$$V(m) = \frac{1}{1 + L(m, m, n) \times \frac{n-m}{360}} \times \left[\overline{R} - L(m, m, n) \right] \times \frac{n-m}{360} \times A$$

The value of the FRA position at time zero is

$$V(0) = \frac{1}{1 + L(0, 0, m) \times \frac{m}{360}} \times V(t)$$

$$= \frac{1}{1 + L(0, 0, n) \times \frac{n}{360}} \left[\overline{R} - L(m, m, n) \right] \times \frac{n - m}{360} \times A$$

$$= 0$$

by construction since $\overline{R} = L(m, m, n)$ *(see Example 3.4.1). If all rates decrease by 1 basis point (0.01%) instantaneously at time 0, then the new value is*

$$V_1(0) = \frac{1}{1 + 4.19\% \times \frac{183}{360}} [4.35\% - 4.34\%] \times \frac{92}{360} \times 100 \, mn$$

$$= 2,502 \, USD$$

How many Eurodollar futures will have the same interest rate sensitivity as the above FRA? We know that one contract earns 25 USD per basis point: we therefore need $2502/25 = 100.08$ *contracts. Let us now calculate the change in value of both contracts for large interest rate changes: if rates fall instantaneously by 100 basis point (1%), then the value of the FRA is*

$$V_2(0) = \frac{1}{1 + 3.2\% \times \frac{183}{360}} [4.35\% - 3.35\%] \times \frac{92}{360} \times 100 \, million$$

$$= 251,465 \, USD$$

whereas the value of the Eurodollar futures is

$$25 \times 100 \times 100.08 = 250,200 \, USD$$

The convexity advantage is therefore $251,465 - 250,200 = 1,265 \, USD$. *If all rates rose instantaneously by 100 basis points relative to their initial values, then the value of the FRA is*

$$V_3(0) = \frac{1}{1 + 5.2\% \times \frac{183}{360}} [4.35\% - 5.35\%] \times \frac{92}{360} \times 100 \, million$$

$$= -248,974 \, USD$$

The value of the Eurodollar futures is: $25 \times (-100) \times 100.08 = -250,200 \, USD$. *Here again, the FRA has a convexity advantage equal*

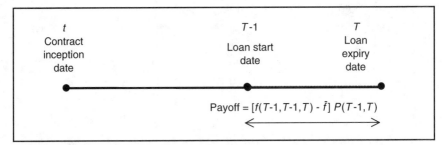

Figure 3.10. Figure accompanying derivation of the convexity adjustment for FRAs

to: $-248,974 - (-250,200) = 1,226\ USD$. *When rates either rise or fall, therefore, one gains more from paying LIBOR and receiving fixed in an FRA than from buying a Eurodollar futures contract. Conversely, paying fixed and receiving LIBOR in an FRA will lose money relative to a sale of Eurodollar futures.*

The next question is how to size a convexity adjustment that will compensate for the discrepancy between FRAs and futures. We show below a simple model (Campbell and Temel, 2000) that gives a rule of thumb for the convexity adjustment.

We assume continuous compounding and a flat yield curve. All forward rates are equal to f and have the following dynamics:[9]

$$df = \sigma dW \tag{3.48}$$

Under these assumptions, the value of a bond $P(t, T)$ is

$$P(t, T) = e^{-f(T-t)} \tag{3.49}$$

where the time variables are defined on the timeline (in years) shown in Figure 3.10. The payoff at $(T - 1)$ is the discounted value of a payoff $(f - \bar{f})$ at T where $\bar{f}$ is the prespecified strike rate and $f(T - 1, T - 1, T)$ is the one-year rate prevailing at $T - 1$. $P(T - 1, T)$ is the value at $T - 1$ of a bond maturing at T with face value 1. It is easy to see, using previous arguments, that the value of

---

[9] The assumptions behind equation (3.48) are similar to those of the simple duration model: flat term structure and parallel shifts of this term structure. We have shown in Section 3.3 that this model is not arbitrage free. However, like the duration model, the rule of thumb for the convexity adjustment developed here is widely used by fixed income traders.

the FRA at time t is

$$V = P(t, T) \times \left[f(t, T - 1, T) - \overline{f} \right] \tag{3.50}$$

For simplicity we denote $f(t, T - 1, T)$ by f. For V to be equal to zero at t, date of inception of the FRA, we set $\overline{f} = f$. Also for ease of notation, set $P(t, T) = P$. If both f and P follow Itô processes, then we note from (3.48) that the change in V can be obtained using a two-dimensional Itô's lemma

$$dV = \left(f - \overline{f} \right) dP + Pdf + dPdf = Pdf + dPdf \tag{3.51}$$

Consider now a futures contract valued at F, with the same characteristics as the FRA. As explained above, we need to subtract from the rate f a convexity adjustment κ_f to do away with the forward-futures discrepancy. The futures contract pays M when rates change by one unit. Then the change in F is

$$dF = -M(df - d\kappa_f) \tag{3.52}$$

We now construct a portfolio composed of one FRA contract and N futures contracts. The change $d\Pi$ in the value of the portfolio is

$$d\Pi = dV + NdF = Pdf + dPdf - NMdf + NMd\kappa_f \tag{3.53}$$

We pick $N = P/M$ to get

$$d\Pi = dPdf + Pd\kappa_f \tag{3.54}$$

$d\pi = 0$ will set the futures-forward discrepancy to zero. Then

$$d\kappa_f = -\frac{dP}{P}df \tag{3.55}$$

Applying Itô's lemma to (3.49)

$$\begin{aligned} dP &= -(T - t)Pdf + (T - t)^2 P(df)^2 + fPdt \\ &= -(T - t)Pdf + [(T - t)^2 P\sigma^2 + fP]dt \end{aligned} \tag{3.56}$$

where the last line follows from (3.48) : $(df)^2 = (\sigma dW)^2 = \sigma^2 dt$. Therefore

$$dPdf = -(T - t)P(df)^2 = -(T - t)P\sigma^2 dt \tag{3.57}$$

From (3.55) and (3.57)

$$d\kappa_f = (T - t)\sigma^2 dt \tag{3.58}$$

and the convexity adjustment $\kappa_f(T)$ applicable to a contract with accrual until T is

$$\kappa_f(T) = \kappa_f(t) + \int_t^T (T-t)\sigma^2 dt$$

$$= \left[\left(Tt - \frac{t^2}{2}\right)\sigma^2\right]_t^T = -\frac{\sigma^2}{2}(T-t)^2 \qquad (3.59)$$

Example 3.4.4. The Eurodollar futures contract on the three-month LIBOR is expiring in 14 months. The futures rate is 4.2%. What is the forward rate applicable to a 14 × 17 FRA, when the basis point (or normal) volatility[10] is $\sigma = 1\%$?

First note that $(T - t) = 17/12$ years. The forward hence should be lower than the futures by

$$\frac{(1\%)^2}{2} \times \left(\frac{17}{12}\right)^2 = 1 \text{ basis point} = 0.01\%$$

The convexity adjustment is 1 basis point. The forward rate is

$$4.20\% - 0.01\% = 4.19\%$$

3.4.5 Swaps

A swap, generically, is an exchange. In financial parlance, it refers to an exchange of a series of cash flows against another series of cash flows. For example, party A can pay party B on a yearly basis the return on a stock index (such as the S&P 500 index) on a notional principal amount of 100mn USD for the next ten years. In exchange, party B can pay to party A the 12-month USD LIBOR on 100mn USD yearly over the next 10 years.

Most famous in the swap family is the *interest rate swap*. An interest rate swap involves typically an exchange of fixed cash flows against floating cash flows where the floating leg is calculated in reference to an index such as the LIBOR index.

Example 3.4.5. Party A enters an interest rate swap with party B whereby A receives the six-month USD LIBOR every six months against a fixed

---

[10] In this case, basis point volatility refers to the fact that $\sigma = 0.01 = 1/100 = 1\%$.

rate of 6% yearly. The notional principal amount is 10mn USD. The maturity is five years. Specifically, every six months, party A receives

$$L \times 10mn \times \frac{N}{360} \, USD \qquad (3.60)$$

where L is the six-month USD LIBOR observed six months prior to the payment date[11] and N is the number of days in the six-month period. The LIBOR leg follows therefore the N/360 money market convention, much like FRAs. Every year, party A pays

$$6\% \times 10mn \, USD = 600,000 \, USD$$

At swap maturity, there is no exchange of principal. If there were such an exchange, the amounts (10mn USD paid and received by each party) would cancel each other anyway.

We proceed to the valuation of an interest rate swap. It is useful to think of the value of a swap as the difference between two bond prices. For example, a swap receiving fixed cash flows and paying floating cash flows has value.

$$V_{swap} = P_{fixed} - P_{floating} \qquad (3.61)$$

Consider the case of a T-year swap receiving a fixed coupon C, also called a swap rate, and paying the six-month LIBOR on a notional amount A. For analytical convenience, we assume that the i period zero-coupon rates R_i used to discount the fixed and floating cash flows are based on the LIBOR curve. This curve is generally derived from Eurostrip futures or FRAs when futures are unavailable.

The value of the fixed leg at swap inception is then

$$P_{fixed} = \frac{CA}{1 + R_1} + \cdots + \frac{(1 + C) A}{(1 + R_T)^T}$$

The value of the floating leg is

$$P_{floating} = A$$

---

[11] When the floating rate leg is paid in reference to the n-month LIBOR observed at payment date (as opposed to n months prior to payment date), the swap is called "LIBOR in arrears swap."

The floating rate leg is valued at par at LIBOR setting dates because, in this instance, the LIBOR curve is both the discount curve and the reference curve for setting the coupon.[12] Because the value of a swap at inception is conventionally zero, the swap rate can be obtained from the above:

$$C = \frac{1 - (1 + R_T)^{-T}}{\sum_{i=1}^{T}(1 + R_i)^{-i}} \tag{3.62}$$

Example 3.4.6. The zero-coupon rates based on the LIBOR curve for years 1, 2, and 3 are respectively 5.11%, 5.35%, and 5.47%. What is the three-year swap rate?

Based on (3.62), the swap rate is

$$C_3 = \frac{1 - (1.0547)^{-3}}{(1.0511)^{-1} + (1.0535)^{-2} + (1.0547)^{-3}} = 5.46\%$$

3.4.6 Caps and Floors

A *cap* is a collection of *caplets*. A caplet is a call option on a reference rate L, such as the three-month LIBOR rate, struck at rate K, on a notional amount A. A typical K-period cap has $(K - 1)$ caplets. Caplet i $(i = 1, \ldots, K - 1)$ has a payoff:

$$A \max(L_i - K, 0) \Delta t$$

where L_i is observed at $i \Delta t$ and the payoff is made at $(i + 1) \Delta t$. The value of the cap at time zero is

$$V_{cap} = \sum_{i=1}^{K-1} V_i^C$$

where V_i^C is the value of caplet i. We shall discuss later in this chapter models to value interest rate options such as caplets.

---

[12] To see why, consider the last setting date of a floating rate bond. Its value is then:
$$\frac{A\left(1 + L_{T-\frac{1}{2}} \times \frac{N}{360}\right)}{\left(1 + L_{T-\frac{1}{2}} \times \frac{N}{360}\right)} = A$$ where $L_{T-1/2}$ is the last six-month LIBOR setting. On the setting date that is before last, because the bond will be worth A with certainty in six months, the value is similarly: $\frac{A\left(1 + L_{T-1} \times \frac{N'}{360}\right)}{\left(1 + L_{T-1} \times \frac{N'}{360}\right)} = A$. N and N' are the respective numbers of days for interest daycount. We can recursively proceed to get a par price at inception in a similar way.

A *floor* is a collection of *floorlets*. A floorlet is a put option on the reference rate L. Retaining the cap and caplet notation, we have the following payoff for a floorlet:

$$A \max(K - L_i, 0) \Delta t$$

Similarly

$$V_{floor} = \sum_{i=1}^{K-1} V_i^F$$

where V_i^F is the value of floorlet i.

3.4.7 Swaptions

A *swaption* is an option on a swap. A *receiver swaption* is an option to enter a swap that receives a fixed rate and pays a floating rate. Conversely, a *payer swaption* is an option to enter a swap that receives a floating rate (say 6-month LIBOR) and pays a fixed rate. A swaption contract must specify the nature of the swaption (receiver or payer), the time to expiration of the option, the maturity of the underlying swap, the notional amount, and the strike rate. For example a 5-year–10-year payer swaption on $100 million struck at 7% is a 5-year option on a swap that would pay 7% annually and receive the 6-month LIBOR semiannually on $100 million for 10 years at expiration of the option and should that option be exercised. In this example, if the swap rate is above 7% in 5 years, then the owner of the swaption should exercise it because the 7% coupon to be paid under the swaption would then be below the prevailing swap rate. A swaption payoff at expiration is $max(0, V_{swap})$, where V_{swap} is the value (at expiration of the swaption) of a swap with fixed rate coupon equal to the strike rate.

Example 3.4.7. A 5-year–2-year receiver swaption on $100 million struck at 6.5% has just expired. The prevailing curve of swap rates is flat at 5%. What is the value of the swaption at expiration?

$$V_{swap} = P_{fixed} - P_{floating}$$

$$P_{fixed} = \frac{6.5}{1.05} + \frac{106.5}{(1.05)^2} = \$102.79 \ million$$

$$P_{floating} = \$100 \ million$$

The swaption is worth $\max(0, 102.79 - 100)$, *or $2.79 million.*

3.5 YIELD CURVE SWAPS

This section describes the mechanics of so-called *yield curve swaps*. We focus on two types of yield curve swaps: the *CMS (constant maturity swap)* and the *quanto swap*. We shall present the topic through two examples with actual market data.

3.5.1 The CMS Swap

Consider a five-year CMS swap where an investor pays the five-year swap rate plus or minus a spread annually, against receiving the six-month LIBOR semiannually. The notional is 100. The LIBOR receive leg is priced at par as seen in the previous section. As is the convention, the investor observes the five-year swap at the beginning of each year and makes the CMS payment one year later.

The aim of the exercise is to determine the spread over or below the five-year swap rate to be paid by the investor to equate the initial value of the swap to zero. We proceed in four steps.

CMS Step 1. We start with the term structure of swap rates shown in Table 3.5. We derive zero-coupon rates from the swap rates. As explained earlier in the chapter, zero-coupon rates are obtained iteratively. The one-year zero-coupon swap rate Z_1 is obtained by setting

$$100 = \frac{103.2034}{1 + Z_1}$$

Table 3.5

Term (years)	Swap Rate (%)
1	3.2034
2	3.4966
3	3.9362
4	4.3858
5	4.8058
6	5.1461
7	5.4249
8	5.6567
9	5.8469
10	5.9773
11	6.0500

Table 3.6

Term (years)	Swap Rate (%)	Zero-Coupon Swap Rate (%)
1	3.2034	3.2034
2	3.4966	3.5018
3	3.9362	3.9577
4	4.3858	4.4349
5	4.8058	4.8925
6	5.1461	5.2726
7	5.4249	5.5919
8	5.6567	5.8645
9	5.8469	6.0935
10	5.9773	6.2496
11	6.0500	

yielding $Z_1 = 3.2034\%$. The two-year zero-coupon rate Z_2 is obtained from the following equation:

$$100 = \frac{3.4966}{1 + Z_1} + \frac{103.4966}{(1 + Z_2)^2}$$

We know that $Z_1 = 3.2034\%$. This yields $Z_2 = 3.5018\%$. Similarly, the three-year zero-coupon rate Z_3 is a solution to the equation

$$100 = \frac{3.9362}{1 + Z_1} + \frac{3.9362}{(1 + Z_2)^2} + \frac{103.9362}{(1 + Z_3)^3}$$

where $Z_1 = 3.2034\%$ and $Z_2 = 3.5018\%$; and so on for the remaining zero-coupon rates. The term structure can be written as shown in Table 3.6.

CMS Step 2. We now calculate five-year swap rates one, two, three, and four years forward. These rates are needed because the five cash flows of the CMS leg of the swap are based on the five-year spot swap rate (observed today and used to calculate the first payment) and on these forward rates. The five-year forward swap rate in one year, F_5^1, is obtained from the equation

$$\frac{100}{1 + Z_1} = \frac{100 F_5^1}{(1 + Z_2)^2} + \frac{100 F_5^1}{(1 + Z_3)^3} + \frac{100 F_5^1}{(1 + Z_4)^4}$$
$$+ \frac{100 F_5^1}{(1 + Z_5)^5} + \frac{100 \left(1 + F_5^1\right)}{(1 + Z_6)^6}$$

We know $Z_1, \ldots, Z_6$. The above calculation gives F_5^1 equal to 5.5958%. Similarly, the value of the five-year forward rate in two years, F_5^2, is found to be 6.3568% from the following equation:

$$\frac{100}{(1 + Z_2)^2} = \frac{100 F_5^2}{(1 + Z_3)^3} + \frac{100 F_5^2}{(1 + Z_4)^4} + \frac{100 F_5^2}{(1 + Z_5)^5}$$

$$+ \frac{100 F_5^2}{(1 + Z_6)^6} + \frac{100 \left(1 + F_5^2\right)}{(1 + Z_7)^7}$$

We find $F_5^2 = 6.3568\%$. We can proceed similarly to get F_5^3 and F_5^4. The results are

$$F_5^0 = 4.8058\%$$
$$F_5^1 = 5.5966\%$$
$$F_5^2 = 6.3562\%$$
$$F_5^3 = 6.9618\%$$
$$F_5^4 = 7.3980\%$$

CMS Step 3. The five-year forward rates calculated in step 2 are close enough to the coupon rates we shall use to price the CMS leg of the swap. As in the FRA futures case, we need to adjust these rates by a convexity factor.

The intuitive reason for this adjustment can be explained as follows: Consider a CMS coupon received under a swap. The hedge should be a forward starting swap receiving fixed and paying LIBOR.[13] When rates decrease, the CMS coupon received is lower whereas the swap value increases. The problem is that while the CMS coupon is a linear function of rates, the swap value is a (decreasing) convex function of these rates. Convexity means that the swap payoff is higher than the linear payoff if the CMS leg of rates moves either way. This means that the portfolio comprised of the long CMS leg and the swap will always make money as rates move. The counterparty receiving the CMS leg of

---

[13] Consider the second CMS coupon under the five-year CMS swap. The five-year CMS rate on which this coupon is based will only be observed in one year. To hedge this coupon, one could enter a five-year swap – receiving fixed and paying LIBOR – with a forward start in one year. Both the CMS coupon and the forward swap value are sensitive to the five-year swap rate in one year.

the swap should therefore have to compensate the CMS payer owing to the convexity advantage. The adjustment factor should increase with volatility and time.

We now provide a rule-of-thumb calculation of the convexity adjustment. The rule relies on a number of approximations but is widely used by market participants. At time zero, we look at a specific CMS coupon to be observed at time T and paid at $T_1 > T$. At time 0, the change in the value of this CMS coupon on a one dollar principal is

$$dC_{CMS} = P(0, T_1)(dF + d\kappa_\varepsilon)$$

where dF is the change in the forward swap rate, $P(0, T)$ is the price at time 0 of a zero-coupon paying a dollar at time T, and $d\kappa_\varepsilon$ is the change in the convexity adjustment. (Recall that the aim of the exercise is to find κ_ε, the size of the convexity adjustment.) As stated above, the coupon can be hedged by a forward swap. The change in value of the forward swap is

$$dV_{FS} = P(0, T_1)\left(P'(F)dF + \frac{1}{2}P''(F)(dF)^2 + \text{higher order terms}\right)$$

where $P(F)$ is the price of the fixed rate leg of the forward swap. If the swap rate F follows a driftless geometric Brownian motion

$$dF = \sigma F dW$$

then $(dF)^2 = \sigma^2 F^2 dt$. The *hedge ratio* h^* that represents the dollar notional amount of the forward swap necessary to hedge the CMS coupon is set so that the random part is eliminated:

$$dC_{CMS} + h^* dV_{FS} = P(0, T_1)$$
$$\times \left(\sigma F dW + d\kappa_\varepsilon + h^* P'(F)\sigma F dW + h^* \frac{1}{2}P''(F)\sigma^2 F^2 dt\right)$$

Setting $h^* = -1/P'(F)$, the hedge is efficient if

$$dC_{CMS} - \frac{1}{P'(F)}dV_{FS} = 0$$

in other words, if

$$d\kappa_\varepsilon = -\frac{1}{2}\frac{P''(F)}{P'(F)}\sigma^2 F^2 dt$$

Integrating from 0 to T and evaluating the derivatives around the forward rate, we get

$$\kappa_\varepsilon = -\frac{1}{2}\frac{P''(F)}{P'(F)}\sigma^2 F^2 T \tag{3.63}$$

κ_ε is the adjustment we need to add to the forward rate in order to get the CMS coupon. Because $P''(F) > 0$ and $P'(F) < 0$, κ_ε is positive. This confirms our initial intuition.

As the reader may have noted, the calculation above makes a number of assumptions: $P(0, T_1)$ is left constant; $P''(F)\sigma^2 F^2/P'(F)$ is treated as independent of time when we integrate $d\kappa_\varepsilon$; the duration and convexity measures assume parallel displacements of the yield curve and we assume that F varies while $P(0, T_1)$ does not. These assumptions turn out to be relatively benign, as comparisons with more sophisticated models have shown.[14]

We now apply (3.63) to each one of the forward rates calculated in step 2. First note that the fixed leg of a five-year swap with coupon C is priced at

$$P(F) = \sum_{i=1}^{5} \frac{C}{(1+F)^i} + \frac{100}{(1+F)^5}$$

Then

$$P'(F) = \sum_{i=2}^{6} \frac{-(i-1)C}{(1+F)^i} - \frac{500}{(1+F)^6} \tag{3.64}$$

and

$$P''(F) = \sum_{i=3}^{7} \frac{(i-1)(i-2)C}{(1+F)^i} + \frac{3000}{(1+F)^7} \tag{3.65}$$

Table 3.7 gives the input values and the resulting convexity adjustment for the forward rates. We use a 6% flat yield throughout to calculate the adjustment. The values of the adjusted CMS coupons are in column (7). Column (2) is the term structure of lognormal volatilities. Columns (4), (5), and (6) are calculated from equations (3.64), (3.65), and (3.63), respectively. Column (7) gives the CMS coupons.

---

[14] See Brotherton-Ratcliffe and Iben (1993).

Table 3.7

(1) Forward Swap Rate (%)	(2) σ (%)	(3) T (yrs)	(4) $P'(F)$	(5) $P''(F)$	(6) Convexity Adj. (%)	(7) CMS Coupon [(1) + (6)(%)]
$F_5^0 = 4.8058$	17.0	0	-352	1995	0	$CMS_1 = 4.8058$
$F_5^1 = 5.5966$	15.2	1	-408	2233	0.0198	$CMS_2 = 5.6164$
$F_5^2 = 6.3562$	12.8	2	-417	2272	0.0361	$CMS_3 = 6.3923$
$F_5^3 = 6.9618$	11.5	3	-425	2309	0.0522	$CMS_4 = 7.0140$
$F_5^4 = 7.3980$	10.5	4	-432	2339	0.0653	$CMS_5 = 7.4633$

CMS Step 4. We can now price the CMS swap. At inception, the swap value should be zero. This means that the LIBOR leg (valued at par, or 100) should be equal to the CMS leg. We calculate a spread α such that

$$100 = 100 \left(\frac{CMS_1 - \alpha}{1 + Z_1} + \frac{CMS_2 - \alpha}{1 + Z_2} + \frac{CMS_3 - \alpha}{1 + Z_3} \right.$$
$$\left. + \frac{CMS_4 - \alpha}{1 + Z_4} + \frac{1 + CMS_5 - \alpha}{1 + Z_5} \right)$$

or

$$100 = \frac{4.8058 - 100\alpha}{1.032034} + \frac{5.6164 - 100\alpha}{(1.035018)^2} + \frac{6.3923 - 100\alpha}{(1.039577)^3}$$
$$+ \frac{7.014 - 100\alpha}{(1.044349)^4} + \frac{107.4633 - 100\alpha}{(1.048925)^5}$$

We get $\alpha = 1.38\%$. In other words, the investor pays five-year CMS minus 138 basis points against receiving LIBOR at swap inception.

Last, but not least, note that a swap paying CMS and receiving LIBOR will gain from a flattening of the swap curve. As this happens, forward swap rates decline at the long end of the curve. This lowers the value of the CMS paying leg and therefore increases the swap value.

3.5.2 The Quanto Swap

We now analyze a swap[15] where an investor pays the six-month US dollar LIBOR in US dollars and receives the six-month EURIBOR in

---

[15] See Brotherton-Ratcliffe and Iben (1993).

US dollars. The notional amount for both legs is one US dollar. Every six months, the investor receives (or pays if the amount is negative)

$$(L_{EUR} - L_{USD}) \times \frac{\text{number of days in the six-month period}}{360} USD$$

How do we value this swap? First, consider the USD LIBOR leg. If we do not take the spread into account, this leg is valued at par at swap inception as seen before. The problem is therefore to value the EURIBOR leg payable in USD, discounted at USD rates because it is paid in USD. This leg is called the *quanto leg*. The investor's risk is twofold: The EUR rates may drop resulting in lower coupons, or the USD rates may rise, decreasing the present value of the coupons. The investor can hedge the quanto leg (and therefore the quanto swap) by

• receiving fixed and paying floating on a EUR interest rate swap, and
• receiving floating and paying fixed on a USD interest rate swap.

The EUR swap would profit from a drop in EUR rate, while the USD swap would profit from increased USD rates. The only trouble with this hedge is that EUR swap proceeds are in EUR. If a drop in EUR rates tends to happen when the EUR gets weaker, then the gains from the hedge will not live up to the expectations in USD terms. Similarly, if a rise in EUR rates is associated with a stronger EUR, then losses on the hedge will be too high compared to the underlying quanto position. Both these problems will occur if the correlation coefficient between the EUR rates and the USD/EUR exchange rate is positive. So in the event of positive correlation, the investor needs to be compensated. How do we calculate the quanto convexity adjustment to account for the correlation effect?

As the reader can see from the above hedging strategies, the complication comes from the EUR interest rate swap part of the hedge. Let us then assume constant USD interest rates and neglect the USD interest rate swap part of the hedge. In this case, if we posit a multiplicative convexity adjustment for the coupon of the quanto: $F^* = \alpha F$, where F^* is the adjusted coupon, F is the forward EUR interest rate, and α is a convexity adjustment factor, then the change in the value of a quanto leg coupon (set at time T and paid at $T_1 > T$) is

$$dQ = (\alpha dF + F d\alpha) e^{-L_{USD} T_1}$$

By Itô's lemma, we can express the EUR interest rate swap change in value (in USD) as

$$dV = h^* (XdF + FdX + dFdX) e^{-L_{USD}T_1}$$

where h^* is the hedge ratio (i.e., the USD notional amount of the EUR interest rate swap in this case) and X is the USD/EUR exchange rate. Both X and F are assumed to follow geometric Brownian motions. The change in the value of the hedged portfolio is

$$dP = dV + dQ$$
$$= e^{-L_{USD}T_1} [\alpha dF + Fd\alpha + h^* XdF + Fh^* dX + h^* dFdX]$$

Setting $h^* = -\alpha / X$, we get

$$dP = e^{-L_{USD}T_1} \left[Fd\alpha - \frac{\alpha F}{X} dX - \alpha dF \frac{dX}{X} \right]$$

The $\alpha F (dX/X)$ term can be hedged through a simple currency forward as a consequence of the geometric Brownian motion assumption. We are left with the convexity adjustment term and the cross-correlation term. For the hedge to be efficient, the terms need to cancel each other. This means

$$\frac{d\alpha}{\alpha} = \frac{dF}{F} \times \frac{dX}{X}$$

If

$$\frac{dF}{F} = \sigma_F dW_F$$

and

$$\frac{dX}{X} = \sigma_X dW_X$$

with $dW_X dW_F = \rho dt$, then

$$\frac{d\alpha}{\alpha} = \rho \sigma_F \sigma_X dt$$

with boundary condition $\alpha (T) = 1$, this differential equation can be solved for $\alpha (t)$:

$$\alpha (t) = e^{-\rho \sigma_F \sigma_X (T-t)}$$

and the adjusted coupon of the quanto leg of the swap is then

$$F^* = Fe^{-\rho\sigma_F\sigma_X(T-t)}$$

As a final step, we show a numerical application. As in the preceding example, the investor is paying USD six-month LIBOR (plus or minus a spread) in USD and receiving EUR six-month LIBOR in USD for 18 months. Six-month rates are given below:

	EUR	USD
Spot	3%	5%
6-month forward	3.6%	5.42%
12-month forward	3.9%	5.70%

In addition, we know that the volatility of the EUR forward interest rates is 20%.

The volatility of the USD/EUR exchange rate is 10%. The correlation between these rates is −50%. The notional is, USD LIBORs are set six months prior to payment. There are three payment periods (18/6) under the swap. These periods comprise 182, 183, and 182 days, respectively. As shown before, the USD LIBOR leg (before any spread is added or subtracted) is valued at par. The spread x that we need to subtract from the USD LIBOR coupon is the solution to the equation

$$1 = \frac{(F_0^* + x)\frac{182}{360}}{\left(1 + 5\% \times \frac{182}{360}\right)} + \frac{\left(F_{\frac{1}{2}}^* + x\right)\frac{183}{360}}{\left(1 + 5\% \times \frac{182}{360}\right)\left(1 + 5.42\% \times \frac{183}{360}\right)}$$
$$+ \frac{1 + \left(F_1^* + x\right)\frac{182}{360}}{\left(1 + 5\% \times \frac{182}{360}\right)\left(1 + 5.42\% \times \frac{183}{360}\right)\left(1 + 5.70\% \times \frac{182}{360}\right)}$$

where

$$F_0^* = 3\%$$
$$F_{\frac{1}{2}}^* = 3.6\% \times e^{-\left(-50\% \times 20\% \times 10\% \times \frac{1}{2}\right)} = 3.62\%$$
$$F_0^* = 3.9\% \times e^{-\left(-50\% \times 20\% \times 10\% \times 1\right)} = 3.94\%$$

We get $x = 1.87\%$. The above equation says that the USD LIBOR leg value (equal to 1) must be equal to the quantoed leg value plus the value of a USD LIBOR spread, so that the quanto swap value at inception is zero. Under the swap, therefore, the investor pays six-month USD LIBOR-187 basis points in USD and receives six-month EUR LIBOR in USD every six months for 18 months.

3.6 FACTOR MODELS

3.6.1 A General Single-Factor Model

We now present models of the term structure of interest rates in continuous time. Factor models are predicated on the idea that the whole term structure of interest rates can be generated by, and is a function of, a unique single factor, generally the instantaneous interest rate r. This short rate r follows a general Itô process:

$$dr = \mu(r, t)dt + \sigma(r, t)dW \qquad (3.66)$$

Much like the contingent claims in Chapter 2, a bond price P can be expressed as a function of an underlying variable, r in this case, and time. If the bond matures at T, then

$$P = P(r, t, T) \qquad (3.67)$$

By Itô's lemma, we can get an expression for the bond return. This expression allows us to identify the drift a and the volatility b of the bond return:

$$\frac{dP}{P} = a(r, t, T) \, dt + b(r, t, T) \, dW \qquad (3.68)$$

where a and b are

$$a(r, t, T) \equiv \frac{\frac{\partial P}{\partial r}\mu(r, t) + \frac{\partial P}{\partial t} + \frac{1}{2}\frac{\partial^2 P}{\partial r^2}\sigma^2(r, t)}{P} \qquad (3.69)$$

and

$$b(r, t, T) \equiv \frac{\frac{\partial P}{\partial r}\sigma(r, t)}{P} \qquad (3.70)$$

Defining the duration D of a bond in a single-factor model as

$$D \equiv -\frac{1}{P}\frac{\partial P}{\partial r} \qquad (3.71)$$

the reader will notice that the volatility of a bond is equal to (minus) its duration multiplied by the volatility of the short rate. Indeed, from

(3.70) and (3.71), we obtain

$$b(r, t, T) = -\sigma(r, t) D \tag{3.72}$$

Note that b is negative for most bonds.[16]

Consider now two bonds, "Bond 1" and "Bond 2," priced at P_1 and P_2, maturing at T_1 and T_2, with drifts a_1 and a_2 and volatilities b_1 and b_2. We form a self-financing portfolio comprised of:

- Bonds 1 worth V_1
- Bonds 2 worth V_2
- an amount $(V_1 + V_2)$ borrowed at the riskless short rate r.

There is no restriction on the sign of V_1 and V_2. Call the value of this portfolio π. The instantaneous change in the portfolio value π is

$$
\begin{aligned}
d\pi &= V_1 \frac{dV_1}{V_1} + V_2 \frac{dV_2}{V_2} - (V_1 + V_2) r \, dt \\
&= V_1 (a_1 - r) \, dt + V_2 (a_2 - r) \, dt + (V_1 b_1 + V_2 b_2) \, dW
\end{aligned} \tag{3.73}
$$

If we choose a portfolio such that

$$V_1 = -V_2 \frac{b_2}{b_1} \tag{3.74}$$

then the stochastic term in dW disappears. $d\pi$ is therefore deterministic when portfolio weights are chosen according to (3.74). Moreover, because the portfolio is riskless and self-financed, it can only earn an instantaneous rate of zero. Equation (3.73) becomes

$$-\frac{V_2 b_2}{b_1} (a_1 - r) \, dt + V_2 (a_2 - r) \, dt = 0 \tag{3.75}$$

or

$$\frac{a_1 - r}{b_1} = \frac{a_2 - r}{b_2} \tag{3.76}$$

Equation (3.76) states that the expected bond return in excess of the risk-free rate per unit of volatility is the same for all interest-rate-sensitive securities. We can call this ratio λ. Note that because λ is the

---

[16] To conform this result with the conventional intuition that a volatility should be positive, define $dW' \equiv -dW$ to get

$$\frac{dP}{P} = a(r, t, T) \, dt + b(r, t, T) \, dW', \text{ with } b(r, t, T) \geq 0$$

same for bonds of all maturities, it does not depend on T. We reformulate equation (3.76) as

$$\frac{a_i - r}{b_i} = \lambda(r, t) \tag{3.77}$$

where a_i and b_i are the expected return and volatility of any bond i. $\lambda(r, t)$ can be viewed as the market price of the risk attached to long bonds. Because b_i is generally negative, a negative λ means that long bond expected returns are higher than short rates.

We can now combine equation (3.77) with equations (3.69) and (3.70) to get the general pricing equation for interest-rate-sensitive securities:

$$\frac{\partial P}{\partial r}\left[\mu(r, t) - \lambda(r, t)\sigma(r, t)\right] + \frac{\partial P}{\partial t} + \frac{1}{2}\frac{\partial^2 P}{\partial r^2}\sigma^2(r, t) = rP \tag{3.78}$$

As mentioned above, equation (3.78) has broad applications in that it prices any interest-rate-dependent security. Whereas equation (3.78) is general, the economics (or payoff) of a specific security will be reflected in the boundary condition that will complement the partial differential equation in (3.78). For example, the boundary condition for a zero-coupon bond with a face value of 1 is

$$P(r, T, T) = 1 \tag{3.79}$$

The solution of (3.78) subject to boundary condition (3.79) is

$$P(t, T)$$
$$= \tilde{\mathbb{E}}_t\left\{\exp\left[-\int_t^T r(s)\,ds - \int_t^T \lambda(r, s)\,dW(s) - \frac{1}{2}\int_t^T \lambda^2(r, s)\,ds\right]\right\} \tag{3.80}$$

To prove (3.80), consider the expression[17]

$$X(u, W(u))$$
$$= \exp\left[-\int_t^u r(s)\,ds - \int_t^u \lambda(r, s)\,dW(s) - \frac{1}{2}\int_t^u \lambda^2(r, s)\,ds\right] \tag{3.81}$$

---

[17] See Vasicek (1977) for the original proof.

By Itô's lemma, the differential of $X(u, W(u))$ is

$$dX(u, w(u)) = \frac{\partial X}{\partial u} du + \frac{\partial X}{\partial W} dW(u) + \frac{1}{2} \frac{\partial^2 X}{\partial W^2} du \qquad (3.82)$$

But

$$\frac{\partial X}{\partial u} = -r(u) X(u) - \frac{1}{2}\lambda^2(r, u) X(u)$$

$$\frac{\partial X}{\partial W} = -\lambda(r, u) X(u)$$

and

$$\frac{\partial^2 X}{\partial W^2} = \lambda^2(r, u) X(u)$$

Therefore

$$dX(u, W(u)) = -r(u) X(u) du - \lambda(r, u) X(u) dW(u) \qquad (3.83)$$

From (3.68), we also know that

$$dP(r, u, T)$$
$$= \left[\frac{\partial P}{\partial r} \mu(r, u) + \frac{\partial P}{\partial u} + \frac{1}{2} \frac{\partial^2 P}{\partial r^2} \sigma^2(r, u) \right] du + \frac{\partial P}{\partial r} \sigma(r, u) dW(u)$$
$$(3.84)$$

From Itô's lemma, (3.83), and (3.84), and using short form, we get

$$d[P(r, u, T) X(u)] = XdP + PdX + dXdP$$
$$= \left[\frac{\partial P}{\partial r} \mu + \frac{\partial P}{\partial u} + \frac{1}{2} \frac{\partial^2 P}{\partial r^2} \sigma^2 - rP - \lambda\sigma \frac{\partial P}{\partial r} \right] Xdu$$
$$+ \left(\frac{\partial P}{\partial r} \sigma X - \lambda XP \right) dW \qquad (3.85)$$

By (3.78), the term in du disappears. We integrate from t to T, the remaining expression in (3.85)

$$\int_t^T d[P(r, u, T) X(u)] = \int_t^T \left(\frac{\partial P}{\partial r} \sigma X - \lambda XP \right) dW(u) \qquad (3.86)$$

Taking expectations on both sides, the right-hand side disappears. We then obtain

$$\tilde{\mathbb{E}}_t[P(r, T, T) X(T) - P(r, t, T) X(t)] = 0 \qquad (3.87)$$

Because $P(r, T, T) = 1$ and $X(t) = 1$, equation (3.80) follows:

$$
\begin{aligned}
P(r, t, T) &= \tilde{\mathbb{E}}_t [X(T)] \\
&= \tilde{\mathbb{E}}_t \left\{ \exp \left[-\int_t^T r(s) \, ds - \int_t^T \lambda(r, s) \, dW(s) \right. \right. \\
&\qquad\qquad \left. \left. -\frac{1}{2} \int_t^T \lambda^2(r, s) \, ds \right] \right\}
\end{aligned}
$$

Equation (3.80) is the solution of our general model. To get a closed-form formula for zero-coupon bonds, we need to specialize this model by specifying the $\mu(r, t)$, $\sigma(r, t)$, and $\lambda(r, t)$ functions. We study three models that postulate specific forms for these functions: the Merton model, the Vasicek model, and the Cox-Ingersoll-Ross model.

3.6.2 The Merton Model

The Merton model posits a simple arithmetic Brownian motion for the short rate

$$
dr = \mu dt + \sigma dW \tag{3.88}
$$

Additionally, the market price of risk is assumed to be a constant λ. In the parlance of the general model, $\mu(r, t) = \mu$; $\sigma(r, t) = \sigma$; and $\lambda(r, t) = \lambda$. The general pricing equation (3.78) becomes

$$
\frac{\partial P}{\partial r}(\mu - \lambda\sigma) + \frac{\partial P}{\partial t} + \frac{1}{2}\sigma^2 \frac{\partial^2 P}{\partial r^2} = rP \tag{3.89}
$$

To price a zero-coupon bond, we impose the boundary condition $P(r, T, T) = 1$. We set $\tau \equiv T - t$ and try a solution of the form

$$
P(r, t, T) = A(\tau) \exp[-B(\tau)r] \tag{3.90}
$$

The derivatives of P can be calculated from (3.90):

$$
\frac{\partial P}{\partial r} = -AB \exp(-rB) \tag{3.91}
$$

$$
\frac{\partial^2 P}{\partial r^2} = AB^2 \exp(-rB) \tag{3.92}
$$

$$
\frac{\partial P}{\partial t} = rAB' \exp(-rB) - A' \exp(-rB) \tag{3.93}
$$

Equation (3.90) can then be reformulated as

$$-AB\left(\mu - \lambda\sigma\right) + \frac{\sigma^2}{2}AB^2 - A' = rA\left(1 - B'\right) \tag{3.94}$$

Because both sides of the equation must be equal for all values of r, it follows that both sides are equal to zero:

$$-AB\left(\mu - \lambda\sigma\right) + \frac{\sigma^2}{2}AB^2 - A' = 0 \tag{3.95}$$

and

$$A\left(1 - B'\right) = 0 \tag{3.96}$$

We have collapsed partial differential equation (3.90) into two separable ordinary differential equations. Also note that, because $P\left(r, T, T\right) = 1$, we have

$$A\left(0\right)\exp\left(-B\left(0\right)r\right) = 1 \text{ for all } t \tag{3.97}$$

The boundary conditions are therefore $A\left(0\right) = 1$ and $B\left(0\right) = 0$. Solving equation (3.96) subject to $B\left(0\right) = 0$ gives

$$B = \tau \tag{3.98}$$

To solve for A, we substitute the value of B in (3.95):

$$\frac{A'}{A} = -\tau\left(\mu - \lambda\sigma\right) + \frac{\sigma^2\tau^2}{2} \tag{3.99}$$

subject to $A\left(0\right) = 1$. This gives the solution for A:

$$A = \exp\left[-\frac{\tau^2}{2}\left(\mu - \lambda\sigma\right) + \frac{\sigma^2\tau^3}{6}\right] \tag{3.100}$$

The price of a zero-coupon bond follows:

$$P = \exp\left[-r\tau - \left(\mu - \lambda\sigma\right)\frac{\tau^2}{2} + \frac{\sigma^2}{6}\tau^3\right] \tag{3.101}$$

Equation (3.101) determines the entire spectrum of zero-coupon bond prices according to their maturity. The zero-coupon rate $R\left(t, T\right)$ is related to the zero-coupon price $P\left(r, t, T\right)$ by the equation

$$P\left(r, t, T\right) = \exp\left[-R\left(t, T\right)\tau\right] \tag{3.102}$$

or equivalently

$$R(t, T) = \frac{-\ln P(r, t, T)}{\tau} = r + (\mu - \lambda\sigma)\frac{\tau}{2} - \frac{\sigma^2\tau^2}{6} \qquad (3.103)$$

A major drawback of this model is that zero-coupon rates become negative for long maturities, as can be seen from (3.103).

The shape of the term structure is better understood by calculating $\partial R/\partial\tau$:

$$\frac{\partial R}{\partial \tau} = \frac{\mu - \lambda\sigma}{2} - \frac{1}{3}\sigma^2\tau \qquad (3.104)$$

If $\mu \leq \lambda\sigma$, the term structure is downward sloping. For $\mu > \lambda\sigma$, the term structure is humped with a maximum at

$$\tau = \frac{3(\mu - \lambda\sigma)}{2\sigma^2} \qquad (3.105)$$

We can also infer the duration $D = \frac{-\partial P}{\partial r}/P$. Because $\frac{\partial P}{\partial r} = -\tau P$, then the *Merton duration D* is

$$D = \tau \qquad (3.106)$$

The Merton duration of a zero-coupon bond, like the Macaulay duration, is equal to maturity. Note, however, that, unlike the Macaulay duration which assumes parallel displacements of a flat term structure, the Merton duration measures the sensitivity of bond price to the instantaneous short rate r.

We now turn to the calculation of short forward rates in Merton's model. We define a forward rate at time t for the period $[T_1, T_2]$, with $t < T_1 < T_2$, as $f(t, T_1, T_2)$. It is straightforward to see that

$$P(t, T_2) = P(t, T_1)e^{-f(t, T_1, T_2)(T_2 - T_1)} \qquad (3.107)$$

or

$$f(t, T_1, T_2) = \frac{-1}{T_2 - T_1}\ln\frac{P(t, T_2)}{P(t, T_1)} \qquad (3.108)$$

Define the short forward rate as the instantaneous forward rate at time t for the period $[T, T + dt]$. Then this short forward, denoted $f(t, T)$ is equal to

$$f(t, T) = \lim_{T_2 \to T_1}\frac{-\ln\frac{P(t, T_2)}{P(t, T_1)}}{T_2 - T_1} = \frac{-\partial \ln P}{\partial T} \qquad (3.109)$$

Equation (3.109) always holds in continuous time, regardless of the pricing model used. Specializing this equation to Merton's model, we get

$$f(t, T) = \frac{-\partial \ln P}{\partial T} = r + (\mu - \lambda\sigma)\tau - \frac{\sigma^2\tau^2}{2} \qquad (3.110)$$

At this juncture, we may ask whether the forward rate is an unbiased predictor of the short rate. This is equivalent to comparing $f(t, T)$ and $\tilde{\mathbb{E}}_t[r(T)]$. From (3.88), it can be seen that

$$r(T) = r + \mu\tau + \sigma[W(T) - W(t)] \qquad (3.111)$$

The expected short rate is therefore

$$\tilde{\mathbb{E}}_t[r(T)] = r + \mu\tau \qquad (3.112)$$

A direct comparison of equation (3.110) and (3.112) shows that $f(t, T)$ and $\tilde{\mathbb{E}}_t[r(T)]$ are not equal in general. In other words, the so-called "unbiased expectations hypothesis" does not hold. The forward premium, that is, the difference between the forward rate and the expected short rate, is

$$q(t, T) = f(t, T) - \tilde{\mathbb{E}}_t[r(T)] = -\lambda\sigma\tau - \frac{\sigma^2\tau^2}{2} \qquad (3.113)$$

when $\lambda \geq 0$, $q(t, T)$ is negative. When $\lambda < 0$, which is what one would expect if long bonds are considered riskier than short bonds., the forward premium $q(t, T)$ has a maximum at $\tau = \frac{-\lambda}{\sigma}$ with $q_{max} = \frac{\lambda^2}{2}$. Note that $q(t, T)$ is zero in a world of certainty ($\sigma = 0$). Indeed, it is easy to show that the forward rate and the expected rate must coincide in a world without uncertainty because any other outcome would give rise to a straightforward arbitrage.

Last, note that we can infer from the model the term structure of volatilities, in other words, the volatility of zero-coupon rates of various maturities. To answer this question, first apply Itô's lemma to get $d\ln P$ from equation (3.68):

$$d\ln P = \left(a - \frac{b^2}{2}\right)dt + b\,dW \qquad (3.114)$$

where a and b are defined in (3.69) and (3.70). From (3.114) and the definition of zero-coupon rates in (3.103), it follows that the volatility

$v(t, T)$ of a zero-coupon rate $R(t, T)$ is

$$v(t, T) = \frac{-\sqrt{Var(d \ln P)}}{\tau} = \frac{-b}{\tau} = \frac{-\frac{\partial P}{\partial r} \sigma}{\tau P} \tag{3.115}$$

But we know from (3.106) that $\frac{-\partial P}{\partial r}/P = \tau$. The term structure of volatility is hence flat with the volatility of all rates equal to σ:

$$v(t, T) = \sigma \tag{3.116}$$

3.6.3 The Vasicek Model

The Vasicek model differs from the Merton model in the specification of the drift term of the stochastic differential equation followed by the short rate:

$$dr = k(\theta - r)dt + \sigma dW \tag{3.117}$$

This is the Ornstein-Uhlenbeck process described in Chapter 4. k is the speed of mean reversion ($k > 0$) and θ is the long-term target for r. When $r < \theta$, the drift is positive. When $r > \theta$, the drift is negative. In both cases, r is pulled back by the drift term toward the long-term target θ. The market price of risk is constant in the Vasicek model.

In terms of our general model, $\mu(r, t) = k(\theta - r)$; $\sigma(r, t) = \sigma$; and $\lambda(r, t) = \lambda$. The general pricing equation (3.78) becomes:

$$\frac{\partial P}{\partial r}[k(\theta - r) - \lambda\sigma] + \frac{\partial P}{\partial r} + \frac{1}{2}\sigma^2\frac{\partial^2 P}{\partial r^2} = rP \tag{3.118}$$

subject to $P(r, T, T) = 1$ for a zero-coupon bond with face value 1.

To solve the zero-coupon prices, we try the same solution as in Merton's model:

$$P(r, t, T) = A(\tau)\exp[-B(\tau)r]$$
$$\frac{\partial P}{\partial r} = -AB\exp(-rB)$$
$$\frac{\partial^2 P}{\partial r^2} = AB^2\exp(-rB)$$
$$\frac{\partial P}{\partial t} = rAB'\exp(-rB) - A'\exp(-rB)$$

Equation (3.118) can be rewritten as

$$r\left(kAB + AB' - A\right) + \left[\left(\lambda\sigma - k\theta\right)B + \frac{1}{2}\sigma^2 B^2\right]A - A' = 0 \quad (3.119)$$

Because this equation needs to hold for all values of r, the values of A and B can be obtained by solving two separable ordinary differential equations:

$$kB + B' = 1 \quad (3.120)$$

subject to $B(0) = 0$, and

$$\left[\left(\lambda\sigma - k\theta\right)B + \frac{1}{2}\sigma^2 B^2\right]A - A' = 0 \quad (3.121)$$

subject to $A(0) = 1$. The choice of the boundary conditions is, as before, motivated by equation (3.97). The reader can easily check that the solution is

$$A = \exp\left\{B\left(\theta - \frac{\lambda\sigma}{k} - \frac{\sigma^2}{k^2}\right) - \left(\theta - \frac{\lambda\sigma}{k} - \frac{\sigma^2}{2k^2}\right)\tau + \left(1 - e^{-2k\tau}\right)\frac{\sigma^2}{4k^3}\right\}$$
$$(3.122)$$

and

$$B = \frac{1 - e^{-k\tau}}{k} \quad (3.123)$$

The zero-coupon bond price is

$$P(r, t, T) = \exp\left\{\frac{1 - e^{-k\tau}}{k}\left(\theta - \frac{\lambda\sigma}{k} - \frac{\sigma^2}{k^2} - r\right)\right.$$
$$\left. - \left(\theta - \frac{\lambda\sigma}{k} - \frac{\sigma^2}{2k^2}\right)\tau + \left(1 - e^{-2k\tau}\right)\frac{\sigma^2}{4k^3}\right\} \quad (3.124)$$

A bit of algebra shows that P can be reformulated as

$$P(r, t, T) = \exp\left\{-R(t, \infty)\tau + [R(t, \infty) - r]\left(\frac{1 - e^{-k\tau}}{k}\right)\right.$$
$$\left. - \frac{\sigma^2}{4k}\left(\frac{1 - e^{-k\tau}}{k}\right)^2\right\} \quad (3.125)$$

with

$$R(t, \infty) = \theta - \frac{\lambda\sigma}{k} - \frac{\sigma^2}{2k^2} \qquad (3.126)$$

Why the above expression is baptized $R(t, \infty)$ becomes clear when we calculate the zero-coupon yields

$$R(t, T) = \frac{-\ln P(r, t, T)}{\tau}$$

$$= R(r, \infty) + [r - R(t, \infty)] b(\tau) + \frac{\sigma^2\tau}{4k} b^2(\tau) \qquad (3.127)$$

with

$$b(\tau) = \frac{1 - e^{-k\tau}}{k\tau} \qquad (3.128)$$

$b(\tau)$ goes to zero for infinite τ. It is easy to check that $\lim_{\tau \to \infty} R(t, T)$ is indeed $R(t, \infty)$. Unlike the Merton model, the term structure tends asymptotically toward a value that is positive for the right choice of the parameters in (3.126).

It can also be shown that the term structure is upward sloping when

$$r < \theta - \frac{\lambda\sigma}{k} - \frac{3\sigma^2}{4k^2} \qquad (3.129)$$

It is humped when

$$\theta - \frac{\lambda\sigma}{k} - \frac{3\sigma^2}{4k^2} < r < \theta - \frac{\lambda\sigma}{k} \qquad (3.130)$$

and it is downward sloping if

$$r > \theta - \frac{\lambda\sigma}{k} \qquad (3.131)$$

The Vasicek duration is

$$D = \frac{-\frac{\partial P}{\partial r}}{P} = \frac{\left(\frac{1 - e^{-k\tau}}{k}\right) P}{P} = \frac{1 - e^{-k\tau}}{k} \qquad (3.132)$$

For small k, $D = \tau$. For large k, the duration is zero reflecting the speedy mean-reversion of rates toward the long-run target θ. For long maturities, the duration converges to $1/k$. The short forward rate can also be calculated from (3.125):

$$f(t, T) = \frac{-\partial \ln P}{\partial T}$$

(3.133)

$$= R(r, \infty) - (R(t, \infty) - r) e^{-k\tau} + \frac{\sigma^2}{k^2} \left(e^{-k\tau} - e^{2k\tau} \right)$$

We know from Chapter 4 that the expected short rate is

$$\tilde{\mathbb{E}}_t [r(T)] = \theta + (r - \theta) e^{-k\tau}$$

(3.134)

The forward premium is therefore

$$q(t, T) = f(t, T) - \tilde{\mathbb{E}}_t [r(t)]$$

$$= [R(t, \infty) - \theta] (1 - e^{-k\tau}) + \frac{\sigma^2}{k^2} \left(e^{-k\tau} - e^{2k\tau} \right)$$

(3.135)

Again, it appears that $q(t, T) \neq 0$ except for pathological cases such as $\sigma = 0$. Last, we calculate the volatility of the zero-coupon rates. As in the Merton model

$$v(t, T) = \frac{-\sqrt{var(d \ln P)}}{\tau} = \frac{\frac{-\partial P}{\partial r} \sigma}{\tau P}$$

(3.136)

From (3.133), we infer the term structure of volatilities:

$$v(t, T) = \frac{1 - e^{-k\tau}}{k\tau} \sigma$$

(3.137)

As τ goes to infinity, $v(t, T)$ goes to zero, reflecting the fact that $R(t, \infty)$ is constant.

3.6.4 The Cox-Ingersoll-Ross Model

In both the Merton and Vasicek specifications [equations (3.88) and (3.117)], the short rate can become negative if the realization of the Wiener process dW is negative enough. The Cox-Ingersoll-Ross process has no such drawback as the volatility of the short rate is proportional to the square root of this rate. The stochastic process for the short rate is

$$dr = K(\theta - r) dt + \sigma \sqrt{r} dW$$

(3.138)

This is the square-root process encountered in Chapter 4. As in the Vasicek model, K is the speed of mean-reversion ($K > 0$) and θ is the long-term target for r. In reference to the general model, $\mu(r, t) = K(\theta - r)$ and $\sigma(r, t) = \sigma\sqrt{r}$. Cox, Ingersoll, and Ross also derive from a general equilibrium model a specific formulation for the market price of risk:

$$\lambda(r, t) = \frac{\lambda\sqrt{r}}{\sigma} \tag{3.139}$$

Under the above specifications, the general pricing equation (3.78) is

$$\frac{\partial P}{\partial r}[K(\theta - r) - \lambda r] + \frac{\partial P}{\partial r} + \frac{1}{2}\sigma^2 r \frac{\partial^2 P}{\partial r^2} = rP \tag{3.140}$$

subject to $P(r, T, T) = 1$ for a zero-coupon bond paying 1 at maturity. As in previous single-factor models, we can guess a solution of the form

$$P(r, t, T) = A(\tau)\exp[-B(\tau)r]$$

Here again, partial differential equation (3.140) can be tackled by solving two separable ordinary differential equations. The fearless reader can check that

$$A = \left\{ \frac{\alpha \exp\left[\left(\frac{K+\lambda+\alpha}{2}\right)\tau\right]}{\left(\frac{K+\lambda+\alpha}{2}\right)[\exp(\alpha\tau) - 1] + \alpha} \right\}^{\beta} \tag{3.141}$$

and

$$B = \frac{\exp(\alpha\tau) - 1}{\left(\frac{k+\lambda+\alpha}{2}\right)[\exp(\alpha\tau) - 1] + \alpha} \tag{3.142}$$

with

$$\alpha \equiv \sqrt{2\sigma^2 + (K + \lambda)^2}$$

and

$$\beta \equiv \frac{2K\theta}{\sigma^2}$$

The zero-coupon rates can be inferred directly:

$$R(t, T) = \frac{-\log A(\tau) + rB(\tau)}{\tau} \tag{3.143}$$

As T goes to infinity, it can be shown that

$$R(t, \infty) = \frac{2K\theta}{K + \lambda + \alpha} \tag{3.144}$$

The term structure of zero-coupon rates is upward sloping when $r < R(t, \infty)$, humped when $R(t, \infty) < r < \frac{K\theta}{K+\lambda}$, and downward sloping when $r > \frac{K\theta}{K+\lambda}$.

The duration of a zero-coupon bond is

$$D = \frac{\frac{-\partial P}{\partial r}}{P} = B(\tau) = \frac{\exp(\alpha\tau) - 1}{\left(\frac{K+\lambda+\alpha}{2}\right)[\exp(\alpha\tau) - 1] + \alpha}$$

It can be reexpressed as

$$D = \frac{1}{\left(\frac{K+\lambda+\alpha}{2}\right) + \frac{\alpha}{\exp(\alpha\tau) - 1}} \tag{3.145}$$

For large maturities

$$\lim_{\tau \to \infty} D = \frac{2}{K + \lambda + \alpha}$$

The calculation of short forwards and rate volatilities is similar to the Merton and Vasicek models, but the algebra is more tedious. As in these models, the forward rate turns out to be different from the expected future spot rate, with the certainty case ($\sigma = 0$) being an obvious counterexample. As in the Vasicek model, the term structure of rate volatilities declines to zero because $R(t, \infty)$ is a constant independent of the initial short rate.

3.6.5 Risk-Neutral Valuation

We now attempt a thought experiment: Picture a risk-neutral world, that is, a world where the market price of risk is zero, where the short rate r follows a general Itô process as in equation (3.66) of the general single-factor model

$$dr = \tilde{\mu}(r, t)\,dt + \tilde{\sigma}(r, t)\,d\tilde{W} \tag{3.146}$$

Choose $\tilde{\mu}(r, t)$ and $\tilde{\sigma}(r, t)$ as follows:

$$\tilde{\mu}(r, t) \equiv \mu(r, t) - \sigma(r, t)\lambda(r, t) \tag{3.147}$$

and

$$\tilde{\sigma}(r, t) \equiv \sigma(r, t) \tag{3.148}$$

Apply Itô's lemma to $P = P(r, t)$:

$$\frac{dP}{P} = \frac{\frac{\partial P}{\partial r}\tilde{\mu} + \frac{\partial P}{\partial r} + \frac{1}{2}\frac{\partial^2 P}{\partial r^2}\tilde{\sigma}^2(r, t)}{P}dt + \frac{\frac{\partial P}{\partial r}\tilde{\sigma}(r, t)}{P}d\tilde{W} \quad (3.149)$$

But recall that, in our thought experiment, the market price of risk, $\tilde{\lambda}$, is zero by definition of a risk-neutral world. From equation (3.77), it can be seen that the expected return $\tilde{a}_i$ on all interest-rate-sensitive securities is equal to r in a risk-neutral world. Said differently, because $\tilde{a}_i = \tilde{\mathbb{E}}\left(\frac{dP}{P}\right)/dt = r$, we have

$$\tilde{\mathbb{E}}\left(\frac{dP}{P}\right) = r\,dt \quad (3.150)$$

From equations (3.149) and (3.150), we have

$$\frac{\partial P}{\partial r}\tilde{\mu}(r, t) + \frac{\partial P}{\partial r} + \frac{1}{2}\frac{\partial^2 P}{\partial r^2}\tilde{\sigma}^2(r, t) = rP \quad (3.151)$$

and, from the definitions of $\tilde{\mu}$ and $\tilde{\sigma}$:

$$\frac{\partial P}{\partial r}[\mu(r, t) - \lambda(r, t)\sigma(r, t)] + \frac{\partial P}{\partial t} + \frac{1}{2}\frac{\partial^2 P}{\partial r^2}\sigma^2(r, t) = rP \quad (3.152)$$

Equation (3.152) is identical to (3.78). Because they lead to the same pricing equation, the real world leading to equation (3.78) and the risk-neutral world described in this paragraph are equivalent for the purpose of pricing interest-rate-sensitive instruments.

Under the risk-neutral approach, it is convenient to use equation (3.80) with $\tilde{\lambda}(r, t) = 0$ to price zero-coupon bonds:

$$P(t, T) = \tilde{\mathbb{E}}_t\left[\exp\left\{-\int_t^T r(s)\,ds\right\}\right] \quad (3.153)$$

More generally, to price a contingent claim $C(t, T)$ with payoff $f(P(T), T)$ at time T, a similar formula can be used:

$$C(t, T) = \tilde{\mathbb{E}}_t\left[f(T, P(T))\exp\left\{-\int_t^T r(s)\,ds\right\}\right] \quad (3.154)$$

Equations (3.153) and (3.154) are used extensively to price zero-coupon bonds and interest-rate-derivative securities. As an example of the risk-neutral approach, we now attempt to recover the formula for zero-coupon bonds in the Merton model.

Example 3.6.1. We calculated bond prices in Merton's model using the risk-neutral approach. In the risk-neutral world described above, the short rate follows the stochastic differential equation

$$dr = (\mu - \lambda\sigma)\,dt + \sigma\,d\tilde{W} \qquad (3.155)$$

The integral form of (3.155) is

$$r(T) = r(t) + (\mu - \lambda\sigma)(T - t) + \sigma\left[\tilde{W}(T) - \tilde{W}(t)\right]$$

Because the expression $-\int_t^T r(s)\,ds$ *in (3.153) is the limit of the sum of normal variables, it follows a normal distribution. We know from the moment generating function of a normal distribution (see Chapter 4) that*

$$\tilde{\mathbb{E}}_t\left[\exp - \int_t^T r(s)\,ds\right] \qquad (3.156)$$

$$= \exp\left\{\tilde{\mathbb{E}}_t\left[-\int_t^T r(s)\,ds\right] + \frac{1}{2}\widetilde{Var}\left[-\int_t^T r(s)\,ds\right]\right\}$$

From (3.155), we can infer

$$\tilde{\mathbb{E}}_t\left[-\int_t^T r(s)\,ds\right] = \int_t^T -\left[r(t) + (\mu - \lambda\sigma)(s - t)\right]ds$$

$$= -r\tau - (\mu - \lambda\sigma)\frac{\tau^2}{2} \qquad (3.157)$$

where $\tau = T - t$*, as before. We can similarly calculate the variance term*

$$\widetilde{Var}\left[-\int_t^T r(s)\,ds\right] = \widetilde{Cov}\left[\left(-\int_t^T r(s)\,ds\right), \left(-\int_t^T r(s)\,ds\right)\right]$$

$$= \int_t^T \int_t^T \widetilde{Cov}\left[r(\alpha), r(\beta)\right]d\alpha\,d\beta$$

$$= \sigma^2 \int_t^T \int_t^T \tilde{\mathbb{E}}_t\left\{\int_t^\alpha d\tilde{W}(u) \int_t^\beta d\tilde{W}(v)\right\}d\alpha\,d\beta$$

$$= \sigma^2 \int_t^T \int_t^T \min(\alpha - t, \beta - t)\,d\alpha\,d\beta$$

$$= \sigma^2 \int_t^T \left[\int_t^\beta (\alpha - t)\,d\alpha + \int_\beta^T (\beta - t)\,d\alpha\right]d\beta$$

$$= \frac{\sigma^2 \tau^3}{3}$$

Replacing the values of the expectation and variance terms into (3.156), we get the price of a zero-coupon bond maturing in τ years:

$$P = \exp\left[-r\tau - (\mu - \lambda\sigma)\frac{\tau^2}{2} + \frac{\sigma^2}{6}\tau^3\right] \qquad (3.158)$$

This is of course the same formula as in (3.101) which we had obtained by solving directly partial differential equation (3.89).

Risk-neutral valuation also allows us to calculate the futures rate in a specific pricing model. For example, the futures short rate prevailing at t for time T in Merton's model is, using (3.155)

$$\begin{aligned}
g(t, T) &= \tilde{\mathbb{E}}_t\left[r(T)\right] \\
&= \tilde{\mathbb{E}}_t\left\{r + (\mu - \lambda\sigma)(T - t) + \sigma\left[\tilde{W}(T) - \tilde{W}(t)\right]\right\} \\
&= r + (\mu - \lambda\sigma)\tau \qquad (3.159)
\end{aligned}$$

Comparing the futures rate to the forward rate in (3.104), the difference is

$$g(t, T) - f(t, T) = \frac{\sigma^2\tau^2}{2} \qquad (3.160)$$

This is the convexity adjustment discussed previously. The reason we adjust for convexity is that forward contracts get discounted unlike futures contracts.

3.7 TERM-STRUCTURE-CONSISTENT MODELS

3.7.1 "Equilibrium" Versus "Fitting"

The factor models presented in Section 3.6 are sometimes called *equilibrium models*. The reason is they can be embedded within an equilibrium model of the economy that optimizes the production plans and the utility functions of agents subject to technology and budget constraints. In the Cox, Ingersoll, and Ross framework, there is an explicit economic model that is the backbone of the pricing model presented in the previous section. One of the outputs of an economic model can be the equilibrium value of the market price of risk λ. In practice, factor models can be used to form a judgment about the yield curve. For example, they can give hints as to whether the observed yield curve is too steep or too high vis-à-vis the equilibrium position predicted by the factor model. In the world of banking and money management, single-factor models are generally too parsimonious to discuss accurately the reality of a yield curve. Multifactor models are typically used, where volatility of the short rate or the long rate serve as factors in addition to the short rate. Needless to say, the econometric work behind the estimation of parameters (speeds of mean-reversion, market prices of risk, long-term targets for various factors, volatility functions) is daunting and will not be discussed here.

By contrast, so-called fitting models are less ambitious in scope. They attempt to replicate the observed yield curve and bond prices. However, as in factor models, future rates follow a prespecified stochastic process. Fitting models are generally used to price contingent claims, such as options and complex swaps. Because these models do not make a statement about the observed yield curve and, unlike equilibrium models, stick to this yield curve, they are also called *term-structure-consistent models*. See Tuckman (1995) for a full discussion of these models.

We illustrate the difference between "equilibrium" and "fitting" models with a detailed example.

Example 3.7.1. The observed rates and prices in an economy are

Maturity (years)	Zero-Coupon Rate	Zero-Coupon Bond Prices
1	5%	$100/1.05 = 95.24$
2	5.75%	$100/(1.0575)^2 = 89.42$

We define the short rate as the one-year rate. How can we go about constructing a tree of future short rates? As mentioned above, the equilibrium approach will generate an output that, unlike the fitting approach, will not necessarily be consistent with observed bond prices. We show below how these approaches differ.

THE EQUILIBRIUM APPROACH. *We use the Merton model. The short rate follows therefore an arithmetic Brownian motion:*

$$dr = \mu dt + \sigma dW \qquad (3.161)$$

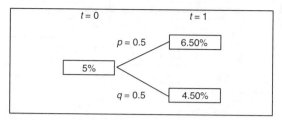

Figure 3.11. Equilibrium vs. fitting – rate tree (one-year rate) for the equilibrium approach

The corresponding risk-neutral dynamics are, as specified in the previous section

$$dr = (\mu - \lambda\sigma)\,dt + \sigma d\tilde{W} \qquad (3.162)$$

Our estimates of the parameters are

$$\hat{\mu} = 0; \ \hat{\sigma} = 1\%; \ and \ \hat{\lambda} = -\frac{1}{2}$$

We discretize the model to get a binomial tree corresponding to the estimated risk-neutral process (Figure 3.11). Indeed, we can check that

$$\tilde{\mathbb{E}}_0(r_1) = r_0 + (\hat{\mu} - \hat{\lambda}\hat{\sigma})$$

since $5.5\% = 5\% + \left[0 - \left(-\frac{1}{2} \times 1\%\right)\right]$ *and*

$$\widetilde{Var}_0\,(r_1) = \tilde{\mathbb{E}}_0\left[r_1 - \tilde{\mathbb{E}}_0\,(r_1)\right]^2 = \hat{\sigma}^2$$

since $1/2\,(6.5\% - 5.5\%)^2 + 1/2\,(4.5\% - 5.5\%)^2 = (1\%)^2$. *Note that the probabilities* $(1/2 \ and \ 1/2)$ *are risk-neutral probabilities, because they fit the discrete version of the risk-neutral process in (3.162).*

This model also allows us to calculate the equilibrium value of a two-year zero-coupon bond with face value 100 (Figure 3.12): In two years, this bond will be worth its face value 100 with certainty. In one year, it will be worth $100/1.065 = 93.9$ *when the short rate is 6.5% and* $100/1.045 = 95.69$ *when the short rate is 4.5%. Today, the equilibrium value of the two-year bond is*

$$\frac{\frac{1}{2} \times (93.9 + 95.69)}{1.05} = 90.28$$

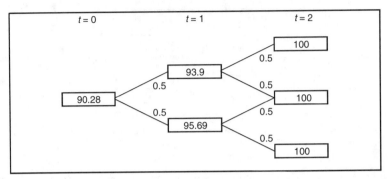

Figure 3.12. Equilibrium vs. fitting – price tree (two-year zero-coupon bond) for the equilibrium approach

The model is therefore stating that the two-year zero-coupon bond is cheap because its equilibrium price of 90.28 is higher than its market price of 89.42.

THE FITTING APPROACH. *This approach does not claim to identify mispricings in the bond markets. Rather, it posits a short-rate process that has enough degrees of freedom to stick to the actual market data. For example, we can work with a slightly modified version of Merton's equation (3.161):*

$$dr = \mu(t)\,dt + \sigma\,dW \qquad (3.163)$$

to recover observed market prices. The drift is now time-dependent and chosen to accommodate actual bond prices. The estimate of σ is $\hat{\sigma} = 1\%$, as before. By contrast with the equilibrium model, the price tree starts with the observed two-year zero-coupon price (89.42) and diffuses future prices that are compatible with observed prices and with equation (3.163), with r^u and r^d defined as the values of the short rate in one year (Figure 3.13). The tree of short rates compatible with (3.163) is shown in Figure 3.14.

From these two trees, we can infer the value of the unknown $\mu(1)$ by setting

$$
\begin{aligned}
89.42 &= \frac{\frac{1}{2}P^u + \frac{1}{2}P^d}{1.05} \\
&= \frac{\frac{1}{2} \times \left(\frac{100}{1+5\%+\mu(1)+1\%}\right) + \frac{1}{2} \times \left(\frac{100}{1+5\%+\mu(1)-1\%}\right)}{1.05}
\end{aligned}
$$

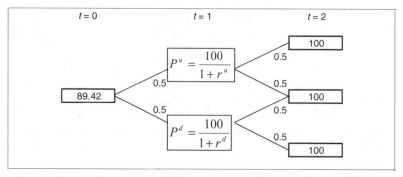

Figure 3.13. Equilibrium vs. fitting – price tree (2y ZCB) for the fitting approach

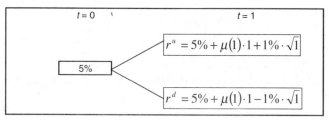

Figure 3.14. Equilibrium vs. fitting – construction of a rate tree consistent with the price tree

We find

$$\mu(1) = 1.51\%$$
$$r^u = 5\% + 1.51\% + 1\% = 7.51\%$$
$$P^u = \frac{100}{1.0751} = 93.01$$
$$r^d = 5\% + 1.51\% - 1\% = 5.51\%$$
$$P^d = \frac{100}{1.0551} = 94.78$$

The tree implied by equation (3.163) and by observed bond prices is shown in Figure 3.15. Future short rates are higher than in the equilibrium model. This reflects the fact that the market price of the two-year zero-coupon bond is cheaper than the equilibrium price given by Merton's model.

Last, note that processes (3.162) and (3.163) are risk-adjusted. The actual process is described by (3.161). With $\hat{\mu} = 0$ and $\hat{\sigma} = 1\%$, this

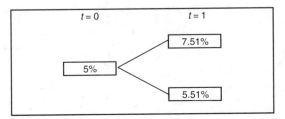

Figure 3.15. Equilibrium vs. fitting – rates consistent with observed prices (fitting approach)

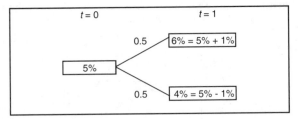

Figure 3.16. Equilibrium vs. fitting – actual rate tree from the short rate dynamics

means that actual dynamics of the short rate are

$$dr = 1\% \times dW \qquad (3.164)$$

The tree for the actual short rate movements corresponding to (3.164) is shown in Figure 3.16. Then, $P^u_{actual} = 100/1.06 = 94.34$ and $P^d_{actual} = 100/1.04 = 96.15$. The expected value discounted at today's short rate is therefore

$$\frac{\frac{1}{2} \times (94.34 + 96.15)}{1.05} = 90.71$$

The observed price for the two-year zero coupon is 89.42, which is lower than 90.71, even though the price of this two-year zero coupon will be 94.34 (with 50% probability) or 96.15 (with 50% probability) next year. This occurs because the two-year bond is viewed as riskier than the one-year bond by investors who require a risk premium over the one-year bond in order to detain it. The price they are willing to pay for the two-year bond is hence lower than its expected value.

3.7.2 The Ho-Lee Model

The "fitting" model using Merton's extended equation (3.163) in Example 3.7.1 is called the *Ho-Lee model*. One might ask: if these fitting models stick to bond prices, why are they useful? The short answer is: to price interest rate derivatives. In a sense, they are no different from the Black-Scholes-Merton model, because they take the price of the underlying asset (in this case, bonds) as a given. We give another worked example that is similar to Example 3.7.1, where we develop a tree for short rates and where we price an option using the Ho-Lee model.

Example 3.7.2(a). We observe the following rates and prices:

Maturity (years)	Zero-Coupon Rate	Zero-Coupon Bond Price
1	5.78%	94.54
2	6.20%	88.66.

We work with the following parameters:

$$\sigma = 1.5\%$$

$$\Delta t = 1 \ (one\text{-}year \ spacing, \ as \ in \ the \ previous \ example)$$

The tree of bond prices can be represented as shown in Figure 3.17. The tree of short rates is shown in Figure 3.18.

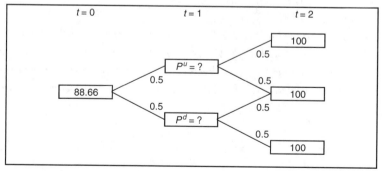

Figure 3.17. Ho-Lee model – price tree construction (2*y* ZCB)

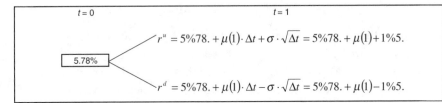

Figure 3.18. Ho-Lee model – construction of short rate tree

The expressions for P^u and P^d are

$$P^u = \frac{\left(\frac{1}{2} \times 100\right) + \left(\frac{1}{2} \times 100\right)}{1 + r^u} = \frac{100}{1.0728 + \mu(1)}$$

$$P^d = \frac{\left(\frac{1}{2} \times 100\right) + \left(\frac{1}{2} \times 100\right)}{1 + r^d} = \frac{100}{1.0428 + \mu(1)}$$

Rolling back one period

$$88.66 = \frac{\frac{1}{2}P^u + \frac{1}{2}P^d}{1.0578} = \frac{\frac{1}{2}\frac{100}{1.0728+\mu(1)} + \frac{1}{2}\frac{100}{1.0428+\mu(1)}}{1.0578}$$

Solving for $\mu(1)$, we get: $\mu(1) = 0.87\%$. The solutions for up and down rates and prices are

$$r^u = 8.15\%$$
$$r^d = 5.15\%$$
$$P^u = 92.47$$
$$P^d = 95.10$$

The bond tree is therefore as given in Figure 3.19, and the rate tree is shown in Figure 3.20.

We now proceed to price a European one-year call on the two-year zero-coupon bond with strike 93. The payoffs of the call are represented in the tree shown in Figure 3.21. Because the probabilities are risk-neutral probabilities, we can price the call by discounting at the risk-free rate the risk-neutral expected payoff:

$$\text{Call price} = \frac{\left(\frac{1}{2} \times 2.1\right) + \left(\frac{1}{2} \times 0\right)}{1.0578} = 0.99$$

The unconvinced reader can justify the above answer by resorting to

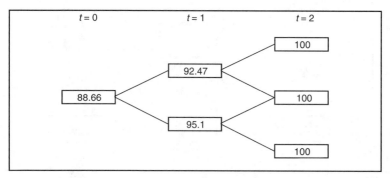

Figure 3.19. Ho-Lee model – bond price tree

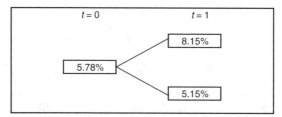

Figure 3.20. Ho-Lee model – short rate tree

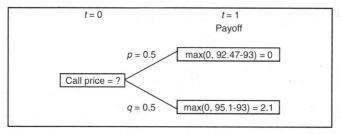

Figure 3.21. Ho-Lee model—construction of option-pricing tree

the following replication strategy: Buy N_1 one-year bonds and N_2 two-year bonds to replicate the call payoff. N_1 and N_2 can be either positive or negative numbers. The tree in Figure 3.22 values this portfolio. To replicate the call payoff, set N_1 and N_2 so that

$$(N_1^* \times 100) + (N_2^* \times 92.47) = 0$$
$$(N_1^* \times 100) + (N_2^* \times 95.10) = 2.1$$

Solving for N_1^* and N_2^*, we get: $N_1^* = -0.738$; $N_2^* = 0.798$. The original

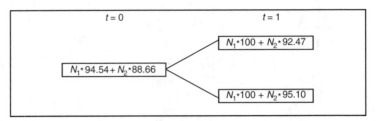

Figure 3.22. Ho-Lee model – replicating porfolio argument

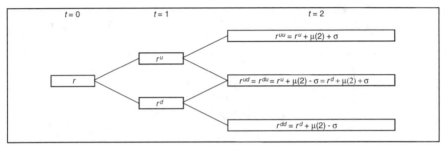

Figure 3.23. Ho-Lee model – extending the rate tree to three periods

portfolio should have the same value as the call since both the portfolio and the call produce the same payoff in a year. Therefore, the call price is given by

$$(-0.738 \times 94.54) + (0.798 \times 88.66) = 0.99$$

which is the same value as the one found previously.

Example 3.7.2(b). The tree of short rates can be extended to any number of periods through successive iterations. For example, if we know the price of a three-year zero-coupon P_3, this should allow us to extend the tree in Example 3.7.2 by one more period. The tree for short rates (where r, r^u and r^d are known) is shown in Figure 3.23. The corresponding zero-coupon-bond tree is given in Figure 3.24.
   Then

$$P_3 = \frac{\frac{1}{2}P^u + \frac{1}{2}P^d}{1+r} = \frac{\frac{1}{2}\left(\frac{\frac{1}{2}P^{uu} + \frac{1}{2}P^{ud}}{1+r^u}\right) + \frac{1}{2}\left(\frac{\frac{1}{2}P^{ud} + \frac{1}{2}P^{dd}}{1+r^d}\right)}{1+r} \tag{3.165}$$

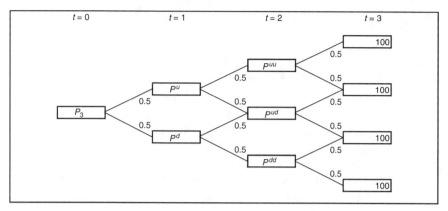

Figure 3.24. Ho-Lee model – three-period bond price tree

where in turn

$$P^{uu} = \frac{100}{1 + r^{uu}} = \frac{100}{1 + r^u + \mu(2) + \sigma} \qquad (3.166)$$

$$P^{ud} = \frac{100}{1 + r^{ud}} = \frac{100}{1 + r^u + \mu(2) - \sigma} \qquad (3.167)$$

and

$$P^{dd} = \frac{100}{1 + r^{dd}} = \frac{100}{1 + r^d + \mu(2) - \sigma} \qquad (3.168)$$

Equation (3.165), complemented by (3.166), (3.167), and (3.168), is an equation in one unknown, namely $\mu(2)$. P_3 is an observed price, and r^u and r^d have been calculated in a previous iteration as in Example (3.7.2). The volatility σ is kept unchanged from the previous iteration (1.5% in Example 3.7.2).

Equation (3.165) is best resolved numerically. We leave it to the reader to plug in numbers and solve for a three-period tree based on this example.

3.7.3 The Ho-Lee Model with Time-Varying Volatility

We now fit the interest rate tree to both a term structure of interest rates and a term structure of volatilities. Before we proceed to an illustrative

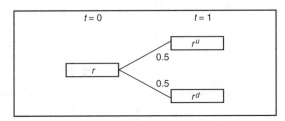

Figure 3.25. Ho-Lee model with time-varying volatility – tree prototype

example, recall that, for a tree of the form shown in Figure 3.25, we have

$$\mathbb{E}_0\left(r\right) = \frac{1}{2}r^u + \frac{1}{2}r^d \tag{3.169}$$

$$\mathbb{E}_0\left(r^2\right) = \frac{1}{2}\left(r^u\right)^2 + \frac{1}{2}\left(r^d\right)^2 \tag{3.170}$$

$$Var_0\left(r\right) = \mathbb{E}\left(r^2\right) - \left[\mathbb{E}\left(r\right)\right]^2 = \frac{1}{4}\left(r^u - r^d\right)^2 \tag{3.171}$$

and

$$\sigma_0\left(r\right) = \sqrt{Var_0\left(r\right)} = \frac{r^u - r^d}{2} \tag{3.172}$$

Equation *(3.172)* gives the expression of the so-called *basis point (or normal) volatility* $\sigma_0\left(r\right)$. This equation will be used to ensure that the interest rate tree fits the observed volatility.

Example 3.7.3. We want to build a tree fitting the following data:

Maturity (years)	Zero-Coupon Rate (%)	Zero-Coupon Price	Normal Volatility (%)
1	5.78	94.54	1.5
2	6.20	88.66	1.3
3	6.43	82.95	1.2

We first generate the future one-year rates. To this effect, we start with the tree of bond prices, as in Figure 3.26. This is the exact same tree as

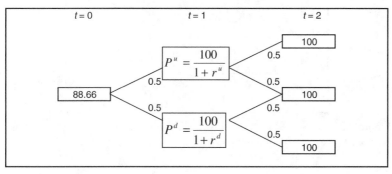

Figure 3.26. Ho-Lee model with time-varying volatility – tree prototype for bond prices

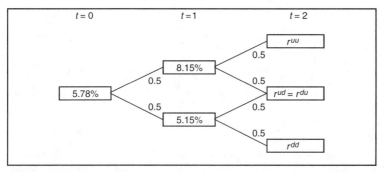

Figure 3.27. Ho-Lee model with time-varying volatility – extending the tree of one-year rates to the second period

in the previous example. We solve for r^u and r^d. First, note that

$$88.66 = \frac{\left(\frac{1}{2}\frac{100}{1+r^u}\right) + \left(\frac{1}{2}\frac{100}{1+r^d}\right)}{1.0578}$$

Moreover, the fitting condition on the one-year normal volatilities is

$$1.5\% = \frac{r^u - r^d}{2}$$

Solving the above equations for r^u and r^d, we get $r^u = 8.15\%$ and $r^d = 5.15\%$. Note that this is equivalent to the result in the previous example, because the one-year rate level and volatility are unchanged.

We now expand the tree of one-year rates to two years (Figure 3.27). To solve for r^{uu}, r^{ud}, and r^{dd}, we first need to generate the tree of

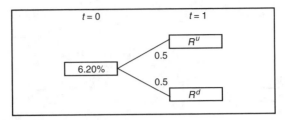

Figure 3.28. Ho-Lee (HL) model with time-varying volatility – generating a tree of two-year zero-coupon yields

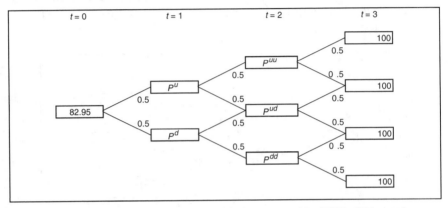

Figure 3.29. HL with time-varying volatility – tree of 3y ZCB prices used to solve for 2y zero rates (see previous figure)

two-year zero-coupon yields (Figure 3.28): where R^u and R^d are the two-year zero-coupon rates in one year in the up state and down state respectively. In turn, to solve for R^u and R^d, consider the tree showing the evolution of the three-year zero-coupon bond price (Figure 3.29). We find R^u and R^d by solving the following two equations:

$$82.95 = \frac{\frac{1}{2}P^u + \frac{1}{2}P^d}{1.0578} = \frac{\frac{1}{2}\frac{100}{(1+R^u)^2} + \frac{1}{2}\frac{100}{(1+R^d)^2}}{1.0578}$$

and

$$1.3\% = \frac{R^u - R^d}{2}$$

The solution is: $R^u = 8.08\%$ and $R^d = 5.48\%$. Hence, $P^u = 100/(1.0808)^2 = 85.61$ and $P^d = 100/(1.0548)^2 = 89.88$. The last step of *this three-period calibration is to solve for one-year rates two years from now: r^{uu}, r^{ud}, and r^{dd}. The three equations providing the solution are*

$$P^u = 85.61 = \frac{\frac{1}{2}\frac{100}{1+r^{uu}} + \frac{1}{2}\frac{100}{1+r^{ud}}}{1.0815}$$

$$P^d = 89.88 = \frac{\frac{1}{2}\frac{100}{1+r^{ud}} + \frac{1}{2}\frac{100}{1+r^{dd}}}{1.0515}$$

and

$$\frac{r^{uu} - r^{ud}}{2} = \frac{r^{ud} - r^{dd}}{2}; \text{ or } r^{ud} = \frac{r^{uu} + r^{dd}}{2}$$

This last equation holds because we want the tree to recombine, that is, $r^{ud} = r^{du}$. This means that the "local" volatility viewed from a given period is the same at each node of the tree. The solution is: $r^{uu} = 9.11\%$; $r^{ud} = 6.92\%$; and $r^{dd} = 4.74\%$. The following tree summarizes the results. The tree for one-year rates is shown in Figure 3.30, and the tree for two-year rates is shown in Figure 3.31.

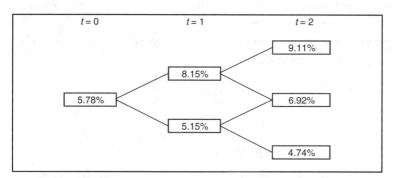

Figure 3.30. HL with time-varying volatility – tree of one-year rates

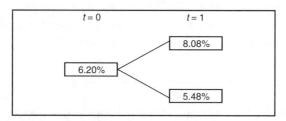

Figure 3.31. HL with time-varying volatility – tree of two-year rates

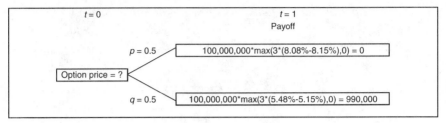

Figure 3.32. Pricing an interest rate option using HL on a binomial tree

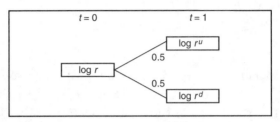

Figure 3.33. Black-Derman-Toy (BDT) lognormal model – prototypical tree

We can use these trees to price a variety of options. For example, a one-year European yield curve option with payoff Max [3 × (*two-year rate – one-year rate*), 0] *on a notional amount of 100 million can be easily priced. The terminal payoffs of this option are given in Figure 3.32. The value of the option is therefore*

$$V = \frac{\left(\frac{1}{2} \times 990{,}000\right) + \left(\frac{1}{2} \times 0\right)}{1.0578} = 467{,}952$$

3.7.4 The Black-Derman-Toy Model

The Black-Derman-Toy (BDT) model is similar to the Ho-Lee model with time-varying volatility. The main distinction is that short rates are lognormally distributed in BDT whereas they are normally distributed in Ho-Lee. A lognormal tree can be represented as in Figure 3.33. Then the lognormal volatility can be calculated as in (3.172):

$$\sigma_0 (\ln r) = \frac{\ln r^u - \ln r^d}{2} = \frac{\ln \left(r^u / r^d\right)}{2} \tag{3.173}$$

To illustrate the BDT model, we show an example along the same lines as Example (3.7.3).

Example 3.7.4. We want to fit the BDT model to the following data:

Maturity (years)	Zero-Coupon Rate (%)	Zero-Coupon Price	Lognormal Vol (%)
1	5.78	94.54	25%
2	6.20	88.66	22%
3	6.43	82.95	21%

Again, we start with the tree of bond prices, as in Figure 3.34.

To find r^u and r^d, we solve two equations with two unknowns:

$$88.66 = \frac{\frac{1}{2}\frac{100}{1+r^u} + \frac{1}{2}\frac{100}{1+r^d}}{1.0578}$$

and

$$25\% = \frac{\ln\left(r^u/r^d\right)}{2}$$

We obtain $r^u = 8.28\%$ and $r^d = 5.02\%$.

We expand the tree of one-year rates to two years, shown in Figure 3.35.

As in the previous example, prior to solving for r^{uu}, r^{ud}, and r^{dd}, we first need to generate a tree for two-year zero-coupon rates (see Figure 3.36), where R^u and R^d are the two-year zero-coupon rates in one year in the up state and down state respectively. To solve for R^u and R^d, consider the tree retracing the process for the three-year zero-coupon bond (Figure 3.37). R^u and R^d are the solutions of the following

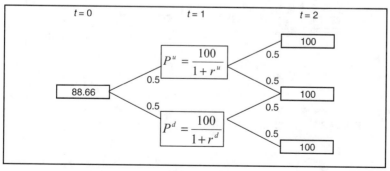

Figure 3.34. BDT model fitting – bond price tree (2y ZCB)

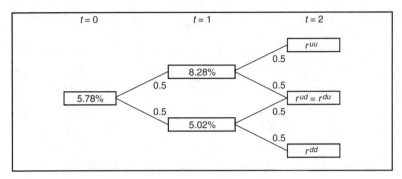

Figure 3.35. BDT model – tree for one-year rates

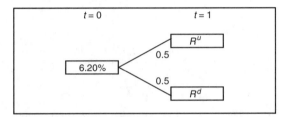

Figure 3.36. BDT model – tree for two-year zero rates

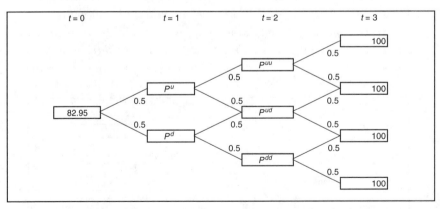

Figure 3.37. BDT model – three-year zero-coupon-bond price tree

equations:

$$82.95 = \frac{\frac{1}{2}P^u + \frac{1}{2}P^d}{1.0578} = \frac{\frac{1}{2}\frac{100}{(1+R^u)^2} + \frac{1}{2}\frac{100}{(1+R^d)^2}}{1.0578}$$

and

$$22\% = \frac{\ln\left(R^u/R^d\right)}{2}$$

We find $R^u = 8.26\%$ and $R^d = 5.32\%$. It follows that $P^u = \frac{100}{(1.0826)^2} = 85.32$ and $P^d = \frac{100}{(1.0532)^2} = 90.15$. We now solve for one-year rates two years from now, r^{uu}, r^{ud}, and r^{dd}. These are given by the following equations:

$$P^u = 85.32 = \frac{\frac{1}{2}\frac{100}{1+r^{uu}} + \frac{1}{2}\frac{100}{1+r^{ud}}}{1.0828}$$

$$P^d = 90.15 = \frac{\frac{1}{2}\frac{100}{1+r^{ud}} + \frac{1}{2}\frac{100}{1+r^{dd}}}{1.0502}$$

and

$$\frac{\ln\left(r^{uu}/r^{ud}\right)}{2} = \frac{\ln\left(r^{ud}/r^{dd}\right)}{2} \text{ or } r^{ud} = \sqrt{r^{uu}r^{dd}}$$

This last equation, as in the previous example, describes a recombining tree. The solution is

$$r^{uu} = 10.14\%; \ r^{ud} = 7.01\%; \ and \ r^{dd} = 4.85\%$$

To summarize, the tree for one-year rates is shown in Figure 3.38, and the tree for two-year rates is represented in Figure 3.39. Let us now

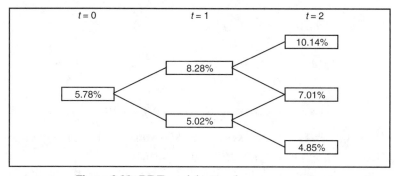

Figure 3.38. BDT model – tree for one-year rates

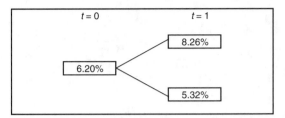

Figure 3.39. BDT model – tree for two-year rates

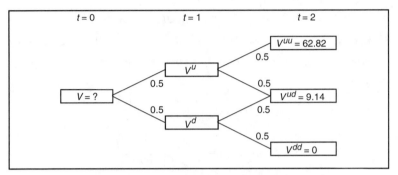

Figure 3.40. BDT model – tree for pricing power options

price a power option based on these trees. The option is European, pays

$$\max[(100 \times \textit{one-year rate})^2 - 40, 0]$$

and expires in two years. The payoff at year 2 is given in Figure 3.40.
Rolling back one period:

$$V^u = \frac{\frac{1}{2}V^{uu} + \frac{1}{2}V^{ud}}{1 + r^u} = \frac{\left(\frac{1}{2} \times 62.82\right) + \left(\frac{1}{2} \times 9.14\right)}{1.0828} = 33.23$$

$$V^d = \frac{\frac{1}{2}V^{ud} + \frac{1}{2}V^{dd}}{1 + rd} = \frac{\left(\frac{1}{2} \times 9.14\right) + \left(\frac{1}{2} \times 0\right)}{1.0502} = 4.35$$

The price of the power option is therefore

$$V = \frac{\frac{1}{2}V^u + \frac{1}{2}V^d}{1 + r} = \frac{\left(\frac{1}{2} \times 33.23\right) + \left(\frac{1}{2} \times 4.35\right)}{1.0578} = 17.76$$

3.8 RISKY BONDS AND THEIR DERIVATIVES

Much like riskless bonds, risky (or *credit sensitive*) bonds can be priced
by *structural* models and *fitting* models. Structural models value risky
bonds in the context of the corporate balance sheet: In these models,

risky bonds are priced relative to the assets (or value) of the firm, the volatility of these assets, the bond maturity, and face value. The structural model par excellence is the Merton model presented below. By contrast, fitting models take risky bond prices as a given and are generally used to price credit-sensitive derivatives. From this perspective, fitting models of risky bonds are similar to the Ho-Lee and Black-Derman-Toy models. An example of a fitting model is the Jarrow-Turnbull model that we also describe here.

3.8.1 The Merton Model

Consider a corporation with the following balance sheet at time t:

A		L	
Value		Value	
Assets	A	Equity	E
		Zero-coupon	P^R

The zero-coupon bond matures at time T. The corporation does not pay dividends and cannot issue debt other than the existing zero coupon. The face value of the zero coupon is Z. The term structure of riskless interest rates is flat at r. In the case of a limited liability company, if the asset value is lower than Z at time T, the bondholders take ownership of the company assets and the equityholders receive nothing. Said in equations:

$$E_T = \max(A_T - Z, 0) \tag{3.174}$$

and

$$P_T^R = \min(A_T, Z) = Z - \max(Z - A_T, 0) \tag{3.175}$$

Equation (3.174) states that equity is a European call on the assets of the firm with the strike price equal to the debt face value. Equation (3.175) expresses the value of a risky bond P^R as the value of a riskless bond with similar characteristics minus a European put on the assets of the firm with the strike price equal to the debt face value.

It is therefore straightforward to price the equity and the zero coupon, using the Black-Scholes-Merton formula explained in Chapter 2:

$$E = A\Phi(d_1) - Ze^{-r\tau}\Phi(d_2) \tag{3.176}$$

with

$$d_1 \equiv \frac{\ln(A/Z) + \left(r + \frac{\sigma^2}{2}\right)\tau}{\sigma\sqrt{\tau}}; d_2 \equiv d_1 - \sigma\sqrt{\tau}; \tau \equiv T - t$$

and σ is the volatility of the firm assets A (assumed to follow a geometric Brownian motion: $dA/A = \mu dt + \sigma dW$). The risky (zero-coupon) debt price is then

$$\begin{aligned}
P^R = A - E &= Ze^{-r\tau}\left[\Phi(d_2) + \frac{A}{Ze^{-r\tau}}\Phi(-d_1)\right] \\
&= Ze^{-r\tau}\left[\Phi\left(-\frac{\frac{\sigma^2\tau}{2} + \log d}{\sigma\sqrt{\tau}}\right) + \frac{1}{d}\Phi\left(-\frac{\frac{\sigma^2\tau}{2} - \log d}{\sigma\sqrt{\tau}}\right)\right]
\end{aligned} \quad (3.177)$$

where $d \equiv \frac{Ze^{-r\tau}}{A}$ is the "quasi-debt to asset ratio." The risky yield $Y^R(t, T)$ is given by

$$P^R = Ze^{-Y^R(t,T)\tau} \quad (3.178)$$

or

$$Y^R(t, T) = -\frac{1}{\tau}\ln\left(\frac{P^R}{Z}\right) \quad (3.179)$$

The credit spread is

$$\begin{aligned}
\pi(t, T) &\equiv Y^R(t, T) - r \\
&= -\frac{1}{\tau}\left[\Phi\left(-\frac{\frac{\sigma^2\tau}{2} + \log d}{\sigma\sqrt{\tau}}\right) + \frac{1}{d}\Phi\left(-\frac{\frac{\sigma^2\tau}{2} - \log d}{\sigma\sqrt{\tau}}\right)\right]
\end{aligned} \quad (3.180)$$

The reader can check that $\partial\pi/\partial d > 0$, reflecting the positive relationship between credit risk premium and "leverage." Also $\partial\pi/\partial\sigma^2 > 0$. Indeed, equityholders get richer (and bondholders poorer) as assets become more volatile because they hold a call on these assets (while bondholders are short a put on these assets). Last, it can be shown that $\partial\pi/\partial\tau \gtrless 0$ for $d < 1$ (the credit spread term structure is humped with a maximum) and $\partial\pi/\partial\tau < 0$ for $d \geq 1$ (the credit spread term structure is downward sloping).

3.8.2 The Jarrow-Turnbull Model

While structural models like the Merton model are theoretically consistent, their practical implementation remains rather limited owing to the restrictive nature of their assumptions. Fitting models, like the Jarrow-Turnbull model, are calibrated to the market value of risky bonds. Generally, these models superpose an interest rate process with a default process. An example will best illustrate the Jarrow-Turnbull model.

Example 3.8.1. In emerging market XYZ, the one-year risk-free rate is 15%. The one-year debt of a major corporation trades at 80. Its face value is 100. What is the value of a one-year European option that pays 10 should the corporation default and nothing otherwise? The reader should assume that, in case of default, the redemption value is 30.

To answer the question, we build a simple binomial tree (Figure 3.41), where λ_1 is the risk-neutral probability of default. λ_1 can be easily inferred from the tree:

$$80 = \frac{(1 - \lambda_1) \times 100 + \lambda_1 \times 30}{1.15}$$

and $\lambda_1 = 11.43\%$. The price of the option P, like the bond itself, is the expected value of the payoff in a risk-neutral world. The payoff is described in the tree shown in Figure 3.42. The price of the option

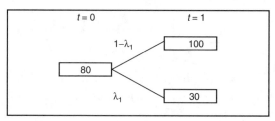

Figure 3.41. Jarrow-Turnbull model – tree for defaultable bonds

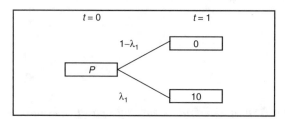

Figure 3.42. Jarrow-Turnbull model – tree for options on defaultable bonds

follows:

$$P = \frac{\lambda_1 \times 10}{1.15} = \frac{0.1143 \times 10}{1.15} = 0.99$$

Multiperiod trees tend to be fairly complicated when stochastic interest rates are assumed. We assume for the purpose of the next example that the interest rate process and the default process are independent.

Example 3.8.2. We observe the following risk-free rates, risk-free zero-coupon, and risky zero-coupon prices.

Maturity (years)	Zero-Coupon Rate	Risk-Free Zero-Coupon Price	Risky Zero-Coupon Price
1	5.78%	94.54	92.57
2	6.20%	88.66	84.30

Note that the data are compatible with those in Example 3.7.2. As in Example 3.7.2, we work with the Ho-Lee tree for one-year rates shown in Figure 3.43. As in Example 3.8.1, we extract the risk-neutral probability of default over the first year λ_1 from observed prices. Assume a redemption value of 30 in case of default.

$$92.57 = \frac{(1 - \lambda_1) \times 100 + \lambda_1 \times 30}{1.0578}$$

Hence $\lambda_1 = 2.97\%$. To solve for λ_2, the conditional risk neutral probability of default over the second year, first note that there are four possible outcomes in year 1:

Outcome	One-Year Risk-Free Rate	Default During the First Year
1	8.15%	No
2	5.15%	No
3	8.15%	Yes
4	5.15%	Yes

Also note that, should default occur in year 1, then bondholders will be paid 30 (the redemption value), no matter what, in year 2. The tree in

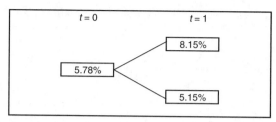

Figure 3.43. HL-type tree for one-year rates – used in the Jarrow-Turnbull model for defaultable bonds

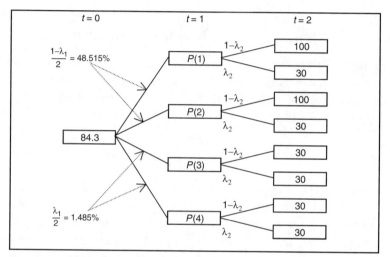

Figure 3.44. Jarrow-Turnbull model – tree for the price of a defaultable bond

Figure 3.44 traces the evolution of the two-year risky zero-coupon bond over its life. Then

$$P(1) = \frac{(1 - \lambda_2) 100 + \lambda_2 \times 30}{1.0815}; P(2) = \frac{(1 - \lambda_2) 100 + \lambda_2 \times 30}{1.0515}$$

$$P(3) = \frac{30}{1.0815} = 27.74; P(4) = \frac{30}{1.0515} = 28.53$$

and the two-year risky zero-coupon price today is equal to

$$84.30 = \frac{48.515\% [P(1) + P(2)] + 1.485\% [27.74 + 28.53]}{1.0578}$$

This is one equation in one unknown, λ_2. The reader can check that $\lambda_2 = 4.177\%$. It follows that $P(1) = 89.76$ and $P(2) = 92.32$. This tree can of course be used to price options on this bond. For example, a *one-year European call on this two-year bond with strike 90 would be worth*

$$\frac{(48.515\% \times 0) + (48.515\% \times 2.32) + (1.485\% \times 0) + (1.485\% \times 0)}{1.0578}$$
$$= 1.06$$

and a two-year zero-coupon bond callable in one year at 90 with otherwise similar characteristics should be priced at: $84.30 - 1.06 = 83.24$.

3.9 THE HEATH, JARROW, AND MORTON APPROACH

Factor models presented earlier in this chapter had a major drawback: a central input in these models, the market price of risk, is unobservable and hard to estimate. The Heath, Jarrow, and Morton (HJM) approach bypasses this difficulty by relying on the simple relationship[18]

$$P(t, T) = \exp\left[-\int_t^T f(t, u)\, du\right] \tag{3.181}$$

where $f(t, u)$ is the instantaneous forward rate prevailing at time t for time interval $[u, u + dt]$. HJM then model the dynamics of the short forward rates in a way that precludes arbitrage. These dynamics allow us to price derivative securities in a straightforward manner without having to use the market price of risk "artifact." In continuous time, HJM models the evolution of instantaneous forward rates as a diffusion driven by a multidimensional Brownian motion.

$$f(t, T) = f(0, T) + \int_0^t \alpha(s, T, \omega)\, ds + \sum_{j=1}^n \int_0^t \sigma_j(s, T, \omega)\, dW_j(t)$$

---

[18] How do we get this equation? Recall from (3.109) that $f(t, T) = \frac{-\partial \ln P(t, T)}{\partial T}$. We can integrate this equation between t and T to get:

$$-\int_t^T f(t, u)du = \int_t^T -d\ln P(t, u)$$

or

$$-\int_t^T f(t, u)du = \ln P(t, T) - \ln P(t, t)$$
$$= \ln P(t, T) \text{ since } P(t, t) = 1$$

Taking exponentials, equation (3.181) obtains.

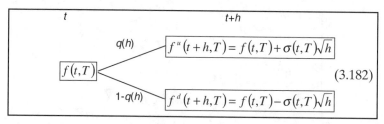

Figure 3.45. Heath-Jarrow-Morton (HJM) – basic tree for forward rates

ω is a state variable that can in general depend on the whole history of the process.

We shall first present the discrete-time version of the HJM approach.[19] We posit a simple binomial tree where short forward rates today are chosen to fit the observed forward curve, and where these forward rates $f(t, T)$ evolve as shown in Figure 3.45, with $q(h) = 1/2 + o(h)$. We show in an example that this binomial process is not arbitrage-free and will need to be amended accordingly.

Example 3.9.1. We suppose a flat yield curve at 5%. Hence $f(t, T) = 5\%$. $f(t, T)$ evolves according to (3.182), with $\sigma(t, T) = 1\%$ and $h = 1$ (see Figure 3.46). Consider the following portfolio at time t:

- *Buy N_1 zero-coupon bonds expiring at $t + 1$.*
- *Sell N_2 zero-coupon bonds expiring at $t + 2$.*
- *Buy N_3 zero-coupon bonds expiring at $t + 3$.*

Then the cash flow from this portfolio today is

$$\pi = -N_1 \exp(-0.05) + N_2 \exp(-0.1) - N_3 \exp(-0.15)$$

At $t + 1$, in the up state, the cash flow is

$$\pi^u = N_1 - N_2 \exp(-0.06) + N_3 \exp(-0.12)$$

In the down state

$$\pi^d = N_1 - N_2 \exp(-0.04) + N_3 \exp(-0.08)$$

Set $\pi = 0$ (to get a self-financed portfolio), $\pi^u = \pi^d$ (to get a sure cash

---

[19] We use continuous compounding in this section. Obviously, the choice of the compounding convention does not matter when time steps are very small.

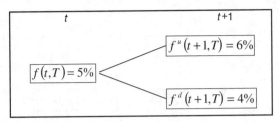

Figure 3.46. Schematic HJM implementation – binomial tree

flow at t + 1), and N_2 equal to one (because we have a degree of freedom)
to obtain

$$N_3^* = \frac{\exp(-0.06) - \exp(-0.04)}{\exp(-0.12) - \exp(-0.08)} = 0.525609268$$

$$N_1^* = \exp(-0.05) - N_3^* \exp(-0.1) = 0.475638493$$

and $N_2^* = 1$, as mentioned. These values of N_1^*, N_2^*, and N_3^* give $\pi^u =$
$\pi^d = 0.0000476$, a positive amount. The process in (3.182) is therefore
not arbitrage-free.

Note that Example 3.9.1 is similar to Example 3.3.11, where it was
shown that the conventional duration assumptions allowed an arbitrage. It turns out that the process in (3.182) can be made arbitrage-free
if we modify it to include a drift term. Consider the tree in Figure 3.47,
with $q(h) = \frac{1}{2} + o(h)$.

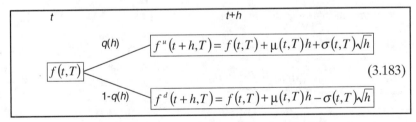

$$(3.183)$$

Figure 3.47. HJM for arbitrage-free bond pricing

We now show that the arbitrage-free drift term must be

$$\mu(t, T) = \frac{\sigma(t, T) \times \tanh h}{\sqrt{h}} \left[\sqrt{h} \int_{t+h}^{T} \sigma(t, u)\, du \right] \qquad (3.184)$$

with

$$\tanh(x) = \frac{e^x - e^{-x}}{e^x + e^{-x}} \qquad (3.185)$$

To show that (3.184) holds, first recall from Section 3.6 that no-arbitrage led to the following relationship in a risk-neutral world:

$$\mathbb{E}^* \left(\frac{dP}{P} \right) = r \, dt$$

where P is a bond price, r is the instantaneous short rate, and $\mathbb{E}^*$ is the expectations operator in a risk-neutral world. This relationship is equivalent to[20]

$$\mathbb{E}_t^* \left[P(t+h, T) \right] = \frac{P(t, T)}{P(t, t+h)} \tag{3.186}$$

Therefore, from (3.183)

$$\frac{1}{2} \{ e^{- \int_{t+h}^{T} \left[f(t,u) + \mu(t,u)h + \sigma(t,u)\sqrt{h} \right] du} + e^{- \int_{t+h}^{T} \left[f(t,u) + \mu(t,u)h - \sigma(t,u)\sqrt{h} \right] du} \}$$

$$= e^{- \int_{t}^{T} f(t,u) du} e^{\int_{t}^{t+h} f(t,u) du} \tag{3.187}$$

Rearranging equation (3.187), and eliminating identical terms on both sides, we obtain

$$\cosh \left(\int_{t+h}^{T} \sigma(t, u) \sqrt{h} \, du \right) = e^{\int_{t+h}^{T} \mu(t,u) h \, du} \tag{3.188}$$

where $\cosh(x) = \frac{e^x + e^{-x}}{2}$. Taking logarithms gives

$$\ln \cosh \int_{t+h}^{T} \sigma(t, u) \sqrt{h} \, du = \int_{t+h}^{T} \mu(t, u) h \, du \tag{3.189}$$

Last, we differentiate both sides with respect to T to get

$$\frac{\sigma(t, T) \sqrt{h} \sinh \int_{t+h}^{T} \sigma(t, u) \sqrt{h} \, du}{\cosh \int_{t+h}^{T} \sigma(t, u) \sqrt{h} \, du} = \mu(t, T) h \tag{3.190}$$

where $\sinh(x) = \frac{d \cosh(x)}{dx} = \frac{e^x - e^{-x}}{2}$. Equation (3.184) follows directly.

---

[20] To see this, note that, for a small time interval h

$$\mathbb{E}_t^* \left[\frac{P(t+h, T) - P(t, T)}{P(t, T)} \right] = rh \implies \mathbb{E}_t^* \left[\frac{P(t+h, T)}{P(t, T)} \right] = 1 + rh$$

Because h is small

$$(1 + rh)^{-1} \approx e^{-rh} = P(t, t+h)$$

The result follows.

Example 3.9.2. Consider a tree with one-year increments $(h = 1)$, and constant volatility σ. The one-year rate is $r_0 = f(0,0) = 6.2\%$. We use (3.184) to get the drift adjustment term

$$\mu(t, T) = \sigma \tanh \left[\int_{t+1}^{T} \sigma\, du \right] = \sigma \tanh[\sigma(T - t - 1)]$$

$$= \sigma \frac{e^x - e^{-x}}{e^x + e^{-x}}, \ \text{with } x \equiv \sigma(t - t - 1) \qquad (3.191)$$

With $\sigma = 1.5\%$, we get the following drift adjustment factors:

$$\mu(0, 1) = 0$$
$$\mu(0, 2) = 0.0225\%$$
$$\mu(1, 2) = 0$$

We use these factors to generate a two-period tree. Assume the observed (continuously compounded) one-year forward rates at year 1 and year 2 are, respectively

$$f(0, 1) = 6.41\%$$
$$f(0, 2) = 6.66\%$$

To build a tree of spot rates, we simply apply (3.183) and (3.191). The tree shown in Figure 3.48 gives us one-year spot rates one year from now, r^u, and r^d. Similarly, to get one-year spot rates two years from now $(r^{uu}, r^{ud}, \text{and } r^{dd})$, we start with $f(02)$ and apply the same equations (3.183) and (3.191) (Figure 3.49). Note that the tree is recombining here (i.e., $r^{ud} = r^{du}$). However, the tree does not have to recombine in the HJM model when the volatility function (a constant in this example) gets more complex. The tree shown in Figure 3.50 summarizes the evolution of one-year spot rates.

We can easily price derivative instruments in the HJM framework. As in all term-structure-consistent models, the first step is to build a tree for rates as illustrated by the previous example.

Example 3.9.3. Using the tree built in Example 3.9.2, price a two-year European call (strike price = 93) on a three-year zero-coupon bond with face value 100.

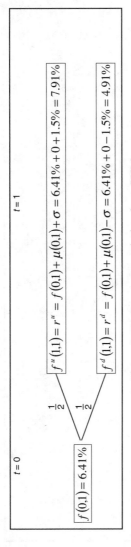

Figure 3.48. Spot rate evolution from HJM

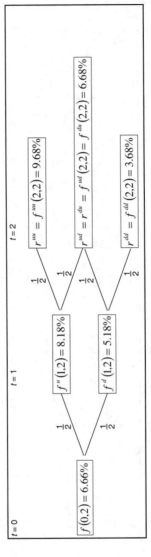

Figure 3.49. Spot rates from HJM – two-period example

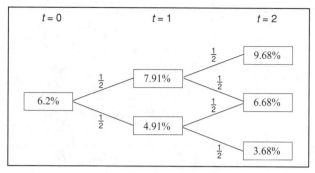

Figure 3.50

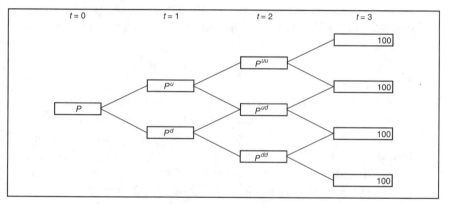

Figure 3.51. Bond price tree – recombining HJM prototype

From Example 3.9.2, we know that $r^{uu} = 9.68\%$, $r^{ud} = r^{du} = 6.68\%$,
and $r^{dd} = 3.68\%$. *The price tree for the three-year zero-coupon will have
the shape depicted in Figure 3.51. Then*

$$P^{uu} = 100 \times e^{-0.0968} = 90.77$$
$$P^{ud} = 100 \times e^{-0.0668} = 93.54$$
$$P^{dd} = 100 \times e^{-0.0368} = 96.39$$

*For the purposes of this example, this is all the information we need. The
European call can then be priced as given in Figure 3.52. The European
call is therefore worth 1.*

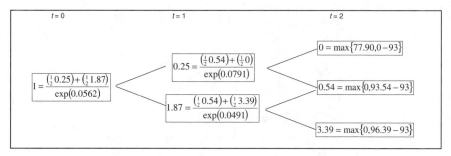

Figure 3.52. Bond option pricing with HJM

3.10 INTEREST RATES AS OPTIONS

A short-term interest rate r^* can be thought of as the sum of a real short-term rate R^*, expected inflation π^e (and a risk premium, which we neglect for the purpose of this analysis):

$$r^* = R^* + \pi^e \tag{3.192}$$

Think about a country facing severe depression like the United States in the 1930s or Japan in the late 1990s: It is entirely conceivable that the real short-term rate R^* be negative: Owing to the falling demand of goods and services, most projects are money losers. Additionally, expected (and actual) inflation is negative: For example, based on consensus 1998 economic forecasts, the inflation rate was expected to reach -2% in 1999 in Japan. Obviously, if both R^* and π^e are negative, r^* is negative as well. However, as the reader may suspect, it is virtually impossible for the actual nominal interest rate to be negative. Why? If the nominal rate were negative, investors would immediately withdraw their money from their bank account and fill their safes with currency rather than incur passively negative accruals on their savings. Therefore, in a world with cash, the actual nominal short interest rate r cannot be negative. It is equal to r^* if r^* is positive and it is zero otherwise:

$$r = \max(r^*, 0) = \max(R^* + \pi^e, 0) \tag{3.193}$$

r^* can therefore be redefined as the shadow nominal short rate. The actual rate is a call option on the shadow rate with strike zero. Note that this optional feature is due to the existence of cash. In a world

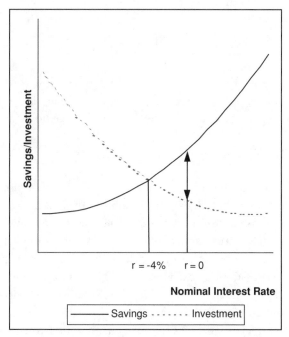

Figure 3.53. Savings-investment recessionary gap: zero rate is too high.

with electronic money, agents cannot withdraw their cash. In such a world, it is conceivable that the short-term nominal interest rate be negative.

What are the implications of this optional feature of interest rates? The economic implication of the option-like property is that rates can be driven, because of the existence of cash, out of the equilibrium as defined by (3.192). For example, if $R^* = -2\%, \pi^e = -2\%$, then the interest rate should be at $r^* = -4\%$ to ensure equality between supply and demand of loanable funds. Because $r = 0\% > r^* = -4\%$, the actual interest rate is too high, encouraging savings and discouraging investment, as shown by Figure 3.53. One way to drive r^* into positive territory is to increase expected inflation via, for example, the money supply.

The financial implication of the optionality in interest rates is that bond analysis and interest rate volatility analysis should be radically different. Recall the standard formula for the price of a default-free zero-coupon bond:

$$P(t, T) = \mathbb{E}_t^* \left\{ \exp - \int_t^T r(s)\, ds \right\} \qquad (3.194)$$

where $P(t, T)$ is the price at time t of a zero-coupon bond maturing at time T and $\mathbb{E}_t^*$ is the expectation operator at time t in a risk-neutral world. Owing to the option property in (3.193), we now have

$$P(t, T) = \mathbb{E}_t^* \left(\exp \left\{ - \int_t^T \max[0, r^*(s)]\, ds \right\} \right) \qquad (3.195)$$

In other words, the price of a zero-coupon bond is discounted at future short rates that all exhibit the option property. The higher the volatility of these future short rates, the more in-the-money the option, the higher these rates, and hence the higher the slope of the term structure. Last, note that, to the extent that r^* is very negative, the option is out-of-the-money. Hence, the short rate should remain at zero for a long time and its volatility should therefore be low.

To model the first exit time of r^* into positive territory, one can model R^* and π^e as variables following arithmetic Brownian motions

$$dR^* = \mu_1 dt + \sigma_1 dW_1 \qquad (3.196)$$

and

$$d\pi^e = \mu_2 dt + \sigma_2 dW_2 \qquad (3.197)$$

with $dW_1 dW_2 = \rho dt$. From these equations, it follows that

$$dr^* = a\, dt + b\, dW \qquad (3.198)$$

with

$$a = \mu_1 + \mu_2 \qquad (3.199)$$

$$b = \sqrt{\sigma_1^2 + \sigma_2^2 + 2\rho\sigma_1\sigma_2} \qquad (3.200)$$

and

$$dW = \frac{\sigma_1 dW_1 + \sigma_2 dW_2}{b} \qquad (3.201)$$

Then, it is easy to see that the time it takes for r^* (recall that $r^* < 0$) to reach zero will be low if a is high. Because r^* moves by a per unit time, it is easy to see that

$$\mathbb{E}[\tau] = \frac{|r^*|}{a} \tag{3.202}$$

where τ is the first exit time of the shadow rate r^* into positive domain. In terms of the economic analysis above, $\mathbb{E}[\tau]$ is the average time needed to close the savings-investment gap.

4

Mathematics of Asset Pricing

For much of this text, we have strived to keep the mathematics as simple as possible so that readers with basic preparation in calculus (ordinary, not stochastic) and probability theory could learn from the book productively. But modern financial research can be more demanding than has been suggested so far. This chapter presents more advanced mathematics to enable students to read and understand current research in asset pricing. The chapter begins with a mathematical description of random walks and goes on to introduce Itô calculus, Poisson processes, dynamic programming, and solution techniques for partial differential equations.

4.1 RANDOM WALKS

4.1.1 Description

An interesting metaphor of asset returns in financial markets is that of the "random walk." A random unidentified object (you may think of a drunkard, a particle, or an asset return) starts at point zero and time zero and travels along a line. At each step, the object moves forward by a small (positive) distance Δx with probability p, or backward by a small (negative) "distance" $-\Delta x$ with probability $q = 1 - p$. Put more formally, at each step i of the random walk where $i = 1, 2 \ldots$, there is a random variable Z_i that can take the values $+1$ or -1 with probabilities p and q, respectively. The Z variables are independent and identically distributed. The object moves with metronomic regularity: one step per unit time Δt.

At time $t = n\Delta t$, that is, n steps into the game, $X(t)$, the position of the random walk away from the origin, is the sum of the realizations of the n steps, $Z_1, Z_2, \ldots Z_n$.

$$X(t) = Z_1 + Z_2 + \cdots + Z_n \tag{4.1}$$

We might now ask: Where can we expect the object to be after n steps? How far will it deviate from the origin? These questions can be reexpressed mathematically as: What is the mathematical expectation of $X(t)$, $\mathbb{E}[X(t)]$? What is its variance, $Var[X(t)]$? Before we answer, it is useful to compute the expectation and the variance if the position changes from a generic step i

$$\mathbb{E}(Z_i) = (p - q)\Delta x \tag{4.2}$$

and

$$\begin{aligned} Var(Z_i) &= \mathbb{E}(Z_i^2) - [\mathbb{E}(Z_i)]^2 \\ &= (\Delta x)^2[1 - (p - q)^2] \\ &= 4pq(\Delta x)^2 \end{aligned} \tag{4.3}$$

Because the expectation operator is additive, the expected total distance is n times the expectation of Z_i:

$$\mathbb{E}[X(t)] = n(p - q)\Delta x \tag{4.4}$$

When $p = q = 1/2$, the object is *expected* to remain at point zero. This result makes intuitive sense because the object is equally likely to go in either direction.

An expectation has to be understood, however, as an average over a large number of experiments. Of course an expected value may never materialize. For example, when $p = q = 1/2$, $X(\Delta t)$, the position after the first step is either Δx or $-\Delta x$, but it will never equal zero, its expected value. Further intuition suggests that the random variable will tend to drift away from the origin as time goes by. A pertinent measure to check this intuition is $Var[X(t)]$. Because $X(t)$ is the sum of n independent variables with variance $4pq(\Delta x)^2$, the variance of the sum is the sum of the variances

$$Var[X(t)] = 4npq(\Delta x)^2 \tag{4.5}$$

The variance of the distance away from the origin is therefore proportional to the number of steps. But remember that each step corresponds exactly to a time unit. *It follows that the variance of the position is proportional to time.*

In the special case where $p = q = 1/2$, we have $4pq = 1$. If we think of n as the number of time units, (4.5) can be rewritten as:

$$Var[X(t)] = \text{number of time units} * (\triangle x)^2 \qquad (4.6)$$

and $(\triangle x)^2$ can then be interpreted as the variance of $X(t)$ per unit of time, or as an instantaneous variance when the time unit is very small. $\triangle x$ is then the instantaneous standard deviation of $X(t)$.

4.1.2 Gambling Recreations

Gambler's Ruin. A gambler with k dollars to spend bets one dollar at each play of a game with probability p to win and $q = 1 - p$ to lose the dollar. The game stops when the gambler's fortune either vanishes or reaches $N > k$ dollars. It can be proved that the probability of winning, which is the probability of reaching N before reaching zero, is[1]

$$P_W = \frac{1 - (q/p)^k}{1 - (q/p)^N} \qquad \text{if } p \neq \frac{1}{2} \qquad (4.7)$$

$$P_W = \frac{k}{N} \qquad \text{if } p = \frac{1}{2} \qquad (4.8)$$

Evidently, *deep pockets are good for you.* The higher k, the higher the probability of winning: Picture a coin-tossing game between a prince

---

[1] The result can be obtained by solving the difference equation

$$P_W(k) = pP_W(k+1) + qP_W(k-1)$$

subject to

$$P_W(0) = 0$$

and

$$P_W(N) = 1$$

where $P_W(k)$ is the probability of reaching N before reaching zero given a fortune k.

and a pauper. The prince gains a dollar if the outcome is "tails" and loses a dollar if it is "heads." The prince has 1,000,000 dollars, the pauper has 10,000, and the game must go on until one of the players goes bankrupt. Here

$$N = 1,000,000 + 10,000 = 1,010,000$$

Assuming the coin is fair ($p = 1/2$), the prince will win with a probability of

$$1,000,000/1,010,000 = 99.01\%$$

This is also the probability of the pauper going bankrupt. However, as the reader may want to check, both players have a mathematical expectation of zero.

More powerful is the idea that players can influence their probability of winning and their mathematical expectation by choosing specific strategies. This idea can be illustrated with a roulette game. A player has an initial fortune of 3,000 dollars and would like to stop at a 4,000-dollar figure. The roulette game is characterized by 37 possible outcomes[2] $(0, 1, 2, \ldots, 36)$. If the player bets one dollar on the even number, the probability to get two dollars is 18/37. The favorable outcomes are 2, 4, \ldots, 36, with the casino always winning on a zero outcome. What is the probability of winning if the gambler plays 1 dollar, 10 dollars, 100 dollars, 500 dollars, or 1,000 dollars at a time?

To answer this question, we use equation (4.7) with $p = 18/37$ and $q = 19/37$. If the player bets one dollar at a time, then $k = 3,000$ and $N = 4,000$. In the 10-dollar case, $k = 300$ and $N = 400$ (remember that (4.7) assumes that one dollar is played at a time. If 10 dollars are played at each step, k and N must be scaled back by a factor of 10 for the formula to apply). Similarly, $k = 300$ and $N = 400$ in the 100-dollar case and so on. Table 4.1 gives the probability of winning for each strategy.

Clearly, the 1,000-dollar betting strategy yields the highest probability of success among the five strategies considered. It can be proved,

---

[2] This is the European version of the roulette game. In its American version, there are 38 possible outcomes $(00, 0, 1, 2, \ldots, 36)$.

Table 4.1 *Bet Size and
Probability of Success*

Dollar Bet	Win Probability
1	0
10	0.45%
100	52.81%
500	70.81%
1000	72.94%

Table 4.2

Dollar Bet	Expectation
1	$1000 \times 0 + (-3000) \times 1 = -3000$
10	$1000 \times 0.45\% + (-3000) \times 99.55\% = -2982$
100	$1000 \times 52.81\% + (-3000) \times 47.19\% = -887.6$
500	$1000 \times 70.81\% + (-3000) \times 29.19\% = -167.6$
1000	$1000 \times 72.94\% + (-3000) \times 27.06\% = -82.4$
Bold play	$1000 \times 73.63\% + (-3000) \times 26.37\% = -54.8$

however, that the optimal strategy is the so-called bold play:[3] This consists in betting at each step whatever amount it takes to reach the desired objective.[4] In this example, the player should bet 1,000 dollars at the first step, since this should allow him to reach 4,000 dollars in case of success. If he loses, he should then bet the remaining 2,000 dollars. The probability of winning is then $1 - (19/37)^2 = 73.63\%$.

Table 4.2 gives the mathematical expectations associated with the betting strategies.

The bold play technique of course yields the highest (the least negative) expectation. Note that expectations must be negative because the player's probability of success *at each step* of the game is $18/37 < 1/2$. We know therefore that probabilities in Table 4.1 can never exceed 75%, that is, the probability corresponding to zero expectation in Table 4.2. The 73.63% probability delivered by the bold play comes as close as it gets.

---

[3] See Dubins and Savage (1965).
[4] Or else, if this is beyond budget, whatever money is left.

The Arcsine Law. That nature abhors equality should not be a matter of doubt after you read about the arscine law.

We focus on two players, 1 and 2, engaged in a coin-tossing contest. As before, the coin is fair and player 1 wins (loses) one dollar at each step of the way if heads (tails) comes up. For obvious reasons, player 1's fortune S_1 is equally likely to be positive or negative after n tosses. We are interested in the proportion of time (or, equivalently, the proportion of the n tosses) where player 1 is ahead of the game (i.e., when $S_1 > 0$). This proportion, which we denote as A, is of course random. In other words, if we toss the coin 1,000 times, A could happen to be 55%, meaning that player 1's *cumulative* fortune was positive 550 times out of 1,000. Then, if we repeat the experiment, A could be 47%. Consider now the following question: What is the probability distribution of A? To most of us, crude intuition about laws of averages and fair games suggests a clustering of A around a value of 50%. Right? Blatantly wrong. It turns out that, for a large number of coin tosses, the probability distribution of A is[5]

$$\Pr(A < \alpha) = \frac{1}{\pi} \int_0^\alpha \frac{1}{\sqrt{x(1-x)}} = \frac{2}{\pi} \arcsin \sqrt{\alpha} \qquad (4.9)$$

The arcsin function – as you may remember from basic trigonometry – gives the angle (measured in radians) with a sine equal to $\sqrt{\alpha}$. For example, when $\alpha = 1$, arcsin of 1 is $\pi/2$ (or 90 degrees) and $\Pr(A < 1) = 2/\pi \times \pi/2 = 1$, which makes obvious sense. Similarly, for $\alpha = 0.5$, arcsin of $\sqrt{2}/2$ is $\pi/4$ and $\Pr(A < 0.5) = 2/\pi \times \pi/4 = 1/2$, another intuitive result. Table 4.3 may not quite agree with our intuition.

Let us examine our earlier assertion that A should remain close to 50%. From Table 4.3, the probability that A is between 40% and 60% is

$$A(0.6) - A(0.4) = 56.41\% - 43.59\% = 12.82\%$$

If our initial intuition is any guide, this figure seems remarkably low. By contrast, the probability of one of the players leading more than 70% of the time is

$$[A(1) - A(0.7)] + [A(0.3) - A(0)] = 73.8\%$$

[5] See Feller (1968).

Table 4.3 *Arcsin*
Probabilities

α	$\Pr(A < \alpha)(\%)$
0	0
0.01	6.38
0.1	20.48
0.2	29.52
0.3	36.90
0.4	43.59
0.5	50
0.6	56.41
0.7	63.10
0.8	70.48
0.9	79.52
1	100

Even though the game is fair and both players start with identi-cal chances, it appears that one of the players is persistently lucky while the opponent is stubbornly in the red. Now for a mathematical interpretation: from (4.9), recall that the probability density function is

$$f(x) = \frac{1}{\pi\sqrt{x(1-x)}} \qquad (4.10)$$

This function "explodes" for extreme values of x, that is, $x = 0$ or $x = 1$, while showing considerable "restraint" in-between. This trans-lates into a high-probability mass in the tails of the probability density function as shown in Figure 4.1.

The arcsine law can be given a slightly different interpretation.[6] It can be shown that both players will reach exactly y ties in $2n$ tosses with probability

$$P_{y,2n} = \binom{2n-y}{n} 2^{y-2n} \qquad (4.11)$$

---

[6] See Epstein (1977).

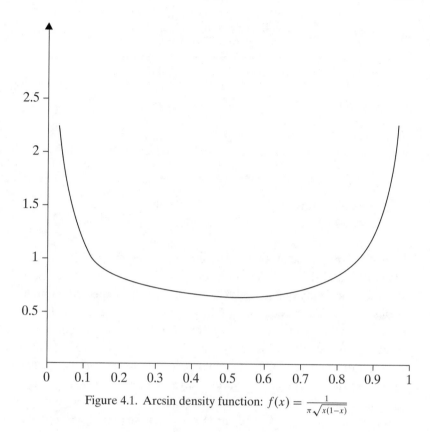

Figure 4.1. Arcsin density function: $f(x) = \frac{1}{\pi\sqrt{x(1-x)}}$

The expected number of ties corresponding to a sequence of $2n$ tosses is

$$\mathbb{E}(y) = \sum_{y=0}^{n} y \binom{2n-y}{n} 2^{y-2n} \qquad (4.12)$$

$$= \binom{2n}{n} \frac{2n+1}{2^{2n}} - 1$$

From Stirling's formula

$$n! \approx \sqrt{2\pi n}\, e^{-n}\, n^n \text{ for large } n \qquad (4.13)$$

we can infer an expression for $\mathbb{E}(y)$ when n is large:

$$\mathbb{E}(y) \approx 2\sqrt{\frac{n}{\pi}} \qquad (4.14)$$

Table 4.4 *Probability of Ties in a*
Sequence of Ten Tosses

Number of Tosses	Probability (%)
0	24.61
1	24.61
2	21.88
3	16.41
4	9.38
5	3.13

The probabilities given by equation (4.11) can be ranked as follows:

$$P_{0,2n} = P_{1,2n} > P_{2,2n} > P_{3,2n} > \cdots > P_{n,2n} \qquad (4.15)$$

Table 4.4 shows these probabilities for $n = 5$ (a sequence of 10 tosses).

The probabilities of no ties or one tie are 24.61% and decline quickly, with the probability of five ties as low as 3.13%. The expected number of ties is 1.71. For a sequence of 10 million tosses, we use (4.14) to get an expected number of ties of 3,568.25. Whereas the length of the sequence has been multiplied by a million – from 10 to 10 million – the ratio of expected values is 2,090 only. *The longer the game, the lower the probability of a tie and the longer the periods when a player is ahead.* These results show that the outcome of a fair game tends to be unfair, and go a long way toward explaining the persistence of luck and misfortune on trading floors, in casinos, and in other walks of life.

4.2 ARITHMETIC BROWNIAN MOTION

4.2.1 Arithmetic Brownian Motion as a Limit of a Simple Random Walk

We revert to our description of the simple random walk. Recall that we had computed the expectation and variance of the object position at time $t = n\Delta t$ after n steps:

$$\mathbb{E}[X_n] = n(p - q)\Delta x \qquad (4.16)$$

and

$$Var[X_n] = 4npq(\Delta x)^2 = 4\frac{t}{\Delta t}pq(\Delta x)^2 \qquad (4.17)$$

We now look at the properties of the random walk in a world where time is continuous. In such a world, for a given t, the length of a time interval Δt and the step size Δx will be made arbitrarily small (tend to zero). The number of corresponding steps n therefore becomes very large (goes to infinity). How can we then "calibrate" the parameters of the random walk, $p, q,$ and Δx to obtain a continuous time distribution of $X(t)$ with constant *intantaneous* mean μ and variance σ^2? Stated in equations, this is equivalent to

$$\mathbb{E}[X(t)] = \frac{t}{\Delta t}(p - q)\Delta x \longrightarrow \mu t \qquad (4.18)$$

and

$$Var[X(t)] = 4\frac{t}{\Delta t}pq\,(\Delta x)^2 \longrightarrow \sigma^2 t \qquad (4.19)$$

The reader can check that the solution of (4.18) and (4.19) is given by

$$p = \frac{1}{2} + \frac{\mu\sqrt{\Delta t}}{2\sigma} \qquad (4.20)$$

$$q = \frac{1}{2} - \frac{\mu\sqrt{\Delta t}}{2\sigma} \qquad (4.21)$$

$$\Delta x = \sigma\sqrt{\Delta t} \qquad (4.22)$$

Note that everything is written in terms of the time step. In the above derivation, we chose the step sizes and probabilities to be consistent with a continuous-time limit. The limiting process for X is called an *arithmetic Brownian motion* with drift μ and volatility σ. It is similar to the discrete-time random walk process discussed earlier:

1. $X(0) = 0$.
2. Increments are independent: Where the walk has led you so far has nothing to do with your path in the future. We can say equivalently: $X(t) - X(0)$ and $X(t + h) - X(t)$ are independent for all $h > 0$.
3. $X(t)$ has mean μt and variance $\sigma^2 t$ by the above construction. What is more, it can be shown using the central limit theorem[7] that $X(t)$ is normally distributed. We prove this result by calculating the moment generating function of $X(t)$. The moment

---

[7] More precisely, the de Moivre-Laplace early version of the central limit theorem.

generating function of a single step Z_i is

$$\mathbb{E}\left(e^{\lambda Z_i}\right) = pe^{\lambda \Delta x} + qe^{-\lambda \Delta x} \tag{4.23}$$

The moment generating function of X_n is the nth power of the above expression. Formally

$$\mathbb{E}\left[e^{\lambda X_n}\right] = \mathbb{E}\left[e^{\lambda(Z_1 + Z_2 + \cdots + Z_n)}\right] \tag{4.24}$$

$$= \mathbb{E}\left(e^{\lambda Z_1}\right)\mathbb{E}\left(e^{\lambda Z_2}\right)\cdots\mathbb{E}\left(e^{\lambda Z_n}\right)$$

$$= \left(pe^{\lambda \Delta X} + qe^{-\lambda \Delta X}\right)^n$$

$$= \left[\left(\frac{1}{2} + \frac{\mu\sqrt{\Delta t}}{2\sigma}\right)e^{\lambda\sigma\sqrt{\Delta t}} + \left(\frac{1}{2} - \frac{\mu\sqrt{\Delta t}}{2\sigma}\right)e^{-\lambda\sigma\sqrt{\Delta t}}\right]^n$$

where the first equality comes from (4.1), the second equality from the independence of the steps, the third equality from (4.23) and the fourth one from the solution to the limiting distribution in continuous time (4.20), (4.21), and (4.22). Because Δt can be made as small as we wish, it is the smallest time unit of interest to us. Any quantity of order $(\Delta t)^n$, with $n > 1$, is negligible for our purpose and is called $o(\Delta t)$, which means

$$\lim \frac{(\Delta t)^n}{\Delta t} = 0 \text{ when } \Delta t \longrightarrow 0 \tag{4.25}$$

For example, $(\Delta t)^2 = o(\Delta t)$, $(\Delta t)^{3/2} = o(\Delta t)$, but $\sqrt{\Delta t} \neq o(\Delta t)$ because its ratio to Δt goes to infinity when Δt goes to zero. With this point made, we can write the Taylor expansion of the exponentials in (4.24) as

$$e^{\lambda\sigma\sqrt{\Delta t}} = 1 + \lambda\sigma\sqrt{\Delta t} + \frac{\lambda^2\sigma^2\Delta t}{2} + o(\Delta t) \tag{4.26}$$

and

$$e^{-\lambda\sigma\sqrt{\Delta t}} = 1 - \lambda\sigma\sqrt{\Delta t} + \frac{\lambda^2\sigma^2\Delta t}{2} + o(\Delta t) \tag{4.27}$$

Plugging (4.26) and (4.27) back into (4.24), we get after a bit of algebra

$$\mathbb{E}\left[e^{\lambda X(t)}\right] = \left[1 + \left(\lambda\mu + \frac{\lambda^2\sigma^2}{2}\right)\Delta t + o\left(\Delta t\right)\right]^n \qquad (4.28)$$

But $\Delta t = t/n$. Because the number of steps n goes to infinity as the time increment Δt goes to zero, the moment generating function becomes in the continuous time limit[8]

$$\lim_{n\longrightarrow\infty} E\left[e^{\lambda X t}\right] = \left[1 + \frac{\left(\lambda\mu + \frac{\lambda^2\sigma^2}{2}\right)}{n}\right]^n \qquad (4.29)$$

$$= e^{\left(\lambda\mu + \frac{\lambda^2\sigma^2}{2}\right)t}$$

This is precisely the moment generating function of a normal distribution with mean μt and variance $\sigma^2 t$. As claimed, $X(t)$ is normally distributed and can be standardized by subtracting its mean and dividing by its standard deviation

$$\frac{X(t) - \mu t}{\sigma\sqrt{t}} = \phi \qquad (4.30)$$

where ϕ is a normal variable with mean zero and variance one.

We can rewrite the arithmetic Brownian motion in (4.30) as

$$X(t) = \mu t + \sigma W(t) \qquad (4.31)$$

with $X(0) = 0$, as in the discrete-time random walk. $W(t)$ is called a *standard Brownian motion* – a special case of the arithmetic Brownian motion where $\mu = 0$ and $\sigma = 1-$ or a Wiener process (after Norbert Wiener from MIT who formalized the theory of Brownian motion in 1923). $W(t)$ is therefore the continuous time limit of a basic random walk where $p = q = 1/2$ and $\Delta x = \sqrt{\Delta t}$.

---

[8] Recall that

$$\lim_{n\to\infty}\left(1 + \frac{x}{n}\right)^n = e^x$$

4.2.2 Moments of an Arithmetic Brownian Motion

As shown above, $W(t)$ is normally distributed with

$$\mathbb{E}[W(t)] = 0 \tag{4.32}$$

$$Var[W(t)] = t$$

$$
\begin{aligned}
Cov[W(t), W(t+h)] &= Cov[W(t), W(t+h) - W(t) + W(t)] \\
&= Cov[W(t), W(t+h) - W(t)] + Var[W(t)] \\
&= 0 \text{ (by independent increments)} + t \tag{4.33} \\
&= t
\end{aligned}
$$

$$
\begin{aligned}
Var[W(t) - W(t+h)] &= Var[W(t)] + Var[W(t+h)] - 2Cov \\
&\quad \times [W(t), W(t+h)] \\
&= t + (t+h) - 2t = h \tag{4.34}
\end{aligned}
$$

also note from (4.30) with $\mu = 0$ and $\sigma = 1$ that $W(t)$ can be written as

$$W(t) = \phi\sqrt{t} \tag{4.35}$$

To calculate higher-order moments of a standard Brownian motion, consider the higher order moments of a standard normal distribution. It is well known from standard statistics that

$$
\mathbb{E}(\phi^n) = \begin{cases} 0 & \text{for } n \text{ odd} \\ (n-1)!! = (n-1)(n-3)\cdots 1 & \text{for } n \text{ even} \end{cases}
$$

The moments of $W(t)$ are therefore

$$
\mathbb{E}[W^n(t)] = \begin{cases} 0 & \text{for } n \text{ odd} \\ (n-1)!!t^{n/2} = t^{n/2}(n-1)(n-3)\cdots 1 & \text{for } n \text{ even} \end{cases} \tag{4.36}
$$

Example 4.2.1. The vagaries of a return $R(t)$ on a stock can be described by the following arithmetic Brownian motion:

$$R(t) = 0.1t + 0.3W(t), \quad R(0) = 0$$

The expected return is

$$\mathbb{E}[R(t)] = \mathbb{E}(0.1t) + \mathbb{E}[0.3W(t)] = 0.1t$$

The variance of the return is

$$Var[R(t)] = Var(0.1t) + Var[0.3W(t)] = 0.09t$$

with a standard deviation equal to $0.3\sqrt{t}$. Higher order moments can be calculated by expanding the $R(t)$ polynomial and using equation (4.36). For example

$$\mathbb{E}[R^3(t)] = E[0.001t^3 + 3(0.01)t^2(0.03)W(t)$$
$$+ 3(0.1)t0.09W^2(t) + 0.0027W^3(t)]$$
$$= 0.001t^3 + 0.0027t^2$$

The process for $R(t)$ can be rewritten as

$$R(t) = 0.1t + 0.3\phi\sqrt{t}$$

where ϕ is a standard normal variable with mean zero and variance one. How do we infer the properties of, say, the one-year return? We know that

$$R(1) = 0.1 + 0.3\phi$$

It is the sum of a deterministic component (10%) and a random component ϕ scaled by the standard deviation per unit time (30%). ϕ can take any real value. As you may recall from standard probability textbooks, ϕ will live in the $[-1.96, +1.96]$ interval with probability 95%; in the $[-1.645, +1.645]$ interval with probability 90%; and in the $[-1, +1]$ interval with probability 68%. A corresponding statement about the one-year return $R(1)$ is: The realization of $R(1)$ will fall in the $[-48.8\%, +68.8\%]$ interval with probability 95%; in the $[-39.35\%, +59.35\%]$ interval with probability 90%; and in the $[-20\%, +40\%]$ with probability 68%. Last, note that, strictly speaking, a stock return cannot be described by the above process because there is a positive probability of the return being lower than -100%.

4.2.3 Why Sample Paths Are Not Differentiable

Equation (4.31) – slightly "reworded" – is

$$X(t) = X(0) + \mu t + \sigma W(t) \tag{4.37}$$

or, in a differential form[9]

$$dX(t) = \mu dt + \sigma dW(t) \tag{4.38}$$

where $dX(t)$ and $dW(t)$ are defined as[10]

$$dX(t) \equiv X(t + dt) - X(t) \tag{4.39}$$

and

$$dW(t) \equiv W(t + dt) - W(t) = \phi\sqrt{dt} \tag{4.40}$$

Equation (4.38) is called a *stochastic differential equation*. It begs a basic question: Is the variable $X(t)$ differentiable with respect to t? In other words, does $dX(t)/dt$ converge? A simple calculation reveals that this is not the case:

$$\lim_{\Delta t \to 0} \frac{\Delta X(t)}{\Delta t} = \mu + \frac{\sigma\phi}{\sqrt{\Delta t}} \longrightarrow \pm\infty \tag{4.41}$$

The expression goes to plus or minus infinity depending on the sign of ϕ. Brownian motion is fundamentally unpredictable over short time intervals. This means that a typical sample path – in other words, a realization of X as a function of time – is not differentiable. The expression $dX(t)/dt$ is therefore decreed not acceptable for the remainder of this textbook.

4.2.4 Why Sample Paths Are Continuous

We want to prove the continuity of the sample path of a Wiener process. The path is continuous in probability if, and only if, for every $\delta > 0$ and t

$$\lim_{\Delta t \to 0} \Pr\left\{ |W(t + \Delta t) - W(t)| > \delta \right\} = 0 \tag{4.42}$$

---

[9] The section on Itô calculus in this chapter will explain how integral and differential versions of a process interrelate.

[10] We shall write interchangeably dX and $dX(t)$; dW and $dW(t)$.

Recalling that, at time t

$$\mathbb{E}_t \left[W(t + \Delta t) \right] = W(t) \tag{4.43}$$

We use Chebyshev's inequality[11] to get

$$\Pr \left\{ \left| W(t + \Delta t) - \mathbb{E}_t W(t + \Delta t) \right| > \delta \right\} \leq \frac{Var_t \left[W(t + \Delta t) \right]}{\delta^2} \tag{4.44}$$

$$= \frac{\Delta t}{\delta^2} \longrightarrow 0 \text{ when } \Delta t \longrightarrow 0$$

This establishes the continuity of the Wiener process.

4.2.5 Extreme Values and Hitting Times

We now look at the properties of extreme values of an arithmetic Brownian motion. We start with the case of a driftless Brownian motion $X(t) = W(t)$, that is, $\mu = 0$, and ask the following question: What is the probability – calculated at time zero – that $X(t)$ reaches a point a $(a > X(0))$ by time T?

Let T_a denote the first such time when $X(t)$ hits point a. As a preamble, we discuss a principle widely used in the theory of random walks Brownian motions, called the "reflection principle": It states that if point a was hit at time $T_a < t$, then it is equally likely, by symmetry, that $X(t)$ will be either above or below a. Stated differently, for every sample path starting at T_a and ending *above a* at time t, there exists a symmetrical sample path starting at T_a and ending *below a* at time t. The mathematical expression of the reflection principle is

$$\Pr \left\{ X(t) \geq a, \ T_a \leq t \right\} = \Pr \left\{ X(t) \leq a, \ T_a \leq t \right\} = 0.5 \tag{4.45}$$

---

[11] Chebyshev's inequality states that for a random variable X, and any $\delta > 0$

$$\Pr \left\{ |X - \mathbb{E} X| \geq \delta \right\} \leq \frac{Var(X)}{\delta^2}$$

By the law of total probabilities[12]

$$\Pr\{X(t) \geq a\} = \Pr\{X(t) \geq a,\ T_a \leq t\}\Pr\{T_a \leq t\} \quad (4.46)$$
$$+ \Pr\{X(t) \geq a,\ T_a \geq t\}\Pr\{T_a \geq t\}$$

But it is tautologically true that

$$\Pr\{X(t) \geq a,\ T_a \geq t\} = 0 \quad (4.47)$$

Plugging (4.45) and (4.47) into (4.47) gives

$$\Pr\{T_a \leq t\} = 2\ \Pr\{X(t) \geq a\} \quad (4.48)$$

If we denote by M_t the maximum reached by the sample path trajectory over the period $[0, t]$, that is, $M(t) \equiv \max X(u)$ for $u \in [0, t]$, then the statements $\{T_a \leq a\}$ and $\{M(t) \geq a\}$ are equivalent. This is to say

$$\Pr\{M(t) \geq a\} = \Pr\{T_a \leq t\} = 2\ \Pr\{X(t) \geq a\} \quad (4.49)$$

Recall that we are solving for the case of a driftless arithmetic Brownian motion, where

$$X(t) = X(0) + \sigma\phi\sqrt{t} \quad (4.50)$$

Replacing $X(t)$ by its value in (4.49) allows us to derive an explicit solution for the probability of a maximum hitting a given point by a given time:

$$\Pr\{M(t) \geq a\} = \Pr\{T_a \leq t\} = 2\ \Pr\{X(t) \geq a\} \quad (4.51)$$
$$= 2\ \Pr\left\{X(0) + \sigma\varepsilon\sqrt{t} \geq a\right\}$$
$$= 2\Phi\left\{\frac{X(0) - a}{\sigma\sqrt{t}}\right\}$$

where $\Phi(.)$ is the cumulative standard normal distribution function

---

[12] The law of total probabilities states that for any pair of events (A, B)

$$P(A) = P(A\ /\ B)\,P(B) + P(A\ /\ B^c)\,P(B^c)$$

where B^c is the set of all events excluding event B.

$$\Phi(x) \equiv \frac{1}{\sqrt{2\pi}} \int_{-\infty}^{x} e^{-\frac{1}{2}u^2} du \tag{4.52}$$

Example 4.2.2. $X(t)$, *the short-term interest rate differential between the United States and Germany, follows the process*

$$X(t) = X(0) + \sigma\phi\sqrt{t} \tag{4.53}$$

with $X(0) = 1\%$ *and* $\sigma = 0.5\%$. *What is the probability that this differential hits 2% at any point during the next year (*$a = 2\%$ *and* $t = 1$)? *Equation (4.51) then yields*

$$\begin{aligned}
\Pr\{M(1) \geq 2\%\} &= \Pr\{T_{2\%} \leq 1\} \\
&= 2\Phi\left(\frac{1\% - 2\%}{0.5\%\sqrt{1}}\right) \\
&= 2\Phi(-2) \\
&= 4.56\%
\end{aligned}$$

The probability of the differential hitting 1.5% can be similarly calculated to yield $2\Phi(-1) = 31.73\%$.

We now generalize the result in (4.51) to the case of an arithmetic Brownian motion *with drift* as defined in equation (4.37) above:

$$X(t) = X(0) + \mu t + \sigma W(t)$$

The probability of the path hitting point a ($a > X(0)$) is then[13]

$$\Pr\{M(t) \geq a\} = \Pr\{T_a \leq t\} = \Phi\left(\frac{X(0) - a + \mu t}{\sigma\sqrt{t}}\right) \tag{4.54}$$
$$- e^{2\mu[a-X(0)]/\sigma^2}\Phi\left(\frac{X(0) - a - \mu t}{\sigma\sqrt{t}}\right)$$

or, equivalently

$$P\{M(t) \leq a\} = P\{T_a \geq t\}$$
$$= \Phi\left\{\frac{a - X(0) - \mu t}{\sigma\sqrt{t}}\right\} - e^{2\mu[a-X(0)]/\sigma^2}\Phi\left\{\frac{X(0) - a - \mu t}{\sigma\sqrt{t}}\right\}$$

---

[13] See Harrison (1985) for the proofs of subsequent results in this paragraph.

Example 4.2.3. X(t), the short-term interest rate differential between the
United States and Mexico, follows the process described in (4.37) with
$X(0) = -5\%$, $\mu = 0.5\%$, *and* $\sigma = 1\%$. *What is the probability that this*
differential vanishes at any point during the next five years (a = 0 and
$t = 5$)? *Plugging the parameter in (4.54) gives*

$$P\{M(5) \geq 0\} = P\{T_0 \leq 5\}$$
$$= \Phi\left(\frac{5\% - 0.5\% \times 5}{1\% \times \sqrt{5}}\right)$$
$$+ e^{2 \times 0.5\% \frac{-5\%}{(1\%)^2}} \Phi\left(\frac{-5\% - 0.5\% \times 5}{1\% \times \sqrt{5}}\right)$$
$$= 19.12\%$$

A related useful result gives the joint probabiltity of M(t) not reaching
point a during the time interval $[0, t]$ *and X(t) being below point b:*

$$P\{M(t) < a, X(t) < b\} = \Phi\left\{\frac{b - X(0) - \mu t}{\sigma\sqrt{t}}\right\} \qquad (4.55)$$
$$- e^{2\mu[a - X(0)]/\sigma^2} \Phi\left\{\frac{b - 2a + X(0) - \mu t}{\sigma\sqrt{t}}\right\}$$

Example 4.2.4. Back to the previous example: What is now the proba-
bility of the differential never reaching zero at any point during the next
five years (a = 0 and t = 5) and being below −2% at the end of year
5 (b = −2%)? We use (4.45) with $X(0) = -5\%$; $\mu = 0.5\%$; $\sigma = 1\%$;
$a = 0$; $b = -2\%$; *and* $t = 5$ *to get*

$$P\{M(5) < 0, X(5) < -2\%\} = \Phi(0.5/\sqrt{5}) - e^5\Phi(-9.5/\sqrt{5})$$
$$= 58.85\%$$

Note that, by setting $b = 0$, *we have*

$$P\{M(5) < 0, X(5) < 0\} = P\{M(5) < 0\} = 80.88\%$$

which is essentially the same result as in the previous example (1 −
19.12%). The reason is obviously that the event "X(5) < 0" is implied
by the event "M(5) < 0."

The reader can check that, more generally,

$$\Pr\{M(t) < a, X(t) < a\} = \Pr\{M(t) < a\} \qquad (4.56)$$

and the equation (4.55) with $b = a$ reduces to the expression for $P\{M(t) \le a\}$.

4.2.6 The Arcsine Law Revisited

We revisit an old friend – the arcsine law – and sketch a proof of the law for Brownian motion processes.[14] We want to compute the probability of $X(t)$ hitting zero at least once in a given time interval (t_1, t_2), given that $X(0) = 0$. Call such an event E. To calculate $\Pr(E)$, we use the law of total probabilities by conditioning on all possible values of $X(t_1)$

$$\Pr(E) = \frac{1}{\sqrt{2\pi t_1}} \int_R \Pr(E \mid X(t_1) = x)e^{-x^2/2t_1}dx \qquad (4.57)$$

with

$$\Pr(E \mid X(t_1) = x) = P(T_{|x|} \le t_1 - t_2) \qquad (4.58)$$

where the subscript in absolute value follows from the symmetry of arithmetic Brownian motion about the x-axis. Combining (4.51) and (4.57) gives

$$\Pr(E) = \frac{1}{\pi\sqrt{t_1(t_2 - t_1)}} \int_{R^+} \int_x^{+\infty} e^{-x^2/2t_1} e^{-y^2/2(t_2-t_1)}dxdy \qquad (4.59)$$

After a bit of algebra, the intrepid reader will get

$$\Pr(E) = \frac{2}{\pi} \arccos\sqrt{\frac{t_1}{t_2}} \qquad (4.60)$$

and the probability of $X(t)$ being always positive or negative in the time interval (t_1, t_2) is

$$\Pr(E^c) = \frac{2}{\pi} \arcsin\sqrt{\frac{t_1}{t_2}}, \qquad (4.61)$$

---

[14] See Karlin and Taylor (1975) and Ross (1996).

a result you should relate to the arcsine law described in the discrete-time framework of the previous section.

4.3 GEOMETRIC BROWNIAN MOTION

4.3.1 Description

Geometric Brownian motion is the benchmark process used to describe values of assets underlying option contracts. A variable $X(t)$ follows a geometric Brownian motion if it obeys a stochastic differential of the form

$$dX(t) = \mu X(t)dt + \sigma X(t)dW(t) \tag{4.62}$$

With $X(0) = x_0$, the integral expression of (4.62) is:[15]

$$X(t) = x_0 e^{(\mu - \sigma^2/2)t + \sigma\phi\sqrt{t}} \tag{4.63}$$

where ϕ is a normal variable with the mean of zero and variance 1. $X(t)$ is always positive. Once zero, the value of $X(t)$ will be zero forever.[16]

Example 4.3.1. A stock price $X(t)$ follows a geometric Brownian motion of the form

$$dX(t) = 0.12 X(t)dt + 0.4 X(t)dW(t)$$

The stock is worth 100 today. What are the bounds on the stock price in three months with a 95% confidence interval? We know that the stock price satisfies (4.63). Hence

$$X(t) = 100 e^{0.04t + 0.4\phi\sqrt{t}}$$

The standard normal variable ϕ is in the $[-1.96, +1.96]$ interval with 95% probability. With $t = 0.25$ year, the price will be between 73.20

---

[15] A proof is provided in the section on Itô calculus.

[16] The intuititive reason why zero is an absorbing state is that, if the price of an asset were zero today with even the slightest prospect of it becoming strictly positive later, an arbitrageur could buy the asset at will for free, creating a money machine.

and 160.32 with a 95% probability. It can be seen from (4.63) that the logarithm of $X(t)$ is normally distributed (conditional on $X(0) = x_0$). From (4.63)

$$\log[X(t)] = \log x_0 + (\mu - \sigma^2/2)t + \sigma\phi\sqrt{t} \qquad (4.64)$$

As of time zero, the mean and variance of $\log[X(t)]$ are

$$\mathbb{E}\{\log[X(t)\} = \log x_0 + (\mu - \sigma^2/2)t \qquad (4.65)$$

and

$$Var\{\log[X(t)]\} = \sigma^2 t \qquad (4.66)$$

$X(t)$, in turn, is obviously the exponential of the normal variable defined in (4.64). It follows therefore a lognormal distribution (a lognormal variable – to this extent a misnomer – can be defined as the exponential of a normal variate). More specifically, the lognormal cumulative distribution function is

$$\Pr\{X(t) \leq x\} = \int_{-\infty}^{x} \frac{1}{\sigma X \sqrt{2\pi t}}$$
$$\times \exp\left\{-\frac{(\log X - [\log x_0 + (\mu - \sigma^2/2)t])^2}{2\sigma^2 t}\right\} dX$$
$$(4.67)$$

Because a lognormal $X(t)$ also means a normal $\log X(t)$, expression (4.67) can be redefined with a normal probability density function as an integrand. Indeed, a change of variables

$$u \equiv \frac{\log X - [\log x_0 + (\mu - \sigma^2/2)t]}{\sigma\sqrt{t}} \qquad (4.68)$$

produces the desired result:[17]

$$\Pr\{X(t) \le x\} = \frac{1}{\sqrt{2\pi}} \int_{-\infty}^{\frac{\log X - [\log x_0 + (\mu - \sigma^2/2)t]}{\sigma\sqrt{t}}} e^{\frac{-u^2}{2}} \, du \tag{4.69}$$

$$= \Phi\left\{ \frac{\log X - \left[\log x_0 + \left(\mu - \frac{1}{2}\sigma^2\right)t\right]}{\sigma\sqrt{t}} \right\}$$

We show in Figure 4.2 a lognormal probability density function. It is

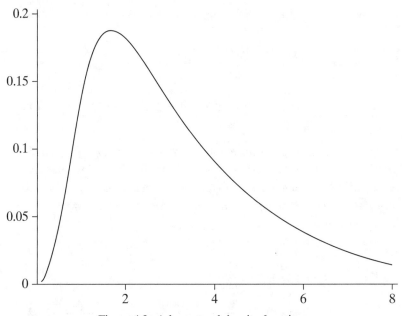

Figure 4.2. A lognormal density function

[17] The lognormal probability density functions can be obtained by using the general formula for two probability density functions $f(X)$ and $g(Y)$, with $Y = h(X)$:

$$f(X) = g(Y)\left|\frac{dY}{dX}\right| = g[h(X)]|h'(x)|$$

In the case at hand, $Y = \log X$ and

$$g(Y) = \frac{1}{\sigma\sqrt{2\pi t}} \exp\left\{ \frac{-\left(\log X - \left[\log x_0 + \left(\mu - \frac{\sigma^2}{2}\right)t\right]\right)^2}{2\sigma^2 t} \right\}$$

With

skewed to the left and is defined only for positive values of the random variable.

4.3.2 Moments of a Geometric Brownian Motion

Recall from the previous section that the moment generating function of a normal random variable Y with mean m and variance v^2 is

$$\mathbb{E}[e^{\lambda Y}] = \exp(m\lambda + v^2\lambda^2/2) \tag{4.70}$$

If we define

$$Y \equiv \log X(t) \tag{4.71}$$

then, it appears that the moment generating function of a *normal* is a straightforward expression of the statistical moments of a *lognormal* distribution

$$\mathbb{E}[X^\lambda(t)] = \exp(m\lambda + v^2\lambda^2/2) \tag{4.72}$$

with

$$m = \log x_0 + (\mu - \sigma^2/2)t, \tag{4.73}$$

$$v^2 = \sigma^2 t \tag{4.74}$$

From these equations we obtain the moment of order λ, calculated at time zero.

$$\mathbb{E}[X^\lambda(t)] = x_0^\lambda \exp[\lambda(\mu - \sigma^2/2)t + \lambda^2\sigma^2 t/2] \tag{4.75}$$

_____

$$|h'(X)| = \frac{1}{|X|}$$

we get

$$f(X) = \frac{1}{\sigma X\sqrt{2\pi t}} \exp\left\{ \frac{-\left(\log X - \left[\log x_0 + \left(\mu - \frac{\sigma^2}{2}\right)t\right]\right)^2}{2\sigma^2 t} \right\}$$

for $X > 0$ and $f(X) = 0$, otherwise.

We now compute the mathematical expectation of $X(t)$, conditional on $X(0) = x_0$:

$$\mathbb{E}[X(t)] = x_0 \exp(\mu t) \tag{4.76}$$

the second moment

$$\mathbb{E}[X(t)^2] = x_0^2 \exp(2\mu t + \sigma^2 t) \tag{4.77}$$

and the variance

$$Var[X(t)] = \mathbb{E}[X(t)^2] - \{\mathbb{E}X(t)\}^2 \tag{4.78}$$
$$= x_0^2 \exp(2\mu t)[\exp(\sigma^2 t) - 1]$$

Higher-order moments obtain similarly. The median, that is, the value of $X(t)$ at which the cumulative probability defined in (4.69) is 50%, is

$$median[X(t)] = x_0 \exp(\mu - \sigma^2/2)t \tag{4.79}$$

This is equation (4.63) with $\phi = 0$ (the median point of a standard normal distribution). More generally, the quantile of a lognormal distribution is

$$\text{Quantile}_k[X(t)] = x_0 \exp(\mu - \sigma^2/2 + z_k \sigma)t \tag{4.80}$$

where z_k is defined by

$$k \equiv \Phi(z_k) \tag{4.81}$$

At $k = 50\%$, $z_k = 0$, and (4.80) reduces to (4.79). The mode – the maximum point of the probability density function – is obtained by setting the derivative of the density function (i.e., of the integrand in 4.67) with respect to X equal to zero:

$$\text{Mode}[X(t)] = x_0 \exp(\mu - 3\sigma^2/2)t \tag{4.82}$$

Hence

$$mode < median < mean$$

The "median < mean" inequality is just an expression of the skewness to the left of the lognormal distribution. It means that it is more likely than not that a realization of $X(t)$ will be smaller than its mathematical expectation $x_0 e^{\mu t}$.

Reexpressing equation (4.62) as

$$\frac{dX(t)}{X(t)} = \mu dt + \sigma dW(t) \tag{4.83}$$

and looking at how dX/X will evolve over time, it appears that the mean will increase with time for a positive μ. The variance will keep increasing with time. As the time horizon goes to infinity, the normal distribution degenerates toward a straight line, reflecting a probability distribution with infinite variance.

On a different note, it is evident from (4.83) that the return dX/X is normally distributed with mean μdt and variance $\sigma^2 dt$. A comparison of (4.83) and (4.64) shows that the drift of dX/X and $d\log X$ differ by $0.5\sigma^2 dt$. Unlike in ordinary calculus where $d\log X = dX/X$, we need new rules of calculus to tackle Brownian motion. Section 4.4 will elaborate upon this topic.

4.4 ITÔ CALCULUS

4.4.1 Riemann-Stieljes, Stratonovitch, and Itô Integrals

Recall from Sections 4.2 and 4.3 that we represented arithmetic and geometric Brownian motions both in their differential and integral forms, without explaining the rites of passage between the two forms. To this end, we need to give meaning to the expression

$$\int_0^t f(s)dW(s) \tag{4.84}$$

where, to give examples, $f(s)$ is σ in the model of arithmetic Brownian motion and σS in the model of geometric Brownian motion. Someone with a knowledge of calculus may be tempted to use the conventional Riemann-Stieljes definition of an integral to evaluate (4.84). Let us try our hand at that. First, partition the time interval $(0, t)$ into subintervals, with $0 = s_0 < s_1 < \cdots < s_{n-1} < s_n = t$. The integral can be defined in this context as

$$\int_0^t f(s)dW(s) = \lim_{\max_i |s_{i+1}-s_i| \to 0} \sum_{i=0}^{n-1} f(\hat{s}_i)[W(s_{i+1}) - W(s_i)] \tag{4.85}$$

where $s_i \leq \hat{s}_i \leq s_{i+1}$, for $i = 0, 1, \ldots, n - 1$. It is a well-known result that in a deterministic context, no matter where $\hat{s}_i$ is in the (s_i, s_{i+1}) subinterval, the Riemann-Stieljes integral converges toward the same value.[18] It can also be proved that, as long as f is nonstochastic in (4.85), the position of $\hat{s}_i$ is irrelevant and the Riemann-Stieljes integral exists. For example, consider the differential form of an arithmetic Brownian motion

$$dX(t) = \mu dt + \sigma dW(t) \tag{4.86}$$

Because σ is nonstochastic, we can use the Riemann-Stieljes integral

$$\int_0^t dX(s) = \mu \int_0^t ds + \sigma \int_0^t dW(s) \tag{4.87}$$

and the integral form of an arithmetic Brownian motion follows:

$$X(t) = X(0) + \mu t + \sigma W(t) \tag{4.88}$$

However, when $f(s)$ is stochastic, for example, in a geometric Brownian motion where $f(s) = \sigma S(s)$, the use of the Riemann-Stieljes integral can be problematic, as shown in the following example.

Example 4.4.1. We want to evaluate $\int_0^t W(s) dW(s)$. For the Riemann-Stieljes integral to converge, we need to verify that the position of $\hat{s}_i$ in the (s_i, s_{i+1}) subinterval does not affect the value of the integral as defined in (4.85). To do this, we calculate the difference between the integral – denoted J – at $\hat{s}_i = s_{i+1}$, and the integral – denoted I – at $\hat{s}_i = s_i$. Also, for simplicity, we assume n equal subintervals of length Δs each, that is, $\Delta s = s_{i+1} - s_i$, for $i = 0, 1, \ldots, n - 1$, and $n\Delta s = t$.

$$I \equiv \lim_{\Delta s \to 0} \sum_{i=0}^{n-1} W(s_i)[W(s_{i+1}) - W(s_i)] \tag{4.89}$$

and

---

[18] When convergence conditions are met.

$$J \equiv \lim_{\Delta s \to 0} \sum_{i=0}^{n-1} W(s_{i+1})[W(s_{i+1}) - W(s_i)] \qquad (4.90)$$

then

$$J - I = \lim_{\Delta s \to 0} \sum_{i=0}^{n-1} [W(s_{i+1}) - W(s_i)]^2 \qquad (4.91)$$

Because Wiener increments are independent, we get

$$\mathbb{E}(J - I) = \sum_{i=0}^{n-1} (s_{i+1} - s_i) = n\Delta s = t \qquad (4.92)$$

The difference between the two integrals will therefore average t. We now calculate the variance of the difference. We start by calculating $E(J - I)^2$. First, observe that

$$\left\{ \sum_{i=0}^{n-1} [W(s_{i+1}) - W(s_i)]^2 \right\}^2 \qquad (4.93)$$

$$= \left[\phi_1^2(s_1 - s_0) + \phi_2^2(s_2 - s_1) + \cdots + \phi_n^2(s_n - s_{n-1}) \right]^2$$

$$= (\Delta s)^2 \sum_{i=0}^{n-1} \phi_i^4 + \sum \sum_{i \neq j} \phi_i^2 \phi_j^2 (s_i - s_{i-1})(s_j - s_{j-1})$$

where ϕ_i's are independent standard normal variables. It follows that

$$\mathbb{E}(J - I)^2 = \lim_{\Delta s \to 0} \left[(\Delta s)^2 \mathbb{E} \left\{ \sum_{i=0}^{n-1} \phi_i^4 \right\} \right. \qquad (4.94)$$

$$\left. + \mathbb{E} \left\{ \sum \sum_{i \neq j} \phi_i^2 \phi_j^2 (s_i - s_{i-1})(s_j - s_{j-1}) \right\} \right]$$

$$= \lim_{\Delta s \to 0} \left[3n(\Delta s)^2 + n(n - 1)(\Delta s)^2 \right]$$

$$= \lim_{\Delta s \to 0} \left[2t\Delta s + t^2 \right]$$

$$= t^2$$

The variance of the difference between the integrals is then

$$\text{Var}(J - I) = \mathbb{E}(J - I)^2 - [\mathbb{E}(J - I)]^2 = t^2 - t^2 = 0 \qquad (4.95)$$

The difference $(J - I)$ has a mean of t and a variance of zero. We say it converges to t in mean square. Formally, we can define convergence in mean-square in this context as

$$\lim_{n \to \infty} \mathbb{E} \left\{ \sum_{i=0}^{n-1} [W(s_{i+1}) - W(s_i)]^2 - t \right\}^2 = 0 \qquad (4.96)$$

By looking at the definition of I and J, the reader will notice that (4.95) and (4.96) are equivalent statements. The above convergence results still obtain if time subintervals are unequal.

Because the limit changes with the position of $\hat{s}_i$, the Riemann-Stieljes integral does not converge. We therefore have to define a new integral to "fit the bill." Such an integral should – unlike the Riemann-Stieljes integral – include in its definition the position of $\hat{s}_i$. Obviously, there are an infinite number of positions that $\hat{s}_i$ could take in the (s_i, s_{i+1}) subinterval; so, we could technically define an infinite number of integrals. Two of these have actually caught the probabilists' fancy:

- the Stratonovitch integral, where $\hat{s}_i = \frac{1}{2}(s_i + s_{i+1})$:

$$_{S-}\int_0^t f(s)dW(s) = \lim_{\Delta s \to 0} \sum_{i=0}^{n-1} f\left(\frac{s_i + s_{i+1}}{2}\right)[W(s_{i+1}) - W(s_i)]$$
$$(4.97)$$

- and the Itô integral, where $\hat{s}_i = s_i$:

$$_{I-}\int_0^t f(s)dW(s) = \lim_{\Delta s \to 0} \sum_{i=0}^{n-1} f(s_i)[W(s_{i+1}) - W(s_i)] \qquad (4.98)$$

Note. For convenience, we shall drop the "$I-$" when dealing with Itô integrals from now on. All stochastic integrals will be assumed to be Itô integrals unless stated otherwise.

The integral I in equation (4.89) is an example of an Itô integral. The function $f(s_i)$ is then said to be nonanticipating, because it is evaluated at the beginning of the (s_i, s_{i+1}) time subinterval. Also worth mentioning is the significance of the symbol "$=$" in (4.97) and (4.98).

Unlike in the Riemann-Stieljes definition of an integral in a deterministic context (where the integral is equal to a number), the Stratonovitch and Itô integrals can be random, and are "equal" to a quantity in the sense that they converge toward that quantity in mean-square. We now discuss the Stratonovitch and Itô integrals in reference to our previous example.

Example 4.4.2. How can we calculate explicitly the value of $\int_0^t W(s)$ $dW(s)$ in Itô's sense? By definition of the Itô integral

$$\int_0^t W(s)dW(s) \equiv \lim_{\Delta s \to 0} \sum_{i=0}^{n-1} W(s_i)[W(s_{i+1}) - W(s_i)] = I \qquad (4.99)$$

as in equation (4.89). We already know from the previous example that $J - I$ is equal to t (in the mean-square sense). Let us now evaluate $I + J$:

$$I + J \equiv \lim_{\Delta s \to 0} \sum_{i=0}^{n-1} [W(s_{i+1}) + W(s_i)][W(s_{i+1}) - W(s_i)]$$

$$= \lim_{\Delta s \to 0} \sum_{i=0}^{n-1} [W(s_{i+1})^2 - W(s_i)^2] = W(t)^2 \qquad (4.100)$$

From the values of $(J - I)$ and $(J + I)$, we infer I and J:

$$I = \frac{W(t)^2 - t}{2} \qquad (4.101)$$

and

$$J = \frac{W(t)^2 + t}{2} \qquad (4.102)$$

The reader can check that the Stratonovitch integral, evaluated at $\hat{s}_i = \frac{1}{2}[s_i + s_{i+1}]$, is

$$S - \int_0^t W(s)dW(s) = \lim_{\Delta s \to 0} \sum_{i=0}^{n-1} W\left(\frac{s_i + s_{i+1}}{2}\right)[W(s_{i+1}) - W(s_i)]$$

$$= \frac{1}{2}W(t)^2 \qquad (4.103)$$

Table 4.5

	1	*dW*	*dt*
1	1	*dW*	*dt*
dW	*dW*	*dt*	0
dt	*dt*	0	0

which is the value of the integral $\int_0^t W(s)dW(s)$ from standard calculus, had W(.) been a deterministic function.

This characteristic of the Stratonovitch integral – namely, that it preserves the rules of standard calculus – has often been viewed as an advantage. The Itô integral, however, happens to conform better with economic intuition. For example, the conditional mean and variance of a process are calculated by economic agents at time t on the basis of the information set available to them at time t. By contrast, there is an element of perfect foresight in the Stratonovitch definition that is difficult to justify intuitively in the world of economics and finance. In addition, the martingale properties of the Itô integral – to be discussed later in the book – prove to be computationally desirable. As mentioned above, we shall use exclusively the Itô formulation when discussing stochastic integrals and differentials.

4.4.2 Itô's Lemma

Itô's lemma will be the tool of the trade in a number of subsequent developments and, as such, deserves the reader's undivided attention. In its heuristic[19] incarnation, it is just a Taylor expansion *cum* a multiplication table. We discuss in turn the multiplication table and the lemma, then give examples and applications.

The multiplication table consists of the results reproduced in Table 4.5.

Recall from the arithmetic Brownian motion section that any quantity smaller than dt (called $o(dt)$) was deemed negligible. With this

---

[19] In other words, says the mathematician, incorrect. As a counterpoint, it is also said that a little inaccuracy saves tons of explanation.

background, we prove the multiplication rules:

- Rule 1: $(dt)^2 = 0$

$$(dt)^2 = o(dt) \tag{4.104}$$

because $\lim_{\Delta t \to 0} \frac{(\Delta t)^2}{\Delta t} = 0$. The result follows.
- Rule 2: $dW \times dt = dt \times dW = 0$: $dW \times dt$ is a random variable with

$$\mathbb{E}(dWdt) = dt\mathbb{E}(dW) = 0 \tag{4.105}$$

and

$$
\begin{aligned}
\text{Var}(dWdt) &= (dt)^2\text{Var}(dW) \\
&= (dt)^2\text{Var}(\phi\sqrt{dt}) \\
&= (dt)^3 \\
&= o(dt)
\end{aligned}
$$

A random variable with infinitesimally small variance "equals" its expectation, in this instance zero.[20] Because a random variable cannot, strictly speaking, equal a known quantity, we use quotation marks. "Equals zero" is meant here as "converges toward zero in mean-square."[21]
- Rule 3: $(dW)^2 = dt$: $(dW)^2$ has expectation

$$\mathbb{E}(dW)^2 = \mathbb{E}(\phi\sqrt{dt})^2 = dt \tag{4.106}$$

and variance

$$
\begin{aligned}
\text{Var}[(dW)^2] &= \mathbb{E}(dW)^4 - [\mathbb{E}(dW)^2]^2 \tag{4.107} \\
&= (dt)^2\mathbb{E}(\phi^4) - (dt)^2 \\
&= 2(dt)^2 \\
&= o(dt)
\end{aligned}
$$

The random variable $(dW)^2$ converges therefore toward dt in mean-square ("equals" dt).

---

[20] The reader can check that higher-order moments do not matter, i.e., are $o(dt)$, using the formulae in the arithmetic Brownian motion section.

[21] See Example 4.4.1 for a discussion of mean-square convergence.

We now establish Itô's lemma. We start with a general stochastic process, called an *Itô process*, of the form

$$dX(t) = \mu[X(t), t]dt + \sigma[X(t), t]dW(t) \tag{4.108}$$

and want to calculate the total differential of a function $f[X(t), t]$. f is twice continuously differentiable with respect to $X(t)$ and t. A Taylor expansion of the function f gives

$$df[X(t), t] = \frac{\partial f}{\partial X}dX + \frac{\partial f}{\partial t}dt + \frac{1}{2}\frac{\partial^2 f}{\partial X^2}(dX)^2 \tag{4.109}$$
$$+ \frac{\partial^2 f}{\partial X \partial t}dXdt + \frac{1}{2}\frac{\partial^2 f}{\partial t^2}(dt)^2$$
$$+ \text{higher-order terms}$$

From the multiplication rules established above, we have

$$\frac{1}{2}\frac{\partial^2 f}{\partial X^2}(dX)^2 = \frac{1}{2}\frac{\partial^2 f}{\partial X^2}\sigma^2[X(t), t] \tag{4.110}$$

$$\frac{\partial^2 f}{\partial X \partial t}dXdt = 0 \tag{4.111}$$

and

$$\frac{1}{2}\frac{\partial^2 f}{\partial t^2}(dt)^2 = 0 \tag{4.112}$$

Plugging (4.108), (4.110), (4.111), and (4.112) into (4.109), we get Itô's lemma:

$$df[X(t), t] = \left\{ \frac{\partial f}{\partial X}\mu[X(t), t] + \frac{\partial f}{\partial t} + \frac{1}{2}\frac{\partial^2 f}{\partial X^2}\sigma^2[X(t), t] \right\} dt$$
$$+ \frac{\partial f}{\partial X}\sigma[X(t), t]dW \tag{4.113}$$

The lemma is also expressed in its integral form as

$$f[X(t), t] = f[X(0), 0]$$
$$+ \int_0^t \left\{ \frac{\partial f}{\partial X}\mu[X(s), s] + \frac{\partial f}{\partial s} + \frac{1}{2}\frac{\partial^2 f}{\partial X^2}\sigma^2[X(s), s] \right\} ds$$
$$+ \int_0^t \frac{\partial f}{\partial X}\sigma[X(s), s]dW(s) \tag{4.114}$$

When f is not an explicit function of t, we get a simpler version of

(4.113):

$$df[X(t)] = \left\{ \frac{\partial f}{\partial X} \mu[X(t), t] + \frac{1}{2} \frac{\partial^2 f}{\partial X^2} \sigma^2[X(t), t] \right\} dt$$
$$+ \frac{\partial f}{\partial X} \sigma[X(t), t] dW \qquad (4.115)$$

The above formulations apply to Itô processes in general and will be used in the context of specific random processes. For a geometric Brownian motion, for example, $\mu[X(t), t] = \mu X$ and $\sigma[X(t), t] = \sigma X$. Equations (4.113) and (4.115) become

$$df[X(t), t] = \left\{ \frac{\partial f}{\partial X} \mu X + \frac{\partial f}{\partial t} + \frac{1}{2} \frac{\partial^2 f}{\partial X^2} \sigma^2 X^2 \right\} dt + \frac{\partial f}{\partial X} \sigma X dW$$
$$(4.116)$$

and

$$df[X(t)] = \left\{ \frac{\partial f}{\partial X} \mu X + \frac{1}{2} \frac{\partial^2 f}{\partial X^2} \sigma^2 X^2 \right\} dt + \frac{\partial f}{\partial X} \sigma X dW \qquad (4.117)$$

Example 4.4.3: Integral Form of a Geometric Brownian Motion. We want to obtain the integral form corresponding to the stochastic differential equation

$$dX(t) = \mu X(t) dt + \sigma X(t) dW(t)$$

We first find the process followed by $f[X(t)] = \log X(t)$. Then

$$\frac{\partial f}{\partial X} = \frac{1}{X} \text{ and } \frac{\partial^2 f}{\partial X^2} = -\frac{1}{X^2}$$

Replacing the values of the derivatives in (4.117) gives

$$d \log X(t) = (\mu - \frac{1}{2}\sigma^2) dt + \sigma dW(t) \qquad (4.118)$$

We integrate (4.118) from 0 to t

$$\int_0^t d \log X(s) = \int_0^t (\mu - \frac{1}{2}\sigma^2) ds + \int_0^t \sigma dW(s)$$

to get

$$\log X(t) = \log X(0) + (\mu - \frac{1}{2}\sigma^2) t + \sigma W(t)$$

Taking exponentials of both sides gives the integral form

$$X(t) = X(0) \exp\left[(\mu - \frac{1}{2}\sigma^2)t + \sigma W(t) \right]$$

Example 4.4.4: Siegel's Paradox. The US dollar/Euro exchange rate X follows a geometric Brownian motion

$$\frac{dX}{X} = \mu dt + \sigma dW$$

Denote by Y the Euro/US dollar exchange rate. Then $Y \equiv 1/X$, and

$$\frac{\partial Y}{\partial X} = -\frac{1}{X^2} \ and \ \frac{\partial^2 Y}{\partial X^2} = \frac{2}{X^3}$$

By (4.117), we obtain the dynamics of the Euro/dollar exchange rate:

$$\frac{dY}{Y} = (\sigma^2 - \mu)dt - \sigma dW$$

A comparison of the stochastic differential equations for X and Y may reveal a paradox of interesting dimensions:

1. *If $\sigma^2 > \mu > 0$, then both $E(dY/Y)$ and $E(dX/X)$ are positive, and both X and Y go to infinity as time goes to infinity, even though $Y = 1/X$.*
2. *If $\sigma^2 = 2\mu$, then $E(dY/Y) = E(dX/X)$. In other words, one should expect the Euro/dollar exchange rate and dollar/Euro exchange rate to grow at the same rate. For example, if $\sigma^2 = 2\mu = 0.1\%$, and $X_0 = Y_0 = 1$ at year zero, then one should expect both X and Y to be 1.0005 (or e^μ) a year later.*
3. *The "intuitive" result: $E(dY/Y) = -E(dX/X)$ (or equivalently $E(Y) = 1/E(X)$ for all t) obtains only when $\sigma = 0$, that is, in a deterministic world.*

The paradox is called Siegel's paradox and is the expression of the so-called Jensen's inequality.[22] This example is discussed in more detail in Chapter 1.

---

[22] Jensen's inequality states that, for a convex function f and a random variable X:

$$\mathbb{E}[f(X)] \geq f[\mathbb{E}(X)]$$

Example 4.4.5: Power Functions. A variable X follows a geometric Brownian motion:

$$\frac{dX}{X} = \mu dt + \sigma dW$$

and we want the process followed by the variable $Y = X^n$. We have

$$\frac{\partial Y}{\partial X} = nX^{n-1} \text{ and } \frac{\partial^2 Y}{\partial X^2} = n(n-1)X^{n-2}$$

By (4.117), the process followed by Y will be

$$\frac{dY}{Y} = (n\mu + \frac{1}{2}n(n-1)\sigma^2)dt + n\sigma dW \qquad (4.119)$$

Hence, a lognormal random variable raised to the nth power is also a lognormal random variable. Note two applications of (4.119):

1. *The expectation of $Y = X^n$ follows directly:*

$$\mathbb{E}[X(t)]^n = X(0)^n \exp[n\mu + \frac{1}{2}n(n-1)\sigma^2]t \qquad (4.120)$$

   This is the formula for the moments of a lognormal random walk. We have therefore recovered through Itô's lemma equation (4.75), that we had reached in the previous section by using the moment generating function of a normal random variable. It turns out that Itô's lemma provides a way to calculate the moments of more general processes. We shall elaborate further upon this point in the next section.

2. *The expected present value P*

$$P = \mathbb{E}\left[\int_0^\infty e^{-rt} X^n dt\right]$$
$$= \int_0^\infty e^{-rt} \mathbb{E}(X^n) dt$$

   can also be calculated. From equation (4.120), the expected present value is

$$P = \int_0^\infty X(0)^n \exp[n\mu + \frac{1}{2}n(n-1)\sigma^2 - r]t \, dt$$

$$= \frac{X(0)^n}{r - n\mu - \frac{1}{2}n(n-1)\sigma^2}$$

Provided the denominator is positive and $n > 1$, the expected present value increases with μ and σ.

Example 4.4.6: Forward Contracts. We know from standard finance that a forward price F at time t of a non-dividend-paying asset with value X to be delivered at time $T \geq t$ is

$$F = Xe^{r(T-t)}$$

Assuming X follows a geometric Brownian motion:

$$\frac{dX}{X} = \mu dt + \sigma dW$$

and noting that

$$\frac{\partial F}{\partial X} = e^{-r(T-t)}$$

$$\frac{\partial F}{\partial t} = -rXe^{-r(T-t)}$$

$$\frac{\partial^2 F}{\partial X^2} = 0$$

we can use equation (4.116) to write the dynamics for F:

$$\frac{dF}{F} = (\mu - r)dt + \sigma dW$$

Example 4.4.7: The Integral $\int_0^t W(s)dW(s)$. We revert to a direct calculation of the integral $\int_0^t W(s)dW(s)$, that we had computed rather laboriously from first principles in the previous subsection. To this end, the integral form of Itô's lemma will be used. Set

$$X(t) \equiv W(t) \text{ and } f[X(t)] \equiv W(t)^2$$

Hence

$$\frac{\partial f}{\partial X} = 2W$$

$$\frac{\partial f}{\partial t} = 0$$

$$\frac{\partial^2 f}{\partial X^2} = 2$$

From equation (4.114), with $\mu = 0$ and $\sigma = 1$, we can write

$$W^2(t) = W^2(0) + \int_0^t ds + \int_0^t 2W(s)dW(s)$$

The result is therefore

$$\int_0^t W(s)dW(s) = \frac{W(t)^2 - t}{2}$$

Example 4.4.8: The Integral $\int_0^t s\,dW(s)$. As in the previous example, we need the integral version of Itô's lemma. We define

$$X(t) \equiv W(t)$$

and

$$f[X(t), t] \equiv t W(t)$$

and get the derivatives

$$\frac{\partial f}{\partial X} = t$$

$$\frac{\partial f}{\partial t} = W(t)$$

$$\frac{\partial^2 f}{\partial X^2} = 0$$

The integral under study then obtains directly from (4.114):

$$\int_0^t s\,dW(s) = t W(t) - \int_0^t W(s)ds$$

Example 4.4.9: The Expression $\mathbb{E}\{\exp[\int_0^t(-\frac{1}{2}\lambda^2 ds + \lambda dW(s))]\}$. We posit a variable X following an arithmetic Brownian motion

$$dX = -\frac{1}{2}\lambda^2 dt + \lambda dW$$

with $X(0) = 0$. As shown above, the integral form for $X(t)$ is

$$X(t) = \int_0^t \left[-\frac{1}{2}\lambda^2 ds + \lambda dW(s) \right]$$

With $Y(t) \equiv \exp[X(t)]$, we have

$$\frac{\partial Y}{\partial X} = \frac{\partial^2 Y}{\partial X^2} = \exp[X(t)]$$

By equation (4.117), we get

$$\frac{dY}{Y} = \lambda dW$$

The mathematical expectation at time zero is thus

$$\mathbb{E}[Y(t)] = Y(0) = 1$$

By substitution, this implies the following equality at time zero:

$$\mathbb{E}\left\{ \exp\left[\int_0^t (-\frac{1}{2}\lambda^2 ds + \lambda dW(s)) \right] \right\} = 1 \qquad (4.121)$$

As we shall discuss later, $Y(t)$ is said to be a martingale since its expected value is always 1. Equation (4.121) is particularly relevant to the Girsanov theorem and related topics. Also note that equation (4.121) could have been deduced directly from the expression of the moment generating function of an arithmetic Brownian motion.

We now discuss the multidimensional version of Itô's lemma and give related illustrative examples.

4.4.3 Multidimensional Itô's Lemma

We posit several variables $X_1, X_2, \ldots, X_n$ following Itô processes of the form

$$dX_i(t) = \mu_i[\tilde{X}(t), t]dt + \sigma_i[\tilde{X}(t), t]dW_i(t)$$

for all $i = 1, 2, \ldots, n$. $\tilde{X}(t)$ is an n-dimensional row vector defined as $(X_1, X_2, \ldots, X_n)$. Each variable X_i is characterized by its own drift μ_i, variance σ_i, and Wiener process dW_i. While these Wiener processes dW_i follow normal distributions with means of zero and variance dt as explained before, they are not identical in the sense that each of them is drawn from a different standard normal distribution. We assume constant correlation coefficients among Wiener processes to yield, for all $i, j = 1, 2, \ldots, n$:

$$dW_i dW_j = \rho_{ij} dt \tag{4.122}$$

where $-1 \le \rho_{ij} \le 1$, and $\rho_{ij} = 1$ when $i = j$. We can easily infer Itô's lemma for a function of the form $f(X_1, X_2, t)$. Recall that:

$$dW_i dt = 0 \tag{4.123}$$

A Taylor expansion of the f function gives:

$$df(X_1, \ldots, X_n, t) = \frac{\partial f}{\partial X_1} dX_1 + \cdots + \frac{\partial f}{\partial X_n} dX_n$$
$$+ \frac{\partial f}{\partial t} dt + \frac{1}{2} \sum_{i,j=1}^{n} \frac{\partial^2 f}{\partial X_i \partial X_j} dX_i dX_j$$

This can be rewritten, as can be easily verified, as follows:

$$df = \left\{ \sum_{i=1}^{n} \mu_i \frac{\partial f}{\partial X_i} + \frac{\partial f}{\partial t} + \frac{1}{2} \sum_{i=1}^{n} \sigma_i^2 \frac{\partial^2 f}{\partial X_i^2} + \sum_{i \ne j} \rho_{ij} \sigma_i \sigma_j \frac{\partial^2 f}{\partial X_i \partial X_j} \right\} dt$$
$$+ \sum_{i=1}^{n} \sigma_i \frac{\partial f}{\partial X_i} dW_i \tag{4.124}$$

In the particular case of a two-dimensional geometric Brownian motion

$$\mu_1[\tilde{X}(t), t] = \mu_1 X_1; \mu_2[\tilde{X}(t), t] = \mu_2 X_2;$$
$$\sigma_1[\tilde{X}(t), t] = \sigma_1 X_1; \sigma_2[\tilde{X}(t), t] = \sigma_2 X_2$$

where $\tilde{X}(t)$ is (X_1, X_2). Then

$$df[X_1, X_2, t] = \left[\frac{\partial f}{\partial X_1} \mu_1 X_1 + \frac{\partial f}{\partial X_2} \mu_2 X_2 + \frac{\partial f}{\partial t} + \frac{\partial^2 f}{\partial X_1 \partial X_2} \sigma_1 \sigma_2 \rho_{12} X_1 X_2 \right.$$
$$\left. + \frac{1}{2} \frac{\partial^2 f}{\partial X_1^2} \sigma_1^2 X_1^2 + \frac{1}{2} \frac{\partial^2 f}{\partial X_2^2} \sigma_2^2 X_2^2 \right] dt \tag{4.125}$$
$$+ \frac{\partial f}{\partial X_1} \sigma_1 X_1 dW_1 + \frac{\partial f}{\partial X_2} \sigma_2 X_2 dW_2$$

Example 4.4.10: The Foreign Currency Price of An Asset. We want to identify the stochastic process followed by, say, the U.S. dollar price of a British asset. If X_1 and X_2, defined respectively as the asset price in

British pounds and the exchange rate (measured as the number of U.S. dollars per British pound), obey the following processes:

$$\frac{dX_1}{X_1} = \mu_1 dt + \sigma_1 dW_1$$

and

$$\frac{dX_2}{X_2} = \mu_2 dt + \sigma_2 dW_2$$

with

$$dW_1 dW_2 = \rho_{12} dt$$

We designate by $Y \equiv f(X_1, X_2) = X_1 X_2$ the U.S. dollar price of the British asset. Then we can use equation (4.125) with

$$\frac{\partial f}{\partial X_1} = X_2; \frac{\partial f}{\partial X_2} = X_1; \frac{\partial f}{\partial t} = 0; \frac{\partial^2 f}{\partial X_1 \partial X_2} = 1; \frac{\partial^2 f}{\partial X_1^2} = \frac{\partial^2 f}{\partial X_2^2} = 0$$

to get the process followed by Y:

$$\frac{dY}{Y} = (\mu_1 + \mu_2 + \rho_{12}\sigma_1\sigma_2)dt + \sigma_1 dW_1 + \sigma_2 dW_2$$

The process for Y can also be expressed as a function of a single Wiener process W:

$$\frac{dY}{Y} = (\mu_1 + \mu_2 + \rho_{12}\sigma_1\sigma_2)dt + \sqrt{\sigma_1^2 + \sigma_2^2 + 2\rho_{12}\sigma_1\sigma_2}\,dW \quad (4.126)$$

with dW defined as

$$dW = \frac{\sigma_1 dW_1 + \sigma_2 dW_2}{\sqrt{\sigma_1^2 + \sigma_2^2 + 2\rho_{12}\sigma_1\sigma_2}} \quad (4.127)$$

The reader can easily verify that the moments of dW, as defined above, are indeed the moments of a standard Wiener process ($E(dW) = 0$; $E[dW^2] = dt$).

4.5 MEAN-REVERTING PROCESSES

4.5.1 Introduction

In Section 4.3 on a geometric Brownian motion, we saw that the variance of returns would explode to infinity over long time horizons. This might not square with our intuitive grasp of asset returns in the long run. Indeed, the optimists among us like to think that some inherent stability in financial markets keeps the variance of long-term returns away from infinity. This stability can be modeled like a force pulling asset returns back to some mean whenever they deviate from it. This is the so-called mean-reversion phenomenon. This idea is just one example among many that depart from the traditional Brownian motion model. There are a host of "exotic" phenomena related to asset return dynamics that have been described, documented, or conjectured. Hence the need for competing random processes – the subject of Sections 4.5 and 4.6 – to describe these alternative phenomena. In Section 4.5, we illustrate the mean-reversion idea with two processes – both of which turn out to be helpful when we discuss interest rates. See Chapter 3 for an illustration. These processes, called the *Ornstein-Uhlenbeck process* and the *square-root process*, will be presented in turn.

4.5.2 The Ornstein-Uhlenbeck Process

A variable $X(t)$ is said to follow an Ornstein-Uhlenbeck process[23] when

$$dX(t) = k[\theta - X(t)]dt + \sigma dW(t) \qquad (4.128)$$

subject to $X(0) = x_0$ and $k \geq 0$. Equation (4.128) describes a motion for $X(t)$ that gets pulled back with "speed" k toward a long-term mean value θ whenever $X(t)$ deviates from θ. To obtain the integral version of (4.128), note, by Itô's lemma, that

$$d(Xe^{kt}) = e^{kt}(k\theta dt + \sigma dW)$$

---

[23] This is a "rescaled" version of the Ornstein-Uhlenbeck process. What is usually referred to as the Ornstein-Uhlenbeck process is (4.128) with $\theta = 0$.

Integrating both sides

$$\int_0^t d(Xe^{ks}) = \int_0^t e^{ks}(k\theta \, ds + \sigma \, dW(s))$$

we get an explicit solution for $X(t)$

$$X(t) = \theta + (x_0 - \theta)e^{-kt} + \sigma \int_0^t e^{-k(t-s)} dW(s) \qquad (4.129)$$

Note that $\mathbb{E}_0 \int_0^t e^{-k(t-s)} dW = 0$. The expectation of $X(t)$ at time zero is therefore

$$\mathbb{E}[X(t)] = \theta + (x_0 - \theta)e^{-kt} \qquad (4.130)$$

and the variance at time zero is

$$Var[X(t)] = \mathbb{E}\{X(t) - \mathbb{E}[X(t)]\}^2 \qquad (4.131)$$

$$= \sigma^2 \mathbb{E}\left\{ \int_0^t e^{-k(t-s)} dW(s) \right\}^2$$

$$= \sigma^2 \int_0^t \mathbb{E}\{e^{-k(t-s)} dW(s)\}^2$$

$$= \sigma^2 \int_0^t e^{-2k(t-s)} ds$$

$$= \frac{\sigma^2(1 - e^{-2kt})}{2k}$$

From (4.129), it can be seen that $X(t)$ follows a normal distribution.[24] The distribution of $X(t)$ is

$$\Pr\left(X(t) \le x\right) = \int_{-\infty}^x \frac{1}{\sqrt{2\pi \, Var(X(t))}} \exp\left[-\frac{X(t) - \mathbb{E}[X(t)]}{2Var(X(t))} \right] dX(t)$$

$$(4.132)$$

4.5.3 Calculations of Moments with the Dynkin Operator

We explore below an alternative technique to calculate the moments of an Itô process. This technique makes use of the so-called Dynkin

---

[24] You can think of an integral as the limit of a sum. In the case at hand, $X(t)$ is the sum of normal terms: Indeed, each term ΔW is normal and multiplied by a deterministic factor (the exponential term). The product is therefore normal. The sum of normal variables is in turn a normal variable.

operator, which is defined as:

$$D(X(t)) \equiv \frac{d}{dt}\mathbb{E}(X(t)) \qquad (4.133)$$

To see how the expectation and variance of $X(t)$ can be obtained, consider the Ornstein-Uhlenbeck process:

$$dX = k(\theta - X)dt + \sigma dW$$

Because

$$\frac{\mathbb{E}(dX(t))}{dt} = \frac{d\mathbb{E}(X(t))}{dt}$$

it follows that

$$\frac{d\mathbb{E}(X(t))}{dt} = k\theta - k\mathbb{E}(X(t)) \qquad (4.134)$$

This is a simple differential equation which can be solved subject to the boundary condition, $\mathbb{E}(X(0)) = x_0$, to get

$$\mathbb{E}(X(t)) = \theta + (x_0 - \theta)e^{-kt}$$

We have therefore obtained the same result as in (4.130). To calculate the variance of $x(t)$, we first compute the second moment of X, $\mathbb{E}(X^2)$ from Itô's lemma:

$$dX^2 = 2X[k(\theta - X)dt + \sigma dW] + \sigma^2 dt$$

and, as before,

$$\frac{d\mathbb{E}(X^2)}{dt} = 2k\theta\mathbb{E}(X) - 2k\mathbb{E}(X^2) + \sigma^2$$

The differential equation is therefore

$$\frac{d\mathbb{E}(X^2)}{dt} = -2k\mathbb{E}(X^2) + 2k\theta^2 + 2k\theta(x_0 - \theta)e^{-kt} + \sigma^2 \qquad (4.135)$$

subject to: $\mathbb{E}\left(X^2(0)\right) = x_0^2$. The solution is

$$\mathbb{E}(X^2) = \frac{\sigma^2(1 - e^{-2kt})}{2k} + \theta^2 + (x_0 - \theta)^2 e^{-2kt} + 2\theta(x_0 - \theta)e^{-kt}$$

The variance of $X(t)$ follows:

$$Var(X(t)) = \mathbb{E}(X^2) - (\mathbb{E}(X))^2 = \frac{\sigma^2\left(1 - e^{-2kt}\right)}{2k} \qquad (4.136)$$

as in equation (4.131).

4.5.4 The Square-Root Process

The square-root process is written as

$$dX(t) = k\left[\theta - X(t)\right]dt + \sigma\sqrt{X(t)}dW(t) \qquad (4.137)$$

The process is defined for positive values of X, when $k > 0$, the drift term $k\left[\theta - X(t)\right]dt \gtrless 0$ if $X(t) \lessgtr \theta$: There is a tendency for $X(t)$ to revert to θ at a speed k.

We make use of the Dynkin operator to calculate the mean and variance of $X(t)$, conditional on information at time zero. As in the Ornstein-Uhlenbeck process:

$$\mathbb{E}(dX(t)) = k\left[\theta - X(t)\right]dt$$

and

$$\frac{d\mathbb{E}(X(t))}{dt} = k\theta - k\mathbb{E}\left(X(t)\right)$$

subject to $\mathbb{E}(X(0)) = x_0$ The expectation is therefore

$$\mathbb{E}\left(X(t)\right) = \theta + (x_0 - \theta)e^{-kt} \qquad (4.138)$$

As before, we need an expression of dX^2 to infer the second moment and the variance of $X(t)$:

$$dX^2 = 2X\left[k(\theta - X)dt + \sigma\sqrt{X}dW\right] + \sigma^2 X dt \qquad (4.139)$$

From (4.139),

$$\frac{d\mathbb{E}(X^2)}{dt} = (2k\theta + \sigma^2)\mathbb{E}(X) - 2k\mathbb{E}(X^2) \qquad (4.140)$$

subject to $\mathbb{E}(X(0)^2) = x_0^2$ combining (4.138) and (4.140), and solving the differential equation, we find

$$\mathbb{E}\left(X(t)^2\right) = x_0 e^{-2kt} + x_0\left(\frac{\sigma^2}{k} + 2\theta\right)\left(e^{-kt} - e^{-2kt}\right) \qquad (4.141)$$

$$+ \left(\frac{\theta\sigma^2}{2k} + \theta^2\right)\left(1 - e^{-kt}\right)^2$$

and

$$Var\left[X(t)^2\right] = \mathbb{E}\left[X(t)^2\right] - \left\{\mathbb{E}\left[X(t)\right]\right\}^2 \qquad (4.142)$$

$$= \frac{x_0\sigma^2}{k}(e^{-kt} - e^{-2kt}) + \frac{\theta\sigma^2}{2k}(1 - e^{-kt})^2$$

It turns out[25] that the probability density function of $X(t)$, conditional on $X(0) = x_0$, is

$$f(X(t), t; x_0, 0) = ce^{-(u+v)} \left(\frac{v}{u}\right)^{\frac{q}{2}} I_q\left(2\sqrt{uv}\right) \tag{4.143}$$

where

$$c \equiv \frac{2k}{\sigma^2 \left(1 - e^{-kt}\right)}$$

$$u \equiv cx_0 e^{-kt}$$

$$v \equiv cX(t)$$

$$q \equiv \frac{2k\theta}{\sigma^2} - 1$$

and

$$I_q(y) \equiv \left(\frac{y}{2}\right)^q \sum_{n=0}^{q} \frac{\left(\frac{y}{2}\right)^{2n}}{n!\,\Gamma(q+n+1)} \tag{4.144}$$

with the gamma function Γ defined as

$$\Gamma(q+n+1) \equiv \int_0^\infty u^{(q+n+1)}e^{-u}du \tag{4.145}$$

4.6 JUMP PROCESS

4.6.1 Pure Jumps

We characterize a jump or Poisson process by the number of occurrences $q(t)$ at time t of a counting process. Events are expected to occur singly and at an average rate of λ per unit time. The increments of the process $q(t + n\Delta t) - q(t + (n-1)\Delta t), \ldots, q(t + \Delta t) - q(t)$ are independent. The process starts at $q(0) = 0$ and jumps are expected at a rate, or probability, $\lambda \Delta t$ in a short interval $(t, t + \Delta t)$. We can define the Poisson process by

$$q(0) = 0$$

$$\Pr(q(t + \Delta t) - q(t) = 0) = 1 - \lambda \Delta t + o(\Delta t) \tag{4.146}$$

---

[25] See Cox, Ingersoll, and Ross (1985).

$$\Pr(q\,(t + \Delta t) - q\,(t) = 1) = \lambda \Delta t + o\,(\Delta t) \qquad (4.147)$$

$$\Pr(q\,(t + \Delta t) - q\,(t) > 1) = o(\Delta t) \qquad (4.148)$$

and, as outlined above, independent increments. This is called a Poisson process with intensity or rate parameter λ. We now seek to determine the probability distribution of $q\,(t)$. Define

$$P_n\,(t) \equiv \Pr\,(q\,(t) = n)$$

Then, from (4.146)–(4.148) and the property of independent increments

$$P_n\,(t + \Delta t) = P_n\,(t)\,(1 - \lambda \Delta t + o\,(\Delta t)) + P_{n-1}(t)\lambda \Delta t + P_{n-2}(t)o\,(\Delta t) \qquad (4.149)$$

Equation (4.149) implies that

$$\lim_{\Delta t \to 0} \frac{P_n\,(t + \Delta t) - P_n\,(t)}{\Delta t} = \frac{P_{n-1}(t)\lambda \Delta t - P_n\,(t)\,\lambda \Delta t}{\Delta t}$$

or, equivalently,

$$P_n'(t) = -\lambda P_n(t) + \lambda P_{n-1}(t) \qquad (4.150)$$

When $n = 0$, $P_{-1}(t) = 0$ and (4.150) becomes

$$P_0'(t) = -\lambda P_0(t) \qquad (4.151)$$

subject to: $P_0\,(0) = 1$. The solution to this equation is

$$P_0(t) = e^{-\lambda t} \qquad (4.152)$$

When $n > 0$, we can show inductively that the solution is

$$P_n(t) = \frac{e^{-\lambda t}(\lambda t)^n}{n!} \qquad (4.153)$$

Indeed, from (4.150)

$$e^{\lambda t}\,(P_n'(t) + \lambda P_n(t)) = \lambda e^{\lambda t} P_{n-1}(t)$$

But $\qquad\qquad e^{\lambda t}\,(P_n'(t) + \lambda P_n(t)) = \dfrac{d\,(e^{\lambda t} P_n\,(t))}{dt}$

and $P_{n-1}(t)$ is assumed to equal $\frac{e^{-\lambda t}(\lambda t)^{n-1}}{(n-1)!}$. We can integrate both sides of the equation above to get

$$\int \frac{d\left(e^{\lambda t} P_n(t)\right)}{dt} dt = \int \frac{\lambda^n t^{n-1}}{(n-1)!} dt$$

or

$$P_n(t) = \frac{e^{-\lambda t}(\lambda t)^n}{n!} + K$$

subject to $P_n(0) = 0$, which implies that $K = 0$. We have therefore shown by induction equation (4.153).

4.6.2 Time Between Two Jumps

We are now interested in the probability density function of the time to the first jump. We call this period of time T_1. Then

$$\Pr(t < T_1 < t = \Delta t) = \Pr(\text{no jump in } (0, t))$$
$$\times \Pr(\text{one jump in } (t, t + \Delta t)) + o(\Delta t)$$

$$= P_0(t) \lambda \Delta t + o(\Delta t)$$
$$= e^{-\lambda t} \lambda \Delta t + o(\Delta t)$$

The probability density function of T_1 is

$$f_{T_1}(t) = \lim_{\Delta t \to 0} \frac{e^{-\lambda t} \lambda \Delta t + o(\Delta t)}{\Delta t} = \lambda e^{-\lambda t} \tag{4.154}$$

More generally, if T_n is the time it takes to reach the nth jump,

$$\Pr(t < T_n < t + \Delta t) = P_{n-1}(t) \lambda \Delta t + o(\Delta t)$$

Therefore, the probability density function of T_n is

$$f_{T_n}(t) = \frac{e^{-\lambda t}(\lambda t)^{n-1}}{(n-1)!} \lambda \tag{4.155}$$

Note that the moment generating function of T_1 is

$$\mathbb{E}\left(e^{-\theta T_1}\right) = \int_0^\infty \lambda e^{-\lambda t} e^{-\theta t} dt = \frac{\lambda}{\lambda + \theta} \tag{4.156}$$

Because of the independence of increments of a Poisson process, the moment generating function of T_n is

$$\mathbb{E}\left(e^{-\theta T_n}\right) = \left\{\mathbb{E}\left(e^{-\theta T_1}\right)\right\}^n = \left(\frac{\lambda}{\lambda + \theta}\right)^n \qquad (4.157)$$

From the properties of a moment generating function, we can infer

$$\mathbb{E}(T_n) = \frac{n}{\lambda} \text{ and } Var(T_n) = \frac{n}{\lambda^2} \qquad (4.158)$$

Example 4.6.1. A Poisson process has a parameter $\lambda = 0.5$. What is the probability of three jumps exactly occurring over the next four periods? We use (4.153) to compute:

$$P_3(4) = \frac{e^{-(0.5 \times 4)}(0.5 \times 4)^3}{3!} \approx 18\%$$

Example 4.6.2. T_3 designates the time till the third jump for a Poisson process with parameter $\lambda = 0.1$. What are the expectation and variance of T_3? From (4.158),

$$\mathbb{E}(T_3) = \frac{3}{0.1} = 30$$

and

$$Var(T_3) = \frac{3}{0.01} = 300$$

4.6.3 Jump Diffusions

If we define

$$dq(t) \equiv q(t + \Delta t) - q(t)$$

with related probabilities stated in equations (4.146)–(4.148), we can describe a jump-diffusion process by

$$dX(t) = \mu(X, t) \, dt + \sigma(X, t) \, dW(t) + J(X, t) \, dq(t) \qquad (4.159)$$

where J is the size of the jump and is a random variable. When J is nonzero, the process is no longer continuous. In financial markets, jump components generally describe sudden news or events such as Fed intervention or unforeseen currency devaluations. In practice, it is often difficult to decide whether a movement in an asset price is a jump or an emanation of a smooth diffusion process.

4.6.4 Itô's Lemma for Jump Diffusions

Recall that, in the diffusion case, that is, in equation (4.159) with $J = 0$, for a function $f(X, t)$, Itô's lemma is written as

$$df = \left(\frac{\partial f}{\partial X} \mu(X, t) + \frac{\partial f}{\partial t} + \frac{1}{2} \frac{\partial^2 f}{\partial X^2} \sigma^2(X, t) \right) dt + \frac{\partial f}{\partial X} \sigma(X, t) dW$$

The expectations version of the equation above is

$$\mathbb{E}(df) = \left(\frac{\partial f}{\partial X} \mu(X, t) + \frac{\partial f}{\partial t} + \frac{1}{2} \frac{\partial^2 f}{\partial X^2} \sigma^2(X, t) \right) dt$$

In the jump diffusion case ($J \neq 0$), the contribution of the jump term to $\mathbb{E}(df)$ is

$$\lambda dt \mathbb{E}_J (f(X + J, t) - f(X, t)) + (1 - \lambda dt) \times 0 + o(dt)$$

where $\mathbb{E}_J$ is the expectation operator with respect to the jump size $J(X, t)$. The expectations version for jump diffusions as defined by (4.159) is therefore

$$\mathbb{E}(df) = \left[\frac{\partial f}{\partial X} \mu(X, t) + \frac{\partial f}{\partial t} + \frac{1}{2} \frac{\partial^2 f}{\partial X^2} \sigma^2(X, t) \right. \qquad (4.160)$$
$$\left. + \lambda \mathbb{E}_J (f(X + J, t) - f(X, t)) \right] dt$$

When J is constant, equation (4.161) becomes

$$\mathbb{E}(df) = \left[\frac{\partial f}{\partial X} \mu(x, t) + \frac{\partial f}{\partial t} + \frac{1}{2} \frac{\partial^2 f}{\partial X^2} \sigma^2(X, t) \right. \qquad (4.161)$$
$$\left. + \lambda (f(X + J, t) - f(X, t)) \right] dt$$

We now state without proof Itô's lemma for jump diffusions:

$$df = \left[\frac{\partial f}{\partial X} \mu(X, t) + \frac{\partial f}{\partial t} + \frac{1}{2} \frac{\partial^2 f}{\partial X^2} \sigma^2(X, t) \right. \qquad (4.162)$$
$$\left. + \lambda (f(X + J, t) - f(X, t)) \right] dt + \frac{\partial f}{\partial X} \sigma(X, t) dW$$

Example 4.6.3. Consider a mixed square-root-jump process of the form

$$dX(t) = k\left[\theta - X(t)\right]dt + \sigma\sqrt{X(t)}dW(t) + J\,dq(t)$$

Define $f \equiv f(X, t)$. What is $df(X, t)$? This is a direct application of equation (4.162):

$$df = \left[\frac{\partial f}{\partial X}k\,(\theta - X) + \frac{\partial f}{\partial t} + \frac{1}{2}\frac{\partial^2 f}{\partial X^2}\sigma^2 X\right.$$
$$\left. + \lambda\,(f(X+J, t) - f(X, t))\right]dt + \frac{\partial f}{\partial X}\sigma\,X\,dW$$

4.7 KOLMOGOROV EQUATIONS

We shall now derive a set of equations called the Kolmogorov forward and backward equations that will allow us to infer the probability density functions associated with specific diffusion processes. This should enable us, for example, to calculate from first principles the probability density function of a simple arithmetic Brownian motion, of an Ornstein-Uhlenbeck process, or of a Brownian motion with absorbing barriers.

4.7.1 The Kolmogorov Forward Equation

We go back to the discrete model developed in the second section of this chapter. Recall that the variable under consideration was allowed to move by $+\Delta x$ with probability p and by $-\Delta x$ with probability q. To calibrate the discrete model to a Brownian motion with mean μt and standard deviation $\sigma\sqrt{t}$, we found

$$p = \frac{1}{2} + \frac{\mu\sqrt{\Delta t}}{2\sigma} \tag{4.163}$$

$$q = \frac{1}{2} - \frac{\mu\sqrt{\Delta t}}{2\sigma}$$

$$\Delta x = \sigma\sqrt{\Delta t}$$

If we call $p\,(x, t, x_0)\,\Delta x$ the probability of reaching x at time t given that we started at x_0 at time zero, then the discrete version of the forward equation is

$$p(x, t, x_0) = pp(x - \Delta x, t - \Delta t, x_0) + qp(x + \Delta x, t - \Delta t, x_0)$$
$$(4.164)$$

Expanding (4.164) up to $o(\Delta t)$ terms:

$$p(x, t, x_0) = p\left[p(x, t, x_0) - \Delta x \frac{\partial p}{\partial x}(x, t, x_0) - \Delta t \frac{\partial p}{\partial t}(x, t, x_0) \right.$$
$$\left. + \frac{1}{2}(\Delta x)^2 \frac{\partial^2 p(x, t, x_0)}{\partial x^2} + o(\Delta t) \right]$$
$$+ q\left[p(x, t, x_0) + \Delta x \frac{\partial p}{\partial x}(x, t, x_0) - \Delta t \frac{\partial p}{\partial t}(x, t, x_0) \right.$$
$$\left. + \frac{1}{2}(\Delta x)^2 \frac{\partial^2 p}{\partial x^2}(x, t, x_0) + o(\Delta t) \right] \quad (4.165)$$

Replacing p, q, and Δx by their values, we obtain the continuous-time version of the Kolmogorov forward equation:

$$\frac{1}{2}\sigma^2 \frac{\partial^2 p}{\partial x^2}(x, t, x_0) - \frac{\partial p}{\partial t}(x, t, x_0) - \mu \frac{\partial p}{\partial x}(x, t, x_0) = 0 \quad (4.166)$$

This is called a *partial differential equation* – a topic we shall discuss in a later section. To solve for the probability density function $p(x, t, x_0)$, we need boundary conditions. One such condition is

$$p(x, 0, x_0) = \delta(x - x_0) \quad (4.167)$$

which means that at $t = 0$, $x = x_0$ with probability 1. We therefore equate the initial probability density function to $\delta(x - x_0)$, also called a *Dirac delta function*. This function is infinitely large at point x_0 and zero elsewhere. It always satisfies

$$\int_{-\infty}^{\infty} \delta(x - x_0)\, dx = 1$$

More generally, it can be proved that if μ and σ are functions of x and t, then $p(x, t, x_0)$ will obey the following Kolmogorov forward equation:

$$\frac{1}{2}\frac{\partial^2 [\sigma^2(x, t)\, p(x, t, x_0)]}{\partial x^2} - \frac{\partial p(x, t, x_0)}{\partial t} - \frac{\partial [\mu(x, t)\, p(x, t, x_0)]}{\partial x} = 0$$
$$(4.168)$$

4.7.2 The Dirac Delta Function

The Dirac delta is not really a function in the true sense of the word. Rather, it is a distribution which is defined through the relation

$$\int_{-\infty}^{\infty} \delta(x - x_0) f(x)\, dx = f(x_0)$$

However, we can think of the Dirac delta as a limit of a probability density function. The two properties of the Dirac delta that we will use are

$$\delta(x) = 0 \text{ for } x \neq 0$$

and

$$\int_{-\infty}^{\infty} \delta(x)\, dx = 1$$

which follows directly from the definition. If $q(t, x)$ denotes the normal density function with mean μt and variance $\sigma^2 t$

$$q(t, x) = \frac{1}{\sqrt{2\pi\sigma^2 t}} e^{-(x-\mu t)^2/2\sigma^2 t}$$

then we know that as $\sigma \to 0$, the density function becomes small outside a narrow interval, while still integrating to 1.

4.7.3 The Kolmogorov Backward Equation

The discrete version of the backward equation, that is, the "backward equivalent" of equation (4.164), is

$$p(x, t + \Delta t, x_0) = pp(x, t, x_0 + \Delta x) + qp(x, t, x_0 - \Delta x) \qquad (4.169)$$

We expand (4.169) up to $o(\Delta t)$ terms to get

$$p(x, t, x_0) + \frac{\partial p(x, t, x_0)}{\partial t}$$
$$= p\left[p(x, t, x_0) + \frac{\partial p(x, t, x_0)}{\partial x_0} \Delta x + \frac{1}{2} \frac{\partial^2 p(x, t, x_0)}{\partial x_0^2} (\Delta x)^2 + o(\Delta x) \right]$$
$$+ q\left[p(x, t, x_0) - \frac{\partial p(x, t, x_0)}{\partial x_0} \Delta x + \frac{1}{2} \frac{\partial^2 p(x, t, x_0)}{\partial x_0^2} (\Delta x)^2 + o(\Delta t) \right]$$

$$(4.170)$$

Plugging in the values of p, q, and Δx, we can write the continuous-time version of the Kolmogorov backward equation

$$\frac{1}{2}\sigma^2 \frac{\partial^2 p(x, t, x_0)}{\partial x_0^2} - \frac{\partial p(x, t, x_0)}{\partial t} + \frac{\mu \partial p(x, t, x_0)}{\partial x_0} = 0 \qquad (4.171)$$

As in the forward equation case, the backward equation can be generalized to processes where μ and σ are the functions of x and t. The general form of the backward equation can be written as

$$\frac{1}{2}\sigma^2(x_0, 0) \frac{\partial p^2(x, t, x_0)}{\partial x_0^2} - \frac{\partial p(x, t, x_0)}{\partial t} + \frac{\mu(x_0, 0) \partial p(x, t, x_0)}{\partial x_0} = 0$$

$$(4.172)$$

Example 4.7.1. Show that the probability density function

$$p(x, t, x_0) = \frac{1}{\sigma\sqrt{2\pi t}} \exp\left[-\frac{(x - x_0 - \mu t)^2}{2\sigma^2 t}\right] \qquad (4.173)$$

is the solution of the Kolmogorov forward equation (4.166) with boundary condition (4.167). To check the solution, we first compute the relevant derivatives:

$$\frac{\partial p(x, t, x_0)}{\partial x} = -\frac{(x - x_0 - \mu t)}{\sigma^2 t} p(x, t, x_0)$$

$$\frac{\partial^2 p(x, t, x_0)}{\partial x^2} = \frac{(x - x_0 - \mu t)^2}{(\sigma^2 t)^2} p(x, t, x_0) - \frac{p(x, t, x_0)}{\sigma^2 t}$$

$$\frac{\partial p(x, t, x_0)}{\partial t} = -\frac{p(x, t, x_0)}{2t} - p(x, t, x_0)$$
$$\times \frac{2(x - x_0 - \mu t)(-2\mu\sigma^2 t) - 2\sigma^2(x - x_0 - \mu t)^2}{(2\sigma^2 t)^2}$$

Replacing the derivatives by their values in (4.166), the result is straightforward. Indeed

$$
0 = \frac{1}{2}\sigma^2 \left[\frac{(x - x_0 - \mu t)^2}{(\sigma^2 t)^2} p(x, t, x_0) - \frac{p(x, t, x_0)}{\sigma^2 t} \right]
$$

$$
+ \left[\frac{p(x, t, x_0)}{2t} + p(x, t, x_0) \right.
$$

$$
\left. \times \frac{2(x - x_0 - \mu t)(-2\mu\sigma^2 t) - 2\sigma^2 (x - x_0 - \mu t)^2}{(2\sigma^2 t)^2} \right]
$$

$$
+ \mu p(x, t, x_0) \frac{(x - x_0 - \mu t)}{\sigma^2 t}
$$

Example 4.7.2. Show that the probability density function

$$
p(x, t, x_0) = \frac{1}{\sigma\sqrt{2\pi t}} \exp \left[\frac{-(x - x_0 - \mu t)^2}{2\sigma^2 t} \right] \tag{4.174}
$$

is the solution of the Kolmogorov backward equation (4.171) with boundary condition (4.167). As in the previous example, we compute the derivatives:

$$
\frac{\partial p(x, t, x_0)}{\partial x_0} = \frac{(x - x_0 - \mu t)}{\sigma^2 t} p(x, t, x_0)
$$

$$
\frac{\partial p^2(x, t, x_0)}{\partial x_0^2} = \frac{p(x, t, x_0)(x - x_0 - \mu t)^2}{(\sigma^2 t)^2} - \frac{p(x, t, x_0)}{\sigma^2 t}
$$

$$
\frac{\partial p(x, t, x_0)}{\partial t} = -\frac{p(x, t, x_0)}{2t} - p(x, t, x_0)
$$

$$
\times \frac{2(x - x_0 - \mu t)(-2\mu\sigma^2 t) - 2\sigma^2 (x - x_0 - \mu t)^2}{2(\sigma^2 t)^2}
$$

By plugging the above values into equation (4.171), it is easy to check the following result:

$$
0 = \frac{1}{2}\sigma^2 \left[\frac{p(x, t, x_0)(x - x_0 - \mu t)^2}{(\sigma^2 t)^2} - \frac{p(x, t, x_0)}{\sigma^2 t} \right] + \left[\frac{p(x, t, x_0)}{2t} \right.
$$

$$
\left. + p(x, t, x_0) \frac{2(x - x_0 - \mu t)(-2\mu\sigma^2 t) - 2\sigma^2 (x - x_0 - \mu t)^2}{(2\sigma^2 t)^2} \right]
$$

$$
+ \mu p(x, t, x_0) \frac{(x - x_0 - \mu t)}{\sigma^2 t}
$$

Example 4.7.3. We want to obtain the probability density function for a Brownian motion with an absorbing barrier at $x = b < \infty$.
We can solve the forward equation

$$\frac{1}{2}\sigma^2 \frac{\partial^2 p(x, t, x_0)}{\partial x^2} - \frac{\partial p(x, t, x_0)}{\partial t} - \frac{\mu \partial p(x, t, x_0)}{\partial x} = 0$$

subject to the boundary conditions

$$p(x, t, x_0) = \delta(x - x_0)$$

and

$$p(b, t, x_0) = 0$$

The reader can check the solution:

$$p(x, t, x_0) = \frac{1}{\sigma\sqrt{2\pi t}} \left[\exp\left\{ \frac{-(x - x_0 - \mu t)^2}{2\sigma^2 t} \right\} - \exp\left\{ \frac{2\mu(b - x_0)}{\sigma^2} \right\} \right.$$

$$\left. \times \exp\left\{ \frac{-(x - 2b + x_0 - \mu t)^2}{2\sigma^2 t} \right\} \right] \tag{4.175}$$

4.8 MARTINGALES

4.8.1 Definitions and Examples

A random process $\{M_n : n \geq 1\}$ is a martingale if $\mathbb{E}[M_n]$ is finite for all n and if

$$\mathbb{E}[M_{n+t} | M_0, M_1, \dots, M_n] = M_n \tag{4.176}$$

In words, today's observation of the process is an unbiased estimator of future values of M. If

$$\mathbb{E}[M_{n+t} | M_0, M_1, \dots, M_n] \geq M_n \tag{4.177}$$

then $\{M_n : n \geq 1\}$ is called a *submartingale*. It is a supermartingale if

$$\mathbb{E}[M_{n+t} | M_0, M_1, \dots, M_n] \leq M_n \tag{4.178}$$

The above definitions hold for a discrete process M. We can similarly define a continuous-time martingale M as a process where $\mathbb{E}(M_t)$ is finite for all t and

$$\mathbb{E}_t[M_T] = \mathbb{E}[M_T|\mathcal{F}_t] = M_t \qquad (4.179)$$

where $\mathcal{F}_t$ is, loosely speaking, all the information accumulated till time t.

Example 4.8.1. As in Section 4.1, consider a random walk where

$$M_n = Z_1 + Z_2 + \ldots, +Z_n$$

$M(t)$ is the sum of random variables Z_i that take the values $\Delta X > 0$ and $-\Delta X$ with probability p and q, respectively. Hence, $E(Z_i) = (p - q)\,\Delta X$. The conditional expectation of M_{n+1}, is

$$\mathbb{E}(M_{n+1}|M_0, M_1, \ldots, M_n) = \mathbb{E}(M_n|M_0, \ldots, M_n) + \mathbb{E}(Z_{n+1}|M_0, \ldots, M_n)$$
$$= M_n + (p - q)\,\Delta X \qquad (4.180)$$

The sequence $[M_n - n(p - q)\,\Delta X]$ is a martingale since

$$\mathbb{E}[M_{n+1} - (n + 1)(p - q)\,\Delta X|M_0, \ldots, M_n] = M_n - n(p - q)\,\Delta X$$
$$(4.181)$$

This follows directly from (4.180). Evidently, if $p = q = 1/2$, then M_n is a submartingale. If $p > q$, M_n is a submartingale. If $p < q$, M_n is a supermartingale.

Example 4.8.2. Consider the sequence M_n defined by

$$M_n = Z_1 Z_2 \ldots Z_n$$

where

$$\mathbb{E}(Z_i) = 1$$

Then

$$\mathbb{E}_n[M_{n+1}] = \mathbb{E}_n[M_n Z_{n+1}]$$
$$= M_n \mathbb{E}_n[Z_{n+1}]$$
$$= M_n$$

It follows that M_n is a martingale.

Example 4.8.3. An asset price S follows a geometric Brownian motion:

$$\frac{dS}{S} = \mu dt + \sigma dW$$

Recall that, under these circumstances

$$\mathbb{E}_t [S_T] = S_t e^{\mu(T-t)}$$

We conclude that $S_t e^{-\mu(T-t)}$ follows a martingale because

$$\mathbb{E}_t \left[S_T e^{-\mu(T-t)} \right] = S_t$$

This is not surprising since the increments are driven by a Brownian motion, which is a martingale. If the Brownian motion is driftless ($\mu = 0$), then the asset price S_t is a martingale.

4.8.2 Some Useful Facts About Martingales

Prior to enumerating a few results of martingale theory, we define a stopping time: a *stopping time T* is a positive random variable that indicates the end of a game or of a procedure. For example, a gambler may decide to play until she is ruined. We now state without proof three theorems involving martingales and show related applications.

- OPTIONAL SAMPLING THEOREM: M_n is a martingale ($n = 0, 1, \ldots$) and T is a stopping time. If T is bounded, then under quite general conditions

$$\mathbb{E}(M_T) = \mathbb{E}(M_0) \qquad (4.182)$$

  In words, the optional sampling theorem states that no matter when a player decides to stop a fair game, her fortune when the game ends will equal on average her original fortune. This is the mathematical version of the "no free-lunch" principle.

- WALD'S EQUATION: If Z_i ($i = 1, 2 \ldots$) is a sequence of independent, identically distributed random variables with $\mathbb{E}(Z_i) = \mu < \infty$, if T is a finite stopping time, and if $\mathbb{E}(X_T)$ is finite with $X_T \equiv Z_1 + Z_2 + \cdots + Z_T$, then

$$\mathbb{E}(X_T) = \mu \mathbb{E}(T) \qquad (4.183)$$

- MARTINGALE CONVERGENCE THEOREM: If M_n is a martingale such that $\mathbb{E}[|M_n|]$ is finite for all n, then $\lim_{n\to\infty} M_n$ converges with probability one.

Example 4.8.4. We revisit the gambler's ruin problem discussed in the first section of this chapter. A gambler has k dollars to spend and will stop playing when he has N dollars or when he is penniless. At each play, he gains one dollar with probability $p\ \left(p \neq \frac{1}{2}\right)$ and loses one dollar with probability $q = 1 - p$. What is the expected stopping time (or expected number of plays) $E(T)$?

If X_T is the gambler's final fortune and P_w the probability of reaching N before zero, then

$$\mathbb{E}(X_T) = (N - k)P_w - k(1 - P_w) = NP_w - k \qquad (4.184)$$

But from Wald's equality (4.183),

$$\mathbb{E}(X_T) = (p - q)\mathbb{E}(T)$$

Therefore

$$\mathbb{E}(T) = \frac{NPw - k}{p - q}$$

where P_w is given by (see first section of this chapter)

$$P_w = \frac{1 - \left(\frac{q}{p}\right)^k}{1 - \left(\frac{q}{p}\right)^n}$$

4.8.3 Martingales and Brownian Motion

We shall establish that some Brownian motion expressions are martingales. We then use these results to discuss first-passage time results for Brownian motion. See Ross (1996) for a detailed explanation of these results.

Consider the three expressions:

$$M_1(t) = W(t) \qquad (4.185)$$

$$M_2(t) = W^2(t) - t \qquad (4.186)$$

$$M_3(t) = \exp\left(\lambda W(t) - \frac{1}{2}\lambda^2 t\right) \qquad (4.187)$$

We claim that these three expressions are martingales. We start with expression (4.185):

$$\mathbb{E}_s[W(t)] = \mathbb{E}_s[W(t) - W(s)] + \mathbb{E}_s[W(s)]$$
$$= 0 + W(s)$$
$$= W(s)$$

As for expression (4.186):

$$\mathbb{E}_s\left(W^2(t)\right) = \mathbb{E}_s\left[(W(t) - W(s) + W(s))^2\right]$$
$$= \mathbb{E}_s\left[(W(t) - W(s))^2\right] + 2\mathbb{E}_s\left[(W(t) - W(s))W(s)\right]$$
$$+ 2\mathbb{E}_s\left[W(s)^2\right]$$
$$= (t - s) + 2W(s) \times 0 + 2W(s)^2$$
$$= W^2(s) + (t - s)$$

Therefore

$$\mathbb{E}_s\left(W^2(t) - t\right) = W^2(s) - s$$

and $M_2(t)$ is a martingale.

The expectation of $M_3(t)$ is in turn:

$$\mathbb{E}_s\left[\exp\left(\lambda W(t) - \frac{1}{2}\lambda^2 t\right)\right]$$
$$= \mathbb{E}_s[\exp(\lambda W(t))] + \exp\left(-\frac{1}{2}\lambda^2(t - s)\right)$$

We know the moment generating function of a Wiener process from (4.29) with $\mu = 0$ and $\sigma = 1$ we have

$$\mathbb{E}_s[\exp(\lambda W(t))] = \exp\left\{\frac{1}{2}\lambda^2(t - s)\right\} \qquad (4.188)$$

which gives

$$\mathbb{E}_s(M_3(t)) = 1 \qquad (4.189)$$

But $M_3(s) = 1$. It follows that $M_3(t)$ is a martingale. Note that this result was derived using a different method in Example (4.4.9).

We can combine the above results with the optional sampling theorem (equation (4.182)) to calculate the moment generating function of the first passage time of a Brownian motion.

Example 4.8.5. We want to calculate the moment generating function of T_a where T_a is the first passage time of a Wiener process at point a. Formally

$$T_a = \min \{t > 0 : W(t) = a\}$$

from (4.188) and (4.189)

$$\mathbb{E}_0 (M_3 (t)) = \mathbb{E}_0 \{\exp \lambda W(t)\} \times \exp \left(-\frac{1}{2}\lambda^2 t\right)$$

But the optional sampling theorem implies

$$\mathbb{E}_0 (M_3 (T_a)) = \mathbb{E}_0 (M_3 (0)) = 1 \tag{4.190}$$

Because at $t = T_a$, $W(T_a) = a$, we have

$$\mathbb{E}_0 (M_3 (T_a)) = \mathbb{E}_0 \{\exp \lambda a\} \left\{\exp -\frac{1}{2}\lambda^2 T_a\right\} \tag{4.191}$$

Combining (4.190) and (4.191) and letting $\theta = \lambda^2/2$, we get the moment generating function of T_a:

$$\mathbb{E} [\exp (-\theta Ta)] = \exp \left(-a\sqrt{2\theta}\right) \tag{4.192}$$

Example 4.8.6. A Wiener process is at point x_0. What is the probability that it reaches point a before it reaches point b ($a < x < b$)? We define

$$T_a = \min \{t > 0 : W(t) = a\}$$

and

$$T_b = \min \{t > 0 : W(t) = b\}$$

It can be shown that $W(\min \{T_a, T_b\})$ is a martingale. We apply the *optional sampling theorem to get*

$$\mathbb{E}\left\{M_1\left(\min\left(T_a, T_b\right)\right)\right\} = \left\{M_1\left(0\right)\right\} = x_0 \qquad (4.193)$$

where $M_1(t) = W(t)$ from (4.185). We also have

$$\mathbb{E}\left\{M_1\left(\min\left(T_a, T_b\right)\right)\right\} = a \Pr\left(T_a < T_b\right) + b\left\{1 - \Pr\left(T_a < T_b\right)\right\})$$

Because the above is equal to x_0 from (4.193), we obtain directly the result:

$$\Pr\left(T_a < T_b\right) = \frac{x_0 - a}{b - a} \qquad (4.194)$$

4.9 DYNAMIC PROGRAMMING

4.9.1 The Traveling Salesman

To explain the intuition behind dynamic programming, it may be easiest to proceed by example. A traveling salesman wants to identify the shortest route from town 1 to town 7. The route network is pictured in Figure 4.3. In this example, the salesman must make three decisions to optimize his route. First, he must choose among towns 2, 3, and 4. Second, he must pick either of towns 5 or 6. Third, he must go to town 7 (a "nondecision" that we shall treat as a decision). One way to reach a solution is complete enumeration of all possible routes between 1

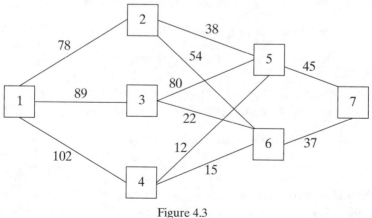

Figure 4.3

and 7 (in this case, a total of 6. You should realize, however, that the dimensionality of these problems can quickly get out of control).

The alternative way – the dynamic programming solution – is a partial enumeration of the routes. This partial enumeration follows the so-called Bellman's principle of optimality, which, in this case, states that the optimal route has the property that, whatever the initial town and the initial decisions are, the remaining decisions must constitute an optimal route with respect to the town resulting from the first decision.

Stated differently, if the optimal route from 1 to 7 were 1-3-6-7, then 3-6-7 would have to be the optimal route from 3 to 7. That is, 3-6-7 needs to be shorter than 3-5-7. Before reaching the 1-3-6-7 solution, we therefore must check the optimality of the 3-6-7 subsolution. You may have guessed that we should then proceed using backward induction. In mathematical parlance, the principle of optimality translates as

$$M_n(i) = \min_{j \in J(i)} \{D_{ij} + M_{n-1}(j)\} \qquad (4.195)$$

where $M_n(i)$ is the minimum distance to the final point given that the salesman is in town i and has to make n more decisions, D_{ij} is the distance from town i to j, $J(i)$ is the set of towns the salesman can choose from when in town i (for example $J(1) = 2, 3, 4$ and $J(4) = 5, 6$).

We are now ready to solve the problem recursively in these steps:

Step 1: $M_1(5) = 45 : M_1(6) = 37$

Step 2: $M_2(2) = \min_{j=5,6}(D_{2j} + M_1(j)) = \min(38 + 45, 54 + 37) = 83$

$M_2(3) = \min_{j=5,6}(D_{3j} + M_1(j)) = \min(80 + 45, 22 + 37) = 59$

$M_2(4) = \min_{j=5,6}(D_{4j} + M_1(j)) = \min(12 + 45, 15 + 37) = 52$

The optimal subsolutions corresponding respectively to $M_2(2)$, $M_2(3)$, and $M_2(4)$ are therefore 2-5-7, 3-6-7, and 4-6-7.

Step 3: $M_3(1) = \min_{j=2,3,4}(D_{1j} + M_2(j))$

$= \min\{78 + 83, 89 + 59, 102 + 52\} = 148$

The shortest route is 148 units long and corresponds to the 1-3-6-7 trajectory. The solution is 1-3-6-7. We have found it by rolling backward and using Bellman's principle of optimaltiy (equation 4.195) at every node. We now move to a stochastic, continuous-time world.

4.9.2 Optimal Control of Itô Processes: Finite Horizon

We consider the optimization problem

$$J(X, 0) = \max_y \mathbb{E}_0 \int_0^T f(X, t, y)\, dt + B(X(T), T) \qquad (4.196)$$

subject to the constraints

$$dX = \mu(X, t, y)\, dt + \sigma(X, t, y)\, dW \qquad (4.197)$$

and

$$X(0) = x_0 \qquad (4.198)$$

In words, an agent is maximizing the expected value of a function. This function comprises an integral term and a terminal value. You can, for example, think of the integral term as the present value of cash flows from a project and the $B(X(T), T)$ term as the terminal or salvage value of the project expressed in today's dollars. The agent's "instrument" in this maximization procedure is the variable y, generally called the *control variable*. To follow up on the project example, you can think of y as the amount to be invested at each point in time in order to maximize the value function. X is called the *state variable* and follows an Itô process (equation (4.197)). X could be any variable (or, if in vector form, any set of variables) influencing the value function. Finally $J(X_0, 0)$ is the optimal value function that the agent is seeking to attain in this control problem.[26]

Applying Bellman's principle of optimality to equation (4.196) valued at time t, we get

$$J(X, t) = \max_y \mathbb{E}_t \int_t^{t+\Delta t} f(X, s, y)\, ds + J(X + \Delta X, t + \Delta t) \quad (4.199)$$

Equation (4.199) says that at any time t, for the solution to be optimal, the subsolution needs to be optimal (and therefore deserves the "J"

---

[26] To readers well versed in microeconomics, $J(X_0, t)$ can be viewed as a dynamic indirect utility function.

label) at time $t + \Delta t$. The integral term can be approximated by[27]

$$\int_t^{t+\Delta t} f(X, s, y)\, ds \approx f(X, t, y)\, \Delta t \qquad (4.200)$$

whereas the J term, by a Taylor expansion, can be expressed as

$$J(X + \Delta X, t + \Delta t) = J(X, t) + \frac{\partial J(X, t)}{\partial X} \Delta X + \frac{\partial J(X, t)}{\partial t} \Delta t$$
$$+ \frac{1}{2} \frac{\partial^2 J}{\partial X^2} (\Delta X)^2 + o(\Delta t) \qquad (4.201)$$

Recall, from Section 4.4, that $(\Delta X)^2 = \sigma^2(X, t, y)\, \Delta t$. Replacing the values of the integral term in (4.200) and the J function in (4.201) into (4.199), and noting that $\mathbb{E}_t[\sigma(X, t, y)\, dW] = 0$, we obtain

$$0 = \max_y \left\{ f(X, t, y)\, \Delta t + \frac{\partial J(X, t)}{\partial X} \mu(X, t, y)\, \Delta t + \frac{\partial J(X, t)}{\partial t} \Delta t \right.$$
$$\left. + \frac{1}{2} \frac{\partial^2 J(X, t)}{\partial X^2} \sigma^2(X, t, y)\, \Delta t + o(\Delta t) \right\}$$

Dividing through by Δt, with $\Delta t \to 0$, we get the Bellman equation of optimal control for Itô processes:

$$-\frac{\partial J(X, t)}{\partial t} = \max_y \left\{ f(X, t, y) + \frac{\partial J(X, t)}{\partial X} \mu(X, t, y) \qquad (4.202) \right.$$
$$\left. + \frac{1}{2} \frac{\partial^2 J(X, t)}{\partial X^2} \sigma^2(X, t, y) \right\}$$

This is a partial differential equation with boundary condition

$$J(X(T), T) = B(X(T), T) \qquad (4.203)$$

4.9.3 Optimal Control of Itô Processes: Infinite Horizon

We consider a simpler dynamic program where the agent's horizon is infinite and where f, μ, and σ are just functions of X and y, that is, are time homogeneous. As before, we define an optimal value function

---

[27] Using the mean–value theorem.

$V(X(0))$:

$$V(X(0)) = \max_{y} \mathbb{E}_0 \int_0^\infty e^{-rt} f(X, y)\, dt \qquad (4.204)$$

where r is the discount rate. Equation (4.203) is subject to the constraints

$$dX = \mu(X, y)dt + \sigma(X, y)dW \qquad (4.205)$$

and

$$X(0) = x_0$$

The resolution of this problem is similar to the one in the previous subsection. At time t, Bellman's principle of optimality is now

$$V(X) = \max_{y} \mathbb{E}_t \left\{ \int_t^{t+\Delta t} e^{-r(s-t)} f(X, y)\, ds + e^{-r\Delta t} V(X + \Delta X) \right\} \tag{4.206}$$

Equation (4.206) can be approximated by

$$V(X) = \max_{y} \mathbb{E}_t \left\{ f(X, y)\,\Delta t + e^{-r\Delta t} \right.$$
$$\left. \times \left[V(X(t)) + V'\Delta X + \frac{1}{2}V''(\Delta X)^2 + o(\Delta t) \right] \right\}$$

where V' and V'' are respectively the first and second derivatives of the value function vis-à-vis the state variable X. Multiplying through by $e^{r\Delta t}$ and recalling that $(\Delta X)^2 = \sigma^2(X, y)\,\Delta t$, we get

$$e^{r\Delta t} V(X) = \max_{y} \mathbb{E}_t \left[e^{r\Delta t} f(X, y)\,\Delta t + V(X(t)) \right.$$
$$\left. + V' \left\{ \mu(X, y)\,\Delta t + \sigma(X, y)\,\Delta W \right\} + \frac{1}{2}V''\sigma^2(X, y)\,\Delta t + o(\Delta t) \right]$$

Noting that $\mathbb{E}_t \{\sigma(X, y)\,\Delta W\} = 0$, that $e^{r\Delta t} = 1 + r\Delta t + o(\Delta t)$ and dividing by Δt with $\Delta t \to 0$, we get Bellman's equation for the inifinite horizon, time-homogeneous case:

$$rV = \max_{y} \left\{ f(X, y) + V'\mu(X, y) + \frac{V''}{2}\sigma^2(X, y) \right\} \qquad (4.207)$$

Alternatively, equation (4.207) could be obtained by letting $J(X, t) = e^{-rt} V(X)$ into equation (4.202).

The interpretation of equation (4.207) is fairly intuitive: the left-hand side is the interest on an asset value V. This interest is equal at equilibrium to the maximum attainable dividend and expected capital gain. Indeed, $f(X, y)$ can be interpreted as dividend flow from equation (4.203), whereas the expected capital gain on an asset value $V(X)$ [with X described by (4.204) and (4.205)] is, by Itô's lemma:

$$\mathbb{E}(dV) = V'\mu(X, y) + \frac{V''}{2}\sigma^2(X, y) \qquad (4.208)$$

Last, note that equation (4.207) is computationally simpler than equation (4.202) because the control rule ends up being the solution of an ordinary differential equation in (4.207) as opposed to a partial differential equation in (4.202).

Example 4.9.1. Merton (1969) has established benchmark results on lifetime consumption and portfolio selection under uncertainty. We solve here for a special case of this control problem. An economic agent has instantaneous utility function: $V(C) = \log C(t)$ where $C(t)$ is the flow of consumption. The agent is mazimizing her expected utility:

$$V(Y(0)) = \max_{C,y} \mathbb{E} \int_0^\infty e^{-\rho t} \log C \, dt$$

where y is the fraction of total wealth Y invested in the risky asset, $(1 - y)$ is the fraction of total wealth Y invested in the riskless asset, and ρ is the discount rate. If the risky asset follows a geometric Brownian motion with instantaneous drift (or expected return) μ and volatility σ, and if the riskless rate is r, then the reader can easily verify the constraint on the change in wealth dY:

$$dY = [r(1 - y)Y + \mu y Y - C] \, dt + yY\sigma \, dW$$

with

$$Y(0) = Y_0$$

Equation (4.207) gives in this case

$$\rho V = \max_{C,y} \left\{ \log C + V' \left[r\left(1-y\right)Y + \mu yY - C \right] + y^2 Y^2 \sigma^2 \frac{V''}{2} \right\}$$

where $V = V(Y)$ as noted above.
   The first-order conditions are

$$C = \frac{1}{V'}$$

and

$$Yy = \frac{-V'}{V''} \frac{\mu - r}{\sigma^2}$$

We replace C and Yy by their values in the Bellman equation to get

$$\rho V = -\log V' + V'rY - \frac{(V')^2}{2V''}\left(\frac{\mu-r}{\sigma}\right)^2 - 1$$

We try the solution

$$V = A \log Y + B$$

Then $V' = A/Y$ and $V'' = -A/Y^2$. Plugging the trial solution for V into the previous equation gives

$$\rho A \log Y + \rho B = \log Y - \log A + rA + \frac{A}{2}\left(\frac{\mu-r}{\sigma}\right)^2 - 1$$

Identifying terms in Y and other terms, we find

$$A = \frac{1}{\rho}$$

and

$$B = \frac{\log \rho + \frac{r}{\rho} + \frac{(\mu-r)^2}{2\rho\sigma^2} - 1}{\rho}$$

We also infer the optimal control rules for consumption and asset allocation:

$$C^* = \rho Y$$

and

$$y^* = \frac{\mu - r}{\sigma^2}$$

Optimal consumption is therefore a fraction ρ of current total wealth and the fraction of wealth invested in the risky asset is the excess return over the riskless asset $(\mu - r)$ divided by the variance σ^2 of the risky asset return.

Example 4.9.2. This example derives the control rule for a growth-optimum portfolio (note that we do not need to use the Bellman equation explicitly here). To maximize the expected geometric return of wealth Y, the agent needs to allocate wealth between the risky asset and the riskless asset to

$$\max \mathbb{E}_0 \left[\frac{\log \left(Y(T) / Y(0) \right)}{T} \right]$$

Because $Y(0)$ and T are known positive constants, this is equivalent to the problem

$$\max \mathbb{E}_0 \left\{ \log Y(T) \right\}$$

Recall from the previous example that, in the absence of consumption:

$$\frac{dY}{Y} = [r(1 - y) + \mu y] \, dt + y\sigma \, dW$$

By Itô's lemma:

$$d \log Y = \left[r(1 - y) + \mu y - \frac{y^2 \sigma^2}{2} \right] dt + y\sigma \, dW$$

It follows that

$$\mathbb{E} \left[\log Y(T) \right] = \log Y(0) \exp \left\{ \left[r(1 - y) + \mu y - \frac{y^2 \sigma^2}{2} \right] T \right\}$$

To maximize $E[\log Y(T)]$, we need to pick y so that the exponential term is maximized. This is to say

$$\frac{\partial}{\partial y} \left(r(1 - y) + \mu y - \frac{y^2 \sigma^2}{2} \right) = 0$$

Therefore

$$-r + \mu - y^*\sigma^2 = 0$$

or

$$y^* = \frac{\mu - r}{\sigma^2}$$

As in the previous example, the portfolio allocation rule does not depend on the time horizon T. Note that the geometric rate of return of the growth-optimum portfolio is

$$g^* = r(1 - y^*) + \mu y^* - \frac{y^{*2}\sigma^2}{2} = r + \frac{(\mu - r)^2}{2\sigma^2}$$

whereas the expected return (or drift) of the portfolio is

$$r(1 - y^*) + \mu y^* = r + \left(\frac{\mu - r}{\sigma}\right)^2$$

and its variance is

$$y^{*2}\sigma^2 = \left(\frac{\mu - r}{\sigma}\right)^2$$

It follows that the expected excess return of the growth-optimum portfolio is equal to its variance.

4.10 PARTIAL DIFFERENTIAL EQUATIONS

We describe two fundamental partial differential equations in finance (the Kolmogorov and pricing equations), then proceed to solve them using Laplace transforms. See Shimko (1991) for a discussion of pricing through Laplace transforms.

4.10.1 The Kolmogorov Forward Equation Revisited

We revisit the Kolmogorov equations and derive the forward equation in the context of simple one-dimensional and two-dimensional random walks. While these derivations are essentially similar to the material in Section 4.7, they show the close link between random walks and diffusion equations. Consider first a one-dimensional random walk. As before, we denote by $p(x, t, x_0) \Delta x$ the probability of reaching x at time t given that the process started at x_0 at time zero. We simplify things further by assuming a unit incremental step ($\Delta x = 1$). The probability of moving by $+1$ or -1 is 1/2. The incremental time step is unity ($\Delta t = 1$). This gives

$$p(x, t, x_0) = \frac{1}{2} [p(x + 1, t - 1, x_0) + p(x - 1, t - 1, x_0)] \quad (4.209)$$

Subtracting $p(x, t, x_0)$ from both sides:

$$p(x, t, x_0) - p(x, t - 1, x_0) \quad (4.210)$$
$$= \frac{1}{2} [p(x + 1, t - 1, x_0) - 2p(x, t - 1, x_0) - p(x - 1, t - 1, x_0)]$$

This is the discrete-time approximation of the Kolmogorov forward equation

$$\frac{\partial p(x, t, x_0)}{\partial t} = \frac{1}{2} \frac{\partial^2 p(x, t, x_0)}{\partial x^2} \quad (4.211)$$

Equation (4.211) is equivalent to equation (4.168) with $\mu = 0$ and $\sigma = 1$. As explained in Section 4.7, (4.211) must verify boundary condition

$$p(x, 0, x_0) = \delta(x - x_0)$$

The general form of (4.211)

$$\frac{\partial p}{\partial r} = k \frac{\partial^2 p}{\partial x^2}$$

is called a one-dimensional heat equation or diffusion equation, in reference to heat flow that follows this equation in mathematical physics. Consider now a random walk in two dimensions (see Figure 4.4).

We obtain now

$$p(x, y, t) = \frac{1}{4} [p(x + 1, y, t - 1) + p(x - 1, y, t - 1) \quad (4.212)$$
$$+ p(x, y + 1, t - 1) + p(x, y - 1, t - 1)]$$

where $p(x, y, t)$ is shorthand for $p(x, y, t, x_0, y_0)$ and is the probability of reaching the point (x, y) at time t given that the process started at (x_0, y_0) at the time zero when $\Delta x = \Delta y = 1$. As in the one-dimensional

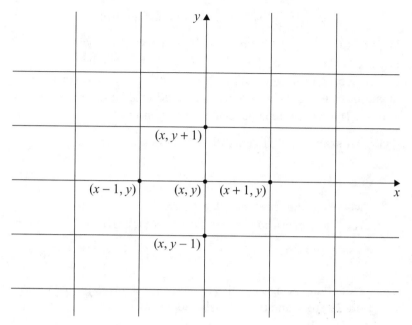

Figure 4.4

case, (4.212) is equivalent to

$$p(x, y, t) - p(x, y, t - 1) \tag{4.213}$$
$$= \frac{1}{4}[p(x+1, y, t-1) - 2p(x, y, t-1) + p(x-1, y, t-1)$$
$$+ p(x, y+1, t-1) - 2p(x, y, t-1) + p(x-1, y, t-1)]$$

This is now the discrete-time approximation of a two-dimensional heat or diffusion equation:

$$\frac{\partial p}{\partial t} = \frac{1}{4}\left(\frac{\partial^2 p}{\partial x^2} + \frac{\partial^2 p}{\partial y^2}\right) \tag{4.214}$$

The result can be generalized to an n-dimensional random walk:

$$\frac{\partial p}{\partial t} = \frac{1}{2n}\sum_{i=1}^{n}\frac{\partial^2 p}{\partial x_i^2} \tag{4.215}$$

We shall solve the one-dimensional forward equation later in this section.

4.10.2 Risk-Neutral Pricing Equation

We now turn to the problem of pricing a derivative product in a risk-neutral world. As was elaborated in Chapter 2, risk-neutral pricing carries considerable generality in option pricing theory. For the moment, let us just imagine a world where all economic agents are risk neutral. There are three financial assets in this economy:

1. A riskless bond priced at B. B follows the equation

$$\frac{dB}{B} = r\,dt \qquad (4.216)$$

 where r is the constant riskless rate.

2. A risky asset priced at S. S follows a geometric Brownian motion:

$$\frac{dS}{S} = r\,dt + \sigma\,dW \qquad (4.217)$$

 Note that because agents are risk neutral, the expected returns on the stock and the bond should be equal:

$$\frac{\mathbb{E}\left(\frac{dB}{B}\right)}{dt} = \frac{\mathbb{E}\left(\frac{dS}{S}\right)}{dt} = r$$

3. A derivative product. Its price P is a function of S and time t, because the payoff of the derivative at some future date T is contractually linked to the price of the risky asset S. By Itô's lemma:

$$\begin{aligned}
dP(S,t) &= \frac{\partial P}{\partial S}dS + \frac{\partial P}{\partial t}dt + \frac{1}{2}\frac{\partial^2 P}{\partial S^2}(dS)^2 \qquad (4.218)\\
&= \left(\frac{\partial P}{\partial S}rS + \frac{\partial P}{\partial t} + \frac{1}{2}\frac{\partial^2 P}{\partial S^2}\sigma^2 S^2\right)dt + \frac{\partial P}{\partial S}dW
\end{aligned}$$

But recall that we live in a risk-neutral world. Therefore, the rate of return on the derivative must be the riskless rate r:

$$\frac{\mathbb{E}\left(\frac{dP}{P}\right)}{dt} = \frac{\frac{\partial P}{\partial S}rS + \frac{\partial P}{\partial t} + \frac{1}{2}\frac{\partial^2 P}{\partial S^2}\sigma^2 S^2}{P} = r \qquad (4.219)$$

Equation (4.219) is the fundamental Black-Scholes-Merton pricing equation. Equation (4.219) is generally written as

$$\frac{1}{2}\sigma^2 S^2 \frac{\partial^2 P}{\partial S^2} + \frac{\partial P}{\partial S}rS + \frac{\partial P}{\partial t} = rP \qquad (4.220)$$

Equation (4.220) was developed in detail in Chapter 2. It is a second-order partial differential equation. To solve for P, we need to specify boundary conditions for equation (4.220). In particular, (4.220) is subject to a boundary condition specifying the contractual payoff of the derivative product. For example, a forward contract on a risky asset with expiration time T and delivery price E will have a payoff:

$$P(T) = S_T - E \qquad (4.221)$$

We have now obtained the pricing equation for derivatives. We have then specialized the problem to a forward contract on a risky asset with terminal payoff described by (4.221). To solve for the value P of the forward contract, we need to step back and learn a technique that facilitates the resolution of partial differential equations. This technique uses the concept of a Laplace transform.

4.10.3 The Laplace Transform

The Laplace transform of a function $f(t)$ is defined as

$$\mathcal{L}[f(t)] \equiv \int_0^\infty e^{-st} f(t)\, dt = F(s) \qquad (4.222)$$

Note that the integral may diverge for some values of s.

Example 4.10.1. The Laplace transform of a constant K is

$$\mathcal{L}(K) = K \int_0^\infty e^{-st} dt = K \left[\frac{e^{-st}}{s} \right]_0^\infty = \frac{K}{s}$$

for $s > 0$. (The Laplace transform does not exist for $s < 0$.)

Example 4.10.2. The Laplace transform of e^{at} is

$$\mathcal{L}(e^{at}) = \int_0^\infty e^{-st} e^{at} dt = \left[\frac{e^{(a-s)t}}{a-s} \right]_0^\infty = \frac{1}{s-a}$$

for $s > a$.

Example 4.10.3. The Laplace transform of t^k is

$$\mathcal{L}(t^k) = \int_0^\infty e^{-st} t^k dt$$

Let $u \equiv st$. Then $dt = \frac{du}{s}$, and

$$\mathcal{L}\left(t^k\right) = \frac{1}{s^{k+1}} \int_0^\infty e^{-u} u^k \, du$$

By definition of the gamma function:

$$\Gamma\left(k+1\right) \equiv \int_0^\infty e^{-u} u^k \, du$$

$\Gamma\left(k+1\right)$ *can be shown to converge for $k > -1$. Therefore*

$$\mathcal{L}\left(t^k\right) = \frac{\Gamma\left(k+1\right)}{s^{k+1}}$$

for $k > -1$. Note that when k is a positive integer, a simple integration by parts shows that $\Gamma\left(k+1\right) = k!$ It then follows that

$$\mathcal{L}\left(t^k\right) = \frac{k!}{s^{k+1}}$$

for $k \in N$, the set of positive integers.

We can now define the inverse Laplace transform. If $\mathcal{L}[f\left(t\right)] = F\left(s\right)$ as in (4.222), then the inverse Laplace transform of $F\left(s\right)$, denoted $\mathcal{L}^{-1}\left[F\left(s\right)\right]$, is

$$\mathcal{L}^{-1}\left[F\left(s\right)\right] = f\left(t\right) \tag{4.223}$$

The inverse Laplace transforms corresponding to Examples (4.10.1), (4.10.2), and (4.10.3) are therefore

$$\mathcal{L}^{-1}\left(\frac{k}{s}\right) = k \tag{4.224}$$

$$\mathcal{L}^{-1}\left(\frac{1}{s-a}\right) = e^{at} \tag{4.225}$$

$$\mathcal{L}^{-1}\left[\frac{\Gamma\left(k+1\right)}{s^{k+1}}\right] = tk \tag{4.226}$$

The techniques to recover inverse Laplace transforms rely on complex analysis. We shall not dwell upon this topic here.

Laplace transforms have a number of properties that will help us solve partial differential equations. We list here two sets of properties for a function of x and t, where

$$\mathcal{L}[f(x,t)] = \int_0^\infty e^{-st} f(x,t)\,dt = F(x,s)$$

1. Linearity of the Laplace operator:

$$\mathcal{L}[af(x,t) + bg(x,t)] = a\mathcal{L}[f(x,t)] + b\mathcal{L}[g(x,t)] \quad (4.227)$$

2. Linearity can be proved trivially from the definition of the Laplace transform

$$\mathcal{L}\left[\frac{\partial f(x,t)}{\partial t}\right] = sF(x,s) - f(x,0) \quad (4.228)$$

$$\mathcal{L}\left[\frac{\partial f(x,t)}{\partial x}\right] = \frac{\partial F(x,s)}{\partial x} \quad (4.229)$$

$$\mathcal{L}\left[\frac{\partial^2 f(x,t)}{\partial x^2}\right] = \frac{\partial^2 F(x,s)}{\partial x^2} \quad (4.230)$$

with

$$F(x,s) \equiv \int_0^\infty \frac{\partial f}{\partial t} e^{-st}\,dt = \mathcal{L}[f(x,t)]$$

To prove (4.228), use integration by parts to get

$$\mathcal{L}\left[\frac{\partial f(x,t)}{\partial t}\right] = \int_0^\infty \frac{\partial f(x,t)}{\partial t} e^{-st}\,dt$$

$$= \left[f(x,t)e^{-st}\right]_0^\infty + s \int_0^\infty f(x,t)e^{-st}\,dt$$

$$= \lim_{t\to\infty} f(x,t)e^{-st} - f(x,0) + sF(x,s)$$

If the function f verifies

$$\lim_{t\to\infty} f(x,t)e^{-st} = 0$$

then (4.228) holds. Such functions are called *functions of exponential order*. To show that (4.229) holds, note that

$$\mathcal{L}\left[\frac{\partial f(x,t)}{\partial x}\right] = \int_0^\infty \frac{\partial f(x,t)}{\partial x} e^{-st}\,dt$$

$$= \frac{\partial}{\partial x} \int_0^\infty f(x,t)e^{-st}\,dt = \frac{\partial F(x,s)}{\partial x}$$

Table 4.6 *Some Common Laplace Transforms*

f(t)	$F(s) = L[f]$
1	$\dfrac{1}{s}$
t	$\dfrac{1}{s^2}$
t^a	$\dfrac{\Gamma(a+1)}{s^{a+1}} = \dfrac{a!}{s^{a+1}}$ if $a = 0, 1, 2, \ldots$
e^{at}	$\dfrac{1}{s-a}$
$\cos \omega t$	$\dfrac{s}{s^2 + \omega^2}$
$\sin \omega t$	$\dfrac{\omega}{s^2 + \omega^2}$
$\cosh at$	$\dfrac{s}{s^2 - a^2}$
$\sinh at$	$\dfrac{a}{s^2 - a^2}$
$1 - erf\frac{k}{2\sqrt{t}}$	$\dfrac{e - k\sqrt{s}}{s}$
$e^{at} t^n$	$\dfrac{n!}{(s-a)^{n+1}}$
$e^{at} \cos \omega t$	$\dfrac{s-a}{(s-a)^2 + \omega^2}$
$e^{at} \sin \omega t$	$\dfrac{\omega}{(s-a)^2 + \omega^2}$

Equation (4.230) can be proven along the same lines. We close this subsection with a summary of the properties of Laplace transforms and a table of common Laplace transforms (see Table 4.6).

Basic Properties of Laplace Transforms

1. LINEARITY: If f and g are functions with well-defined Laplace transforms, and a and b are constants, then

$$\mathcal{L}[af + bg] = a\mathcal{L}[f] + b\mathcal{L}[g]$$

2. LAPLACE TRANSFORM OF A DERIVATIVE: Using integration by parts, it is straightforward to show that

$$\mathcal{L}[f'] = s\mathcal{L}[f] - f(0)$$

Applying this to the second derivative, we can see that

$$\mathcal{L}[f''] = s^2\mathcal{L}[f] - sf(0) - f'(0) \tag{4.231}$$

Now by induction, we obtain the following result for higher order derivatives:

$$\mathcal{L}\left[f^{(n)}\right] = s^n\mathcal{L}[f] - s^{n-1}f(0) - s^{n-2}f'(0) - \cdots - f^{(n-1)}(0) \tag{4.232}$$

3. DERIVATIVE OF A LAPLACE TRANSFORM: Differentiating under the integral sign, we can show that

$$\mathcal{L}[tf(t)] = -F'(s) \tag{4.233}$$

4. LAPLACE TRANSFORM OF AN INTEGRAL: Reversing the result for Laplace transform of the first derivative, we can see that

$$\mathcal{L}\left[\int_0^t f(z)\,dz\right] = \frac{1}{s}\mathcal{L}[f(t)] \tag{4.234}$$

5. INTEGRATION OF LAPLACE TRANSFORMS: Interchanging the order of integration, we can show that

$$\mathcal{L}\left[\frac{f(t)}{t}\right] = \int_s^\infty F(z)\,dz \tag{4.235}$$

6. LAPLACE TRANSFORM OF TRANSLATIONS
   (a) SHIFTING IN SPACE:

$$\mathcal{L}\left[e^{at}f(t)\right] = F(s-a) \tag{4.236}$$

   (b) SHIFTING IN TIME: If $t > a$, then

$$\mathcal{L}[f(t-a)] = e^{-as}\mathcal{L}[f] \tag{4.237}$$

   (c) LAPLACE TRANSFORM OF DIRAC DELTA FUNCTION

$$\mathcal{L}[\delta(t-a)] = e^{-as}, a > 0 \tag{4.238}$$

7. LAPLACE TRANSFORM OF A CONVOLUTION: The convolution of two functions f and g is defined as

$$(f * g)(t) \equiv \int_0^t f(z) g(t - z) dz \qquad (4.239)$$

It can be shown that the Laplace transform of the convolution of two functions is the product of the transforms, that is

$$\mathcal{L}[f * g] = \mathcal{L}[f] \mathcal{L}[g] \qquad (4.240)$$

8. LAPLACE TRANSFORM OF A PERIODIC FUNCTION: If f is periodic with period p, then

$$L[f] = \frac{1}{1 - e^{-ps}} \int_0^p e^{-st} f(t) dt \qquad (4.241)$$

4.10.4 Resolution of the Kolmogorov Forward Equation

Recall the formulation of the forward equation:

$$\frac{\partial p(x, t)}{\partial t} = \frac{1}{2} \frac{\partial^2 p(x, t)}{\partial x^2}$$

When we first derived the Kolmogorov equations in this chapter, we defined p as the probability density function.[28] For reasons of computational convenience, we now redefine p as the cumulative probability function. It is perfectly valid to redefine p in this fashion, because the derivation of the Kolmogorov equation does not restrict p to either definition. However, once p is considered to be a cumulative probability function, boundary conditions need to be altered accordingly. We now specify the boundary conditions for $x(0) = 0$:

$$p(x, 0) = 1 \text{ for positive } x$$

$$p(0, t) = \frac{1}{2} \text{ for positive } t$$

and

$$p(\infty, t) = 0 \text{ for positive } t$$

---

[28] The boundary condition for the probability density function, as noted earlier, is

$$p(x, 0) = \delta(x - x_0)$$

The first boundary condition states that the probability of being below x ($x > 0$) at $t = 0$ is one. This is obviously the case because the process starts at $x(0) = 0$. The second boundary condition is a statement about the symmetry of the random process. The probability of the process taking a negative value at some point in time t is 50%, given that the initial point is zero. Last, the probability is bounded (by zero) as x takes infinite values.

By (4.228) and (4.230), the partial differential equation becomes an ordinary differential equation involving Laplace transforms:

$$s F(x, s) - p(x, 0) = \frac{1}{2} F_{xx}(x, s) \qquad (4.242)$$

where the Laplace transform $F(x, s)$ is

$$F(x, s) \equiv \int_0^\infty e^{-st} p(x, t) \, dt$$

From the first boundary condition, the ordinary differential equation becomes

$$F_{xx}(x, s) - 2s F(x, s) = -2 \qquad (4.243)$$

A linear second-order differential equation is solved by first equating its left-hand side to zero and solving the characteristic equation to find a general solution. In a second step, a particular solution that agrees with the right-hand side term (in this case -2) is found and added to the general solution. The general solution of our problem follows directly from the characteristic equation

$$\lambda^2 - 2s = 0 \qquad (4.244)$$

which has solutions $\lambda = \pm\sqrt{2s}$. The general solution is

$$F^G(x, s) = A e^{x\sqrt{2s}} + B e^{-x\sqrt{2s}} \qquad (4.245)$$

where A and B are to be determined by our second and third boundary conditions. The particular solution $F^P(x, s)$ is guessed easily:

$$F^P(x, s) = \frac{1}{s} \qquad (4.246)$$

The solution is therefore of the form

$$F(x, s) = F^P(x, s) + F^G(x, s)$$
$$= Ae^{x\sqrt{2s}} + Be^{-x\sqrt{2s}} + \frac{1}{s} \qquad (4.247)$$

To solve for A and B, note that the Laplace transforms of the second and third boundary conditions are

$$F(0, t) = \frac{1}{2s}$$

and

$$F(\infty, t) = 0$$

Because $F(\infty, t) = 0$, A must be zero. We now use the condition

$$F(0, t) = \frac{1}{2s}$$

To solve for B:

$$Be^{-0 \times \sqrt{2s}} + \frac{1}{s} = \frac{1}{2s}$$

giving

$$B = -\frac{1}{2s}$$

The solution of the ordinary differential equation is hence

$$F(x, s) = \frac{-e^{-x\sqrt{2s}}}{2s} + \frac{1}{s} \qquad (4.248)$$

From Table 4.6, we note that

$$p(x, t) = \mathcal{L}^{-1}\left(\frac{-e^{-x\sqrt{2s}}}{2s} + \frac{1}{s}\right)$$
$$= \frac{1}{2}\mathcal{L}^{-1}\left(\frac{-e^{-x\sqrt{2}\sqrt{2s}}}{s}\right) + \mathcal{L}^{-1}\left(\frac{1}{s}\right)$$
$$= \frac{1}{2}\left\{\text{erf}\left(\frac{x}{\sqrt{2t}}\right) - 1\right\} + 1$$
$$= \frac{1}{2}\left\{1 + \text{erf}\left(\frac{x}{\sqrt{2t}}\right)\right\}$$

where

$$\text{erf}(a) \equiv \frac{2}{\sqrt{2\pi}} \int_0^a e^{-u^2} du$$

But a little algebra shows that, for any real number a, we have

$$\frac{1 + \text{erf}(a)}{2} = \int_{-\infty}^{a\sqrt{2}} \frac{1}{\sqrt{2\pi}} e^{\frac{-u^2}{2}} du = \Phi\left(a\sqrt{2}\right)$$

The solution follows:

$$p(x, t) = \int_{-\infty}^{\frac{x}{\sqrt{t}}} \frac{1}{\sqrt{2\pi}} e^{\frac{-u}{2}} du = \Phi\left(\frac{x}{\sqrt{t}}\right) \qquad (4.249)$$

This is the normal distribution function with mean zero and standard deviation $\sqrt{t}$.

4.10.5 Resolution of the Risk-Neutral Pricing Equation

Earlier in this section, we showed that the price of a derivative in a risk-neutral world follows the equation

$$\frac{1}{2} \frac{\partial^2 P}{\partial S^2} \sigma^2 S^2 + \frac{\partial P}{\partial S} r S - \frac{\partial P}{\partial \tau} = r P$$

where $\tau \equiv T - t$ is the time to expiration of the derivative contract. Note that we use for convenience $\partial P / \partial \tau = -\partial P / \partial t$. At $\tau = 0$, the boundary condition for the value of a forward contract is $P(S, 0) = S_T - K$. To reexpress the partial differential equation into an ordinary differential equation in Laplace transforms, we use equations (4.228), (4.229), and (4.230) to get

$$\frac{1}{2} \sigma^2 S^2 F_{ss} + r S F_s - (r + s) F = P(S, 0) = K - S_T$$

This is a linear second-order differential equation with general solution

$$F^G = A_1 S^{\lambda_1} + A_2 S^{\lambda_2}$$

where λ_1 and λ_2 can be found by plugging the value of F^G, F_S^G, and F_{SS}^G into the ordinary differential equation. This gives

$$\frac{1}{2} \sigma^2 \lambda (\lambda - 1) + r S \lambda - r - s = 0 \qquad (4.250)$$

and hence

$$\lambda_1 = \frac{-\left(r - \frac{\sigma^2}{2}\right) + \sqrt{\left(r - \frac{\sigma^2}{2}\right)^2 + 2\left(r + s\right)\sigma^2}}{\sigma^2} > 0$$

and

$$\lambda_2 = \frac{-\left(r - \frac{\sigma^2}{2}\right) - \sqrt{\left(r - \frac{\sigma^2}{2}\right)^2 + 2\left(r + s\right)\sigma^2}}{\sigma^2} < 0 \qquad (4.251)$$

The particular solution is of the form

$$F^P = A_3 S + A_4$$

Plugging F^P into the ordinary differential equation, we obtain

$$r S A_3 - (r + s)(A_3 S + A_4) = K - S$$

$\Rightarrow$

$$-s A_3 S = -S; \Rightarrow A_3 = 1/s$$
$$-(r + s) A_4 = K; \Rightarrow A_4 = -K/(r + s)$$

Thus

$$F^P = \frac{S}{s} - \frac{K}{r + s}$$

The complete solution is of the form

$$F = F^G + F^P = A_1 S^{\lambda_1} + A_2 S_2^{\lambda} + \frac{S}{s} - \frac{K}{r + s}$$

The last step is to determine A_1 and A_2. We prescribe to that effect two boundary conditions:

1. $P(S, \tau) \sim S$ as $S \to \infty$. In other words, as the underlying asset becomes more and more valuable, the forward contract tends to behave like the asset. This will prevent F from "exploding" when S grows bigger. Therefore: $A_1 = 0$.
2. $P(0, \tau) \sim |K|$ as $S \to 0$. This boundary condition says that only K, the delivery price, matters as S goes to zero. In particular,

$A_2 S^{\lambda_2}$ should not be allowed to "explode." This constrains A_2 to be equal to zero.

We now have the final solution:

$$F = \frac{S}{s} - \frac{K}{r+s}$$

From the table of Laplace transforms, we get the value of the forward:

$$P(S, \tau) = \mathcal{L}^{-1}(F(s)) = S - Ke^{-r\tau}$$

Bibliography

Chapter 1. Preliminary Mathematics

Aase, K. (1999): "An Equilibrium Model of Catastrophe Insurance Futures and Spreads," *Geneva Papers on Risk and Insurance Theory* 24: 69–96.

Ambarish, R., and L. Seigel (1996): "Time Is the Essence," *Risk* 9(8): 41–42.

Avelleneda, M., P. Laurence, and A. Paras (1999): *Quantitative Modeling of Derivative Securities*, CRC Press.

Barndorff-Nielsen, O. (1997): "Normal Inverse Gaussian Distributions and Stochastic Volatility Modelling," *Scandinavian Journal of Statistics* 24: 1–13.

Bartle, R. (1976): *The Elements of Real Analysis* (2nd ed.), New York: Wiley.

Bertsimas, D., L. Kogan, and A. Lo (1998): "When Is Time Continuous?" Working Paper, MIT Sloan School of Management, *Journal of Financial Economics*.

Billingsley, P. (1986): *Probability and Measure* (2nd ed.), New York: Wiley.

Campbell, J., A. Lo, and C. MacKinlay (1997): *The Econometrics of Financial Markets*, Princeton, NJ: Princeton University Press.

Demange, G., and J.-C. Rochet (1992): *Methodes Mathematique de la Finance*, Paris: Economica.

Dixit, A., and R. Pindyck (1994): *Investment Under Uncertainty*, Princeton, NJ: Princeton University Press.

Dothan, M. (1990): *Prices in Financial Markets*, New York: Oxford University Press.

Duffie, D. (1988b): *Security Markets: Stochastic Models*, New York: Academic Press.

Duffie, D. (1996): *Dynamic Asset Pricing Theory* (2nd ed.), Princeton, NJ: Princeton University Press.

Harrison, M. (1985): *Brownian Motion and Stochastic Flow Systems*, New York: Wiley.

Huang, C.-F., and R. Litzenberger (1988): *Foundations for Financial Economics*, Amsterdam: North-Holland.

Hull, J. (2000): *Options, Futures, and Other Derivative Securities* (4th ed.), Englewood Cliffs, NJ: Prentice-Hall.

Jarrow, R. (1988): *Finance Theory*, Englewood Cliffs, NJ: Prentice-Hall.

Jarrow, R., and A. Rudd (1983): *Option Pricing*, Homewood, IL: Richard D. Irwin.

Jarrow, R., and S. Turnbull (1999): *Derivative Securities* (2nd ed.), Cincinnati: South-Western.

Merton, R. (1990): *Continuous-Time Finance*, Oxford: Basil Blackwell.

Neftci, S. (2000): *An Introduction to the Mathematics of Financial Derivatives*, New York: Academic Press.

Prisman, E. (2000): *Pricing Derivative Securities*, San Diego: Academic Press.

Rubinstein, M. (1974b): "A Discrete-Time Synthesis of Financial Theory," Working Paper, Haas School of Business, University of California, Berkeley.

Rubinstein, M. (1999): *Derivatives: A Power-Plus Picture Book*, Corte Madera, CA: In-The-Money.

Siegel, J. J. (1972): "Risk, Interest Rates and the Forward Exchange," *Quarterly Journal of Economics* 86.

Stokey, N., and R. Lucas (1989): *Recursive Methods in Economic Dynamics* (with Ed Prescott), Cambridge, MA: Harvard University Press.

Wilmott, P., S. Howison, and J. Dewynne (1995): *The Mathematics of Financial Derivatives*, Cambridge: Cambridge University Press.

Chapter 2. Principles of Financial Valuation

Aase, K. (1988): "Contingent Claims Valuation When the Security Price Is a Combination of an Itô Process and a Random Point Process," *Stochastic Processes and Their Applications* 28: 185–220.

Acharya, S., and D. Madan (1993): "Arbitrage-Free Econometric Option Pricing Models in and Incomplete Market with a Locally Risky Discount Factor," Working Paper, Federal Reserve Board.

Ahn, H., M. Dayal, E. Grannan, and G. Swindle (1995): "Hedging with Transaction Costs," *Annals of Applied Probability* 8: 341–366.

Aït-Sahalia, Y., and A. Lo (1998): "Nonparametric Estimation of State-Price Densities Implicit in Financial Asset Prices," *Journal of Finance* 53: 499–547.

Ait-Sahalia, F., and T.-L. Lai (1996): "Approximations for American Options," Working Paper, School of Operations Research and Industrial Engineering, Cornell University.

Ait-Sahalia, F., and T. Lai (1997a): "Random Walk Duality and the Valuation of Discrete Lookback Options," Working Paper, Hewlett-Packard Laboratories.

Ait-Sahalia, F., and T. Lai (1997b): "Valuation of Discrete Barrier and Hindsight Options," Working Paper, Hewlett-Packard Laboratories.

Ait-Sahalia, F., and T.-L. Lai (1998): "Efficient Approximations to American Option Prices, Hedge Parameters and Exercise Boundaries," Working Paper, Hewlett-Packard Laboratories.

Akahari, J. (1993): "Some Formulas for a New Type of Path-Dependent Option," Working Paper, Department of Mathematics, University of Tokyo.

Allegretto, W., G. Barrone-Adesi, and R. Elliott (1993): "Numerical Evaluation of the Critical Price and American Options," Working Paper, Department of Mathematics, University of Alberta.

Amin, K. (1991): "On the Computation of Continuous Time Option Prices Using Discrete Approximations," *Journal of Financial and Quantitative Analysis* 26: 477–495.

Amin, K. (1993a): "Jump-Diffusion Option Valuation in Discrete-Time," *Journal of Finance* 48: 1833–1863.

Amin, K. (1993b): "Option Valuation with Systematic Stochastic Volatility," *Journal of Finance* 48: 881–910.

Amin, K., and A. Khanna (1994): "Convergence of American Option Values from Discrete to Continuous-Time Financial Models," *Mathematical Finance* 4: 289–304.

Amin, K., and J. Bodurtha (1995): "Discrete-Time Valuation of American Options with Stochastic Interest Rates," *Review of Financial Studies* 8: 193–234.

Amin, K., and V. Ng (1993): "Options Valuation with Systematic Stochastic Volatility," *Journal of Finance* 48: 881–910.

Andersen, L. (1995): "Bivariate Binary Options," Working Paper, Research General Re Financial Products Corp.

Andersen, L. (1996): "Monte Carlo Simulation of Barrier and Lookback Options with Continuous or High-Frequency Monitoring of the Underlying Asset," Working Paper, General Re Financial Products Corp.

Andersen, L., and J. Andreasen (1999): "Jump-Diffusion Processes: Volatility Smile Fitting and Numerical Methods for Pricing," Working Paper, General Re Financial Products. Forthcoming in *Review of Derivatives Research*.

Andersen, L., J. Andreasen, and R. Brotherton-Ratcliffe (1998): "The Passport Option," *Journal of Computational Finance* 1(3).

Andersen, L., and R. Brotherton-Ratcliffe (1995): "The Equity Option Volatility Smile: An Implicit Finite Difference Approach," Working Paper, General Re Financial Products Corp.

Andersen, T., L. Benzoni, and J. Lund (2002): "An Empirical Investigation of Continuous-Time Equity Return Models," *Journal of Finance* 57: 1239–1284.

Andreasen, J. (1998): "Fast and Accurate Pricing of Path Dependent Options: A Finite Difference Approach," *Journal of Computational Finance* 2 (Fall).

Andreasen, J., and B. Gruenewald (1996): "American Option Pricing in the Jump-Diffusion Model," Working Paper, Aarhus University, Denmark.

Arrow, K. (1970): *Essays in the Theory of Risk Bearing*, London: North-Holland.

Artzner, P., and D. Heath (1990): "Completeness and Non-Unique Pricing," Working Paper, Department of Operations, Cornell University.

Avellaneda, M., and A. Parás (1994): "Dynamic Hedging Strategies for Derivative Securities in the Presence of Large Transaction Costs," *Applied Mathematical Finance* 1: 165–194.

Bachelier, L. (1990): "Theorie de la Speculation," *Annales de l'Ecole Normale Superieure*, 3, Paris: Gauthier-Villars.

Back, K., and S. Pliska (1991): "On the Fundamental Theorem of Asset Pricing with an Infinite State Space," *Journal of Mathematical Economics* 20: 1–18.

Bajeux-Besnainou, I., and J.-C. Rochet (1996): "Dynamic Spanning: Are Options an Appropriate Instrument?" *Mathematical Finance* 6: 1–16.

Bakshi, G., C. Cao, and Z. Chen (1997): "Empirical Performance of Alternative Option Pricing Models," *Journal of Finance* 52: 2003–2049.

Bakshi, G., and D. Madan (1997): "Pricing Average-Rate Contingent Claims," Working Paper, Department of Finance, College of Business and Management, University of Maryland.

Bakshi, G., and D. Madan (2000): "Spanning and Derivative Security Valuation," *Journal of Financial Economics* 55: 205–238.

Ball, C., and A. Roma (1994): "Stochastic Volatility Option Pricing," *Journal of Financial and Quantitative Analysis* 29: 589–607.

Ball, C., and W. Torous (1985): "On Jumps in Common Stock Prices and their Impact on Call Option Pricing," *Journal of Finance* 40: 155–173.

Bandi, F., and T. Nguyen (2000): "On the Functional Estimation of Jump-Diffusion Models," Mimeo, Graduate School Business, University of Chicago.

Banz, R., and M. Miller (1978): "Prices for State-Contingent Claims: Some Evidence and Application," *Journal of Business* 51: 653–672.

Barles, G., M. Romano, and N. Touzi (1993): "Contingent Claims and Market Completeness in a Stochastic Volatility Model," Working Paper, Département de Mathématiques, Université de Tours, France.

Barles, G., and M. Soner (1998): "Option Pricing with Transaction Costs and a Nonlinear Black-Scholes Equation," *Finance and Stochastics* 2: 369–397.

Barone-Adesi, G., and R. Elliott (1991): "Approximations for the Values of American Options," *Stochastic Analysis and Applications* 9: 115–131.

Barraquand, J. (1993): "Numerical Valuation of High Dimensional Multivariate European Securities," Working Paper, Digital Research Laboratory, Paris.

Barraquand, J., and D. Martineau (1995): "Numerical Valuation of High Dimensional Multivariate American Securities," *Journal of Financial and Quantitative Analysis* 30: 383–405.

Barraquand, J., and T. Pudet (1996): "Pricing of American Path-Dependent Contingent Claims," *Mathematical Finance* 6: 17–51.

Bates, D. (1996): "Jumps and Stochastic Volatility: Exchange Rate Processes Implicit in Deutsche Mark Option," *Review of Financial Studies* 9: 69–107.

Bates, D. (1997): "Post-'87 Crash Fears in S-and-P 500 Futures Options," Working Paper, Finance Department, Wharton School, University of Pennsylvania.

Beckers, S. (1980): "The Constant Elasticity of Variance Model and Its Implications for Option Pricing," *Journal of Finance* 35: 661–673.

Beckers, S. (1981): "Standard Deviations Implied in Option Process as Predictors of Future Stock Price Variability," *Journal of Banking and Finance* 5: 363–382.

Beibel, M., and H. Lerche (1995): "A New Look at Warrant Pricing and Related Optimal Stopping Problems," Working Paper, Institut für Mathematische Stochastik, University of Bonn.

Bensoussan, A. (1984): "On the Theory of Option Pricing," *Acta Applicandae Mathematicae* 2: 139–158.

Bensoussan, A., M. Crouhy, and D. Galai (1995a): "Black-Scholes Approximation of Complex Option Values: The Cases of European Compound Call Options and Equity Warrants," Working Paper, Université Paris Dauphine and INRIA, France.

Bensoussan, A., M. Crouhy, and D. Galai (1995b): "Stochastic Equity Volatility Related to the Leverage Effect II: Valuation of European Equity Options and Warrants," *Applied Mathematical Finance* 2: 43–59.

Benzoni, L. (1998): "Pricing Options under Stochastic Volatility: An Econometric Analysis," Working Paper, J. L. Kellogg Graduate School of Management, Northwestern University.

Bergman, Y., B. Grundy, and Z. Wiener (1996): "Generalized Theory of Rational Optional Pricing," *Journal of Finance* 51: 1573–1610.

Bick, A. (1988): "Producing Derivative Assets with Forward Contracts," *Journal of Financial and Quantitative Analysis* 2: 153–160.

Bick, A. (1994): "Futures Pricing via Futures Strategies," Working Paper, Faculty of Business Administration, Simon Fraser University, Vancouver, Canada.

Bick, A. (1997): "Two Closed-Form Formulas for the Futures Price in the Presence of a Quality Option," *European Finance Review* 1: 81–104.

Bjerksund, P., and G. Stensland (1993): "Closed-Form Approximation of American Options," *Scandinavian Journal of Management* 9: S87–S89.

Björk, T. (1998): *Arbitrage Theory in Continuous Time*, New York: Oxford University Press.

Black, F. (1976): "Studies of Stock Price Volatility Changes," in *Proceedings of the 1976 Meetings of the Business and Economic Statistics Section, American Statistical Association*, pp. 177–181.

Black, F. (1976): "The Pricing of Commodity Contracts," *Journal of Financial Economics* 3: 167–179.

Black, F. (1989): "How We Came Up With the Option Pricing Formula," *Journal of Portfolio Management* 15.

Black, F., and M. Scholes (1973): "The Pricing of Options and Corporate Liabilities," *Journal of Political Economy* 81: 637–654.

Bossaerts, P., E. Ghysels, and C. Gouriéroux (1996): "Arbitrage-Based Pricing when Volatility Is Stochastic," Working Paper, California Institute of Technology, Pasadena, CA.

Bouaziz, Laurent, Eric Briys, and Michel Crouhy (1994): "The Pricing of Forward-Starting Asian Options," *Journal of Banking and Finance* 18(5): 823–839.

Boyarchenko, S., and S. Levendorskii (2000a): "Pricing of the Perpetual American Call Under Lévy Processes," Working Paper, Department of Mathematics, University of Pennsylvania.

Boyarchenko, S., and S. Levendorskii (2000b): "Pricing of the Perpetual American Put Under Lévy Processes," Working Paper, Department of Mathematics, University of Pennsylvania.

Boyle, P. (1977): "Options: A Monte Carlo Approach," *Journal of Financial Economics* 4: 323–338.

Boyle, P. (1988): "A Lattice Framework for Option Pricing with Two State Variables," *Journal of Financial and Quantitative Analysis* 23: 1–23.

Boyle, P. (1990): "Valuation of Derivative Securities Involving Several Assets Using Discrete Time Methods," Working Paper, Accounting Group, University of Waterloo, Waterloo, Canada.

Boyle, P., M. Broadie, and P. Glasserman (1997): "Monte Carlo Methods for Security Pricing," *Journal of Economic Dynamics and Control* 21: 1267–1321.

Boyle, P., J. Evnine, and S. Gibbs (1989): "Numerical Evaluation of Multivariate Contingent Claims," *Review of Financial Studies* 2: 241–250.

Boyle, P., and T. Vorst (1992): "Options Replication in Discrete Time with Transaction Costs," *Journal of Finance* 47: 271–293.

Breeden, D., and R. Litzenberger (1978): "Prices of State-Contigent Claims Implicit in Option Prices," *Journal of Business* 51: 621–651.

Brennan, M., and E. Schwartz (1977): "The Valuation of American Put Options," *Journal of Finance* 32: 449–462.

Broadie, M., J. Cvitanić, and M. Soner (1998): "Optimal Replication of Contingent Claims Under Portfolio Constraints," *Review of Financial Studies* 11: 59–79.

Broadie, M., and J. Detemple (1995): "Amercian Capped Call Options on Dividend-Paying Assets," *Review of Financial Studies* 8: 161–191.

Broadie, M., and J. Detemple (1996): "American Option Valuation: New Bounds, Approximations and a Comparison of Existing Methods," *Review of Financial Studies* 9: 1211–1250.

Broadie, M., and J. Detemple (1997): "The Valuation of American Options on Multiple Assets," *Mathematical Finance* 7: 241–285.

Broadie, M., and P. Glasserman (1996): "Estimating Security Price Derivatives Using Simulation," *Management Science* 42: 269–285.

Broadie, M., and P. Glasserman (1997): "Pricing American Style Securities Using Simulation," *Journal of Economic Dynamics and Control* 21: 1323–1353.

Broadie, M., and P. Glasserman (1998): "A Stochastic Mesh Method for Pricing High Dimensional American Options," Working Paper, Graduate School of Business, Columbia University, New York.

Broadie, M., P. Glasserman, and S. Kou (1997): "A Continuity Correction for Discrete Barrier Options," *Mathematical Finance* 7: 325–349.

Broadie, M., P. Glasserman, and S. Kou (1999): "Connecting Discrete and Continuous Path-Dependent Options," *Finance and Stochastics* 3: 55–82.

Buckdahn, R., and Y. Hu (1995): "Pricing of American Contingent Claims with Jump Stock Price and Constrained Portfolios," Working Paper, Département de Mathématiques, Université de Bretagne Occidentale, Brest, France.

Bunch, D., and H. Johnson (1993): "A Simple and Numerically Efficient Valuation Method of American Puts Using a Modified Geske-Johnson Approach," *Journal of Finance* 47: 809–816.

Campbell, J., and L. Hentschel (1992): "No News Is Good News: An Asymmetric Model of Changing Volatility in Stock Returns," *Journal of Financial Economics* 31: 281–318.

Carr, P. (1989): "European Option Valuation when Carrying Costs Are Unknown," Working Paper, Johnson Graduate School of Management, Cornell University.

Carr, P. (1991): "Deriving Derivatives of Derivative Securities," Working Paper, Johnson Graduate School of Management, Cornell University. Forthcoming in *Journal of Computational Finance*.

Carr, P. (1993a): "European Put Call Symmetry," Working Paper, Johnson Graduate School of Management, Cornell University.

Carr, P. (1994): "On Approximations for the Values of American Options," Working Paper, Johnson Graduate School of Management, Cornell University.

Carr, P. (1995): "Two Extensions to Barrier Option Valuation," *Applied Mathematical Finance* 2: 173–209.

Carr, P. (1998): "Randomization and the American Put," *Review of Financial Studies* 11: 598–626.

Carr, P., and K. Ellis (1994): "Non-Standard Valuation of Barrier Options," Working Paper, Johnson Graduate School of Management, Cornell University.

Carr, P., and D. Faguet (1994): "Fast Accurate Valuation of American Options," Working Paper, Johnson Graduate School of Management, Cornell University.

Carr, P., and D. Faguet (1996): "Valuing Finite-Lived Options as Perpetual," Working Paper, Johnson Graduate School of Management, Cornell University.

Carr, P., and R. Jarrow (1990): "The Stop-Loss Start-Gain Paradox and Option Valuation: A New Decomposition into Intrinsic and Time Value," *Review of Financial Studies* 3: 469–492.

Carr, P., R. Jarrow, and R. Myneni (1992): "Alternative Characterizations of American Put Options," *Mathematical Finance* 2: 87–106.

Carr, P., and D. Madan (1998): "Option Valuation Using the Fast Fourier Transform," *Journal of Computational Finance* 2 (Summer).

Carrasco, M., and J. P. Florens (2000): "Generalization of GMM to a Continuum of Moment Conditions," *Econometric Theory* 16: 797–834.

Carrasco, M., M. Chernov, J. P. Florens, and E. Ghysels (2001): "Estimating Diffusions with a Continuum of Moment Conditions," Working Paper.

Carverhill, A. P., and L. J. Clewlow (1990): "Valuing Average Rate (Asian) Options," *Risk* 3: 25–29.

Chacko, G., P. Tufano, and G. Verter (2001): "Cephalon, Inc., Taking Risk Management Theory Seriously," *Journal of Financial Economics* 60: 449–485.

Chacko, G., P. Tufano, and G. Verter (2002): "Raising Contingent Capital: The Case of Cephalon," *Journal of Applied Corporate Finance* 15: 57–70.

Chacko, G., and L. Viceira (1999): "Dynamic Consumption and Portfolio Choice with Stochastic Volatility in Incomplete Markets," NBER Working Paper 7377.

Chacko, G., and L. Viceira (2002): "Spectral GMM Estimation of Continuous-Time Processes," *Journal of Econometrics*.

Chalasani, P., S. Jha, and A Varikooty (1998): "Accurate Approximations for European Asian Options," *Journal of Computational Finance* 1 (Summer).

Charretour, F., R. Elliott, R. Myneni, and R. Viswanathan (1992): "American Option Valuation Notes," Working Paper, Oberwohlfach Institute, Oberwohlfach, Germany.

Cherian, J., and R. Jarrow (1998): "Options Markets, Self-Fulfilling Prophecies, and Implied Volatilities," *Review of Derivatives Research* 2: 5–37.

Cherif, T., N. El Karoui, R. Myneni, and R. Viswnathan (1995): "Arbitrage Pricing and Hedging of Quanto Options and Interest Rate Claims with Quadratic Gaussian State Variable," Working Paper, Laboratoire de Probabilités, Université de Paris, VI.

Chernov, M., and E. Ghysels (2000): "A Study Towards a Unified Approach to the Joint Estimation of Objective and Risk Neutral Measures for the Purpose of Options Valuation," *Journal of Financial Economics* 56: 407–458.

Chernov, M., R. Gallant, E. Ghysels, and G. Tauchen (2000): "A New Class of Stochastic Volatility Models with Jumps: Theory and Estimation," Working Paper.

Chernov, M., R. Gallant, E. Ghysels, and G. Tauchen (2002): "Alternative Models for Stock Price Dynamics," Working Paper.

Cherubini, U. (1993): "The Orthogonal Polynomial Approach to Contingent Claim Pricing," Working Paper, Banco Commerciale Italiana, Uffcio Studi, Milan.

Chidambaran, N., and S. Figlewski (1995): "Streamlining Monte-Carlo Simulation with the Quasi-Analytic Method: An Analysis of a Path-Dependent Option Strategy," *Journal of Derivatives* 3: 29–51.

Choi, J., and F. Longstaff (1985): "Pricing Options on Agricultural Futures: An Application of the Constant Elasticity of Variance Option Pricing Model," *Journal of Futures Markets* 5: 247–258.

Christensen, P. (1987): "An Intuitive Approach to the Harrison and Kreps Concept of Arbitrage Pricing for Continuous Time Diffusions, Working Paper, Department of Management, Odense University, Denmark.

Christie, Andrew, 1982. "The Stochastic Behavior of Common Stock Variances," *Journal of Financial Economics* 10: 407–432.

Clarke, N., and K. Parrott (1996): "The Multigrid Solution of Two-Factor American Put Options," Working Paper, Oxford University Computing Laboratory.

Clewlow, L. (1990): "Finite Difference Techniques for One- and Two-Dimensional Option Valuation Problems," Working Paper, Financial Options Research Center, University of Warwick.

Clewlow, L., and A. Carverhill (1992): "Efficient Monte Carlo Valuation and Hedging of Contingent Claims," Working Paper, Financial Options Research Centre, University of Warwick.

Clewlow, L., and A. Carverhill (1995): "A Note on the Efficiency of the Binomial Option Pricing Model," Working Paper, Financial Options Research Centre, University of Warwick.

Clewlow, L., and S. Hodges (1996): "Optimal Delta-Hedging under Transaction Costs," Working Paper, Financial Options Research Centre, University of Warwick.

Cohen, H. (1995): "Isolating the Wild Card Option," *Mathematical Finance* 2: 155–166.

Constantinides, G. (1993): "Option Pricing Bounds with Transactions Costs," Working Paper, Graduate School of Business, University of Chicago.

Constantinides, G., and T. Zariphopoulou (1999): "Bounds on Prices of Contingent Claims in an Intertemporal Economy with Proportional Transactions Costs and General Preferences," *Finance and Stochastics* 3: 345–369.

Conze, A., and R. Viswanathan (1991a): "Path Dependant Options: The Case of Lookback Options," *Journal of Finance* 5: 1893–1907.

Cox, J., J. Ingersoll, and S. Ross (1981b): "The Relation between Forward Prices and Futures Prices," *Journal of Financial Economics* 9: 321–346.

Cox, J., and S. Ross (1976): "The Valuation of Options for Alternative Stochastic Processes," *Journal of Financial Economics* 3: 145–166.

Cox, J., S. Ross, and M. Rubenstein (1979): "Option Pricing: A Simplified Approach," *Journal of Financial Economics* 7: 229–263.

Cox, J., and M. Rubenstein (1985): *Options Markets*, Englewood Cliffs, NJ: Prentice-Hall.

Curran, M. (1996): "Adaptive Importance Sampling for Pricing Path Dependent Options," Working Paper, Banque Paribas, London.

Cutland, N., P. Kopp, and W. Willinger (1991): "A Nonstandard Approach to Option Pricing," *Mathematical Finance* 1: 1–38.

Cutland, N., P. Kopp, and W. Willinger (1993a): "From Discrete to Continuous Financial Models: New Convergence Results for Options Pricing," *Mathematical Finance* 3: 101–125.

Cvitanić, J., and I. Karatzas (1993): "Hedging Contingent Claims with Constrained Portfolios," *Annals of Applied Probability* 3: 652–681.

Cvitanić, J., and J. Ma (1996): "Hedging Options for a Large Investor and Forward-Backward SDEs," *Annals of Applied Probability* 6: 370–398.

Daigler, R. (1993): *Financial Futures Markets*, New York: Harper Collins.

Danielsson, J. (1994): "Stochastic Volatility in Asset Prices: Estimation with Simulated Maximum Likelihood," *Journal of Econometrics*, 54.

Davis, M. (1998): "A Note on the Forward Measure," *Finance and Stochastics* 2: 19–28.

Davis, M., and V. Panas (1991): "European Option Pricing with Transaction Costs," Proceedings of the Thirtieth IEEE Conference on Decision and Control, Brighton, December, pp. 1299–1304.

Davis, M., A. Panas, and T. Zariphopoulou (1993): "European Option Pricing with Transaction Costs," *SIAM Journal of Control and Optimization* 31: 470–493.

Davydov, D., and V. Linetsky (1998): "Double Step Options," Working Paper, University of Michigan. Forthcoming in *Journal of Computational Finance*.

Davydov, D., and V. Linetsky (1999a): "Pricing Options on One-Dimensional Diffusions: A Sturm-Liouville Approach," Working Paper, University of Michigan.

Davydov, D., and V. Linetsky (1999b): "The Valuation and Hedging of Barrier and Lookback Options for Alternative Stochastic Processes," Working Paper, University of Michigan.

Davydov, D., and V. Linetsky (1999c): "The Valuation of Path-Dependent Options on One-dimensional Diffusions," Working Paper, University of Michigan.

Décamps, J.-P., and P. Koehl (1994): "Pricing and Hedging Asian Options: A PDE Approach," Working Paper, GREMAQ, Université des Sciences Sociales.

Delbaen, F., and M. Yor (1999): "Passport Options," Working Paper, Presentation at Strobl, Austria.

de Matos, J. A. (1993): "MSM Estimators of American Pricing Models," Working Paper, INSEAD, Fontainebleau, France.

Dempster, M. (1994): "Fast Numerical Valuation of American, Exotic and Complex Options," Working Paper, Finance Research Group, Department of Mathematics and Institute for Studies in Finance, University of Essex.

Dempster, M., and J. Hutton (1997): "Fast Numerical Valuation of American, Exotic and Complex Options," *Applied Mathematical Finance* 4: 1–20.

Dengler, H., and R. Jarrow (1996): "Option Pricing using a Binomial Model with Random Time Steps," *Review of Derivatives Research* 1: 137–138.

Derman, E., and I. Kani (1994): "Riding on the Smile," *Risk* 7 (February): 32–39.

Detemple, J., and S. Murthy (1997b): "Pricing and Trade of Index Options under Heterogeneous Beliefs," Working Paper, Faculty of Management, McGill University and CIRANO.

Detemple, J., and L. Selden (1991): "A General Equilibrium Analysis of Option and Stock Market Interactions," *International Economic Review* 32: 279–303.

Dewynne, J., and P. Wilmott (1994): "Exotic Options: Mathematical Models and Computation," Working Paper, Department of Mathematics, Southampton University.

Dewynne, J. N., and P. Wilmott (1995): "Asian Options as Linear Complementary Problems: Analysis and Finite-Difference Solutions," *Advances in Options and Futures Research* 8: 145–173.

Diener, F., and M. Diener (1999): "Asymptotics of the Binomial Formula for Option Pricing," Working Paper, Université de Nice Sophia-Antipolis.

Duan, J.-C. (1995): The Garch Option Pricing Model," *Mathematical Finance* 5: 13–32.

Duffie, D. (1988a): "An Extension of the Black-Scholes Model of Security Valuation," *Journal of Economic Theory* 46: 194–204.

Dupire, B. (1994): "Pricing with a Smile," *Risk* (January): 18–20.

Eberlein, E., and J. Jacod (1997): "On the Range of Option Prices," *Finance and Stochastics* 1: 131–140.

Eberlein, E., U. Keller, and K. Prause (1998): "New Insights into Smile, Mispricing, and Value at Risk: The Hyperbolic Model," *Journal of Business* 71: 371–405.

Edirisinghe, C., V. Naik, and R. Uppal (1993): "Optimal Replication of Options with Transactions Costs," *Journal of Financial and Quantitative Analysis* 28: 117–138.

El Karoui, N., M. Jeanblanc, and S. Shrever (1998): "Robustness of the Black-Scholes Formula," *Mathematical Finance* 8: 93–126.

Eydeland, A., and H. Geman (1994): "Asian Options Revisited: Inverting the Laplace Transform, Mimeo, ESSEC, Dept of Finance.

Feuerverger, A. (1990): "An Efficiency Result for the Empirical Characteristic Function in Stationary Time-Series Models," *The Canadian Journal of Statistics* 18: 155–161.

Feuerverger, A., and P. McDunnough (1981a): "On Some Fourier Methods for Inference," *Journal of the American Statistical Association* 76: 379–387.

Feuerverger, A., and P. McDunnough (1981b): "On the Efficiency of Empirical Characteristic Function Procedures," *Journal of the Royal Statistical Society, Series* B 43: 20–27.

Fischer, S. (1978): "Call Option Pricing When the Exercise Price is Uncertain, and the Valuation of Index Bonds," *Journal of Finance* 33: 169–176.

Fleming, J., and R. Whaley (1994): "The Value of Wildcard Options," *Journal of Finance* 1: 215–236.

Flesaker, B. (1991): "Valuing European Options when the Terminal Value of the Underlying Asset Is Unobservable," Working Paper, Department of Finance, University of Illinois at Urbana-Champaign.

Föllmer, H., and M. Schweizer (1990): "Hedging of Contingent Claims under Incomplete Information," in M. Davis and R. Elliott (Eds.), *Applied Stochastic Analysis*, pp. 389–414, London: Gordon and Breach.

Föllmer, H., and D. Sondermann (1986): "Hedging on Non-Redundant Contingent Claims," in W. Hildebrand and A. Mas-Collel (Eds.), *Contributions to Mathematical Economics*, pp. 205–244, Amsterdam: North-Holland.

Fournié, E., and J.-M. Lasry (1996): "Some Nonlinear Methods to Study Far-from-the-Money Contingent Claims," Working Paper, Caisse Autonome de Refinancement, Paris.

French, K., G. Schwert, and R. Stambaugh (1987): "Expected Stock Returns and Volatility," *Journal of Financial Economics* 19: 3–30.

Frey, R. (1996): "The Pricing and Hedging of Options in Finitely Elastic Markets, Working Paper, Department of Statistics, Faculty of Economics, University of Bonn.

Frey, R., and C. Sin (1997): "Bounds on European Option Prices under Stochastic Volatility," Working Paper, Department Mathematik, ETH Zentrum, Zürich.

Fu, M., D. Madan, and T. Wang (1999): "Pricing Continuous-Time Asian Options: A Comparison of Monte Carlo and Laplace Transform Methods," *Journal of Computational Finance* 2 (Winter): 49–74.

Galai, D., and M. Schneller (1978): "Pricing of Warrants and the Value of the Firm," *Journal of Finance* 33: 1333–1342.

Gallant, A. R., D. Hsieh, and G. Tauchen (1997): "Estimation of Stochastic Volatility Models with Diagnostics," *Journal of Econometrics* 81: 159–192.

Gallant, R., and G. Tauchen (1996): "Which Moments to Match?" *Econometric Theory* 12: 657–681.

Gandhi, D., A. Kooros, and G. Salkin (1993): "An Improved Analytic Approximation for American Option Pricing," Working Paper, Imperial College, University of London.

Gao, B., J.-Z. Huang, and M. Subrahmanyam (1996): "An Analytical Approach to the Valuation of American Path-Dependent Options," Working Paper, Kenan-Flager Business School, University of North Carolina. Forthcoming in *Journal of Economic Dynamics and Control*.

Geman, H., N. El Karoui, and J. Rochet (1995): "Changes of Numéraire, Changes of Probability Measure and Option Pricing," *Journal of Applied Probability* 32: 443–458.

Geske, H., and H. Johnson (1984): "The American Put Option Valued Analytically," *Journal of Finance* 39: 1511–1524.

Geske, R. (1979): "The Valuation of Compound Options," *Journal of Financial Economics* 7: 63–81.

Ghysels, E., A. Harvey, and E. Renault (1996): "Stochastic Volatility," in G. S. Madala and C. R. Rao (Eds.), *Handbook of Statistics*, Vol. 14, Amsterdam: Elsevier.

Goldman, B., H. Sosin, and M. Gatto (1979): "Path Dependent Options: 'Buy at the Low, Sell at the High'," *Journal of Finance* 34: 1111–1127.

Grabbe, J. (1983): "The Pricing of Call and Put Options on Foreign Exchange," *Journal of International Money and Finance* 2: 239–253.

Grannan, E., and G. Swindle (1996): "Minimizing Transaction Costs of Option Hedging Strategies," *Mathematical Finance* 6: 341–364.

Grauer, F., and R. Litzenberger (1979): "The Pricing of Commodity Futures Contracts, Nominal Bonds, and Other Risky Assets Under Commodity Price Uncertainty," *Journal of Finance* 44: 69–84.

Gukhal, C. (1995a): "American Call Options on Stocks with Discrete Dividends," Working Paper, Graduate School of Business, Columbia University, New York.

Gukhal, C. (1995b): "The Analytic Valuation of American Options on Jump-Diffusion Processes," Working Paper, Graduate School of Business, Columbia University, New York.

Guo, D. (1998): "The Risk Premium of Volatility Implicit in Currency Options," *Journal of Business and Economics Statistics* 16: 498–507.

Hahn, F. (1994): "On Economies with Arrow Securities," Working Paper, Department of Economics, Cambridge University.

Hansen, L. (1982): "Large Sample Properties of Generalized Method of Moments Estimators," *Econometrica* 50: 1029–1054.

Hara, C. (1993): "A Role of Redundant Assets in the Presence of Transaction Costs," Working Paper, Sloan School of Management, Massachusetts Institute of Technology.

Harrison, M., and D. Kreps (1979): "Martingales and Arbitrage in Multiperiod Securities Markets," *Journal of Economic Theory* 20: 381–408.

Harrison, M., and S. Pliska (1981): "Martingales and Stochastic Integrals in the Theory of Continuous Trading," *Stochastic Processes and Their Applications* 11: 215–260.

Harvey, A., E. Ruiz, and N. Shephard (1994): "Multivariate Stochastic Variance Models," *Review of Economic Studies* 61, 247–264.

Haug, E. (1999): "Closed Form Valuation of American Barrier Options," Working Paper, Derivatives Research, Tempus Financial Engineering, Norway.

He, H. (1990): "Convergence from Discrete- to Continuous-Time Contingent Claims Prices," *Review of Financial Studies* 3: 523–546.

Hentschel, L. (1995): "All in the Family: Nesting Symmetric and Asymmetric GARCH Models," *Journal of Financial Economics* 39: 71–104.

Heston, S. (1993): "A Closed-Form Solution for Options with Stochastic Volatility with Applications to Bond and Currency Options," *Review of Financial Studies* 6: 327–344.

Heston, S. (1997): "Option Pricing with Infinitely Divisible Distributions," Working Paper, John M. Olin School of Business, Washington University, St. Louis.

Heston, S., and S. Nandi (1997): "A Closed-Form GARCH Option Pricing Model," Working Paper, Federal Reserve Bank of Atlanta.

Ho, T., R. Stapleton, and M. Subrahmanyam (1997): "The Valuation of American Options with Stochastic Interest Rates: A Generalization of the Geske-Johnson Technique," *Journal of Finance* (June 1997).

Hobson, D. (1998): "Bounds on the Lookback," *Finance and Stochastics* 98: 250–263.

Hodges, S., and A. Carverhill (1992): "The Characterization of Economic Equilibria which Support Black-Scholes Options Pricing," Working Paper, Financial Options Research Centre, University of Warwick.

Hodges, S., and M. Selby (1996): "The Risk Premium in Trading Equilibria Which Support Black-Scholes Option Pricing," in M.A.H. Dempster and S. R. Pliska (Eds.), *Mathematics of Derivative Securities*, pp. 41–52, Cambridge: Cambridge University Press.

Hofmann, N., E. Platen, and M. Schweizer (1992): "Option Pricing Under Incompleteness and Stochastic Volatility," *Mathematical Finance* 2: 153–187.

Huang, J., M. Subrahmanyam, and G. Yu (1996): "Pricing and Hedging American Options: A Recursive Integration Method and Its Implementation," *Review of Financial Studies*.

Huang, J., M. Subrahmanyam, and G. Yu (1996): "Pricing and Hedging American Options: A Recursive Integration Method," *Review of Financial Studies* 9: 277–300.

Hull, J., and A. White (1987): "The Pricing of Options on Assets with Stochastic Volatilities," *Journal of Finance* 2: 281–300.

Hull, J., and A. White (1990b): "Valuing Derivative Securities Using the Explicit Finite Difference Method," *Journal of Financial and Quantitative Analysis* 25: 87–100.

Hull, J., and A. White (1995): "The Impact of Default Risk on the Prices of Options and Other Derivative Securities," *Journal of Banking and Finance* 19: 299–322.

Ibanez, A., and F. Zapatero (1999): "Monte Carlo Valuation of American Options Through Computation of the Optimal Exercise Frontier," Working Paper, Departamento de Administracion, ITAM, Mexico.

Ingersoll, J. (1987): *Theory of Financial Decision Making*, Totowa, NJ: Rowman and Littlefield.

Jacka, S. (1991): "Optimal Stopping and the American Put," *Mathematical Finance* 1: 1–14.

Jackwerth, J. (1997): "Generalized Binomial Trees," *Journal of Derivatives* 5 (2): 7–17.

Jackwerth, J. C. (2000): "Recovering Risk Aversion from Options Prices and Realized Returns," *Review of Financial Studies* 13: 433–452.

Jackwerth, J., and M. Rubinstein (1996a): "Implied Binomial Trees: Generalizations and Empirical Tests," Working Paper, Haas School of Business, University of California, Berkeley.

Jackwerth, J., and M. Rubinstein (1996b): "Recovering Probability Distributions from Option Prices," *Journal of Finance* 51: 1611–1631.

Jackwerth, J., and M. Rubinstein (1996c): "Recovering Stochastic Processes from Option Prices," Working Paper, Haas School of Business, University of California, Berkeley.

Jacquier, E., N. Polson, and P. Rossi (1994): "Bayesian Analysis of Stochastic Volatility Models," *Journal of Business and Economic Statistics* 12: 371–389.

Jagannathan, R. (1984): "Call Options and the Risk of Underlying Securities," *Journal of Financial Economics* 13: 425–434.

Jaillet, P., D. Lamberton, and B. Lapeyre (1990): "Variational Inequalities and the Pricing of American Options," Working Paper, CERMA-ENPC, La Courtine, France.

Jamshidian, F. (1989c): "Free Boundary Formulas for American Options," Working Paper, Financial Strategies Group, Merrill Lynch Capital Markets, New York.

Jamshidian, F. (1993b): "Options and Futures Evaluation with Deterministic Volatilities," *Mathematical Finance* 3: 149–159.

Jamshidian, F. (1997a): "A Note on Analytical Valuation of Double Barrier Options," Working Paper, Sakura Global Capital.

Jamshidian, F., and M. Fein (1990): "Closed Form Solutions for Oil Futures and European Options in the Gibson-Schwartz Model: A Comment," Working Paper, Financial Strategies Group, Merrill Lynch Capital Markets, New York.

Jarrow, R., and A. Rudd (1982): "Approximate Option Valuation for Arbitrary Stochastic Processes," *Journal of Financial Economics* 10: 347–359.

Jiang, G., and J. Knight (2001): "Efficient Estimation of the Continuous Time Stochastic Volatility Model Via the Empirical Characteristic Function," *Journal of Business and Economic Statistics.*

Johnson, H. (1987): "Options on the Maximum or the Minimum of Several Assets," *Journal of Financial and Quantitative Analysis* 22: 277–283.

Johnson, H., and D. Shanno (1987): "The Pricing of Options When the Variance Is Changing," *Journal of Financial and Quantitative Analysis* 22: 143–151.

Johnson, H., and R. Stulz (1987): "The Pricing of Options with Default Risk," *Journal of Finance* 42: 267–280.

Jones, R., and R. Jacobs (1986): "History Dependent Financial Claims: Monte Carlo Valuation," Working Paper, Department of Finance, Simon Fraser University, Vancouver, Canada.

Jorgensen, P. (1994): "American Option Pricing," Working Paper, School of Business, Institute of Management, University of Aarhaus, Denmark.

Jorion, P. (1988): "On Jump Processes in the Foreign Exchange and Stock Markets," *Review of Financial Studies* 1: 427–445.

Ju, N. (1997a): "Fourier Transformation, Martingale, and the Pricing of Average-Rate Derivatives," Working Paper, Haas School of Business, University of California, Berkeley.

Ju, N. (1997b): "Pricing American Perpetual Lookback Options," Working Paper, Haas School of Business, University of California, Berkeley.

Karatzas, I. (1991): "On the Pricing of American Options," *Applied Mathematics and Optimization* 17: 37–60.

Karatzas, I., and S.-G. Kou. (1998): "Hedging American Contingent Claims with Constrained Portfolios," *Finance and Stochastics* 2: 215–258.

Kat, H. (1993): "Hedging Lookback and Asian Options," Working Paper, Derivatives Department, MeesPierson N.V., Amsterdam.

Kemna, A. G. Z., and A. C. F. Vorst (1990): "A Pricing Method for Options Based on Average Asset Values," *Journal of Banking and Finance* 14 (March): 113–129.

Kifer, Y. (2000): "Game Options," *Finance and Stochastics* 4: 443–463.

Kim, I. (1990): "The Analytic Valuation of American Options," *Review of Financial Studies* 3: 547–572.

Kind, P., R. Lipster, and W. Runggaldier (1991): "Diffusion Approximation in Past Dependent Models and Applications to Option Pricing," *Annals of Applied Probability* 1: 379–405.

Kishimoto, N. (1989): "A Simplified Approach to Pricing Path Dependent Securities," Working Paper, Fuqua School of Business, Duke University.

Knight, J., and J. Yu (2002): "Empirical Characteristic Function in Time Series Estimation," *Econometric Theory*.

Kou, S. (1999): "A Jump Diffusion Model for Option Pricing with Three Properties: Leptokurtic Feature, Volatility Smile, and Analytical Tractability," Working Paper, Department of IEOR, Columbia University.

Krasa, S., and J. Werner (1991): "Equilibria with Options: Existence and Indeterminacy," *Journal of Economic Theory* 54: 305–320.

Kreps, D. (1982): "Multiperiod Securities and the Effcient Allocation of Risk: A Comment on the Black-Scholes Option Pricing Model," in J. McCall (Ed.), *The Economics of Uncertainty and Information*, pp. 203–232, Chicago: University of Chicago Press.

Lacoste, V. (1995): "Wiener Chaos: A New Approach to Option Hedging," Working Paper, Department Finance, ESSEC.

Lagnado, R., and S. Osher (1996): "A Technique for Calibrating Derivative Security Pricing Models: Numerical Solution of an Inverse Problem," Working Paper, C-ATS, Palo Alto, CA.

Lamberton, D. (1993): "Convergence of the Critical Price in the Approximation of American Options," *Mathematical Finance* 3: 179–190.

Lamberton, D. (1997): "Error Estimates for the Binomial Approximation of American Put Options," Working Paper, Equipe d'Analyse et de Mathématiques Appliquées, Université De Marne-La-Vallée. Forthcoming in *The Annals of Applied Probability*.

Lando, D. (1994): "Three Essays on Contingent Claims Pricing," Working Paper, Ph.D. dissertation, Statistics Center, Cornell University.

Lando, D. (1995): "On Jump-Diffusion Option Pricing from the Viewpoint of Semimartingale Characteristics," *Surveys in Applied and Industrial Mathematics* 2: 605–625.

Lee, J.-J. (1990): "The Valuation of American Calls," Working Paper, Graduate School of Business, Stanford University.

Lee, J.-J. (1991): "A Note on Binomial Approximation for Contingent Securities," Working Paper, Graduate School of Business, Stanford University.

Leland, H. (1985): "Option Pricing and Replication with Transactions Costs," *Journal of Finance* 40: 1283–1301.

Lesne, J.-P., J.-L. Prigent, and O. Scaillet (2000): "Convergence of Discrete Time Option Pricing Models Under Stochastic Interest Rates," *Finance and Stochastics* 4: 81–93.

Levental, S., and A. Skorohod (1997): "On the Possibility of Hedging Options in the Presence of Transaction Costs," *Annals of Applied Probability* 7: 410–443.

Levy, A., M. Avellaneda, and A. Parás (1994): "A New Approach for Pricing Derivative Securities in Markets With Uncertain Volatilities: A 'Case Study' on the Trinomial Tree," Working Paper, Courant Institute of Mathematical Sciences, New York University.

Levy, E. (1992): "The Valuation of Average Rate Currency Options," *Journal of International Money and Finance* 11: 474–491.

Li, A., P. Ritchken, and L. Sankarasubramanian (1995): "Lattice Models for Pricing American Interest Rate Claims," *Journal of Finance* 50: 719–737.

Linetsky, V. (1999): "Step Options," *Mathematical Finance* 9: 55–96.

Liu, J., J. Pan, and L. Pedersen (1999): "Density-Based Inference in Affne Jump-Diffusions," Working Paper, Graduate School of Business, Stanford University.

Lo, A. (1986): "Statistical Tests of Contingent Claims Asset-Pricing Models: A New Methodology," *Journal of Financial Economics* 17: 143–174.

Lo, A. (1987): "Semi-Parametric Upper Bounds for Option Prices and Expected Payoffs," *Journal of Financial Economics* 19: 373–387.

Lo, A. (1988): "Maximum Likelihood Estimation of Generalized Itô Processes with Discretely Sampled Data," *Econometric Theory* 4: 231–247.

Lo, A., and J. Wang (1995): "Implementing Option Pricing Models When Asset Returns Are Predictible," *Journal of Finance* 50: 87–129.

Longstaff, F., and E. Schwartz (1998): "Valuing American Options By Simulation: A Simple Least-Squares Approach," Working Paper, Anderson Graduate School of Management, University of California, Los Angeles.

Longstaff, F., and E. Schwartz (2001): "Valuing American Options by Simulation: A Simple Least-Squares Approach," *Review of Financial Studies* 14: 113–147.

Lu, S., and G. Yu (1993): "Valuation of Options under Stochastic Volatility: The Garch Diffusion Approach," Working Paper, Department of Mathematics, University of Michigan.

Ma, C.-H. (1991): "Valuation of Derivative Securities with Mixed Poisson-Brownian Information and with Recursive Utility," Working Paper, Department of Economics, University of Toronto.

Ma, J., and J. Cvitanič (1996): "Hedging Options for a Large Investor and Forward Backward SDEs," *Annals of Applied Probability* 6: 370–398.

Madan, D., and E. Chang (1996): "Volatility Smiles, Skewness Premia and Risk Metrics: Applications of a Four Parameter Closed Form Generalization of Geometric Brownian Motion to the Pricing of Options," Working Paper, University of Maryland.

Madan, D., and F. Milne (1991): "Option Pricing with V.G. Martingale Components," *Mathematical Finance* 1: 39–55.

Madan, D., F. Milne, and H. Shefrin (1989): "The Multinomial Option Pricing Model and Its Brownian and Poisson Limits," *Review of Financial Studies* 2: 251–266.

Madan, D., and E. Senata (1987): "Simulation of Estimates Using the Empirical Characteristic Function," *International Statistical Review* 55: 153–161.

Maghsoodi, Y. (1998): "A Closed-Form Analytical Formula for Options with a Non-Linear Stochastic Volatility," Working Paper, University of Southampton, UK.

Magill, M., and W. Shafer (1990): "Characterization of Generically Complete Real Asset Structures," *Journal of Mathematical Economics* 19, 167–194.

Margrabe, W. (1978): "The Value of an Option to Exchange One Asset for Another," *Journal of Finance* 33: 177–186.

Mason, S., and R. Merton (1985): "The Role of Contingent Claims Analysis in Corporate Finance," in E. Altman and M. Subrahmanyam (Eds.), *Recent Advances in Corporate Finance*, Homewood, IL: Richard D. Irwin.

Melino, A. (1994): "Estimation of Continuous-Time Models in Finance," in C. Sims (Ed.), *Advances in Econometrics, Sixth World Congress*, Volume II, Cambridge: Cambridge University Press.

Melino, A., and S. Turnbull (1990): "Pricing Foreign Currency Options with Stochastic Volatility," *Journal of Econometrics* 45: 239–265.

Merton, R. (1973): "The Theory of Rational Option Pricing," *Bell Journal of Economics and Management Science* 4: 141–183.

Merton, R. (1976): "Option Pricing when the Underlying Stock Returns Are Discontinuous," *Journal of Financial Economics* 5: 125–144.

Merton, R. (1976): "The Impact on Option Pricing of Specification Error in the Underlying Stock Price Returns," *Journal of Finance* 31: 333–350.

Merton, R. (1977): "An Analytic Derivation of the Cost of Deposit Insurance and Loan Guarantees: An Application of Modern Option Pricing Theory," *Journal of Banking and Finance* 1: 3–11.

Merton, R. (1977): "On the Pricing of Contingent Claims and the Modigliani-Miller Theorem," *Journal of Financial Economics* 5: 241–250.

Merton, R. (1978): "On the Cost of Deposit Insurance When There Are Surveillance Costs," *Journal of Business* 51: 439–452.

Merton, R. (1980): "On Estimating the Expected Return on the Market: An Explanatory Investigation," *Journal of Financial Economics* 8: 323–361.

Merton, R. C. (1983): "Financial Economics," in E. C. Brown and R. M. Solow (Eds.), *Paul Samuelson and Modern Economic Theory*, New York: McGraw-Hill.

Merton, R. C. (1990): "Capital Market Theory and the Pricing of Financial Securities," in B. Friedman and F. Hahn (Eds.), *Handbook of Monetary Economics*, Amsterdam: North-Holland.

Modigliani, F., and M. Miller (1958): "The Cost of Capital, Corporation Finance, and the Theory of Investment," *American Economic Review* 48: 261–297.

Müller, S. (1985): *Arbitrage Pricing of Contingent Claims*, Lecture Notes in Economics and Mathematical Systems, Vol. 254, New York: Springer-Verlag.

Munk, C. (1997): "No-Arbitrage Bounds on Contingent Claims Prices with Convex Constraints on the Dollar Investments of the Hedge Portfolio," Working Paper, Department of Management, Odense University, Denmark.

Myneni, R. (1992a): "Continuous-Time Relationships between Futures and Forward Prices," Working Paper, Graduate School of Business, Stanford University.

Myneni, R. (1992b): "The Pricing of the American Option," *Annals of Applied Probability* 2: 1–23.

Nahum, E. (1998): "The Pricing of Options Depending on a Discrete Maximum," Working Paper, Department of Statistics, University of California, Berkeley.

Naik, V., and R. Uppal (1994): "Leverage Constraints and the Optimal Hedging of Stock and Bond Options," *Journal of Financial and Quantitative Analysis* 29: 199–222.

Nelson, D., and K. Ramaswamy (1989): "Simple Binomial Processes as Diffusion Approximations in Financial Models," *Review of Financial Studies* 3: 393–430.

Nielsen, J., and K. Sandmann (1996): "The Pricing of Asian Options Under Stochastic Interest Rates," *Applied Mathematical Finance* 3: 209–236.

Ohashi, K. (1991): "A Note on the Terminal Date Security Prices in a Continuous Time Trading Model with Dividends," *Journal of Mathematical Economics* 20: 219–224.

Oliveira, D. (1994): "Arbitrage Pricing of Integral Options," Working Paper, Instituto de Matemática Pura e Applicada, Rio de Janeiro.

Pan, J. (1999): "Integrated Time-Series Analysis of Spot and Options Prices," Working Paper, Graduate School of Business, Stanford University.

Pan, J. (2002): "The Jump-Risk Premia Implicit in Options: Evidence from an Integrated Time-Series Study," *Journal of Financial Economics* 63: 3–50.

Pappalardo, L. (1996): "Option Pricing and Smile Effect when Underlying Stock Prices Are Driven by a Jump Process," Working Paper, Financial Options Research Centre, University of Warwick.

Pham, H. (1995): "Optimal Stopping, Free Boundary and American Option in a Jump Diffusion Model," Working Paper, CEREMADE Université de Paris IX Dauphine. Forthcoming in *Applied Mathematics and Optimization*.

Platen, E., and M. Schweizer (1994): "On Smile and Skewness," Working Paper, School of Mathematical Sciences Centre for Mathematics and Its Applications, The Australian National University, Canberra.

Polemarchakis, H., and B. Ku (1990): "Options and Equilibrium," *Journal of Mathematical Economics* 19: 107–112.

Poteshman, A.M. (1998): "Estimating a General Stochastic Variance Model from Options Prices," Working Paper, Graduate School of Business, University of Chicago.

Prigent, J.-L. (1994): "From Discrete to Continuous Time Finance: Weak Convergence of the Optimal Financial Trading Strategies," Working Paper, Institute of Mathematical Research of Rennes, University of Rennes.

Prigent, J.-L. (1995): "Incomplete Markets: Convergence of Options Values under the Minimal Martingale Measure," Working Paper, THEMA, Université de Cergy-Pontoise, Cergy-Pontoise.

Rady, S. (1993): "State Prices Implicit in Valuation Formula for Derivative Securities: A Martingale Approach," Working Paper, London School of Economics.

Rady, S. (1995): "Option Pricing with a Quadratic Diffusion Term," Working Paper, Financial Markets Group, London School of Economics.

Reiner, E., and M. Rubinstein (1992): "Exotic Options," Berkeley Program in Finance, Working Papers, University of California, Berkeley.

Reisman, H. (1986): "Option Pricing for Stocks with a Generalized Log-Normal Price Distribution," Working Paper, Department of Finance, University of Minnesota.

Renault, E., S. Pastorello, and N. Touzi (2000): "Statistical Inference for Random Variance Option Pricing," *Journal of Business and Economic Statistics* 18: 358–317.

Ritchken, P., and R. Trevor (1999): "Option Pricing Options under GARCH and Stochastic Volatility," *Journal of Finance* 54: 377–402.

Rogers, C., and Z. Shi (1995): "The Value of an Asian Option," *Journal of Applied Probability* 32: 1077–1088.

Rogers, L., and E. Stapleton (1998): "Fast Accurate Binomial Pricing," *Finance and Stochastics* 2: 3–17.

Roll, R. (1977): "An Analytic Valuation Formula for Unprotected American Call Options on Stocks with Known Dividends," *Journal of Financial Economics* 5: 251–258.

Romano, M., and N. Touzi (1997): "Contingent Claims and Market Completeness in a Stochastic Volatility Model," *Mathematical Finance* 7: 399–412.

Ronn, E., and A. Verma (1986): "Pricing Risk-Adjusted Deposit Insurance: An Options-Based Model," *Journal of Finance* 41: 871–895.

Rosenberg, J., and R. Engle (1999): "Empirical Pricing Kernels," Working Paper, Stern School of Business, New York University.

Ross, S. (1978): "A Simple Approach to the Valuation of Risky Streams," *Journal of Business* 51: 453–475.

Rubinstein, M. (1976): "The Valuation of Uncertain Income Streams and the Pricing of Options," *Bell Journal of Economics* 7: 407–425.

Rubinstein, M. (1987): "Derivative Assets Analysis," *Economics Perspectives* 1: 73–93.

Rubinstein, M. (1994): "Implied Binomial Trees," *Journal of Finance* 49: 771–818.

Rubinstein, M. (1995): "As Simple as One, Two, Three," *Risk* 8 (January): 44–47.

Ruttiens, A. (1990): "Average Rate Options, Classical Replica," *Risk* 3: 33–36.

Sbuelz, A. (1998): "A General Treatment of Barrier Options," Working Paper, London Business School.

Schaefer, S., and E. Schwartz (1987): "Time-Dependent Variance and the Pricing of Bond Options," *Journal of Finance* 42: 1113–1128.

Scheinkman, J. (1989): "Market Incompleteness and the Equilibrium Valuation of Assets," in S. Bhattacharya and G. Constantinides (Eds.), *Theory of Valuation*, pp. 45–51, Totowa, NJ: Rowman and Littlefield.

Schoenmakers, J., and A. Heemink (1996): "Fast Valuation of Financial Derivatives," Working Paper, Delft University of Technology, The Netherlands.

Scholes, M. (1976): "Taxes and the Pricing of Options," *Journal of Finance* 31: 319–332.

Schroder, M. (1989): "Computing the Constant Elasticity of Variance Option Pricing Formula," *Journal of Finance* 44(1): 211–219.

Schroder, M. (1999): "Changes of Numeraire of Pricing Futures, Forwards and Options," *Review of Financial Studies* 12: 143–164.

Schröder, M. (1999a): "On the Valuation of Arithmetic-Average Asian Options: Explicit Formulas," Working Paper, Fakultät für Mathematik and Informatik der Universität Mannheim.

Schröder, M. (1999b): "On the Valuation of Double-Barrier Options," Working Paper, Fakultät für Mathematik and Informatik der Universität Mannheim.

Schröder, M. (1999c): "On the Valuation of Paris Options: Foundational Results," Working Paper, Lehrstuhl Mathematik III Universität Mannheim.

Schröder, M. (1999d): "On the Valuation of Paris Options: The First Standard Case," Working Paper, Lehrstuhl Mathematik III Universität Mannheim.

Schwartz, E. (1977): "The Valuation of Warrants: Implementing a New Approach," *Journal of Financial Economics* 4: 79–94.

Schwartz, E. (1982): "The Pricing of Commodity-Linked Bonds," *Journal of Finance* 37: 525–539.

Schwartz, E. (1997): "Presidential Address: The Stochastic Behavior of Commodity Prices: Implications for Valuation and Hedging," *Journal of Finance* 52: 923–973.

Schwert, G. W. (1989): "Why Does Stock Market Volatility Change Over Time?" *Journal of Finance* 44: 1115–1153.

Scott, L. (1987): "Option Pricing when the Variance Changes Randomly: Theory, Estimation, and Application," *Journal of Financial and Quantitative Analysis* 4: 419–438.

Scott, L. (1992): "Stock Market Volatility and the Pricing of Index Options: An Analysis of Implied Volatilities and the Volatility Risk Premium in a Model with Stochastic Interest Rates and Volatility," Working Paper, Department of Finance, University of Georgia.

Scott, L. (1997): "Pricing Stock Options in a Jump-Diffusion Model with Stochastic Volatility and Interest Rates: Applications of Fourier Inversion Methods," *Mathematical Finance* 7: 413–426.

Selby, M., and S. Hodges (1987): "On the Evaluation of Compound Options," *Management Science* 33: 347–355.

Sharpe, W. (1964): "Capital Asset Prices: A Theory of Market Equilibrium under Conditions of Risk," *Journal of Finance* 19: 425–442.

Shephard, N. G. (1991): "From Characteristic Function to Distribution Function: A Simple Framework for the Theory," *Econometric Theory* 7: 519–529.

Singleton, K. (1997): "Estimation of Affine Asset Pricing Models Using the Empirical Characteristic Function," *Journal of Econometrics*.

Singleton, K. (1999): "Estimation of Affine Asset Pricing Models Using the Empirical Characteristic Function," *Journal of Econometrics* 102: 111–141.

Sircar, R. (1996): "Feedback Effects in Option Pricing," Working Paper, SCCM Program, Stanford University.

Soner, M., S. Shreve, and J. Cvitanič (1994): "There Is No Nontrivial Hedging Portfolio for Option Pricing with Transaction Costs," *Annals of Applied Probability* 5: 327–355.

Stapleton, R., and M. Subrahmanyam (1978): "A Multiperiod Equilibrium Asset Pricing Model," *Econometrica* 46: 1077–1093.

Stapleton, R., and M. Subrahmanyam (1984): "The Valuation of Multivariate Contingent Claims in Discrete-Time Models," *Journal of Finance*.

Stapleton, R., and M. Subrahmanyam (1984): "The Valuation of Options When Asset Returns Are Generated by a Binomial Process," *Journal of Finance*.

Steenkiste, R. V., and S. Foresi. (1999): "Arrow-Debreu Prices for Affine Models," Working Paper, Salomon Smith Barney, Inc., Goldman Sachs Asset Management.

Stein, E., and J. Stein (1991): "Stock Price Distributions with Stochastic Volatility: An Analytic Approach," *Review of Financial Studies* 4: 725–752.

Stoll, H., and R. Whaley (1993): *Futures and Options: Theory and Applications*, Cincinnati: Southwestern.

Stulz, R. (1982): "Options on the Minimum or the Maximum of Two Risky Assets: Analysis and Applications," *Journal of Financial Economics* 10: 161–185.

Subramanian, A. (1997): "European Option Pricing with General Transaction Costs," Working Paper, Center for Applied Mathematics, Cornell University.

Subrahmanyam, M. (1989): "Options on Stock Indices and Options on Futures," *Journal of Banking and Finance*.

Taylor, S. (1994): "Modeling Stochastic Volatility: A Review and Comparative Study," *Mathematical Finance* 4: 183–204.

Toft, K., and G. Brown (1996): "Constructing Binomial Trees from Multiple Implied Probability Distributions," Working Paper, Department of Finance, University of Texas, Austin.

Touzi, N. (1995): "American Options Exercise Boundary when the Volatility Changes Randomly," Working Paper, CEREMADE, Université de Paris IX, Dauphine.

Turnbull, S., and L. M. Wakeman (1991): "A Quick Algorithm for Pricing European Average Options," *Journal of Financial and Quantitative Analysis* 26(3): 377–389.

Van Steenkiste, R. J., and S. Foresi (1999): "Arrow-Debreu Prices for Affine Models," Unpublished Manuscript, Goldman Sachs.

Vorst, T. (1990): "Average Rate Exchange Options," Unpublished Manuscript, Erasmus University.

Whaley, R. (1981): "On the Valuation of American Call Options on Stocks with Known Dividends," *Journal of Financial Economics* 9: 207–212.

Whaley, R. (1986): "Valuation of American Futures Options: Theory and Empirical Tests," *Journal of Finance* 41: 127–150.

Whalley, A. E., and P. Wilmott (1997): "An Asymptotic Analysis of an Optimal Hedging Model for Options with Transaction Costs," *Mathematical Finance* 7: 307–324.

Wiggins, J. (1987): "Option Values under Stochastic Volatility: Theory and Empirical Estimates," *Journal of Financial Economics* 19: 351–372.

Willard, G. (1996): "Calculating Prices and Sensitivities for Path-Independent Derivative Securities in Multifactor Models," Working Paper, Washington University, St. Louis.

Wilmott, P., J. Dewynne, and S. Howison (1993): *Option Pricing. Mathematical Models and Computations*, Oxford: Oxford Financial Press.

Yor, M. (1993): "From Planar Brownian Windings to Asian Options," *Insurance: Mathematics and Economics* 13(1): 23–34.

Yu, G. (1993): "Essays on the Valuation of American Options," Working Paper, Stern School of Business, New York University.

Zhang, X. (1994): "Numerical Analysis of American Option Pricing in a Jump-Diffusion Model," Working Paper, CERMA, URA-CNRS 1502, E.N.P.C., Paris.

Zhou, C. (1997): "Path-Dependent Option Valuation when the Underlying Path Is Discontinuous," Working Paper, Divisions of Research and Statistics and Monetary Affairs, Federal Reserve Board, Washington, D.C.

Zvan, R., P. Forsyth, and K. Vetzal (1998): "Robust Numerical Methods for PDE Models of Asian Options," *Journal of Computational Finance* 1 (Winter): 39–78.

Chapter 3. Interest Rate Models

Abken, P. (1993): "Valuation of Default-Risky Interest-Rate Swaps," *Advances in Futures and Options Research* 6: 93–116.

Acharya, V., and J. Carpenter (1999): "Corporate Bonds: Valuation, Hedging, and Optimal Exercise Boundaries," Working Paper, Department of Finance, Stern School of Business.

Adams, K., and D. Van Deventer (1994): "Fitting Yield Curves and Forward Rate Curves with Maximum Smoothness," *Journal of Fixed Income* 4 (June): 52–62.

Ahn, C., and H. Thompson (1988): "Jump-Diffusion Processes and the Term Structure of Interest Rates," *Journal of Finance* 43: 155–174.

Ahn, Dong-Hyun, and Bin Gao (1999): "A Parametric Nonlinear Model of Term Structure Dynamics," *Review of Financial Studies* 12(4): 721–762.

Aït-Sahalia, Y. (1996a): "Do Interest Rates Really Follow Continuous-Time Markov Diffusions?" Working Paper, Graduate School of Business, University of Chicago and NBER.

Aït-Sahalia, Y. (1996b): "Nonparametric Pricing of Interest Rate Derivative Securities," *Econometrica* 64: 527–560.

Aït-Sahalia, Y. (1996c): "Testing Continuous-Time Models of the Spot Interest Rate," *Review of Financial Studies* 9: 382–342.

Amin, K., and A. Morton (1994): "Implied Volatility Functions in Arbitrage-Free Term Structure Models," *Journal of Financial Economics* 35: 141–180.

Amin, K., and R. Jarrow (1993): "Pricing Options on Risky Assets in a Stochastic Interest Rate Economy," *Mathematical Finance* 2: 217–237.

Andersen, L., and J. Andreasen (1998): "Volatility Skew and Extensions of the Libor Market Model," General Re Financial Products, New York. Forthcoming in *Applied Mathematical Finance.*

Anderson, R., Y. Pan, and S. Sundaresan (1995): "Corporate Bond Yield Spreads and the Term Structure," Working Paper, CORE, Belgium.

Anderson, R., and S. Sundaresan (1996): "Design and Valuation of Debt Contracts," *Review of Financial Studies* 9: 37–68.

Apelfield, R., and A. Conze (1990): "The Term Structure of Interest Rates: The Case of Imperfect Information," Working Paper, Department of Economics, University of Chicago.

Artzner, P., and F. Delbaen (1990b): "Term Stucture of Interest Rates: The Martingale Approach," *Advances in Applied Mathematics* 10: 95–129.

Artzner, P., and F. Delbaen (1992): "Credit Risk and Prepayment Options," *ASTIN Bulletin* 22: 81–96.

Artzner, P., and F. Delbaen (1995): "Default Risk and Incomplete Insurance Markets," *Mathematical Finance* 5: 187–195.

Artzner, P., and P. Roger (1993): "Definition and Valuation of Optimal Coupon Reinvestment Bonds," *Finance* 14: 7–22.

Arvantis, A., J. Gregory, and J.-P. Laurent (1999): "Building Models for Credit Spreads," *Journal of Derivatives* 6 (3): 27–43.

Attari, M. (1997): "Discontinuous Interest Rate Processes: An Equilibrium Model for Bond Option Prices," Working Paper, University of Madison, Wisconsin (Ph.D. dissertation, University of Iowa).

Au, K., and D. Thurston (1993): "Markovian Term Structure Movements," Working Paper, School of Banking and Finance, University of New South Wales.

Babbs, S. (1991): "A Family of Itô Process Process Models for the Term Structure of Interest Rates," Working Paper, Financial Options Research Centre, University of Warwick.

Babbs, S., and N. Webber (1994): "A Theory of the Term Structure with an Offcial Short Rate," Working Paper, Midland Global Markets and University of Warwick.

Babcock, G. (1984): "Duration as a Link between Yield and Value," *Journal of Portfolio Management* (Summer).

Back, K. (1996): "Yield Curve Models: A Mathematical Review," Working Paper, Olin School of Business, Washington University, St. Louis.

Backus, D., S. Foresi, and S. Zin (1998): "Arbitrage Opportunities in Arbitrage-Free Models of Bond Pricing," *Journal of Business and Economic Statistics* 16: 13–26.

Bajeux-Besnainou, I., and R. Portait (1998): "Pricing Derivative Securities with a Multi-Factor Gaussian Model," *Applied Mathematical Finance* 5: 1–19.

Balasko, Y., and D. Cass (1986): "The Structure of Financial Equilibrium with Exogenous Yields: The Case of Incomplete Markets," *Econometrica* 57: 135–162.

Balasko, Y., D. Cass, and P. Siconolfi (1990): "The Structure of Financial Equilibrium with Exogenous Yields: The Case of Restricted Participation," *Journal of Mathematical Economics* 19: 195–216.

Balduzzi, P. (1994): "A Second Factor in Bond Yields," Working Paper. Department of Finance, Stern School of Business, New York University.

Balduzzi, P., G. Bertola, S. Foresi, and L. Klapper (1998): "Interest Rate Targeting and the Dynamics of Short-Term Interest Rates," *Journal of Money, Credit, and Banking* 30: 26–50.

Balduzzi, P., S. Das, and S. Foresi (1998): "The Central Tendency: A Second Factor in Bond Yields," *Review of Economics and Statistics* 80: 62–72.

Balduzzi, P., S. Das, S. Foresi, and R. Sundaram (1996): "A Simple Approach to Three Factor Affne Term Structure Models," *Journal of Fixed Income* 6 (December): 43–53.

Ball, C., and W. Torous (1994): "Regime Shifts in Short-Term Interest Rate Dynamics," Working Paper, Owen Graduate School of Management, Vanderbilt University.

Barone, E., and S. Risa (1994): "Valuation of Floaters and Options on Floaters under Special Repo Rates," Working Paper, Instituto Mobiliare Italiano, Rome.

Baxter, M. (1996): "General Interest-Rate Models and the Universality of HJM," Working Paper, Statistical Laboratory, University of Cambridge.

Baxter, M., and A. Rennie (1996): *Financial Calculus*, Cambridge: Cambridge University Press.

Baz, J., and S. Das (1996): "Analytical Approximations of the Term Structure for Jump-Diffusion Processes: A Numerical Analysis," *Journal of Fixed Income* 6: 78–86.

Baz, J., D. Prieul, and M. Toscani (1999): "The Liquidity Trap Revisited," *Risk*.

Beaglehole, D., and M. Tenney (1991): "General Solutions of Some Interest Rate Contingent Claim Pricing Equations," *Journal of Fixed Income* 1: 69–84.

Berardi, A., and M. Esposito (1999): "A Base Model for Multifactor Specifications of the Term Structure," *Economic Notes* 28: 145–170.

Bergman, Y. (1995): "Option Pricing with Differential Interest Rates," *Review of Financial Studies* 8: 475–500.

Bhar, R., and C. Chiarella (1995): "Transformation of Heath-Jarrow-Morton Models to Markovian Systems," Working Paper, School of Finance and Economics, University of Technology, Sydney.

Bielecki, T., and M. Rutkowski (1999a): "Credit Risk Modelling: A Multiple Ratings Case," Working Paper, Northeastern Illinois University and Technical University of Warsaw.

Bielecki, T., and M. Rutkowski (1999b): "Modelling the Defaultable Term Structure: Conditionally Markov Approach," Working Paper, Northeastern Illinois University and Technical University of Warsaw.

Bielecki, T., and M. Rutkowski (2000): "Credit Risk Modelling: Intensity Based Approach," Working Paper, Department of Mathematics, Northeastern Illinois University.

Bierwag, G. O. (1987): *Duration Analysis. Managing Interest Rate Risk*, New York: Ballinger.

Björk, T. (1996): "Interest Rate Theory," Working Paper, Department of Finance, Stockholm School of Economics.

Björk, T., and B. Christensen (1999): "Interest Rate Dynamics and Consistent Forward Rate Curves," *Mathematical Finance* 22: 17–23.

Björk, T., G. DiMasi, Y. Kabanov, and W. Runggaldier (1997): "Towards a General Theory of Bond Markets," *Finance and Stochastics* 1: 141–174.

Björk, T., and A. Gombani (1999): "Minimal Realizations of Interest Rate Model," *Finance and Stochastics* 3: 413–432.

Björk, T., Y. Kabanov, and W. Runggaldier (1995): "Bond Markets Where Prices Are Driven by a General Marked Point Process," Working Paper, Optimization and Systems Theory, Department of Mathematics, Royal Institute of Technology, Stockholm.

Black, F. (1995): "Interest Rates as Options," *Journal of Finance* 50.

Black, F., and J. Cox (1976): "Valuing Corporate Securities: Liabilities: Some Effects of Bond Indenture Provisions," *Journal of Finance* 31: 351–367.

Black, F., E. Derman, and I. Kani (1992): "A Two-Factor Model of Interest Rates," Working Paper, Goldman Sachs and Company, New York.

Black, F., E. Derman, and W. Toy (1990): "A One-Factor Model of Interest Rates and Its Application to Treasury Bond Options," *Financial Analysts Journal* (January–February): 33–39.

Black, F., and P. Karasinski (1991): "Bond and Option Pricing When Short Rates Are Log-Normal," *Financial Analysts Journal* (July–August): 52–59.

Bossaerts, P. (1990): "Modern Term Structure Theory," Working Paper, California Institute of Technology, Pasadena, CA.

Bousoukh, J., M. Richardson, R. Stanton, and R. Whitelaw (1995): "Pricing Mortgage-Backed Securities in a Multifactor Interest Rate Environment: A Multivariate Density Estimation Approach," Working Paper, Institute of Business and Economic Research, University of California, Berkeley.

Boyle, P., and T.Wang (1999): "Valuation of New Securities in an Incomplete Market: The Catch of Derivative Pricing," Working Paper, School of Accountancy, University of Waterloo, Waterloo, Canada.

Brace, A. (1996): "Non-Bushy Trees for Gaussian HJM and Lognormal Forward Models," Working Paper, School of Mathematics, University of New South Wales.

Brace, A., and M. Musiela (1994a): "A Multifactor Gauss Markov Implementation of Heath, Jarrow, and Morton," *Mathematical Finance* 4: 259–284.

Brace, A., and M. Musiela (1994b): "Swap Derivatives In a Gaussian HJM Framework," Working Paper, Treasury Group, Citibank, Sydney, Australia.

Brace, A., and M. Musiela (1995a): "Duration, Convexity and Wiener Chaos," Working Paper, Treasury Group, Citibank, Sydney, Australia.

Brace, A., and M. Musiela (1995b): "Hedging, Duration, Bucketing and Convexity in a Gaussian Heath Jarrow Morton Framework," Working Paper, Treasury Group, Citibank, Sydney, Australia.

Brace, A., and M. Musiela (1995c): "The Market Model of Interest Rate Dynamics," *Mathematical Finance* 7: 127–155.

Brandt, M., and P. Santa-Clara (1998): "Simulated Likelihood Estimation of Diffusions with an Application to Interest Rates," Working Paper, University of California, Los Angeles.

Breeden, D. (1986): "Consumption, Production, Inflation and Interest Rates," *Journal of Financial Economics* 16: 3–39.

Brennan, M., and E. Schwartz (1979): "A Continuous-Time Approach to the Pricing of Bonds," *Journal of Banking and Finance* 3: 133–155.

Brennan, M., and E. Schwartz (1980a): "Analysing Convertible Bonds," *Journal of Financial and Quantitative Analysis* 15: 907–929.

Brennan, M., and E. Schwartz (1980b): "Conditional Predictions of Bond Prices and Returns," *Journal of Finance* 35: 405–419.

Brennan, M., and E. Schwartz (1982): "An Equilibrium Model of Bond Pricing and a Test of Market Effciency," *Journal of Financial and Quantitative Analysis* 17: 301–329.

Brenner, R., R. Harjes, and K. Kroner (1996): "Another Look at Models of the Short-Term Interest Rate," *Journal of Financial and Quantitative Analysis* 31(1): 85–107.

Brotherton-Ratcliffe, R., and B. Iben (1993): "Yield Curve Applications of Swap Products," in R. Schwartz and C. Smith (Eds.), *Advanced Strategies in Financial Risk Management*, New York: New York Institute of Finance.

Brown, R., and S. Schaefer (1994a): "Interest Rate Volatility and the Shape of the Term Structure," *Philosophical Transactions of the Royal Society: Physical Sciences and Engineering* 347: 449–598.

Brown, R., and S. Schaefer (1994b): "The Term Structure of Real Interest Rates and the Cox, Ingersoll, and Ross Model," *Journal of Financial Economics* 35: 3–42.

Brown, R., and S. Schaefer (1996): "Ten Years of the Real Term Structure: 1984–1994," *Journal of Fixed Income* 6 (March): 6–22.

Brown, S., and P. Dybvig (1986): "The Empirical Implications of the Cox, Ingersoll, Ross Theory of the Term Structure of Interest Rates," *Journal of Finance* 41(3): 616–628.

Broze, L., O. Scaillet, and J.-M. Zakoïan (1993): "Testing for Continuous-Time Models of the Short-Term Interest Rate," Working Paper, CORE, Louvain-la-Neuve, Belgium.

Bühler, W., M. Urhig-Homburg, U. Walter, and T. Weber (1995): "An Empirical Comparison of Alternative Models for Valuing Interest Rate Options," Working Paper, Lehrstuehle für Finanzwirtschaft, Universität Mannheim.

Buono, M., R. Gregory-Allen, and U. Yaari (1992): "The Efficacy of Term Structure Estimation Techniques: A Monte Carlo Study," *Journal of Fixed Income* 2: 52–63.

Burnetas, A. N., and P. Ritchken (1996): "On Rational Jump-diffusion Models in the Flesaker-Hughston Paradigm," Working Paper, Case Western Reserve University.

Büttler, H. (1995): "Evaluation of Callable Bonds: Finite Difference Methods, Stability and Accuracy," *Economic Journal* 105: 374–384.

Büttler, H., and J. Waldvogel (1996): "Pricing Callable Bonds by Means of Green's Function," *Mathematical Finance* 6: 53–88.

Calflisch, R., and W. Morokoff (1995): "Valuation of Mortgage Backed Securities Using the Quasi-Monte Carlo Method," Working Paper, Department of Mathematics, University of California, Los Angeles.

Calflisch, R., W. Morokof, and A. Owen (1995): "Valuation of Mortgage Backed Securities Using Brownian Bridges to Reduce Effective Dimension," *Journal of Computational Finance* 1 (Fall).

Campbell, J. (1986a): "Bond and Stock Returns in a Simple Exchange Model," *Quarterly Journal of Economics* 101: 85–103.

Campbell, J. (1986b): "A Defense of Traditional Hypotheses about the Term Structure of Interest Rates," *Journal of Finance* 41: 183–193.

Campbell, J. (1995): "Some Lessons from the Yield Curve," *Journal of Economic Perspectives* 9: 129–152.

Campbell, R., and T. Temel (2000): "Interest Rate Swaps," Lehman Brothers Analytical Research Series.

Carr, P. (1993b): "Valuing Bond Futures and the Quality Option," Working Paper, Johnson Graduate School of Management, Cornell University.

Carr, P., and R.-R. Chen (1993): "Valuing Bond Futures and the Quality Option," Working Paper, Johnson Graduate School of Management, Cornell University.

Carverhill, A. (1986): "Arbitrage, the Term Structure of Volatility, and the Long Forward Rate," Working Paper, Department of Finance, University of Science and Technology, Hong Kong.

Carverhill, A. (1988): "The Ho and Lee Term Structure Theory: A Continuous Time Version," Working Paper, Financial Options Research Centre, University of Warwick.

Carverhill, A. (1990): "A Survey of Elementary Techniques for Pricing Options on Bonds and Interest Rates," Working Paper, Financial Options Research Centre, University of Warwick.

Carverhill, A. (1991): "The Term Structure of Interest Rates and Associated Options: Equilibrium versus Evolutionary Models," Working Paper, Financial Options Research Centre, University of Warwick.

Carverhill, A. (1995): "A Simplified Exposition of the Heath, Jarrow, and Morton Model," *Stochastics* 53: 227–240.

Carverhill, A., and K. Pang (1995): "Efficient and Flexible Bond Option Valuation in the Heath, Jarrow, and Morton Framework," *Journal of Fixed Income* 5 (September): 70–77.

Chacko, G. (1996): "A Stochastic Mean/Volatility Model of Term Structure Dynamics in a Jump-Diffusion Economy," Unpublished Manuscript, Harvard Business School.

Chacko, G. (1998): "Continuous-Time Estimation of Exponential Term Structure Models," Unpublished Manuscript, Harvard Business School.

Chacko, G. (1999): "Estimating Exponential Separable Term Structure Models: A General Approach," Unpublished Manuscript, Harvard University.

Chacko, G., and S. Das (1997): "Average Interest," NBER Working Paper No. 6045.

Chacko, G., and S. Das (1998): "Pricing Average Interest Rate Options: A General Approach," Working Paper, Harvard Business School.

Chacko, G., and S. Das (2002): "Pricing Interest Rate Derivatives: A General Approach," *Review of Financial Studies* 15: 195–241.

Chan, K.-C., A. Karolyi, F. Longstaff, and A. Saunders (1992): "An Empirical Comparison of Alternative Models of the Short-Term Interest Rate," *Journal of Finance* 47: 1209–1227.

Chan, Y.-K. (1992): "Term Structure as a Second Order Dynamical System, and Pricing of Derivative Securities," Working Paper, Bear Stearns and Company, New York.

Chen, L. (1996): *Stochastic Mean and Stochastic Volatility: A Three-Factor Model of the Term Structure of Interest Rates and Its Application to the Pricing of Interest Rate Derivatives: Part I,* Oxford: Blackwell Publishers.

Chen, R.-R., and L. Scott (1992a): "Maximum Likelihood Estimation for a Multi-Factor Equilibrium Model of the Term Structure of Interest Rates," Working Paper, Department of Finance, Rutgers University.

Chen, R.-R., and L. Scott (1992b): "Pricing Interest Rate Options in a Two-Factor Cox-Ingersoll-Ross Model of the Term Structure," *Review of Financial Studies* 5: 613–636.

Chen, R.-R., and L. Scott (1993a): "Multi-Factor Cox-Ingersoll-Ross Models of the Term Structure: Estimates and Tests from a State-Space Model

Using a Kalman Filter," Working Paper, Department of Finance, Rutgers University.

Chen, R.-R., and L. Scott (1993b): "Pricing Interest Rate Futures Options with Futures-Style Margining," *Journal of Futures Markets* 13: 15–22.

Chen, R.-R., and L. Scott (1995): "Interest Rate Options in Multifactor Cox-Ingersoll-Ross Models of the Term Structure," *Journal of Derivatives* 3: 53–72.

Chen, R.-R., and B. Sopranzetti (1999): "The Valuation of Default-Triggered Credit Derivatives," Working Paper, Rutgers Business School, Department of Finance and Economics.

Cheng, S. (1992): "On the Feasibility of Arbitrage-Based Option Pricing when Stochastic Bond Price Processes Are Involved," *Journal of Economic Theory* 53: 185–198.

Cherubini, U., and M. Esposito (1995): "Options in and on Interest Rate Futures Contracts: Results from Martingale Pricing Theory," *Applied Mathematical Finance* 2: 1–15.

Chesney, M., R. Elliott, and R. Gibson (1993): "Analytical Solution for the Pricing of American Bond and Yield Options," *Mathematical Finance* 3: 277–294.

Cheyette, O. (1995): "Markov Representation of the Heath-Jarrow-Morton Model," Working Paper, BARRA Inc., Berkeley, California.

Cheyette, O. (1996): "Implied Prepayments," Working Paper, BARRA Inc., Berkeley, California.

Chiarella, C., and N. E. Hassan (1997): "Evaluation of Derivative Security Prices in the Heath-Jarrow-Morton Framework as Path Integrals," *Journal of Financial Engineering* 6: 121–147.

Clewlow, L., K. Pang, and C. Strickland (1997): "Efficient Pricing of Caps and Swaptions in a Multi-Factor Gaussian Interest Rate Model," Working Paper, Financial Options Research Centre, University of Warwick.

Clewlow, L., and C. Strickland (1996): "Monte Carlo Valuation of Interest Rate Derivatives under Stochastic Volatility," *Journal of Fixed Income* 7 (3): 35–45.

Coleman, T., L. Fisher, and R. Ibbotson (1992): "Estimating the Term Structure of Interest Rates from Data that Include the Prices of Coupon Bonds," *Journal of Fixed Income* 2 (September): 85–116.

Collin-Dufresne, P., and R. Goldstein (1999): "Do Credit Spreads Reflect Stationary Leverage Ratios? Reconciling Structural and Reduced Form Frameworks," Working Paper, GSIA, Carnegie-Mellon University.

Conley, T. G., L. P. Hansen, E. G. J. Luttmer, and J. A. Scheinkman (1997): "Short-Term Interest Rates as Subordinated Diffusions," *Review of Financial Studies* 10: 525–577.

Constantinides, G. (1992): "A Theory of the Nominal Term Structure of Interest Rates," *Review of Financial Studies* 5: 531–552.

Cont, R. (1998): "Modelling Term Structure Dynamics: An Infinite Dimensional Approach," Working Paper, Centre de Mathématiques Appliquées, Ecole Polythechnique, Palaiseau, France.

Cooper, I., and A. Mello (1991): "The Default Risk of Swaps," *Journal of Finance* 46: 597–620.

Cooper, I., and A. Mello (1992): "Pricing and Optimal Use of Forward Contracts with Default Risk," Working Paper, Department of Finance, London Business School, University of London.

Cooper, I., and M. Martin (1996): "Default Risk and Derivative Products," *Applied Mathematical Finance* 3: 53–74.

Cossin, D., and H. Pirotte (2001): *Advanced Credit Risk Analysis*, New York: Wiley.

Courtadon, G. (1982): "The Pricing of Options on Default-Free Bonds," *Journal of Financial and Quantitative Analysis* 17: 75–100.

Cox, J., J. Ingersoll, and S. Ross (1981a): "A Re-examination of Traditional Hypotheses about the Term Structure of Interest Rates," *Journal of Finance* 36: 769–799.

Cox, J., J. Ingersoll, and S. Ross (1985a): "An Intertemporal General Equilibrium Model of Asset Prices," *Econometrica* 53: 363–384.

Cox, J., J. Ingersoll, and S. Ross (1985b): "A Theory of the Term Stucture of Interest Rates," *Econometrica* 53: 385–408.

Dai, Q. (1994): "Implied Green's Function in a No-Arbitrage Markov Model of the Instantaneous Short Rate," Working Paper, Graduate School of Business, Stanford University.

Dai, Q. (1995): "Understanding the Interest Rate Yield Curve Dynamics with the Correlated Three-Factor Vasicek Model," Working Paper, Graduate School of Business, Stanford University.

Dai, Q. (1996): "Technical Notes on CIR Model," Working Paper, Graduate School of Business, Stanford University.

Dai, Q., and K. Singleton (2000): "Specification Anlaysis of Affne Term Structure Models," *Journal of Finance* 55: 1943–1978.

Dai, Q., and K. Singleton (2001): "Expectation Puzzles, Time-Varying Risk Premia, and Dynamic Models of the Term Structure," Working Paper, Stanford University.

Danesi, V., J.-P. Garcia, V. Genon-Catalot, and J.-P. Laurent (1993): "Parameter Estimation for Yield Curve Models Using Contrast Methods," Working Paper, Université Marne-La-Valeé, Noisy-Le-Grand, France.

Das, S. (1993a): "Jump-Diffusion Processes and the Bond Markets," Working Paper, Department of Finance, Harvard Business School.

Das, S. (1993b): "Jump-Hunting Interest Rates," Working Paper, Department of Finance, New York University.

Das, S. (1993c): "Mean Rate Shifts and Alternative Models of the Interest Rate: Theory and Evidence," Working Paper, Department of Finance, New York University.

Das, S. (1995): "Pricing Interest Rate Derivatives with Arbitrary Skewness and Kurtosis: A Simple Approach to Jump-Diffusion Bond Option Pricing," Working Paper, Division of Research, Harvard Business School.

Das, S. (1997): "Discrete-Time Bond and Option Pricing for Jump-Diffusion Processes," *Review of Derivatives Research* 1: 211–243.

Das, S. (1998): "Poisson-Gaussian Processes and the Bond Markets," Working Paper, Department of Finance, Harvard Business School.

Das, S. (1998): "The Surprise Element: Jumps in Interest Rates," *Journal of Econometrics*.

Das, S., and R. Sundaram (1999): "Of Smiles and Smirks: A Term Structure Perspective," *Journal of Financial and Quantitative Analysis* 34: 60–72.

Das, S., and R. K. Sundaram (2000): "A Discrete-Time Approach to Arbitrage-Free Pricing of Credit Derivatives," *Management Science* 46: 46–62.

Das, S., and P. Tufano (1995): "Pricing Credit Sensitive Debt when Interest Rates, Credit Ratings and Credit Spreads are Stochastic," *Journal of Financial Engineering* 5 (2): 161–198.

Das, S., and S. Foresi (1996): "Exact Solutions for Bond and Option Prices with Systematic Jump Risk," *Review of Derivatives Research* 1: 7–24.

Davis, M., and F. Lischka (1999): "Convertible Bonds with Market Risk and Credit Risk," Working Paper, Tokyo-Mitsubishi International.

Davis, M., and V. Lo (1999): "Infectious Defaults," Working Paper, Tokyo-Mitsubishi International.

Davis, M., and V. Lo (2000): "Modelling Default Correlation in Bond Portfolios," Working Paper, Tokyo-Mitsubishi International.

Davis, M., and T. Mavroidis (1997): "Valuation and Potential Exposure of Default Swaps," Working Paper, Tokyo-Mitsubishi International.

Davydov, D., V. Linetsky, and C. Lotz (1999): "The Hazard-Rate Approach to Pricing Risky Debt: Two Analytically Tractable Examples," Working Paper, Department of Economics, University of Michigan.

Décamps, J.-P., and J.-C. Rochet (1997): "A Variational Approach for Pricing Options and Corporate Bonds," *Economic Theory* 9: 557–569.

Deelstra, G., and F. Delbaen (1995): "Long-Term Returns in Stochastic Interest Rate Models," *Insurance: Mathematics and Economics* 17: 163–169.

Delbaen, F. (1993): "Consols in the CIR Model," *Mathematical Finance* 3: 125–134.

Delgado, F., and B. Dumas (1993): "How Far Apart Can Two Riskless Interest Rates Be?" Working Paper, Fuqua School of Business, Duke University.

DeMunnik, J. (1992): *The Valuation of Interest Rate Derivative Securities*, Amsterdam: Tinbergen Institute.

De-Schepper, A., M. Teunen, M. Goovaerts (1994): "An Analytical Inversion of a Laplace Transform Related to Annuities," *Insurance: Mathematics and Economics* 14(1): 33–37.

Diament, P. (1993): "Semi-Empirical Smooth Fit to the Treasury Yield Curve," Working Paper, Graduate School of Business, Columbia University.

Donaldson, J., T. Johnson, and R. Mehra (1990): "On the Term Structure of Interest Rates," *Journal of Economic Dynamics and Control*, 14: 571–596.

Dothan, M. (1978): "On the Term Structure of Interest Rates," *Journal of Financial Economics* 7: 229–264.

Dothan, M., and D. Feldman (1986): "Equilibrium Interest Rates and Multi-period Bonds in a Partially Observable Economy," *Journal of Finance* 41: 369–382.

Duan, J.-C., and J.-G. Simonato (1993): "Estimating Exponential-Affne Term Structure Models," Working Paper, Department of Finance, McGill University and CIRANO.

Duffee, G. (1999a): "Estimating the Price of Default Risk," *Review of Financial Studies* 12: 197–226.

Duffee, G. (1999b): "Forecasting Future Interest Rates: Are Affne Models Failures?" Working Paper, Federal Reserve Board.

Duffie, D. (1996): "Special Repo Rates," *Journal of Finance* 51: 493–526.

Duffie, D., and M. Huang (1996): "Swap Rates and Credit Quality," *Journal of Finance* 51: 921–949.

Duffie, D., and R. Kan (1996): "A Yield-Factor Model of Interest Rates," *Mathematical Finance* 6: 379–406; reprinted in *Options, Markets*, edited by G. Constantinides and A. Malliaris, London: Edward Elgar, 2000.

Duffie, D., J. Pan, and K. Singleton (2000): "Transform Analysis and Asset Pricing for Affne Jump-Diffusions," *Econometrica* 68: 1343–1376.

Duffie, D., and K. Singleton (1997): "An Econometric Model of the Term Structure of Interest Rate Swap Yields," *Journal of Finance* 52: 1287–1321; reprinted in *Options Markets*, edited by G. Constantinides and A. Malliaris, London: Edward Elgar, 2001.

Duffie, D., and K. Singleton (1999): "Modeling Term Structures of Defaultable Bonds," *Review of Financial Studies* 12: 687–720.

Dunn, K., and K. Singleton (1986): "Modeling the Term Structure of Interest Rates under Nonseparable Utility and Durability of Goods," *Journal of Financial Economics* 17: 27–55.

Dybvig, P. (1988): "Bond and Bond Option Pricing Based on the Current Term Structure," Working Paper, School of Business, Washington University, St. Louis.

Dybvig, P., J. Ingersoll, and S. Ross (1996): "Long Forward and Zero-Coupon Rates Can Never Fall," *Journal of Business* 69: 1–25.

Eberlien, E., and S. Raible (1999): "Term Structure Models Driven by General Lévy Processes," *Mathematical Finance* 9: 31–53.

Ederington, L., G. Caton, and C. Campbell (1997): "To Call or Not to Call Convertible Debt," *Financial Management* 26: 22–31.

El Karoui, N., A. Franchot, and H. Geman (1997): "On the Behavior of Long Zero Coupon Rates in a No Arbitrage Framework," *Review of Derivatives Research* 1: 351–369.

El Karoui, N., and H. Geman (1994): "A Probabilistic Approach to the Valuation of General Floating-Rate Notes with an Application to Interest Rate Swaps," *Advances in Futures and Options Research* 7: 47–63.

El Karoui, N., and V. Lacoste (1992): "Multifactor Models of the Term Structure of Interest Rates," Working Paper, Laboratoire de Probabilités, Université de Paris VI.

El Karoui, N., C. Lepage, R. Myneni, N. Roseau, and R. Viswanathan (1991a): "The Pricing and Hedging of Interest Rate Claims: Applications," Working Paper, Laboratoire de Probabilitiés, Université de Paris VI.

El Karoui, N., C. Lepage, R. Myneni, N. Roseau, and R. Viswanathan (1991b): "The Valuation and Hedging of Contingent Claims with Gaussian Markov Interest Rates," Working Paper, Laboratoire de Probabilitiés, Université de Paris VI.

El Karoui, N., R. Myneni, and R. Viswanathan (1992): "Arbitrage Pricing and Hedging of Interest Rate Claims with State Variables I: Theory," Working Paper, Laboratoire de Probabilitiés, Université de Paris VI.

El Karoui, N., and J.-C. Rochet (1989): "A Pricing Formula for Options on Coupon Bonds," Working Paper, October, Laboratoire de Probabilitiés, Université de Paris VI.

Elliott, R., M. Jeanblanc, and M. Yor (1999): "Some Models on Default Risk," Working Paper, Department of Mathematics, University of Alberta. Forthcoming in *Mathematical Finance*.

Ericsson, J., and O. Renault (1999): "Credit and Liquidity Risk," Working Paper, Faculty of Management, McGill University.

Eydeland, A. (1994): "A Special Algorithm for Pricing Interest Rate Options," Working Paper, Department of Mathematics, University of Massachusetts.

Fan, H., and S. Sundaresan (1997): "Debt Valuation, Strategic Debt Service and Optimal Dividend Policy," Working Paper, Columbia University.

Filipović, D. (1999a): "A General Characterization of Affne Term Structure Models," Working Paper, ETH, Zurich. Forthcoming in *Finance and Stochastics*.

Finger, C. (2000): "A Comparison of Stochastic Default Rate Models," Working Paper, The Risk Metrics Group.

Fisher, M., and C. Gilles (1996): "The Term Structure of Repo Spreads," Working Paper, Research and Statistics, Board of Governors of the Federal Reserve System.

Fisher, M., and C. Gilles (1997): "The Equity Premium and the Term Stucture of Interest Rates with Recursive Preferences," Working Paper, Research and Statistics, Board of Governors of the Federal Reserve System.

Fisher, M., and C. Gilles (1998a): "Around and Around: The Expectations Hypothesis," *Journal of Finance* 53: 365–383.

Fisher, M., D. Nychka, and D. Zervos (1994): "Fitting the Term Structure of Interest Rates witn Smoothing Splines," Working Paper, Board of Governors of the Federal Reserve Board, Washington, D.C.

Flesaker, B. (1993): "Testing the Heath-Jarrow-Morton/Ho-Lee Model of Interest Rate Contingent Claims Pricing," *Journal of Financial and Quantitative Analysis* 28: 483–495.

Frachot, A. (1995): "Factor Models of Domestic and Foreign Interest Rates with Stochastic Volatilities," *Mathematical Finance* 5: 167–185.

Frachot, A. (1996): "A Reexamination of the Uncovered Interest Rate Parity Hypothesis," *Journal of International Money and Finance* 15: 419–437.

Frachot, A., D. Janci, and V. Lacoste (1993): "Factor Analysis of the Term Structure: A Probabilistic Approach," Working Paper, Banque de France, Paris.

Frachot, A., and J.-P. Lesne (1993a): "Econometrics of Linear Factor Models of Interest Rates," Working Paper, Banque de France, Paris.

Frachot, A., and J.-P. Lesne (1993b): "Expectations Hypotheses and Stochastic Volatilities," Working Paper, Banque de France, Paris.

Frachot, A., and J.-P. Lesne (1993c): "Factor Models of Interest Rates with Stochastic Volatilities," Working Paper, Banque de France, Paris.

Garbade, K. (1996): *Fixed Income Analytics*, Cambridge, MA: MIT Press.

Gatarek, D., and M. Musiela (1995): "Pricing of American Receiver Swaptions as Optimal Stopping of an Ornstein-Uhlenbeck Process," Working Paper, School of Mathematics, University of New South Wales, Sydney.

Geanakoplos, J., and W. Zame (1999): "Collateral, Default, and Market Crashes," Working Paper, Cowles Foundation Working Papers, Yale University.

Geske, R. (1977): "The Valuation of Corporate Liabilities as Compound Options, *Journal of Financial Economics* 7: 63–81.

Gibbons, M., and K. Ramaswamy (1993): "A Test of the Cox-Ingersoll-Ross Model of the Term Structure of Interest Rates," *Review of Financial Studies* 6: 619–658.

Gibson, R., and S. Sundaresan (1999): "A Model of Sovereign Borrowing and Sovereign Yield Spreads," Working Paper, School of HEC, University of Lausanne.

Glasserman, P., and S. Kou (1999): "The Term Structure of Simple Forward Rates with Jump Risk," Working Paper, Columbia University.

Glasserman, P., and X. Zhao (1999): "Fast Greeks by Simulation in Forward LIBOR Models," *Journal of Computational Finance* 3 (Fall): 5–40.

Goldberg, L. (1998): "Volatility of the Short Rate on the Rational Lognormal Model," *Finance and Stochastics* 2: 199–211.

Goldstein, R. (1995): "On the Term Structure of Interest Rates in the Presence of Reflecting and Absorbing Boundaries," Working Paper, Walter A. Haas School of Business, University of California, Berkeley.

Goldstein, R. (1997): "Beyond HJM: Fitting the Current Term Structure While Maintaining a Markovian System," Working Paper, Fisher College of Business, Ohio State University.

Goldstein, R. (2000): "The Term Structure of Interest Rates as a Random Field," *Review of Financial Studies* 13: 365–384.

Goldys, B., and M. Musiela (1996): "On Partial Differential Equations Related to Term Structure Models," Working Paper, School of Mathematics, University of New South Wales.

Goldys, B., M. Musiela, and D. Sondermann (1994): "Lognormality of Rates and Term Structure Models," Working Paper, School of Mathematics, University of New South Wales.

Gourieroux, C., and O. Scaillet (1994): "Estimation of the Term Structure from Bond Data," Working Paper, CREST and CEPREMAP, Paris.

Gray, S. F. (1996): "Modeling the Conditional Distribution of Interest Rates as a Regime-Switching Process," *Journal of Financial Economics* 42: 27–62.

Grinblatt, M. (1994): "An Analytic Solution for Interest Rate Swap Spreads," Working Paper, Anderson Graduate School of Management, University of California, Los Angeles.

Grinblatt, M., and N. Jegadeesh (1996): "The Relative Pricing of Eurodollar Futures and Forward Contracts," *Journal of Finance* 51, 1499–1522.

Grosen, A., and P. Jorgensen (1995): "The Valuation of Interest Rate Guarantees: An Application of American Option Pricing Theory," Working Paper, Department of Banking and Finance, Aarhus School of Business.

Gupta, A., and M. Subrahmanyam (2000): "An Empirical Examination of the Convexity Bias in the Pricing of Interest Rate Swaps," *Journal of Financial Economics*.

Hamza, K., and F. Klebaner (1995): "A Stochastic Partial Differential Equation for Term Structure of Interest Rates," Working Paper, Department of Statistics, University of Melbourne.

Hansen, A., and P. Jorgensen (1998): "Exact Analytical Valuation of Bonds when Spot Interest Rates are Log-Normal," Working Paper, Centre for Analytical Finance, University of Aarhus, Aarhus School of Business.

Heath, D. (1998): "Some New Term Structure Models," Working Paper, Department of Mathematical Sciences, Carnegie-Mellon University.

Heath, D., R. Jarrow, and A. Morton (1990): "Bond Pricing and the Term Structure of Interest Rates: A Discrete Time Approximation," *Journal of Financial and Quantitative Analysis* 25: 419–440.

Heath, D., R. Jarrow, and A. Morton (1992a): "Bond Pricing and the Term Structure of Interest Rates: A New Methodology for Contingent Claims Valuation," *Econometrica* 60: 77–106.

Heath, D., R. Jarrow, and A. Morton (1992b): "Contingent Claim Valuation with a Random Evolution of Interest Rates," Working Paper, Operations Research Department, Cornell University.

Hemler, M. (1990): "The Quality Delivery Option in Treasury Bond Futures Contracts," *Journal of Finance* 45: 1565–1586.

Heston, S. (1988a): "Generalized Interest Rate Processes for the Goldman, Sachs, and Company Mortgage Valuation Model," Working Paper, Graduate School of Industrial Administration, Carnegie-Mellon University.

Heston, S. (1988b): "Testing Continuous Time Models of the Term Structure of Interest Rates," Working Paper, Graduate School of Industrial Administration, Carnegie-Mellon University.

Heston, S. (1989): "Discrete Time Versions of Continuous Time Interest Rate Models," Working Paper, Graduate School of Industrial Administration, Carnegie-Mellon University.

Heston, S., and S. Nandi (1999): "A Two-Factor Model for Pricing Bonds and Interest Rate Derivatives with GARCH Volatility: Analytical Solutions and their Applications, Working Paper, Goldman Sachs.

Heynen, R., A. Kemna, and T. Vorst (1994): "Analysis of the Term Structure of Implied Volatilities," *Journal of Financial Quantitative Analysis* 1: 31–57.

Ho, T., and S. Lee (1986): "Term Structure Movements and Pricing Interest Rate Contingent Claims," *Journal of Finance* 41: 1011–1029.

Hogan, M. (1993a): "The Lognormal Interest Rate Model and Eurodollar Futures," Working Paper, Citibank, New York.

Hogan, M. (1993b): "Problems in Certain Two-Factor Term Structure Models," *Annals of Applied Probability* 3: 576–581.

Huge, B., and D. Lando (1999): "Swap Pricing with Two-Sided Default Risk in a Rating-Based Model," *European Finance Review* 3: 239–268.

Hull, J., and A. White (1990a): "Pricing Interest Rate Derivative Securities," *Review of Financial Studies* 3: 573–592.

Hull, J., and A. White (1992): "The Price of Default," *Risk* 5: 101–103.

Hull, J., and A. White (1993a): "One-Factor Interest-Rate Models and the Valuation of Interest-Rate Derivative Securities," *Journal of Financial and Quantitative Analysis* 28: 235–254.

Hull, J., and A. White (1993b): "Numerical Procedures for Implementing Term Structure Models," *Journal of Derivatives* 7 (Fall): 7–16; (Winter): 37–48.

Ingersoll, J. (1977): "A Contingent-Claims Valuation of Convertible Securities," *Journal of Financial Economics* 4: 289–322.

Jagannathan, R., and G. Sun (1999): "Valuation of Swaps, Caps and Swaptions," Working Paper, Northwestern University.

Jakobsen, S. (1992): "Prepayment and the Valuation of Danish Mortgage-Backed Bonds," Working Paper, Ph.D. dissertation, Aarhaus School of Business, Denmark.

James, J., and N. Webber (2000): *Interest Rate Modelling*, New York: Wiley.

Jamshidian, F. (1989a): "Closed-Form Solution for American Options on Coupon Bonds in the General Gaussian Interest Rate Model," Working Paper, Financial Strategies Group, Merrill Lynch Capital Markets, New York.

Jamshidian, F. (1989b): "An Exact Bond Option Formula," *Journal of Finance* 44: 205–209.

Jamshidian, F. (1989d): "The Multifactor Gaussian Interest Rate Model and Implementation," Working Paper, Financial Strategies Group, Merrill Lynch Capital Markets, New York.

Jamshidian, F. (1991a): "Bond and Option Evaluation in the Gaussian Interest Rate Model," *Research in Finance* 9: 131–170.

Jamshidian, F. (1991b): "Commodity Option Evaluation in the Gaussian Futures Term Structure Model," *Review of Futures Markets* 10: 324–346.

Jamshidian, F. (1991c): "Forward Induction and Construction of Yield Curve Diffusion Models," *Journal of Fixed Income*, June: 62–74.

Jamshidian, F. (1993a): "Hedging and Evaluating Diff Swaps," Working Paper, Fuji International Finance PLC, London.

Jamshidian, F. (1994): "Hedging Quantos, Differential Swaps, and Ratios," *Applied Mathematical Finance* 1: 1–20.

Jamshidian, F. (1995): "A Simple Class of Square-Root Interest Rate Models," *Applied Mathematical Finance* 2: 61–72.

Jamshidian, F. (1996a): "Bond, Futures and Option Evaluation in the Quadratic Interest Rate Model," *Applied Mathematical Finance* 3: 93–115.

Jamshidian, F. (1996b): "Libor and Swap Market Models and Measures and Models II," Working Paper, Sakura Global Capital, London.

Jamshidian, F. (1997b): "Pricing and Hedging European Swaptions with Deterministic (Lognormal) Forward Swap Volatility," *Finance and Stochastics* 1: 293–330.

Jamshidian, F. (1999): "Libor Market Model with Semimartingales," Working Paper, NetAnalytic Limited.

Jarrow, R., D. Lando, and S. Turnbull (1997): "A Markov Model for the Term Structure of Credit Risk Spreads," *Review of Financial Studies* 10: 481–523.

Jarrow, R., and F. Yu (1999): "Counterparty Risk and the Pricing of Defaultable Securities," Working Paper, Cornell University.

Jarrow, R., and S. Turnbull (1994): "Delta, Gamma, and Bucket Hedging of Interest Rate Derivatives," *Applied Mathematical Finance* 1: 21–48.

Jarrow, R., and S. Turnbull (1995): "Pricing Derivatives on Financial Securities Subject to Credit Risk," *Journal of Finance* 50: 53–85.

Jarrow, R., and S. Turnbull (1997a): "An Integrated Approach to the Hedging and Pricing of Eurodollar Derivatives," *Journal of Risk and Insurance* 64: 271–299.

Jarrow, R., and S. Turnbull (1997b): "When Swaps Are Dropped," *Risk* 10 (May): 70–75.

Jaschke, S. (1996): "Arbitrage Bounds for the Term Structure of Interest Rates," *Finance and Stochastics* 2: 29–40.

Jaschke, S. (1997): "Super-Hedging and Arbitrage Pricing of Bonds and Interest Rate Derivatives," Working Paper, Institut für Mathematik, Humboldt-Universitat zu Berlin.

Jeanblanc, M., and M. Rutkowski (1999): "Modelling of Default Risk: An Overview," Working Paper, University of Evry Val of Essonne and Technical University of Warsaw.

Jeffrey, A. (1995a): "A Class of Non-Markovian Single Factor Heath-Jarrow-Morton Term Structure Models," Working Paper, School of Banking and Finance, University of New South Wales, Sydney.

Jeffrey, A. (1995b): "An Empirical Test of Single Factor Heath-Jarrow-Morton Term Structure Models," Working Paper, School of Banking and Finance, University of New South Wales, Sydney.

Jeffrey, A. (1995c): "Single Factor Heath-Jarrow-Morton Term Structure Models Based on Markov Spot Interest Rate," *Journal of Financial and Quantitative Analysis* 30: 619–643.

Jegadeesh, N. (1993): "An Empirical Analysis of the Pricing of Interest Rate Caps," Working Paper, College of Commerce and Business Administration, University of Illinois at Urbana-Champaign.

Jegadeesh, N., and B. Tuckman (Eds.) (1999): *Advanced Fixed-Income Valuation Tools*, New York: Wiley.

Jin, Y., and P. Glasserman (1998) "Equilibrium Positive Interest Rates: A Unified View," Working Paper, Columbia Business School, New York.

Jong, F.D., and P. Santa-Clara (1999): "The Dynamics of the Forward Interest Rate Curve: A Formulation with State Variables," *Journal of Financial and Quantitative Analysis* 34: 131–157.

Jordan, B. (1995): "On the Relative Yields of Taxable and Municipal Bonds: A Theory of the Tax Structure of Interest Rates," Working Paper, Department of Finance, College of Business and Public Administration, University of Missouri, Columbia.

Jorgensen, P. (1996): "American Bond Option Pricing in One-Factor Spot Interest Rate Models," *Review of Derivatives Research* 1: 245–267.

Kennedy, D. (1994): "The Term Structure of Interest Rates as a Gaussian Random Field," *Mathematical Finance* 4: 247–258.

Kijima, M., and K. Komoribayashi (1998): "A Markov Chain Model for Valuing Credit Risk Derivatives," *Journal of Derivatives* 6 (Fall): 97–108.

Kim, J. (1992): "A Martingale Analysis of the Term Structure of Interest Rates," Working Paper, Graduate School of Industrial Administration, Carnegie-Mellon University.

Kim, J. (1993): "A Discrete-Time Approximation of a One-Factor Markov Model of the Term Structure of Interest Rates," Working Paper, Graduate School of Industrial Administration, Carnegie-Mellon University.

Kim, J. (1994): "A Model of the Term Structure of Interest Rates with the Time-Variant Market Price of Risk," Working Paper, Graduate School of Industrial Administration, Carnegie-Mellon University.

Koedijk, K., F. Nissen, R. Schotman, and C. Wolff (1994): "The Dynamics of Short-Term Interest Rate Volatility Reconsidered," Working Paper, Limburg Institute of Financial Economics, University of Limburg.

Konno, H., and T. Takase (1995): "A Constrained Least Square Approach to the Estimation of the Term Structure of Interest Rates," *Financial Engineering and the Japanese Markets* 2: 169–179.

Konno, H., and T. Takase (1996): "On the De-Facto Convex Structure of a Least Square Problem for Estimating the Term Structure of Interest Rates," *Financial Engineering and the Japanese Market* 3: 77–85.

Korn, R. (1995): "Contingent Claim Valuation in a Market with Different Interest Rates," *Mathematical Methods of Operations Research* 42: 255–274.

Kraus, A., and M. Smith (1993): "A Simple Multifactor Term Structure Model," *Journal of Fixed Income* 3: 19–23.

Kunitomo, N., and A. Takahashi (1996): "The Asymptotic Expansion Approach to the Valuation of Interest Rates Contingent Claims," Working Paper, Faculty of Economics, University of Tokyo.

Kusuoka, S. (1999b): "A Remark on Default Risk Models," *Advances in Mathematical Economics* 1: 69–82.

Kusuoka, S. (2000): "Term Structure and SPDE," *Advances in Mathematical Economics* 2: 67–85.

Lamberton, D., and B. Lapeyre (1996): *Introduction to Stochastic Calculus Applied to Finance*, London: Chapman and Hall.

Lando, D. (1998): "On Cox Processes and Credit Risky Securities," *Review of Derivatives Research* 2: 99–120.

Lang, L., R. Litzenberger, and A. Liu (1996): "Interest Rate Swaps: A Synthesis," Working Paper, Faculty of Business Administration, Chinese University of Hong Kong.

Langetieg, T. (1980): "A Multivariate Model of the Term Structure," *Journal of Finance* 35: 71–97.

Leblanc, B., and O. Scaillet (1998): "Path Dependent Options on Yields in the Affne Term Structure Model," *Finance and Stochastics* 2: 349–367.

Leibowitz, M., E. Sorensen, R. Arnolt, and H. Hanson: "A Total Differential Approach to Equity Duration," *Financial Analysts Journal*, September/October 1989.

Leland, H. (1994): "Corporate Debt Value, Bond Convenants, and Optimal Capital Structure," *Journal of Finance* 49: 1213–1252.

Leland, H., and K. Toft (1996): "Optimal Capital Structure, Endogenous Bankruptcy, and the Term Structure of Credit Spreads," *Journal of Finance* 51: 987–1019.

Lesne, J.-F. (1995): "Indirect Inference Estimation of Yield Curve Factor Models," Working Paper, Universite de Cergy-Pontoise, THEMA.

Levin, A. (1998): "Deriving Closed-Form Solutions for Gaussian Pricing Models: A Systemic Time-Domain Approach," *International Journal of Theoretical and Applied Finance* 1(3): 349–376.

Li, T. (1995): "Pricing of Swaps with Default Risk," Working Paper, Yale School of Management.

Litterman, R., and J. Scheinkman (1988): "Common Factors Affecting Bond Returns," Working Paper, Goldman Sachs, Financial Strategies Group, New York.

Litterman, R., and T. Iben (1991): "Corporate Bond Valuation and the Term Structure of Credit Spreads," *Journal of Portfolio Management* (Spring): 52–64.

Litzenberger, R. (1992): "Swaps: Plain and Fanciful," *Journal of Finance* 47: 831–850.

Longstaff, F. (1989): "A Nonlinear General Equilibrium Model of the Term Structure of Interest Rates," *Journal of Financial Economics* 23: 195–224.

Longstaff, E. (1990): "The Valuation of Options on Yields," *Journal of Financial Economics* 26: 97–121.

Longstaff, F. A. (1995): "Hedging Interest Rate Risk with Options on Average Interest Rates," *Journal of Fixed Income* (March): 37–45.

Longstaff, F., and E. Schwartz (1992): "Interest Rate Volatility and the Term Structure: A Two-Factor General Equilibrium Model," *Journal of Finance* 47: 1259–1282.

Longstaff, F., and E. Schwartz (1993): "Implementing of the Longstaff-Schwartz Interest Rate Model," Working Paper, Anderson Graduate School of Management, University of California, Los Angeles.

Longstaff, E., and E. Schwartz (1995a): "A Simple Approach to Valuing Risky Fixed and Floating Rate Debt," *Journal of Finance* 50: 789–819.

Longstaff, F., and E. Schwartz (1995b): "Valuing Credit Derivatives," *Journal of Fixed Income* 5 (June): 6–12.

Longstaff, F., P. Santa-Clara, and E. Schwartz (2001): "The Relative Valuation of Interest Rate Caps and Swaptions: Theory and Empirical Evidence," *Journal of Finance* 56: 2067–2110.

Loshak, B. (1996): "The Valuation of Defaultable Convertible Bonds under Stochastic Interest Rate," Working Paper, Krannert Graduate School of Management, Purdue University, West Lafayette.

Lund, J. (1999): "A Model for Studying the Effect of EMU on European Yield Curves," *European Finance Review, Journal of the European Finance Association* 2: 321–363.

Madan, D., and H. Unal (1998): "Pricing the Risks of Default," *Review of Derivatives Research* 2: 121–160.

Maghsoodi, Y. (1996a): "Market's Change in Time, Time Change and Time Structured Term Structures," Working Paper, SCINANCE, UK, Southhampton, and University of Southampton.

Maghsoodi, Y. (1996b): "Solution of the Extended CIR Term Structure and Bond Option Valuation," *Mathematical Finance* 6: 89–109.

Maghsoodi, Y. (1997a): "Term Structure, Solutions and Option Valuation Under Marked Point Process Square-Root Interest Rates," Working Paper, Department of Mathematics, University of Southampton, UK.

Maghsoodi, Y. (1997b): "Two-Country Term Structure under Marked Point Process Diffusion Interest and Exchange Rates," Working Paper, Department of Mathematics, University of Southampton, UK.

Marsh, T. (1994): "Term Structure of Interest Rates and the Pricing of Fixed Income Claims and Bonds," Working Paper, Haas School of Business, University of California, Berkeley.

Martin, M. (1997): "Credit Risk in Derivative Products," Working Paper, University of London, London Business School.

Mason, S., and S. Bhattacharya (1981): "Risky Debt, Jump Processes, and Safety Covenants," *Journal of Financial Economics* 9: 281–307.

McConnell, J., and E. Schwartz (1986): "LYON Taming," *Journal of Finance* 41: 561–576.

Mella-Barral, P. (1999): "Dynamics of Default and Debt Reorganization," *Review of Financial Studies* 12: 535–578.

Mella-Barral, P., and W. Perraudin (1997): "Strategic Debt Service," *Journal of Finance* 52: 531–556.

Merrick, J. (1999): "Crisis Dynamics of Russian Eurobond Implied Default Recovery Ratios," Working Paper, Stern School of Business, New York University.

Merton, R. (1970): "A Dynamic General Equilibrium Model of the Asset Market and Its Application to the Pricing of the Capital Structure of the Firm," Working Paper, Sloan School of Management, Massachusetts Institute of Technology.

Merton, R. (1974): "On the Pricing of Corporate Debt: The Risk Structure of Interest Rates," *Journal of Finance* 29: 449–470.

Miltersen, K. (1993): "Pricing of Interest Rate Contingent Claims: Implementing the Simulation Approach," Working Paper, Department of Management, Odense University.

Miltersen, K. (1994): "An Arbitrage Theory of the Term Structure of Interest Rates," *Annals of Applied Probability* 4: 953–967.

Miltersen, K., and S. A. Persson (1997): "Pricing Rate of Return Guarantees in a Heath-Jarrow-Morton Framework," *Insurance: Mathematics and Economics* 25: 307–325.

Miltersen, K., K. Sandmann, and D. Sondermann (1997): "Closed Form Solutions for Term Structure Derivatives with Log-Normal Interest Rates," *Journal of Finance* 52: 409–430.

Miltersen, K., and E. Schwartz (1998): "Pricing of Options on Commodity Futures with Stochastic Term Structures of Convenience Yields and Interest Rates," *Journal of Financial and Quantitative Analysis* 33: 33–59.

Moreleda, J. (1997): *On the Pricing of Interest Rate Options*, Tinbergen Institute Research Series, Rotterdam, The Netherlands: Erasmus University.

Muralidhar, A. (2001): *Innovations in Pension Fund Management*, Stanford: Stanford University Press.

Musiela, M. (1994a): "Nominal Annual Rates and Lognormal Volatility Structure," Working Paper, Department of Mathematics, University of New South Wales, Sydney.

Musiela, M. (1994b): "Stochastic PDEs and Term Structure Models," Working Paper, Department of Mathematics, University of New South Wales, Sydney.

Musiela, M., and D. Sondermann (1994): "Different Dynamical Specifications of the Term Structure of Interest Rates and their Implications," Working Paper, Department of Mathematics, University of New South Wales, Sydney.

Naik, V., and M. H. Lee (1993): "Yield Curve Dynamics with Discrete Shifts in Economic Regimes: Theory and Estimation," Working Paper, University of British Columbia.

Naik, V., and M. Lee (1994): "The Yield Curve and Bond Option Prices with Discrete Shifts in Economic Regimes," Working Paper, University of British Columbia.

Nakagawa, H. (1999): "A Remark on Spot Rate Models Induced by an Equilibrium Model," *University of Tokyo Journal of Mathematical Sciences* 6: 453–475.

Nielsen, L. T., and J. Saá-Requejo (1992): "Exchange Rate and Term Structure Dynamics and the Pricing of Derivative Securities," Working Paper, INSEAD, Fontainebleau, France.

Nielsen, L. T., J. Saá-Requejo, and P. Santa-Clara (1993): "Default Risk and Interest Rate Risk: The Term Structure of Credit Spreads," Working Paper, INSEAD, Fontainebleau, France.

Nielsen, S., and E. Ronn (1995): "The Valuation of Default Risk in Corporate Bonds and Interest Rate Swaps," Working Paper, Department of Management Science and Information Systems, University of Texas, Austin.

Nunes, J., L. Clewlow, and S. Hodges (1999): "Interest Rate Derivatives in a Duffie and Kan Model with Stochastic Volatility: An Arrow Debreu Pricing Approach," *Review of Derivatives Research* 3: 5–66.

Nyborg, K. (1996): "The Use and Pricing of Convertible Bonds," *Applied Mathematical Finance* 3: 167–190.

Pagès, H. (2000): "Estimating Brazilian Sovereign Risk from Brady Bond Prices," Working Paper, Bank of France.

Pang, K. (1996): "Multi-Factor Gaussian HJM Approximation to Kennedy and Calibration to Caps and Swaptions Prices," Working Paper, Financial Options Research Centre, Warwick Business School, University of Warwick.

Pang, K., and S. Hodges (1995): "Non-Negative Affine Yield Models of the Term Structure," Working Paper, Financial Options Research Centre, Warwick Business School, University of Warwick.

Pearson, N., and T.-S. Sun (1994): "An Empirical Examination of the Cox, Ingersoll, and Ross Model of the Term Structure of Interest Rates Using the Method of Maximum Likelihood," *Journal of Finance* 54: 929–959.

Pedersen, H., and E. Shiu (1993): "Pricing of Options on Bonds by Binomial Lattices and by Diffusion Processes," Working Paper, Investment Policy Department, Great West Life Assurance Company.

Pedersen, H., E. Shiu, and A. Thorlacius (1989): "Arbitrage-Free Pricing of Interest Rate Contingent Claims," *Transactions of the Society of Actuaries* 41: 231–265.

Pedersen, L. (1997): "Affine Multifactor Term Structure Models – Theory and Inference," Working Paper, University of Copenhagen.

Pedersen, M. (1999): "Bermudan Swaptions in the LIBOR Market Model," Working Paper, Financial Research Department, SimCorp A/S.

Pennacchi, G. (1991): "Identifying the Dynamics of Real Interest Rates and Inflation: Evidence Using Survey Data," *Review of Financial Studies* 4: 53–86.

Piazzesi, M. (1997): "An Affine Model of the Term Structure of Interest Rates with Macroeconomic Factors," Working Paper, Stanford University.

Pierides, Y. (1997): "The Pricing of Credit Risk Derivatives," *Journal of Economic Dynamics and Control* 21: 1579–1611.

Pikovsky, I., and S. Shreve (1996a): "Callable Convertible Bonds," Working Paper, Department of Mathematics, Courant Institute, New York.

Pikovsky, I., and S. Shreve (1996b): "Perpetual Convertible Debt," Working Paper, Department of Mathematics, Courant Institute, New York.

Pitts, C., and M. Selby (1983): "The Pricing of Corporate Debt: A Further Note," *Journal of Finance* 38: 1311–1313.

Platten, I. (1994): "Non-linear General Equilibrium Models of the Term Structure: Comments and Two-Factor Generalization," *Finance* 15: 63–78.

Pritsker, M. (1998): "Nonparametric Density Estimation of Tests of Continuous Time Interest Rate Models," *The Review of Financial Studies* 11(3): 449–488.

Pye, G. (1966): "A Markov Model of the Term Structure," *Quarterly Journal of Economics* 81: 61–72.

Pye, G. (1974): "Gauging the Default Premium," *Financial Analysts Journal* (January–February): 49–52.

Ramaswamy, K., and S. Sundaresan (1986): "The Valuation of Floating Rate Instruments: Theory and Evidence," *Journal of Financial Economics* 17: 251–272.

Rebonato, R. (1998): *Interest Rate Option Models*, New York: Wiley.

Richard, S. (1978): "An Arbitrage Model of the Term Structure of Interest Rates," *Journal of Financial Economics* 6: 33–57.

Ritchken, B. (1996): *Derivative Markets*, New York: HarperCollins.

Ritchken, P., and L. Sankarasubramaniam (1992): "Valuing Claims when Interest Rates Have Stochastic Volatility," Working Paper, Department of Finance, University of Southern California.

Ritchken, P., and R. Trevor (1993): "On Finite State Markovian Representations of the Term Structure," Working Paper, Department of Finance, University of Southern California.

Rogers, C. (1993): "Which Model for Term-Structure of Interest Rates Should One Use?" Working Paper, Department of Mathematics, Queen Mary and Westfield College, University of London.

Rogers, C., and W. Stummer (1994): "How Well Do One-Factor Models Fit Bond Prices?" Working Paper, School of Mathematical Sciences, University of Bath.

Rumsey, J. (1996): "Comparison of Tax Rates Inferred from Zero-Coupon Yield Curves," *Journal of Fixed Income* 6 (March): 75–81.

Rutkowski, M. (1995): "Pricing and Hedging of Contingent Claims in the HJM Model with Deterministic Volatilities," Working Paper, Institute of Mathematics, Politechnika Warszawska, Warszawa.

Rutkowski, M. (1996): "Valuation and Hedging of Contingent Claims in the HJM Model with Deterministic Volatilities," *Applied Mathematical Finance* 3: 237–267.

Rutkowski, M. (1998): "Dynamics of Spot, Forward, and Futures LIBOR Rates," *International Journal of Theoretical and Applied Finance* 1: 425–445.

Saà-Requejo, J. (1993): "The Dynamics of the Term Structure of Risk Premia in Foreign Exchange Markets," Working Paper, INSEAD, Fontainebleau, France.

Sabarwal, T. (1999): "Default and Bankruptcy in General Equilibrium," Working Paper, Department of Economics, University of California, Berkeley.

Sandmann, K., and D. Sondermann (1997): "On the Stability of Lognormal Interest Rate Models," *Mathematical Finance* 7: 119–125.

Sandroni, A. (1995): "The Risk Premium and the Interest Rate Puzzles: The Role of Heterogeneous Agents," Working Paper, University of Pennsylvania.

Santa-Clara, P., and D. Sornette (1997): "The Dynamics of the Forward Interest Rate Curve with Stochastic String Shocks," Working Paper, University of California, Los Angeles.

Scaillet, O. (1996): "Compound and Exchange Options in the Affne Term Structure Model," *Applied Mathematical Finance* 3: 75–92.

Schaefer, S., and E. Schwartz (1984): "A Two-Factor Model of the Term Structure: An Approximate Analytical Solution," *Journal of Financial and Quantitative Analysis* 19: 413–423.

Schönbucher, P. (1998): "Term Structure Modelling of Defaultable Bonds," *Review of Derivatives Research* 2: 161–192.

Schwartz, E., and W. Torous (1989): "Prepayment and the Valuation of Mortgage-Backed Securities," *Journal of Finance* 44: 375–392.

Scott, L. (1995): "Pricing Stock Options in a Jump-Diffusion Model with Stochastic Volatility and Interest Rates: Applications of Fourier Inversion Methods," Working Paper, University of Georgia.

Scott, L. (1996a): "Simulating a Multi-Factor Term Structure Model over Relatively Long Discrete Time Periods," Working Paper, Department of Banking and Finance, University of Georgia, Athens.

Scott, L. (1996b): "The Valuation of Interest Rate Derivatives in a Multi-Factor Cox-Ingersoll-Ross Model that Matches the Initial Term Structure," Working Paper, Department of Banking and Finance, University of Georgia, Athens.

Sekine, J. (1998): "Mean-Variance Hedging in Continuous-Time with Stochastic Interest Rate," Working Paper, MTP Investment Technology Institute, Tokyo.

Selby, M., and C. Strickland (1993): "Computing the Fong and Vasicek Pure Discount Bond Price Formula," Working Paper, FORC Preprint 93/42, October, University of Warwick.

Shirakawa, H. 1991. "Interest Rate Option Pricing with Poisson-Gaussian Forward Rate Curves," *Mathematical Finance* 1(4): 77–94.

Shimko, D., N. Tejima, and D. van Deventer (1993): "The Pricing of Risky Debt when Interest Rates are Stochastic," *Journal of Fixed Income* 3 (September): 58–65.

Singh, M. (1995): "Estimation of Multifactor Cox, Ingersoll, and Ross Term Structure Model: Evidence on Volatility Structure and Parameter Stability," *Journal of Fixed Income* 5 (September): 8–28.

Sorenson, E., and T. Bollier (1995): "Pricing Default Risk: The Interest-Rate Swap Example," in *Derivative Credit Risk*, London: Risk Publications.

Sornette, D. (1998): "String Formulation of the Dynamics of the Forward Interest Rate Curve," Working Paper, Université des Sciences, Parc Valrose, France, and Institute of Geophysics and Planetary Physics, University of California, Los Angeles.

Stambaugh, R. (1988): "The Information in Forward Rates: Implications for Models of the Term Structure," *Journal of Financial Economics* 21: 41–70.

Stanton, R. (1995a): "A Nonparametric Model of Term Structure Dynamics and the Market Price of Interest Rate Risk," *Journal of Finance* 52: 1973–2002.

Stanton, R. (1995b): "Rational Prepayment and the Valuation of Mortgage-Backed Securities," *Review of Financial Studies* 8: 677–708.

Stanton, R. (1997): "A Nonparametric Model of Term Structure Dynamics and the Market Price of Interest Rate Risk," *Journal of Finance* 52: 1973–2002.

Stanton, R., and N. Wallace (1995): "ARM Wrestling: Valuing Adjustable Rate Mortgages Indexed to the Eleventh District Cost of Funds," *Real Estate Economics* 23: 311–345.

Stapleton, R., and M. Subrahmanyam (1984): "The Analysis and Valuation of Interest Rate Options," *Journal of Banking and Finance*.

Sun, T.-S. (1992): "Real and Nominal Interest Rates: A Discrete-Time Model and Its Continuous-Time Limit," *Review of Financial Studies* 5: 581–612.

Sundaresan, S. (1984): "Consumption and Equilibrium Interest Rates in Stochastic Production Economies," *Journal of Finance* 39: 77–92.

Sundaresan, S. (1991): "Valuation of Swaps," in S. Khoury (Ed.), *Recent Developments in International Banking and Finance*, Amsterdam: North-Holland.

Sundaresan, S. (1997): *Fixed Income Markets and Their Derivatives*, Cincinnati: South-Western.

Svensson, L. E. O., and M. Dahlquist (1993): "Estimating the Term Structure of Interest Rates with Simple and Complex Functional Forms: Nelson and Siegel vs. Longstaff and Schwartz," Working Paper, Institute for International Economic Studies, Stockholm University.

Tanudjaja, S. (1995): "American Swaption Early Exercise Premium Approximation," Working Paper, Global Derivatives, Citibank, London.

Tice, J., and N. Webber (1997): "A Non-Linear Model of the Term Structure of Interest Rates," *Mathematical Finance* 7: 177–209.

Topper, J. (1997): "Solving Term Structure Models with Finite Elements," Working Paper, Fachbereich Wirtschaftwissenschaften der Universität Hannover.

Torous, W. (1985): "Differential Taxation and the Structure of Interest Rates," *Journal of Banking and Finance* 9: 363–385.

Tsiveriotis, K, and C. Fernandes (1998): "Valuing Convertible Bonds with Credit Risk," *Journal of Fixed Income* 8: 95–102.

Tuckman, B. (1995): *Fixed Income Securities*, New York: Wiley.

Turnbull, S. (1993): "Pricing and Hedging Diff Swaps," Working Paper, School of Business, Queen's University.

Turnbull, S. (1994): "Interest Rate Digital Options and Range Notes," Working Paper, School of Business, Queen's University.

Turnbull, S. M. (1995): "Interest Rate Digital Options and Range Notes," *Journal of Derivatives* 3(1): 92–101.

Vasicek, O. (1977): "An Equilibrium Characterization of the Term Structure," *Journal of Financial Economics* 5: 177–188.

Vasicek, O. (1995): "The Finite Factor Model of Bond Prices," Working Paper, KMV Corporation, San Francisco.

Vayanos, D., and J. L. Vila (1999): "Equilibrium Interest Rate and Liquidity Premium with Transaction Costs," *Economic Theory* 13: 509–539.

Wang, J. (1996): "The Term Structure of Interest Rates in a Pure Exchange Economy with Heterogeneous Investors," *Journal of Financial Economics* 41: 75–110.

Webber, N. (1990): "The Term Structure of Spot Rate Volatility and the Behavior of Interest Rate Processes," Working Paper, Financial Options Research Centre, University of Warwick.

Webber, N. (1992): "The Consistency of Term Structure Models: The Short Rate, the Long Rate, and Volatility," Working Paper, Financial Options Research Centre, University of Warwick.

Zapatero, F. (1993): "Interest Rates with Converging Heterogeneous Reliefs," Working Paper, Haas School of Business, University of California, Berkeley.

Zheng, C.-C. (1994): "Pricing Interest Rates Contingent Claims by a Pricing Kernel," Working Paper, NationsBank, New York.

Zhou, C.-S. (2000): "A Jump-Diffusion Approach to Modeling Credit Risk and Valuing Defaultable Securities," Working Paper, Federal Reserve Board, Washington, D.C.

Zhu, Y.-I., and Y. Sun (1999): "The Singularity-Separating Method for Two-Factor Convertible Bonds," *Journal of Computational Finance* 3 (Fall): 91–110.

Chapter 4. Mathematics of Asset Pricing

Aliprantis, C., and O. Burkinshaw (1985): *Positive Operators*, Orlando: Academic Press.

Alvarez, O., and A Tourin (1996): "Viscosity Solutions of Nonlinear Integro-Differential Equations," *Annales de l'"Institut Henri Poincaré Analyse Non Lineaire* 13: 293–317.

Amendinger, J. (1999): "Martingale Representation Theorems for Initially Enlarged Filtrations," Working Paper, Technische Universität Berlin.

Andreasen, J., B. Jensen, and R. Poulsen (1998): "Eight Valuation Methods in Financial Mathematics: The Black-Scholes Formula as an Example," *Mathematical Scientist* 23: 18–40.

Antonelli, F. (1993): "Backward-Forward Stochastic Differential Equations," *Annals of Applied Probability* 3: 777–793.

Artzner, P., and D. Heath (1995): "Approximate Completeness with Multiple Martingale Measures," *Mathematical Finance* 5: 1–11.

Bally, V., and D. Talay (1999): "The Law of the Euler Scheme for Stochastic Differential Equations: II. Convergence Rate of the Density," *Monte Carlo Methods and Applications* 2: 93–128.

Barles, G., R. Buckdahn, and E. Pardoux (1997): "Backward Stochastic Differential Equations and Integral-Partial Differential Equations," *Stochastics and Stochastics Reports* 60: 57–83.

Barles, G., and E. Lisigne (1997): "SDE, BSDE, and PDE," in N. El Karoui and L. Mazliak (Eds.), *Backward Stochastic Differential Equations*, pp. 47–80, Essex: Addison Wesley Longman.

Beibel, M., and H. Lerche (1997): "A New Look at Optimal Stopping Problems Related to Mathematical Finance," *Statistica Sinica* 7: 93–108.

Bernard, P., D. Talay, and L. Tubaro (1994): "Rate of Convergence of a Stochastic Particle Method for the Kolmogorov Equation with Variable Coeffcients," *Mathematics of Computation* 63: 555–587.

Bick, A. (1986): "On Viable Diffusion Price Processes," *Journal of Finance* 45: 673–689.

Bick, A., and W. Willinger (1994): "Dynamic Spanning without Probabilities," *Stochastic Processes and Their Applications* 50: 349–374.

Bouleau, N., and D. Lamberton (1989): "Residual Risks and Hedging Strategies in Markovian Markets," *Stochastic Processes and Their Applications* 33: 131–150.

Bouleau, N., and D. Lépingle (1994): *Numerical Methods for Stochastic Processes*, New York: Wiley.

Brémaud, P. (1981): *Point Processes and Queues: Martingale Dynamics*, New York: Springer.

Buckdahn, R. (1995a): "Backward Stochastic Differential Equations Driven by a Martingale," Working Paper, FB Mathematik der Humboldt-Universität zu Berlin, Berlin.

Buckdhan, R. (1995b): "BSDE with Non-Square Integrable Terminal Value – FBSDE with Delay," Working Paper, Faculté des Sciences, Département de Mathématiques, Université de Bretagne Occidentale, Brest, France.

Bühlmann, H., F. Delbaen, P. Embrechts, and A. Shiryaev (1998): "On Esscher Transforms in Discrete Finance Models," *ASTIN Bulletin* 28: 171–186.

Cassese, G. (1996): "An Elementary Remark on Martingale Equivalence and the Fundamental Theorem of Asset Pricing," Working Paper, Instituto di Economia Politica, Università Commerciale "Luigi Bocconi," Milan.

Cherubini, U., and M. Esposito (1992): "Using Pearson's System to Characterize Diffusion Processes: A Note," Working Paper, Banco Commerciale Italiana, Uffcio Studi, Milan.

Chesney, M., M. Jeanblanc, and M. Yor (1997): "Brownian Excursions and Barrier Options," *Advances in Applied Probability* 29: 165–184.

Chevance, D. (1996): "Discretization of Pardoux-Peng's Backward Stochastic Differential Equations," Working Paper, Université de Provence.

Choulli, T., L. Krawczyk, and C. Stricker (1998): "E-Martingales and Their Applications in Mathematical Finance," *Annals of Probability* 26: 853–876.

Chow, Y., and H. Teicher (1978): *Probability Theory: Independence Interchangeability Martingales*, New York: Springer-Verlag.

Christensen, B. J. (1991): "Statistics for Arbitrage-Free Asset Pricing," Working Paper, Department of Finance, New York University.

Chuang, C. (1994): "Joint Distribution of Brownian Motion and Its Maximum, with a Generalization to Correlated BM and Applications to Barrier Options," Working Paper, Department of Statistics, Stanford University.

Chung, K. (1982): *Lectures from Markov Processes to Brownian Motion*, New York: Springer-Verlag.

Chung, K.-L. (1974): *A Course in Probability Theory* (2nd ed.), New York: Academic Press.

Chung, K.-L., and R. Williams (1990): *An Introduction to Stochastic Integration* (2nd ed.), Boston: Birkhäuser.

Clark, P. (1973): "A Subordianted Stochastic Process with Finite Variance for Speculative Prices," *Econometrica* 41: 135–155.

Conze, A., and R. Viswanathan (1991b): "Probability Measure and Numeraires," Working Paper, CEREMADE, Université de Paris.

Cox, D. R., and H. D. Miller (1965): *The Theory of Stochastic Processes*, London: Chapman and Hall.

Cutland, N., P. Kopp, and W. Willinger (1993b): "Stock Price Returns and the Joseph Effect: Fractional Version of the Black-Scholes Model," Working Paper, School of Mathematics, University of Hull, England.

Cvitanić, J., and I. Karatzas (1996a): "Backward Stochastic Differential Equations with Reflection and Dynkin Games," *Annals of Probability* 24: 2024–2056.

Dalang, R., A. Morton, and W. Willinger (1990): "Equivalent Martingale Measures and No-Arbitrage in Stochastic Securities Market Models," *Stochastics and Stochastic Reports* 29: 185–201.

Daley, D., and D. Vere-Jones (1988): *An Introduction to the Theory of Point Processes*, New York: Springer-Verlag.

Darling, R. (1995): "Constructing Gamma-Martingales with Prescribed Limit, Using Backward SDE," *Annals of Probability* 3: 431–454.

Dassios, A. (1994): "The Distribution of the Quantiles of a Brownian Motion with Drift and the Pricing of Related Path-Dependent Options," Working Paper, Department of Statistics, London School of Economics.

Deelstra, G., and F. Delbaen (1994): "Existence of Solutions of Stochastic Differential Equations Related to the Bessel Process," Working Paper, Department of Mathematics, Vrije Universiteit Brussel.

Deheuvels, P. (1982): *La Probabilité, le Hasard et la Certitude, Que sais-je?* Paris: Presses Universitaires de France.

Delbaen, F., and W. Schachermayer (1994a): "Arbitrage and Free Lunch with Bounded Risk for Unbounded Continuous Processes," *Mathematical Finance* 4: 343–348.

Delbaen, F., and W. Schachermayer (1995a): "Arbitrage Possibilities in Bessel Processes and Their Relations to Local Martingales," *Probability Theory and Related Fields* 102: 357–366.

Delbaen, F., and W. Schachermayer (1995b): "The Existence of Absolutely Continuous Local Martingale Measures," *Annals of Applied Probability* 5: 926–945.

Delbaen, F., and W. Schachermayer (1998): "The Fundamental Theorem of Asset Pricing for Unbounded Stochastic Processes," *Mathematische Annalen* 312: 215–250.

Douglas, J., J. Ma, and P. Protter (1996): "Numerical Methods for Forward-Backward Stochastic Differential Equations," *Annals of Applied Probability* 6: 940–968.

Dubins, L., and L. Savage (1965): *How to Gamble If You Must*, New York: McGraw-Hill.

Duchateau, P., and D. W. Zachmann (1986): *Partial Differential Equations*, Schaum's Outline Series in Mathematics, New York: McGraw-Hill.

Durrett, R. (1991): *Probability: Theory and Examples*, Belmont, CA: Wadsworth Publishing.

Eberlein, E., and U. Keller (1995): "Hyperbolic Distributions in Finance," *Bernoulli* 1: 281–299.

El Karoui, N. (1997): "Backward Stochastic Differential Equations: A General Introduction," in N. El Karoui and L. Mazliak (Eds.), *Backward Stochastic Differential Equations*, pp. 7–26, Essex: Addison Wesley Longman.

El Karoui, N., and S.-J. Huang (1997): "A General Result of Existence and Uniqueness of Backward Stochastic Differential Equations," in N. El Karoui and L. Mazliak (Eds.), *Backward Stochastic Differential Equations*, pp. 27–36, Essex: Addison Wesley Longman.

El Karoui, N., C. Kapoudjian, E. Pardoux, S. Peng, and M. Quenez (1997): "Reflected Solutions of Backward SDE's, and Related Obstacle Problems for PDE's," *Annals of Probability* 2: 702–737.

El Karoui, N., S. Peng, and M. Quenez (1997): "Backward Stochastic Differential Equations in Finance," *Mathematical Finance* 1: 1–71.

Epstein, R. A. (1977): *The Theory of Gambling and Statistical Logic*, New York: Academic Press.

Ethier, S., and T. Kurtz (1986): *Markov Processes: Characterization and Convergence*, New York: Wiley.

Farlow, S. J. (1982): *Partial Differential Equations for Scientists and Engineers*, New York: Dover.

Feller, W. (1951): "Two Singular Diffusion Problems," *Annals of Mathematics* 54: 173–182.

Feller, W. (1968): *An Introduction to Probability Theory and Its Applications*, New York: Wiley.

Filipović, D. (1999b): A Note on the Nelson-Siegel Family," *Mathematical Finance* 9: 349–359.

Fleming, W., and R. Rishel (1975): *Deterministic and Stochastic Optimal Control*, Berlin: Springer-Verlag.

Fleming, W., and M. Soner (1993): *Controlled Markov Processes and Viscosity Solutions*, New York: Springer-Verlag.

Fournié, E. (1993): "Statistiques des Diffussions Ergodiques avec Applications en Finance," Working Paper, Université de Nice-Sophia Antipolis.

Fournié, E., J.-M. Lasry, J. Lebuchoux, P.-L. Lions, and N. Touzi (1999): "Applications of Malliavin Calculus to Monte Carlo Methods in Finance, *Finance and Stochastics* 3: 391–412.

Freedman, D. (1983): *Markov Chains*, New York: Springer-Verlag.

Freidlin, M. (1985): *Functional Integration and Partial Differential Equations*, Princeton, NJ: Princeton University Press.

Friedman, A. (1964): *Partial Differential Equations of the Parabolic Type*, Englewood Cliffs, NJ: Prentice-Hall.

Friedman A. (1975): *Stochastic Differential Equations and Applications, Vol. I*, New York: Academic Press.

Geman, H., D. Madan, and M. Yor (1999): "Time Changes for Lévy Processes," Working Paper, Université Paris IX Dauphine and ESSEC.

Geman, H., and M. Yor (1993): "Bessel Processes, Asian Options and Perpetuities," *Mathematical Finance* 3: 349–375.

Gerber, H., and H. Shiu (1994): "Option Pricing by Esscher Transforms," *Transactions of the Society of Actuaries* 46: 51–92.

Gihman, I., and A. Skorohod (1972): *Stochastic Differential Equations*, Berlin: Springer-Verlag.

Gihman, I. I., and A. V. Skorohod (1979): *Controlled Stochastic Processes*, New York: Springer-Verlag.

Grandell, J. (1976): *Doubly Stochastic Poisson Processes*. Lecture Notes in Mathematics, Number 529, New York: Springer-Verlag.

Ikeda, N., and S. Watanabe (1981): *Stochastic Differential Equations and Diffusion Processes*, Amsterdam: North-Holland.

Jacod, J., and P. Protter (2000): *Probability Essentials*, New York: Springer-Verlag.

Jacod, J., and A. Shiryaev (1987): *Limit Theorems for Stochastic Processes*, New York: Springer-Verlag.

Jarrow, R., and D. Madan (1991): "A Characterization of Complete Security Markets on a Brownian Filtration," *Mathematical Finance* 1: 31–44.

Jarrow, R., and D. Madan (1999): "Hedging Contingent Claims on Semimartingales," *Finance and Stochastics* 3: 111–134.

Karatzas, I. (1997): *Lectures on the Mathematics of Finance*, Providence: American Mathematical Society.

Karatzas, I., and S. Shreve (1988): *Brownian Motion and Stochastic Calculus*, New York: Springer-Verlag.

Karatzas, I., and S. Shreve (1998): *Methods of Mathematical Finance*, New York: Springer-Verlag.

Karlin, S., and H. Taylor (1975): *A First Course in Stochastic Processes*, New York: Academic Press.

Karr, A. (1991): *Point Processes and Their Statistical Inference* (2nd ed.), New York: Marcel Dekker.

Kunitomo, N. (1993): "Long-Term Memory and Fractional Brownian Motion in Financial Markets," Working Paper, Faculty of Economics, University of Tokyo.

Lakner, P. (1993b): "Martingale Measures for a Class of Right-Continuous Processes," *Mathematical Finance* 3: 43–54.

Lawson, J., and J. Morris (1978): "The Extrapolation of First Order Methods for Parabolic Partial Differential Equations I," *SIAM Journal of Numerical Analysis* 15: 1212–1224.

Lipster, R., and A. Shiryaev (1977): *Statistics of Random Processes, I*, New York: Springer-Verlag.

Marcozzi, M. (2000): "On the Approximation of Optimal Stopping Problems with Application to Financial Mathematics," Working Paper, Department of Mathematical Sciences, University of Nevada, Las Vegas.

McKean, H. (1965): "Appendix: Free Boundary Problem for the Heat Equation Arising from a Problem in Mathematical Economics," *Industrial Management Review* 6: 32–39.

Meyer, P.-A. (1966): *Probability and Potentials*, Waltham, MA: Blaisdell Publishing Company.

Milshtein, G. (1974): "Approximate Integration of Stochastic Differential Equations," *Theory of Probability and Its Applications* 3: 557–562.

Milshtein, G. (1978): "A Method of Second-Order Accuracy Integration of Stochastic Differential Equations," *Theory of Probability and Its Applications* 23: 396–401.

Mitchell, A., and D. Griffths (1980): *The Finite Difference Method in Partial Differential Equations*, New York: Wiley.

Morokoff, W., and R. Caflisch (1993): "A Quasi-Monte Carlo Approach to Particle Simulation of the Heat Equation," *SIAM Journal of Numerical Analysis* 30: 1558–1573.

Musiela, M., and M. Rutkowski (1997): *Martingale Methods in Financial Modeling*, New York: Springer.

Newton, N. (1990): "Asymptotically Effcient Runge-Kutta Methods for a Class of Itô and Stratonovich Equations," Working Paper, Department of Electrical Engineering, University of Essex.

Oksendal, B. (1992): *Stochastic Differential Equations*, New York: Springer-Verlag.

Pollard, D. (1984): *Convergence of Stochastic Processes*, New York: Springer-Verlag.

Protter, P. (1990): *Stochastic Integration and Differential Equations*, New York: Springer-Verlag.

Protter, P. (1999): "A Partial Introduction to Finance," Working Paper, Purdue University. Forthcoming in *Stochastic Processes and Their Applications*.

Revuz, D. (1975): *Markov Chains*, Amsterdam: North-Holland.

Revuz, D., and M. Yor (1991): *Continuous Martingales and Brownian Motion*, New York: Springer.

Ricciardi, L., and S. Sato (1988): "First-Passage-Time Density and Moments of the Ornstein-Uhlenbeck Process," *Journal of Applied Probability* 25: 43–57.

Rogers, C. (1994): "Equivalent Martingale Measures and No-Arbitrage," *Stochastics and Stochastic Reports* 51: 1–9.

Ross, S. M. (1996): *Stochastic Processes*, New York: Wiley.

Schachermayer, W. (1993): "A Counterexample to Several Problems in the Theory of Asset Pricing," *Mathematical Finance* 3: 217–230.

Shimko, D. (1991): *Finance in Continuous Time: A Primer*, Oxford: Blackwell Publishers.

Williams, D. (1991): *Probability with Martingales*, Cambridge: Cambridge University Press.

Willinger,W., and M. Tacqu (1989): "Pathwise Stochastic Integration and Application to the Theory of Continuous Trading," *Stochastic Processes and Their Applications* 32: 253–280.

Yor, M. (1993): "The Distribution of Brownian Quantiles," Working Paper, Laboratoires de Probabilités, Université de Paris VI.

Index

327